THE NEW ARABS

How the Millennial Generation
Is Changing the Middle East

JUAN COLE

Simon & Schuster
New York London Toronto Sydney New Delhi

Simon & Schuster
1230 Avenue of the Americas
New York, NY 10020
Copyright © 2014 by Juan Cole

First Simon & Schuster hardcover edition July 2014

For information about special discounts for bulk purchases, please contact Simon & Schuster Special Sales at 1-866-506-1949 or business@simonandschuster.com.

The Simon & Schuster Speakers Bureau can bring authors to your live event. For more information or to book an event contact the Simon & Schuster Speakers Bureau at 1-866-248-3049 or visit our website at www.simonspeakers.com.

Interior design by Akasha Archer
Jacket design by Marc Cohen
Jacket illustration © Anna Poguliaeva/Shutterstock

Manufactured in the United States of America

10   9   8   7   6   5   4   3   2   1

Library of Congress Cataloging-in-Publication Data
  Cole, Juan Ricardo.
  The new Arabs : how the millennial generation is changing the Middle East / Juan Cole.
    pages cm
  1. Arabs—Political activity. 2. Youth—Arab countries—Social life and customs. 3. Youth—Middle East—Social life and customs. 4. Political participation—Technological innovations. 5. Internet—Political aspects. 6. Social media—Political aspects. 7. Online social networks—Political aspects. 8. Arab countries—Politics and government—21st century. 9. Middle East—Politics and government—21st century. I. Title.
  JQ1850.A91C64 2014
  909'.097492708312—dc23   2014005627

ISBN 978-1-4516-9039-2
ISBN 978-1-4516-9041-5 (ebook)

Contents

Preface

While my family and I were paying our respects to the boy pharaoh Tutankhamen and his gold-plated sarcophagus in a side room at the Cairo Museum, one of the guards abruptly forced us out of the room and then out of the building. Soon I learned that what I took for rudeness was desperation: something bad was coming.

That morning, August 1, 2011, my wife, my son, and I had finally found a free moment to visit the venerable museum, a scandalous jumble of poorly labeled precious antiquities less on display than randomly dumped here and there. The building is around the corner from Tahrir Square, where thousands of youth had assembled to push for the trial of deposed dictator Hosni Mubarak and of policemen who had killed demonstrators during the revolution earlier that year. Forty-five minutes before closing time, the guards had begun herding us out, declaring that the museum was closing early for the fasting month of Ramadan. It was a well-intentioned lie.

When we exited the building into the blinding daylight showering Tahrir Square, we discovered shirtless soccer fanatics, called "Ultras," frantically pounding on the metal barricades with plastic bottles and other instruments. They were clearly sending a warning signal, and we did not have to look far to see the reason. Armored vehicles were pulling up on side streets with what looked like ninja police pouring out of them, armed with batons. Now we understood the panic of the museum guards: they had not wanted the tourists to get caught in the middle of the coming melee.

We half-ran, half-walked toward Talaat Harb Square a few blocks away, where we caught a taxi. I told the driver what was going on and that we wanted him to take us away from the scene as quickly as possible. There had been stories of foreigners arrested at Tahrir Square or having their cameras broken by overzealous police, and I imagined all the photos and videos I had taken that summer of the demonstrations, posters, banners, and graffiti being crushed beneath the heel of one of those black boots.

As is frequently the case with Cairo cabbies, he completely disregarded my request. Instead, he circled around and drove us as fast as he could back toward Tahrir Square. Then we got caught in Cairo's notorious traffic, right next to the armored vehicles and the security police, who occasionally peered suspiciously into the taxi. I was petrified that they were going to demand our passports and accuse us of being spies or saboteurs. My camera would have contained all the evidence they needed. They would not have wanted foreign witnesses to what they were about to do.

The taxi inched its tortuous way forward. We could still hear the anxious drumming of the self-appointed guardians of the square, which was festooned with tents, banners, and posters demanding change. The police methodically tapped their open palms with their batons. Two approached our car from the front and I froze. They looked in at us with curiosity. But they were just crossing the street.

After an eternity, the taxi reached the square and turned right, toward the Nile island of Zamalek, and made its way down a highway lined with more armored vehicles, beside which masses of police and soldiers stood. Every inquisitive glance was a threat.

Finally, we were away. I exhaled in relief as we crossed the October 6 Bridge over the languorous Nile. Not long after, we heard that all the protesters had been chased away, all the tents pulled down, and all the banners and posters trampled. Some of the banners had demanded the resignation of the military government, and the military had given its reply.

Young people are the key to the rapid political and social change in the Arab countries that have been in turmoil since 2011.[1] Activist youth returned to Tahrir Square again and again in 2011 to 2013 despite the attempts of the military and various postrevolutionary governments to repress them. In spring–summer 2013, the youth Rebellion Movement against the Muslim Brotherhood managed to unseat its president. The military this time posed as an ally of the youth and made a coup on the backs of the millions of young people who came to the streets. Thereafter, the officers went back to jailing young activists in a continued quest to put the genie back in the bottle. My focus in this book is not on the politics of the presidents, generals, and prime ministers of what some call the "Arab Spring" but rather the networked movements of young people that played such an important role in these events. Not all cohorts of teenagers and twenty-somethings produce movements centered on their identity as youth, with a set of organizations, symbols, repertoires of social action, and demands rooted at least partly in the distinctive problems besetting people of their age. The Arab millennials did, and they forever changed their societies.[2] While they were by no means the only important social actors, youth associations played an outsized role in provoking and shaping these upheavals.[3] This effective activism was all the more remarkable given the patriarchal and regimented character of Arab society. A young Egyptian from the Suez Canal port of Ismailia said after the revolution, "We have made this revolution. Our families were used to keeping quiet. We didn't keep quiet. We went out to get our dream."[4]

The massive crowds that gathered in Tahrir Square in downtown Cairo in January and February 2011 pushed the long-ruling dictator Hosni Mubarak out of power and brought down one of the Middle East's most powerful governments. The protesters in Cairo had taken their inspiration from similar events in Tunisia in December and January. In turn, youthful crowds challenged their rulers in Bahrain, Libya, Yemen, and Syria. Smaller movements produced hurried cosmetic changes in Jordan, Morocco, and Oman. Attempts by the erratic dictator Muammar Gaddafi to crush Libya's protest movement with tanks and artillery led to a United Nations Security Council plea for outside intervention—answered in sometimes problematic ways by NATO and the Arab League—and evolved into civil war. In June and July 2013 millions of Egyptian youth came out for an encore performance, driving from office their first elected president, the Muslim Brotherhood leader Mohamed Morsi, and signaling that Arab youth were not done fashioning their future. The networked youth movements protested the idea of presidents for life being succeeded by their sons in a kind of dynastic succession. They rejected censorship, arbitrary arrest, police brutality, and torture. They developed a concept of personal freedom emphasizing the dignity and autonomy of citizens with regard to their bodies, convictions, and lifestyles (an entire Egyptian nongovernmental organization was formed around this notion). It is unsurprising that they had only partial success in pressing for the implementation of their ideals in the three years after the fall of the dictators. What is surprising is that in societies dominated by police states for decades, these millennials made new social and media spaces in which their demands could be voiced and small steps could be taken toward achieving them.

The most consequential organizations for the overthrow of long-serving dictators in the region's republics were made up of left-liberal youth living in towns and cities, and so they are my primary focus.[5] They were distinguished by their preference for a horizontal model of organization instead of a hierarchy, so that leadership tended not to be centralized. They had years of experience in dissidence, beginning in the early twenty-first century, and in avoiding political taboos. That is, their predecessors had often identified political groups with whom they refused to work, whereas the engaged youth often had wider horizons and were more pragmatic, possibly because their preference for interactive networks and horizontal organization made an inclusive approach easy and a sectarian one difficult.

My travels in Tunisia, Egypt, and Libya have given me a good sense of the issues on the ground. Not only was I able to interview and talk to a wide range of participants in these dramatic events, but I was able to collect rare pamphlets and books and to photograph posters, placards, graffiti, and other visual sources for attitudes and political demands. In Tunisia I found secular middle-class activists firmly confronting militant fundamentalists who were deploying violence to protest film showings and art exhibits, defending the right to be unreligious and warning that the Muslim al-Nahda (Renaissance) Party wanted to turn Tunisia into another Iran. In Egypt I was present on several occasions when the famed Tahrir Square erupted in large protests, in what many youth clearly felt was an unfinished revolution. Tensions between the relatively secular youth movements and the Muslim Brotherhood were palpable and would come to a head in 2013. In Libya I visited a hastily erected war museum in Misrata and Benghazi's symbol of revolt, the city's courthouse, haunted by a generation of the "disappeared," those made political prisoners and done away with by the Gaddafi regime.

Since my concern in this book is with organized youth movements that led to fairly extensive changes in national politics, I will concentrate on Egypt, Tunisia, and Libya. For the same reason I will slight Yemen and Syria. In Yemen the president stepped down in favor of his vice president but remained the leader of the ruling party, which shared some of its power but was not overthrown. Young demonstrators played a key role in these changes in Sanaa, but so too did political parties, tribal groups, and religious and regional movements. In Syria youth played a central role in the March 2011 demonstrations that kicked off a long, grinding political struggle. When the ruling Baath regime deployed armor and the air force to repress those rallies in small towns and cities in the center of the country, the youth turned to military struggle and the country was plunged into years of civil war that is, as of this writing, still unresolved. As the sociologist Manuel Castells observed, "Civil wars not only kill people, they also kill social movements and their ideals of peace, democracy and justice."[6] There was no preexisting youth movement in one-party Syria of the sort I recount in Egypt and Tunisia. Syria's agony requires a different sort of analysis, including that of a military historian, than I offer here. I will not treat Bahrain, both because the demonstrations there were not only generational but also ethnic and political and because my focus is on the Arab republics.

Not all authors writing about the Arab upheavals have put the same emphasis on social movements as does this book. Some see a conspiracy promoted by the United States and/or NATO. Others suspect forces like the Egyptian army of fomenting trouble in early 2011 and again in 2013 to rid itself of rivals. Both theses seem to me absurd. Nothing in the public record suggests that the Obama administration wanted to see Zine El Abidine Ben Ali or Hosni Mubarak deposed, and great powers for the most part are status quo powers. The Egyptian military was opportunistic, using the turmoil where it could to its benefit, but it did not always get its way because of youth opposition to particular policies. The officers were riding a tiger.

The postrevolutionary period in all three countries was rocky, to say the least. Still, it is easy to forget how radical the changes have been. Only a few years ago it was widely expected that ruling families in most Arab republics would manage to install one of their sons in power, creating new dynasties and ensuring their continued dominance of state resources. The notion of presidents for life bequeathing their countries to eldest sons as though the people were a mere heirloom has been tossed on the trash heap of history by Arab youth. There are other, extensive changes with regard to censorship practices and freedom of expression. A prominent newspaper editor was once threatened with jail time for merely speculating about the health of Mubarak. Likewise the slightest criticism of Tunisia's Ben Ali or Libya's Gaddafi could have led to years of imprisonment. For all the continued violations of the rights of journalists and social commentators, the revolutionary countries have a more critical and freewheeling political debate than could have been imagined in 2010, though by 2014 this achievement was imperiled in Egypt. In Tunisia the new constitution guarantees freedom of expression. Hundreds of new political parties have been founded and have contested elections in the three countries, in contrast to the past, when there were no elections in Libya and only phony ones in Tunisia and Egypt that the ruling party always won handily. In the old days a wide range of parties was simply not permitted, and the regimes limited the opposition to a handful of groups that had little popular support. Organizing outside the ruling party was dangerous because it could lead to arrest by the secret police and to arbitrary sentences and even torture. The secret police as a separate institution was abolished in Tunisia and Libya, and the state security police in Egypt experienced dramatic ups and downs from 2011 forward. Torture is not gone, but at least now it is controversial and openly contested (the constitution drafted in late 2013 in Egypt explicitly forbids torture and allows victims to sue government officials if they practice it). The keynote of these changes is what the youth call "dignity" (*karama*), a sense of personal autonomy and rights to freedom of one's person and one's political beliefs that must not be infringed by the security forces.

The rise of the internet may not have been as central to these social movements as some Western press coverage assumed. Nevertheless the revolutions were at least to some extent enabled by blogging, Facebook and Twitter campaigns, satellite television, and smartphones. New media allowed activists to get the word out about torture and corruption in ways that the state-dominated press would not have. The internet worked in tandem with popular social and political movements that moved like deep currents to produce these waves of change. They included leftist and liberal parties, which had youth wings. Among them were long-standing and powerful labor unions, who tended to be ignored by American journalists in particular. Likewise student unions and organizations were often central. And members of the Union of Revolutionary Youth stressed to me that the organic character of urban neighborhoods in the Arab world allowed information to be disseminated through street chants more readily than through the ether. In many cases it was young people on their balconies or lining the streets who passed on the political slogans they heard, functioning as the information highway. Many Arabs live in provincial towns where agricultural jobs and water management matter more than abstract ideals and where the telephone or demonstrations were more important than Twitter for organizing. In Tunisia my informants told me that the offices of the former ruling party had been burned and police stations attacked even in provincial centers; indeed in many ways the youth in the provinces took the lead. "The revolution was everywhere," proclaimed one young enthusiast from Le Kram, working behind the counter at a pizzeria in Tunis; even in his small town on the outskirts of the capital, people had risen up against the old regime.

In this book I tell the story of how the youth movements in North Africa and Egypt arose and describe their protagonists, struggles, passions, and ideas. I paint a broad picture of the revolts in the first half of 2011 in each of the three countries I treat, and I analyze the specific tactics and repertoires the youth used to accomplish their aims.[7] I then assess the aftermath of the political upheavals in the Arab world through winter 2014. How likely is it that these young people taking to the streets, scrawling graffiti, making videos of police brutality, occupying city squares, mounting Facebook protests, and allying with striking workers can build more representative governments bound by the rule of law? Having thrown their societies into turmoil, can they turn to the hard work of institution building in the aftermath? Can the divide between nationalists and religious forces be bridged, or will it derail the transition to democracy? What are their chances of success? Did they really carry out revolutions or merely provoke a change in the personnel manning the ship of state?

Despite acerbic debates about the shape of the new constitutions, there was very little dissent from the ideals of parliamentary democracy among the engaged youth. After decades of dictatorship and an implicit Leninism, in which the people were represented by a self-appointed vanguard, masses of Arab youth were demanding popular sovereignty. They chanted, "Bread, liberty, and social justice." Some wanted a more French-style strong executive and exclusion of overt religious assertion in the state, while others saw Turkey's religiously inflected Justice and Development Party government as their model. Thousands of new nongovernmental organizations have been founded in the three countries, often by engaged young people, working for human rights, women's rights, cultural freedoms, workers' rights, and food and water for the poor. They sought personal freedom and freedom to organize and express oneself in the face of renewed elite repression. Most troubling of all was the repression of the Muslim Brotherhood in Egypt beginning in the summer of 2013, which went well beyond a reaction against the Brotherhood's own dictatorial tendencies to denial of political rights to the country's major party on the religious right. The rise of crime and of political terrorism from Muslim extremists and the constant instability and changes in the executive, while serious problems, should not blind us to the achievements of the youth in putting increased personal autonomy and dignity on the table for societal negotiation. They have kicked off what is likely to be a long intergenerational argument, in which there will be both advances and setbacks. We are still two or three decades from the time when the Arab millennials will come to power, but they have laid down markers on the future of the region.

Because I am a blogger myself, some of the youth activists had followed my work and were happy to meet me and exchange perspectives. I have met some of those whose stories I tell here, and my admiration for these brave and innovative young people who have shaken the world with their rejection of censorship, repression, and torture will be apparent. I dedicate this book to the young men and women who gave their lives for these causes, some of whom did not live to see the revolutions they wrought, while others are still in jail.

THE NEW ARABS

1

The Arab Millennials

New Political Cultures

The Japanese novelist Haruki Murakami observed, "If you're young and talented, it's like you have wings." In the twenty-first century that kind of talent is to be found in the Middle East. The Arab world is young; in some countries the median age is twenty-four, almost half that of graying Japan and Germany. The youth born between 1977 and 2000 are a big part of what I mean by "the new Arabs." The young people, from teenagers through thirty-four-year-olds, spearheaded the large social and political changes that erupted in 2011 and created cultural and political frameworks that their elders often then joined or allied with. Marketers call this cohort "Generation Y" or "millennials," since some of them came of age with the new millennium of the Common Era and the youngest of them were born around then. In the early twenty-first century Gen Y accounts for over a third of the 400 million Arabs. Although the Arab world is not unique in having so many youth (so do sub-Saharan Africa and South and Southeast Asia), it is distinctive compared to the wealthy and powerful northern hemisphere and even when compared to parts of the global South such as China and much of Latin America. Moreover, the Arab youth bulge

faces more and different challenges than their Indian or Indonesian counterparts. Because of low rates of investment and other forms of economic
and political stagnation, Arab youth face an unusually pressing problem of
unemployment.

How is this generation "new"? What distinguishes them from the generation that was born in the mid- to late-1950s? Sociologists and pollsters
have found that the Arab Generation Y has some special and cohesive
characteristics: they are significantly more urban, literate, wired, and secular
than their parents. These are among the characteristics that allowed them
to mount youth movements and political organizations and to challenge
the dictators of their region, sometimes successfully. Arab youth themselves
were conscious of these differences from their predecessors. In a 2012 discussion forum hosted in the Arab Gulf, one young man complained that
his generation was always being told by its elders that it was inferior to
what went before: "Often we hear that this generation is very bad, a failed
generation, a useless generation, a lazy generation, soft and unproductive,
envious, devoid of humanity." Indignant, he countered, "In my opinion our
generation is beautiful and there is nothing wrong with it—it is a creative
generation, innovative, possessing knowledge and culture and awareness,
renewing, developed in every field."[1]

The Youth Bulge and Unemployment

One of the reasons the older generation may have unfairly painted the
millennials as unproductive is that they suffer from Depression-era rates of
forced idleness. In 2011 the average unemployment rate for youth in the
region was 23 percent; for young women it was even worse, 31 percent. The
rates are twice the global average and are unusual even in the global South.
What sociologists call the "youth bulge" is one culprit here. The arrival of
so many eighteen-year-olds on the job market every year requires that Arab
countries create enormous numbers of new jobs if they are to be accom-
modated, something those countries have found impossible to do. Other
regions with high population growth rates suffer less from unemployment,
though, and this discrepancy is explained by remarkably low rates of invest-

ment in the Arab world, the prevalence of corruption and crony capitalism, and unusually low participation of women in the workforce.[2]

Take Libya. In the first decade of this century, petroleum revenues were about 25 percent of the country's gross domestic product, but they provided 60 percent of the money for salaries of government workers and almost all the country's export earnings. The downturn in petroleum prices in 2008 and 2009, with the global financial collapse and mortgage crisis spurred by corrupt practices on Wall Street, caused a significant economic retrenchment in Libya. As in other petroleum states, unemployment was already high in the first decade of the century, generally estimated at 30 percent even though the official figure was 13 percent. Libya is a young country with a young workforce. Over two-thirds are millennials, under thirty-five when the revolution broke out in 2011. About half of the population was born after 1986. The sclerotic state-run economy was treated as a giant piggy bank for the Gaddafis and their hangers-on, inside and outside the country, and despite billions in income it could not provide employment to this annual avalanche of youth coming on the job market. The high unemployment rate therefore primarily hit the youth. The oil wealth allowed the government to give people subsidies of various sorts, making them dependent on such handouts, especially in the absence of a vigorous private sector. When the social security law was passed in 1980, it became almost impossible for a private employer to fire an employee, since termination required provision of severance pay equal to six months of salary. This situation made the small private sector cautious about taking on new employees.[3] If there were so many problems in a wealthy oil state with a small population, imagine the difficulties that faced larger non-oil-exporting countries such as Egypt and Tunisia.

Some observers have wanted to make a larger argument about the effects of this youth bulge, seeking to hang everything from revolutions to a rise of terrorism on it.[4] But we historians are suspicious of one-cause explanations and have long pointed out that although Britain's population tripled in the period 1800–1900, the country suffered no major political upheavals. A similar point could be made about some Middle Eastern countries in the past century and a half. It would be too simplistic to conclude that the Arab upheavals of the second decade of the twenty-first century were caused simply by the low mean age of the population.

The Arab world began its population boom around 1850, and the numbers are jaw-dropping. Egypt had perhaps 5 million people in that year. By 1900 its population had doubled, to 10 million; by 1950 it had doubled again, to about 20 million. This hundred years of population growth is partly owing to the dominance of cotton as an export crop. Before the adoption of combines, cotton harvesting was labor-intensive, and the small hands of children and women were thought better suited to it; farmers thus wanted big families. But in the past sixty years population growth went into overdrive. By 1980 there were 43 million Egyptians, and at the time of the overthrow of Hosni Mubarak in early 2011, Egypt had 83 million people.

This general trajectory is common throughout the Arab world and is not well understood, since the increases began before the impact of modern medicine. In the twentieth century the boom was aided by reductions in death rates because of advances such as inoculation and penicillin. Though some countries, such as Tunisia, saw their birth rate level off as early as the 1970s, in others, such as Egypt, it was not until 2005 that the youth bulge began to decline for the first time in all those decades.[5] Every generation in the Arab world since the middle of the nineteenth century has therefore had a youth bulge. The major revolutionary movements in modern Egypt occurred in 1882, 1919, 1952, and 2011.[6] Given that a generation is about twenty-four years, some generations in modern Egypt were relatively quiet, including those who came of age in the very early twentieth century and those who hit their twenties in the early 1970s. The other generations in modern Egyptian history that mounted major social and political movements on reaching their early twenties for the most part were reacting against British imperialism and foreign economic dominance. The revolution of 2011 was different, being primarily domestic in its concerns and themes, and it announced the advent of a new generation that was decidedly postcolonial.

Urbanism and Cosmopolitanism

It was not only politics that shaped Gen Y but also rapid social, economic, and technological change. Whereas their parents mostly lived in villages, far more Arab millennials live in cities, and consequently far more of them are working in services or industry than as farmers and fishermen.

Colonel Gaddafi and his quirky oil state herded Libyans into cities in droves, raising the rate of urbanization from 50 percent in 1970 to 75 percent in 1985.[7] By 2010 Libya was almost 80 percent urban, similar to Taiwan, Norway, and Spain. Despite the tendency of pundits to analyze the country with regard to tribe and clan, urban migration typically weakens those forms of social organization. The really tribal societies are usually rural. Libyan youth for the most part organized on the basis of occupation or city or city quarter. Sometimes these urban units, as with the city of Zintan in Libya, overlapped with clan loyalties, but often they did not. Urban institutions such as factories provide opportunities for the establishment of unions and the fostering of solidarity across sectarian and clan barriers. The steel workers of Misrata played an important role in that city's 2011 rebellion against the Libyan government.

As in Libya, in the 1970s about half of Tunisians were rural, but by 2009 two-thirds were urban (and even many of the villagers were increasingly encompassed by cities and urban ways of life).[8] Tunisia's rate of urbanization on the eve of revolution neared that of Austria and Italy. The previous generation had been more like Nigeria or Romania. Again, urban unions in industrial cities such as Sfax (on the Mediterranean, south of the capital of Tunis) played a large role in the 2010–11 revolution. Cities often also have big high school and university populations, affording opportunities for campus organization of demonstrations. In Tunisia the main nationwide student organization, the General Union of Tunisian Students (Union générale des étudiants de Tunisie, UGET), appears repeatedly in accounts of demonstrations from late 2010 onward. Soccer games and other cultural and sports events not only gather large numbers of people but allow for rowdy organizations such as the young Ultras (soccer fanatics), who developed a hostile relationship with the police. Institutions such as attorneys' and judges' guilds that have a professional interest in the rule of law attain a critical mass in big cities that can give them political weight in times of crisis. Cities are also places where large numbers of young, middle-class culture workers congregate: bloggers, journalists, software engineers, artists, and other opinion leaders.[9]

Egypt's story with regard to city dwellers is more complex than that of the two North African societies, since it added enormous numbers of new urban residents if we consider the absolute numbers. During the era of the millennials, Egypt's urban population increased from fewer than 20 million to 36 million, nearly doubling from 1980 to 2009. But the proportion of the population that lived in cities on the eve of the 2011 revolution was still only about 50 percent. There were two major reasons for this slowing of urbanization. One was the long period of relative economic and social stagnation beginning in the 1980s. The other was that many Egyptians emigrated abroad in search of work in that era; as much as 10 to 12 percent of the active citizen labor force was overseas, whether in the oil-rich countries of the Gulf or in Europe.[10] The oil price revolution of the 1970s produced huge revenue increases for countries that often did not have the population to put these billions of dollars to work in the local economy. The Gulf imported Egyptian construction workers and schoolteachers on a mammoth scale, people who otherwise would have gone to Egyptian cities in search of work. To a lesser extent, Europe, with its declining rates of population growth and still-strong economies, also brought in large numbers of Egyptians. These Egyptians did become urban, but they did so abroad. When, as often happened, they were forced home by economic downturns in their host countries, they brought urban skills and ways of thinking back to their villages.

Anthropologist Farha Ghannam reports that urban working-class and lower-middle-class young men would make late-night forays into the city, hanging out at coffeehouses, having sexual adventures, getting into fights with other young men, and facing police harassment and arrest. They found the whole city open to them and spent significant amounts of time grooming to ensure an acceptable appearance. They also learned to their dismay that their worth was increasingly measured by their income.[11] This floating population of unmarried young men was not necessarily political or revolutionary, but their discontent with their low economic and employment status and their conflicts with the police made many of them sympathetic to youth movements when those turned revolutionary.

A large textile industry dotted urban Egypt with factories that often had thousands of workers, who attempted to organize on the shop floor, engaging in strikes and factory sit-ins. Thousands of labor actions were launched in the early twenty-first century, and the urban working class had advantages of organization and sheer critical mass that made them important to the January 25 revolution in ways that were not always visible to outside observers concentrating on the middle-class youth in Tahrir Square. Because many of these factories were outside Cairo, in cities such as El Mahalla El Kubra and Alexandria, journalists based in the capital rarely reported on them.

Not only were the young Arabs much more likely to be urban than their parents, but they innovated in creating a cosmopolitan culture. This generation made the pop music video clip (their version of MTV videos) a phenomenon, were interested in American or Arab French hip-hop, adopted the short message service (SMS) texting function on their cell phones, flocked in their millions to social media, grew up watching international news on satellite television, sometimes traveled and worked abroad for a few years, and formed a plethora of civil society organizations that challenged old shibboleths. Some activist youth put these changes in connectivity to political purposes. While the mere existence of a youth bulge does not predict political upheaval, it is also true that where activists can successfully mobilize youth, they have a lot to work with. Single teenagers and twenty-somethings have free time and lack the family and occupational constraints that even young marrieds face, and so are available to join organizations and attend meetings and rallies.[12]

The internet put young Arabs in contact with like-minded youth not only in other Arab countries but throughout the world, contributing to their globalization. Because of the internet and because the small number of government-owned television channels was supplemented by both Arabic-language and international satellite channels, the Arab millennials are the most cosmopolitan Middle Easterners yet. While their parents could get the Arabic service of the BBC and, on shortwave, the old Voice of America, it was possible to live in provincial Egypt and to know little of the outside world. In contrast, for Gen Y, a French, American, or British election is almost a local event.

The young Arabs are also disproportionately likely to have worked outside the country. In 2008, out of some 10 million Tunisians, about 1 million lived abroad as guest workers (over 800,000 of these in Europe, more than half in France).[13] Many of these guest workers earn enough money to change their social status when they return home. While they are abroad the internet and satellite television allow them to remain connected to their friends, their culture, and politics, and when they return home they can keep in touch with developments in their former host country.[14] Having few prospects in their own country led some 8 million Egyptians, mostly youth, to apply for the U.S. immigration lottery in 2006. In the first decade of the century an estimated half a million Egyptians illegally slipped into Greece and Italy, and thence the rest of Europe, putting their lives at risk on rickety Mediterranean vessels to escape economic and political stagnation. At that time too a million Egyptian graduate students were studying in Europe and North America, few of whom planned on returning.[15] In 2008 about a million of Egypt's 25 million workers had taken jobs abroad on temporary visas, about half of them in Saudi Arabia.[16] This statistic does not count Egyptians who had emigrated permanently, who may be as much as 10 percent of Egypt's population. That so many Egyptians live for a while in Saudi Arabia probably has helped make Egyptian Islam and politics more conservative. That Tunisians' main experience abroad is in Europe may explain some of the difference between Egypt and Tunisia. The latter remains far more secular despite advances by the religious Renaissance Party.

The New Arabs Are Wired

The role of the internet in the revolutions that began in 2011 has provoked debate. Some observers argue that calling them "Facebook revolutions" is inaccurate and that traditional street politics was far more important, pointing out that only a little over half of the revolutionaries even had access to the internet. Others question whether the revolutions could even have occurred had the youth been captive to state newspapers and news broadcasts that neglected to report protests or denigrated them as the insignificant acts of a few malcontents or paid agents for shadowy foreign interests.[17] In order to assess these arguments it is important to understand the communication networks in which the millennials were embedded.

The older members of this enormous stratum were in their late teens when the internet was introduced on a significant scale in the Arab world, and they were its pioneers. As will be shown, the dictatorial regimes developed cyber-police to track and imprison or exile dissents. Unlike in previous generations, however, exile did not end their involvement in Tunisian politics. Because of the internet, expatriate dissident websites such as Nawaat, founded by Sami Ben Gharbia from the Netherlands, could benefit from the talents of young activists in several countries yet focused on Tunisia. Tunisians could access these sites if they knew the necessary workarounds that allowed them to bypass Ben Ali's censors.

The internet was regulated by the Tunisian Internet Agency, which reported to the Ministry of Telecommunications. The managers of internet cafés tracked patrons' activities online and could disconnect them at any time. Ben Ali's police were also involved in monitoring those who surfed the web, with plainclothesmen visiting the establishments and recovering the navigation history of patrons from the browsers they had used. The cyber police looked for subversive sites, which they then blocked. They also tried, without much success, to close down proxy sites that allowed users to evade government filtering of sites and to limit licenses for new internet cafés.[18] In fact, any hope Ben Ali and his fellow dictators had that they could slow the penetration of the internet among youth, or closely monitor and control it, rapidly slipped away.

Not all Arab youth, by any means, were wired by the end of the first decade of the century. Although cyber cafés were common in Cairo and Alexandria, the rural areas of Egypt were not as well served. In many governorates at this time computers were still rare in Egyptian schools. In some rural provinces in 2007 only 10 percent of the people had access to computers.[19] But note that if each person in that 10 percent had two hundred family members, friends, and acquaintances with whom to discuss information gained from the web, the effect could be significant. Moreover, access increased rapidly after 2007, even in the countryside.

The internet was only one of many new forms of connectivity encompassing large numbers of youth. At the beginning of 2009 a little over half of Egyptians had a cell phone. By early 2010, nearly three-fourths had one, and there were hundreds of thousands of new connections each month. In

Tunisia by 2009 almost everyone had a cell phone. Even many relatively poor and rural youth had a mobile connection in these two countries.[20] The young people I have talked to in the Arab world often mentioned the importance of cell phones for their activism. News received initially via the internet was then spread by calling around or sending SMS texts to friends. When the Libyan internet was cut off for half a year during the revolution, one young Libyan in Misrata explained to me, the cell phones and SMS were still available to activists. Satellite television was also widely available and opened many horizons. In 2009 19.5 million Egyptian households had televisions, the highest TV penetration in Africa. Of these, some 38 percent had free satellite, and another 4 percent had paid satellite service.[21]

Gen Y eagerly took to the internet. A 2005 article on marketing to Arab youth in a web-based magazine out of Dubai spoke of the Arab Generation Y and how advertisers could reach its members.[22] The author wrote that studies had shown that these youth spent more time surfing the internet or on their mobile phones each week than reading print magazines or watching TV. Search engines offered advertisers an opportunity to piggyback on the inquiries that had become popular with youth obsessively looking for their favorite "celebrities, video games, music and movies." Linda Herrera, a pioneering researcher on the Arab Gen Y, was told by her informants that they felt as though the ability to download text files and films changed their personality. Those dissatisfied with the education they were receiving could supplement it on the internet. They could use torrents to download Hollywood films with subtitles and improve their English. A young Egyptian, Haisam, told Herrera, "Having this knowledge pumped into your head is like the Matrix. . . . Maybe someone who lived for seventy years wouldn't have the chance to know what we were able to learn in two years."[23]

Another opportunity arose from portal sites such as Maktoob, "perhaps the world's biggest community of Arabs aged between 16–26." The site provided subchannels on music, soccer, and social encounters. Other portal sites, such as Mazzika, concentrated on offering MP3 files of pop music, and as the Web 2.0 unfolded, it became possible for sites such as Melody to offer music videos. The "video clip," as young Arabs called it, was to the Middle East what MTV had been to the West's Gen X in the 1980s. In the Middle East, because of cultural conservatism, many popular clips were banned from television by governments, but they circulated freely on the web. The ecology of the internet allowed easy sharing of text, music, and (from about 2005) video and permitted some items to go viral, shared by millions.

Marketing researchers found that younger internet users were the ones likely to share online content with their peers. Apparently older readers growing up in the 1950s and 1960s with inert print media or television thought of information consumption as private and individualistic, whereas the Arab Gen Y wanted to share what they were reading or viewing, seeing information as an interactive group experience. Sultan al-Qassemi, an internet activist based in the United Arab Emirates, pointed to another key part of the interactive media: "Readers of newspapers couldn't argue back."[24] Comment sections and various forms of communication among those experiencing a news item together allowed the emergence of a cooperative critique and what some have called "symmetrical participation." The wired generation played "an active role in the production, alteration, consumption, and dissemination of content; their relationship to the media is more interactive."[25] New media and the internet sharpened critical faculties and encouraged a healthy skepticism. Young people online take apart an urban legend or a propaganda point the way Upper Nile crocodiles strip the flesh off a gazelle that falls into the river. The various forms of media and communications newly available to the millennials were used for many purposes, not just (or even primarily) politics. Still, they made it more difficult for youth to drop out of current affairs because of what those who study the internet call "crisis informatics," in which friends intensively share news updates on social media and the penetration of information becomes inescapable.

Chat rooms and internet forums also attracted millions of young Arabs. The anonymity of the web perhaps allowed for more frank discussions of relationships and religion and for interactions across the sexes. The marketing article enthused about the advent of "instant chat," which "caused a near revolution across both teenagers and adults alike." In 2005 over 1.5 million consumers in the Middle East were logging on to MSN Messenger every day.

Let us flash forward to 2010, when there were tens of millions of young

Arabs on the internet. In that year, throughout the Arab world, the number of Facebook users alone almost doubled, from about 12 million to over 21 million. Tunisian journalist Henda Chennaoui wrote that when she graduated from journalism school in 2007, she discovered Facebook, which she called a "turning point" in her life: "It permitted me and other young dissidents to better organize and structure our networks of struggle. That did not prevent me from retaining a strong contact with the blogosphere through my blog."[26] Youth between the ages of fifteen and twenty-nine made up three-quarters of Facebook users three years later. Nearly a quarter of these Facebook accounts belonged to Egyptians. Young men predominated over girls and women by two to one. Still, by the end of 2010 seven million young Arab women were updating their status, joining pages, and sharing items of interest from their friends. Never before in history had that many young Arab women been visible and active in a public sphere. If the governments' secret police internet units were often outfoxed at the beginning of the century, when they had only relatively small numbers of connections to monitor, imagine how overwhelmed they became in 2010. By December 2010 over 17 percent of Tunisia's population was on Facebook; that same year some 58 percent of Egyptian youth between the ages of eighteen and thirty-five had access to the internet.[27] While social media and the internet did not cause anything to happen by themselves, they had a multiplier effect when deployed by activists. In the week after the fall of Tunisian dictator Ben Ali (the third week of January 2011), one-sixth of Tunisian blog posts treated revolution, and one in ten centered on liberty.[28]

In assessing the impact of the internet and other forms of electronic communication on the youth movements of the Arab world, it may be useful to consider the idea of the multiplier effect, as explained by economists. Let's say you had a company worth $1 billion, and because it did very well last year you put another $30 million into it. That does not seem like a lot of extra funding. That money, however, would raise salaries and produce bonuses and perhaps result in some new hires. So the money would go into the economy when the employees spent it. Then the people working at companies making the things bought with that money would also get raises, and new hires would be made. These people would then buy goods and pass the money on yet again. The money would go through at least five sets of hands before the multiplier effect tapered off. So putting $30 million into the company had a much, much bigger effect than it looked like on the surface. Likewise the internet produces a multiplier effect, recognized implicitly when we speak of an internet posting "going viral," meaning that it is intensively forwarded to ever larger circles of people, until it reaches a saturation point and subsides in popularity. Virality is the way the multiplier effect works with regard to online communications.[29]

The New Arabs Are More Literate

One of the reasons the internet and social media were so much more popular among the youth than among the older generation is that users must be literate. In the beginning of the century they even needed to have a basic grasp of Latin script, since web protocols did not yet allow for web addresses or URLs in Arabic script.

The literacy of the Arab Gen Y upset social hierarchies. Many sons could read and write, while their fathers could not, allowing the sons to take charge of certain areas of life for the family. Many sisters became an intellectual match for their father or brothers in a way unexampled in the generation of their mother and aunts. Anthropologist Farha Ghannam tells the story of Zaki and Zakiya, a brother and sister in a working-class neighborhood of Cairo. Zaki was allowed to run around the neighborhood doing errands and got a part-time job when only seven years old. He dropped out of school after the eighth grade. He was expected to lead a responsible, sober life, forsaking his late-night forays with friends into the city. Because of his limited literacy his prospects were few. In contrast, Zakiya was kept at home or in the neighborhood in her youth and on two occasions was beaten by her brother for staying out too late or going too far away. She studied hard and finished high school, and in her twenties got a good job as an overseer in a factory in a middle-class neighborhood about an hour away from her home. She shopped in malls and could afford more expensive clothing. Her income and mobility actually increased as her brother's declined, in part because of her greater literacy.[30] Literate, urban young women are likely to use birth control and limit family size, helping them achieve a middle-class lifestyle.[31]

Gen Y are far more likely to be able to read and write than their elders, giving them greater access to the internet. In 1980 only about half the citizens of the Arabic-speaking states had these skills.[32] By 2000 the average literacy rate was 61.5 percent in seventeen Arab countries, but among those fifteen to twenty-four, the rate was much higher, around 80 percent, for both men and women. Although in some countries as many as 50 percent of older women still could not read and write in 2000 to 2004, in those years the average literacy rate of Arab women age fifteen to twenty-four in the six countries where there were significant political upheavals, was 82 percent. In three of those countries—Tunisia, Libya, and Bahrain—it was over 90 percent! There is an enormous difference between expecting 50 percent of the people your age to be able to read a newspaper and expecting 80 percent of them to read. Generation Y is the most literate cohort of Arabs ever to exist.[33] This large pool of educated young people in Egypt fueled the rise of newspapers that, despite the country's censorship regime, often demonstrated a streak of independence. The four most popular among the youth tended to have a secular orientation and often took their cues from bloggers and human rights NGOs regarding which stories to pursue.[34]

Psychologist Muhammad Khalil told Al Jazeera television in a 2002 interview on the generational divide, "The ability of the older generation to work with computers, the internet and other modern communications technologies is far less than that of their children in the young generation. It leaves them, really, unable to follow the preoccupations of their children and makes them feel as though the gap has increased, that there is a distance, not just in knowledge or in the sources of knowledge, but rather they feel that there is a distance between the social circles in which they live." The program introduced a young woman who told the anchor, "There isn't good communication between my family and myself. Only on the internet are there a lot of people my age who understand me better. I know how to talk with them in my own style, but with my family I am more reserved when I speak."[35] The expert guests pointed out that a literate, internet-savvy child quickly figured out the limits of what an illiterate mother could teach him or her, compared to the information available through independent reading or interactions on the web. These reversals were all the more significant in heavily patriarchal societies that insist on respect for age and strict obedience to family norms and that usually marginalize the young, as well as guarding the prerogative for parents of choosing a lifestyle, a mate, and an occupation for their children.[36]

An Arab satellite news account illustrated the importance of literacy to social advancement when it told the life story of Muhammad Abu Jaus, an Egyptian born into a poor family whose father died before he was two.[37] At five he began working in a thread-making workshop in his village, as well as in the fields growing and harvesting vegetables. In his late twenties Abu Jaus attended a wedding in his village, and when the notary asked him to sign as a witness to the marriage contract he sheepishly confessed that he was unable to read or write, provoking laughter and ridicule among the wedding guests and the presiding officials. He made a private vow then and there that he would not get married until he had gained an education. He entered an anti-illiteracy program and in a few months had graduated with basic literacy skills. He then went to night school and completed a high school degree. He got married as he was finishing his degree, working in the fields during the day and studying at night. He ultimately went to law school, though after he graduated he had to scrimp and save to afford a license to practice. He managed to sign on as an intern to a law firm and specialized in commercial law. Abu Jaus gradually emerged as one of Egypt's foremost corporate attorneys. One of his three sons became an engineer, while the other two became attorneys. This story of a determined peasant who transformed himself into a successful urban professional through literacy and education is unusual in this generation only because he began so late and achieved such stunning success. But his experience mirrors that of tens of millions of young Arabs.

Majdi Abd al-Azim, also an illiterate peasant, tried to run for president of Egypt in spring 2012.[38] He maintained that all the other candidates were ignoring Egypt's still substantial rural sector and were not attending to the country's agricultural crises. He insisted that being illiterate was no bar to running the country, since he could employ someone to read to him, and, besides, he said, Egyptian peasants have natural street smarts superior to those of urban people. In a country that is now largely urban and literate, however, his inability to read and write was seen as a fatal liability to a political career. Only a small minority of Egyptian youth are illiterate, and they face prejudice from young urban populations. The novelist Alaa Al-Aswany, convinced that illiterate peasants are easier for the Muslim Brotherhood to manipulate, demanded on Twitter in advance of the referendum on the new Egyptian constitution in late fall 2012 that the vote be taken away from anyone who could not read or write.[39] (Al-Aswany's argument is hard to countenance, given that many rural residents of the Egyptian Delta are hostile to political Islam and did not vote for the Muslim Brotherhood candidate Mohamed Morsi in the June 2012 presidential election.)

Literacy has long had implications for political mobilization. One of the keys to the long period of European rule in the global South, from the eighteenth century until after World War II, was that these empires largely presided over territories consisting of small rural villages, the inhabitants of which were unable to read or write and therefore were hampered in uniting against their foreign overlords. Some imperial rulers, such as Lord Cromer, British controller-general of Egypt from 1883 to 1907, were suspicious of educated "natives," and consequently they underfunded education.[40] Cromer was cruel, but his theory was correct: an illiterate Egyptian population was much less likely to be able to unite for anticolonial activities.

The vast increase in literacy in Modern Standard Arabic in this generation over previous ones allowed the millennials to communicate beyond the small groups that use their dialect. Literacy also bestowed on them the confidence to challenge their elders, born in part of a realization that they possessed competencies their parents and grandparents did not. Sometimes these skills gave women advantages, including on the internet.

The Secular-Religious Divide

The distinctive character of today's youth bulge was demonstrated by a large Pew Charitable Trust poll of the world's Muslims, published in 2012, which found that respondents under the age of thirty-five were almost everywhere at least somewhat less observant religiously than those over that age, and in some instances the generational divide was great.[41] In Egypt, Tunisia, and Morocco a little over 50 percent of older respondents said they listen to the Qur'an being recited daily, but among the younger set, only about

40 percent do. An average of 62 percent of middle-aged and older people said they go to mosque once a week, but only 46 percent of young people do. (The biggest spread here is in Tunisia, at 55 versus 38 percent.) Nearly 75 percent of older Arabs claimed to pray "several" times a day, while only about 57 percent of the young people do. The fall-off was in observance, not necessarily in expressed faith. Only in Tunisia, of these three countries, was there a significant difference between the young and the old with regard to the sentiment that religion is very important in their lives. Young Lebanese Muslims are a lot more secular than their counterparts elsewhere, with only 42 percent saying religion is important in their lives; only 25 percent attending mosque regularly, and only 20 percent listening to the Qur'an daily. Tunisian youth are the next most secular in the Arab world.

A decline in religious observance is perhaps not completely unrelated to a willingness to act in a revolutionary way. Secular and leftist youth played a leading role in the revolts, and they were the least likely to have been indoctrinated into the conservative Sunni Muslim mind-set that discourages challenging governmental authority.

A little over a year after the 2011 revolution a young Egyptian activist posted a prose poem at his website, then called The Mother of the Blog, entitled "I Am a Secularist." He belonged to the left-of-center, pro-labor youth group April 6. His poem conveys some of the spirit of the youth culture's disinterest in being observant and its objection to regimented forms of religion:[42]

> *I am secular: That is, for me, religion is for God and the nation is for all.*
> *I am secular: That is, for me, there is no religion in politics and no politics in religion.*
> *I am secular: That is, your name, your title, your religion, your color, your sex are not important for me: all of us are Egyptian and equal before the law.*[43]

He concludes that others should be free to worship in temples or churches, or not worship at all, just as he worships in a mosque.

These sentiments reflect a commitment to tolerance rather than to

French-style militant secularism and even exhibit pious turns of phrase. Yet the author had provocatively put a hammer and sickle next to the name of his blog. Activist youth went back and forth between opposition to political Islam and a willingness to ally with it, but in Egypt by the summer of 2013 there was a decisive split between the two currents. Secularism, or at least an opposition to the Muslim Brotherhood, was becoming not just an attitude but a distinctive youth movement.[44] It is perhaps instructive of the post–Muslim Brotherhood atmosphere in Egypt that the author of the poem, a small part of which is translated above, abandoned his anonymity in fall of 2013, as his secular convictions came to reflect the political direction of the country.

The sociologist Karl Mannheim argued that dramatic political events form one matrix of a generation's common consciousness, and the religious-secular divide has been an important theme of the Arab Gen Y.[45] Its oldest members were born in 1977 and came to consciousness politically in their early teens, so they lived through the collapse of the Soviet Union in 1991. They thereby became the first post-Soviet generation of Arabs since republican Arab nationalism had begun tilting toward Moscow in the 1950s. The old communist model of governance and economy had no attractions for them. At the same time, they were freed to experiment with new ideas about socialism and social democracy as they pushed back against the assertions of the primacy of the market and business classes by the Clinton administration and its successors. From 1992 through the early twenty-first century the secular-religious divide threw Algeria into a civil war between a secular military regime and fundamentalist challengers. They saw the attempted assassination of Mubarak by Muslim radicals at a summit in Addis Ababa in 1995, and they lived through the terrorist attacks of the Egyptian Islamic Jihad of Ayman al-Zawahiri, including one that killed sixty-two foreign tourists in Luxor in 1997 and disgusted most Egyptians. Crucially, they lived through the 9/11 attacks by al-Qaeda on the United States and Washington's invasion and occupation of Iraq and Afghanistan. Many of them got their start in politics by protesting the Iraq War. At the same time, the liberals, leftists, and moderate Muslims were distressed at the hard-line fundamentalism and violence of rising religious movements such as the Salafis and al-Qaeda, as well as the vicious civil war waged by religious forces in Iraq. Engaged youth in Egypt mobilized in the Kefaya (Enough) movement against the 2005 phony presidential and parliamentary elections conducted by Mubarak. Most rooted for Hizbullah in 2006, when Israel attacked Lebanon and failed to dislodge the Shiite party-militia, but their enthusiasm was fueled by Arab nationalism rather than admiration of Shiite Islam or the model of the Islamic Republic of Iran. They lived through 2008, the oldest of them in their early thirties, when major labor strikes were launched in textile factories near Cairo and the mines in Gafsa in southern Tunisia, and the leftists among them gave their support. Struggles between a secular and a religious vision of society had become central to the Middle Eastern experience in this generation, provoking contradictory responses. Some left-liberal youth were determined to create alliances across the secular-religious divide. Others were determined not to let what they saw as fundamentalist terrorism shape their lives.

People in complex societies have more than one social identity, and when challenged they are willing to rank those identities according to which are most important to them. Some identities have to do with social roles or with communities of belief, favored lifestyles, or even hobbies. Moreover, which identities they rank highest can change over time, depending on the social circumstances. When a representative sample of Egyptians was asked in 2001 whether they saw themselves as Muslims first or Egyptians first, an overwhelming 80 percent replied that they saw themselves as Muslims first, with only 8 percent foregrounding their national identity. But remember that in 2001 the vast majority of millennials were too young to be sampled. Similar results were reported in 2007. After the overthrow of Mubarak in 2011, when the sociologist Mansoor Moaddel asked his sample the same question, about 50 percent responded that they were Egyptians first and Muslims second, while 48 percent said that they were Muslims first.[46] The sample probably included many more persons born in the 1980s and early 1990s, and the revolution itself may have contributed to secularization. An impressive 84 percent of Egyptians told one pollster that they regarded democracy and economic prosperity as the main goals of the Arab uprisings of 2011; only 9 percent said they thought that the goal was to set up an Islamic government. Feelings about Islamic law (sharia) followed a similar trajectory. In 2001 nearly 50 percent of Egyptians insisted that it was "very important" for the government to implement Islamic law, but in 2011 only 28 percent held that sentiment. When Moaddel asked a representative sample of 3,500 Egyptians to rate their participation in the demonstrations against Mubarak, those who were active were disproportionately likely to have been users of the internet, consumers of newspapers, urban, and well off. They described themselves as having "modern values" and being willing to have European friends. Those in this poll who were most religious and most intolerant were least likely to have joined the revolutionary movement.[47]

These findings might seem at odds with the electoral victories that the Muslim religious right gained in the elections held in late 2011 and the summer of 2012 in Tunisia and Egypt. Those victories, however, were often exaggerated in the Western press. In Tunisia the religious Renaissance Party got only about 37 percent of the votes (which translated into over 40 percent of the seats in Parliament). It formed a government and gained the office of prime minister only by making a coalition with secular parties. It had to rule as a minority government rather than achieving an overwhelming victory. In Egypt the religious parties gained about 66 percent of the seats in Parliament, and the Muslim Brotherhood candidate later won the presidency. But many of those Egyptians who voted for the religious right were not themselves fundamentalists; instead, they believed that the proponents of political Islam, once in office, would not be corrupt and would form an effective bulwark against the return of the old regime. A starkly different political geography was revealed in the first round of the presidential elections in mid-May 2012. Three of the leading presidential candidates, out of five that had a chance of getting into the run-off, were secularists, and together they garnered 60 percent of the vote. The fundamentalist candidate who did get into the run-offs (Mohamed Morsi of the Muslim Brotherhood) did so by a small margin, and he won by an even smaller margin against a secular candidate who was a man of the old regime. In June 2013 some 22 million Egyptians signed a petition asking Morsi to leave office, far more than the 13 million who voted for him the year before. In Libya the Muslim fundamentalist party fared poorly in the national parliamentary elections of July 2012, though many of the independents elected were religious and conservative. Even in Egypt, where the religious right is obviously strong, its fortunes fluctuated a great deal after the revolution and its victories likely derived from voters and activists of an older generation, whereas the less religious young were less interested in running for Parliament.

All this is not to say that the religious right is unimportant or marginal among young people in the countries of the Arab Spring. Just as leftist groups have emerged into prominence, so too has a new generation of Muslim activists, including the Renaissance movement in Tunisia and the Muslim Brotherhood in Egypt. The Muslim Brotherhood was founded in 1928 by Hasan al-Banna and aimed at removing European influences after the years of British rule (1882–1922). In the 1930s it became popular among the urban lower middle classes as a religious revival movement. In the 1940s, when the British reoccupied Egypt during World War II and the Jewish immigrants into Mandate Palestine began asserting themselves, the Brotherhood leadership formed a "Secret Apparatus" that conducted a campaign of terrorism. This covert violence was discovered by Egyptian police in 1948, and the organization was banned. It responded by assassinating Prime Minister Mahmoud al-Nuqrashi in December 1948. Al-Banna was shot to death in early 1949, probably by Egyptian secret police in reprisal for al-Nuqrashi's assassination. The organization went underground. It was briefly rehabilitated after 1952 by the young officers' coup, but its attempt to assassinate Colonel Gamal Abdel Nasser in 1954 led to another ban, with leaders and rank and file jailed and tortured. In the 1970s President Anwar El Sadat struck a bargain with the Brotherhood that they would forsake political violence and become junior partners in the center-right state he was attempting to create (in reaction against the socialism of the Nasser period). When Sadat restored Parliament, the Brotherhood began fielding candidates (under other party rubrics, since Egyptian law then forbade religiously based parties). Thereafter, the Brotherhood always had a handful of members in Parliament and gained experience in campaigning and canvassing neighborhoods. The Mubarak regime depended on the Muslim Brotherhood as a sort of loyal opposition in cracking down on radical groups such as the al-Gama'a al-Islamiyya and the Egyptian Islamic Jihad of Ayman al-Zawahiri in the 1990s.[48]

The Muslim Brotherhood youth wing produced hundreds of bloggers beginning in 2007, and its tight, cadre-like organization allowed it to play a role in the 2011 revolution. Religious youth were among the voters who propelled Morsi into the presidency in June 2012, and the Tunisian Renaissance Party gained 37 percent of the vote in October 2011, in part because of the support of rural youth. To the right of both of these are the Salafis, hard-line, sometimes violent religious activists. Many of these young men have worked in Saudi Arabia and brought back home the intolerance and rigidity of the Wahhabi tradition.[49] But while Salafis get a lot of press, they are not a big portion of the population, and the secular-minded center and left are far more numerous, especially among the young. What we see is the polarization of youth in this generation, with most of them tending to be less observant but a significant number supporting fundamentalism. Some of the vehemence of the religious right may be in part a reaction against this decline in the proportion of observant Muslims in this generation.

It is possible that members of Generation Y are turning away from religion as the principal guide to their lives because they have other forces competing for their attention. In many Middle Eastern cities the Western-style mall (often populated by many of the same retail outlets as in European or American shopping centers) has become a favored gathering place for middle- and upper-class youth on Fridays, rather than the mosque. Going to the shops has sometimes replaced attending Friday prayers.

They are also heirs to a vague secular philosophical heritage passed on to them from parents who were communists, socialists, liberals, or followers of Arab leftist leaders such as Nasser. Although an explicit secularism is less common than a falling away from strict observance, it is an important strain of youth activism. When Libya elected the first president of its transitional Parliament in the postrevolutionary period, Mohamed al-Magariaf, in the fall of 2012, he gave an interview in which he called for Libya to be a secular (*'almani*) country.[50] Al-Magariaf had defected in 1980 when serving the Gaddafi regime as ambassador to India and joined the leftist group the National Front for the Salvation of Libya, which had tried and failed to assassinate the dictator. Few politicians elsewhere in the Arab world would any longer dare use the term *'almani*, insofar as fundamentalist parties and clerics have associated it with atheism and irreligion. We may, however, be seeing pushback from secularists against more assertive and less repressed religious forces. In October 2012 Lena Ben Mhenni, who blogs as "A Tunisian Girl," posted a short Arabic poem to Twitter, in which she openly spoke of being an atheist and condemned her fundamentalist critics for "backwardness and stupidity," saying that what she disbelieved in above all were their lies and hypocrisy. [51] And in summer of 2013 secular-minded youth opposed to what they saw as creeping theocracy during the Morsi presidency (June 30, 2012 to July 3, 2013) helped provoke a combination of revolution and military coup d'état against him. In the aftermath Egyptians in overtly religious garb were sometimes harassed by outraged secularists.

Still, being an atheist in public and participating in atheistic Facebook sites and blogs is dangerous in countries such as Egypt, and frank unbelief is not only rare but can result in prosecution. The Muslim Brotherhood's rise to political power in 2011–12 made many young atheists cautious for a while, though they insisted that their numbers had greatly increased after the revolution.[52]

My point here is not that Gen Y is deserting religious belief in any numbers but that its members arc on average less observant than their elders and that a majority tend to define themselves in other ways, such as by their nation-state or their political and cultural leanings rather than their religion. As for the committed religious youth, some of them are religious liberals, while others are more hard-line in their fundamentalism than the older generation of Muslim Brothers. The religious divide between the increasing numbers of nonobservant youth and the devotees of hard-line political Islam would be a key theme both during and after the upheavals of 2011.

Networks and Political Culture

This generation of Arab youth movements is characterized by special forms of political breadth and flexibility. Mahmoud Jibril served as an interim prime minister of Libya after the fall of Gaddafi. I heard Jibril speak in Istanbul at a World Forum sponsored by the Turkish government in October 2012. Short, balding, and square-faced, he has something of the bulldog about him. His talk was in part about how the youth had made the revolutions in Libya and elsewhere from 2011 forward. On that warm, sunny day about a year after Gaddafi's death he explained what made these young people distinctive: "My generation had become accustomed to authoritarianism. It had become part of our mentality. If the young people had not mobilized, nothing would have happened."[53] When he was a student, young Arab activists tended to belong to small political parties that declined to have anything to do with one another. "We were divided into insular factions—Marxists, Islamists, nationalists, Nasserists and Baathists." (Nasserists idolized Egypt's left-wing nationalist leader Gamal Abdel Nasser, who died in 1970. Baathists, who belonged to another strain of socialist Arab nationalism, came to rule Syria and Iraq.) These factions, often relatively small and furtive, attempted to organize students on campuses under the nose of the police state. But despite challenging the regime, they found it impossible to abandon their sectarianism long enough to work together. Or at least that was Jibril's experience. What is different about today's youth, he insisted, is that they used the internet to break down those political barriers and to organize themselves across the whole ideological spectrum. "Because of the internet the younger generation has more connectivity, and possesses a broader, more cosmopolitan vision." In his youth Jibril had despaired of organizing for change in Libya, given the fragmentation of the opposition, leaving in his midtwenties for the United States, where he pursued a doctorate in economics at the University of Pittsburgh. In 2007 he finally returned to his homeland, on the promise of Gaddafi's new technocratic elite that things were changing. Jibril joined the revolution early in 2011 and served for seven months as interim prime minister of the transitional government. In May 2013 he and others who had recently served in the Gaddafi government were excluded from politics by an act of the elected Parliament, which was pressured by angry young militiamen insistent that a new, untainted political class come to the fore.

I was excited to hear Jibril's analysis, because it accorded with what I was finding in my own interviews with young Arab activists. In the years leading up to the upheavals that began in 2011, they refused to let themselves be divided and ruled. Among these youth, he said, it was not unusual for secular leftists and Muslim fundamentalists jointly to plan a demonstration, something unheard of thirty years before.

Jibril is certainly right about the leading role of the youth in the uprisings. I had been struck by how the American press called the Libyan revolutionaries seeking to overthrow Gaddafi "rebels," when in Arabic they were invariably called *al-shabab al-thuwwar* (youth revolutionaries). In the summer of 2011 I heard a reporter ask a grizzled old Libyan tribal leader on Arab satellite television how the revolution was going. He replied, "The youth are doing a good job." I suspect the reporter had sought the old man's views because he was venerable and had assumed that he was directing his young tribesmen. But the old man surprised everyone by admitting that his generation wasn't the one making this revolution.

I met with some young Egyptian revolutionaries in a café off Tahrir Square in July 2011, only five months after the fall of the Mubarak regime, and, like Jibril, was struck by their pragmatism and breadth of political vision. At that time their primary goal was to return the Egyptian army to its barracks and firmly subordinate the officer corps to civilian politicians. They seemed genuinely not to care who the civilian politicians might be, as long as they came to power through free, fair, and transparent elections and pledged to go on submitting themselves to such elections. I asked one, a leftist member of April 6, "Aren't you afraid that fundamentalist Muslims will come to power and impose harsh laws and restrict the rights of workers and women?" He smiled, shook his head slowly, and said, "Islam is good." This willingness to work across political divides was context-dependent; it spoke to political pragmatism rather than long-term alliances. The long moment of goodwill between the leftist youth and the Muslim fundamentalist youth that began around 2004 in Egypt sadly came to an end late in 2012, when the Muslim Brotherhood forced a right-wing constitution on the country and began enacting a creeping coup aiming at a new authoritarianism. Even then, many left-liberal youth movements stood up for the right of the Muslim Brothers to play a role in national politics if they were genuinely willing to accept democratic and human rights norms. That is, the basis for shunning a movement did not have to do with the movement's abstract ideology but with whether it seemed like an ally in the search for greater personal freedoms and dignity. Many youth perceived the Brotherhood to be moving in that direction, but when it got into power and behaved dictatorially and cliquishly, they turned on it.

Later in the conversation I asked that member of April 6 for his opinion about a political development, using the Egyptian honorific *hadratak* (literally, "your excellency," but used as a formal *you*, sort of like *usted* in Spanish or *vous* in French). He reacted sharply. "Don't call me 'your excellency,'" he said. "Say 'you.'" The Gen Y Egyptians, especially after the revolution, had an egalitarian way of thinking and disdained social hierarchies and their markers. Sociologist Saad Eddin Ibrahim told me that in February 2011, when he flew back to Egypt and went to Tahrir Square, he asked the demonstrators, "Take me to your leader." He laughed as he told the story. "They looked at me funny." For the most part these social movements are networked and horizontal, not hierarchical. When I was researching the millennials, I came across a manual on the web for Western baby boomer bosses who were hiring and training members of this younger generation in their companies. I was amused that the manual advised the older bosses, "Don't be insulted if the Gen Y employees call you by your first name."[54] Via the internet and social media, many millennials worldwide shared this informal way of addressing one another. After all, a person's age and rank are often opaque in cyberspace.

In much of the Arab world the enormous cohort of youth born after 1977 formed a potential constituency for activists seeking to organize them into a youth movement, appealing to the grievances and aspirations of their generation. This generation was on the whole blocked, with little prospect of gaining real political power or economic betterment. The political systems in the Arab republics were locked up by geriatric, formerly socialist one-party states that had turned into oligarchies. Political positions were given to a relatively small clique of regime sycophants as a form of patronage. The regimes overproduced college graduates, training youth for white-collar and managerial positions that did not exist and had no prospect of existing, forcing the youth to take jobs they felt were beneath them when they did not end up unemployed and living with their parents. Others, in their millions, were forced abroad to find jobs, where they also found new political and social ideas challenging the order at home. Throughout modern history this combination of poor employment prospects, lack of integration into elite structures, and repression has often radicalized intellectuals and contributed to revolutionary upheaval.[55]

Much more urban, literate, wired, and cosmopolitan than their parents, the millennials pioneered new forms of horizontal connectedness and interactivity. They were open to being organized by student unions and the youth wings of activist nongovernmental organizations and small opposition parties, but often attempted to reach out on a generational basis to establish wider linkages. In the first decade of the century Gen Y showed a new ability to form political coalitions across ideological lines, successfully cooperating across the divide between left-liberal groups and those devoted to political Islam. They were most often united against the repression of the police state and outraged by torture and corruption. Evidence of these abuses could now be presented on the internet with a visceral impact that went beyond the human rights reports and print journalism of the 1990s. The new generation's experience with literacy and the internet sometimes also emboldened them to challenge the authority of their often much less educated elders.

The three-way contest between relatively secular dictatorships, left-liberal middle-class activists, and supporters of political Islam produced strange bedfellows as the revolutions unfolded. Before the revolutions the left-liberal youth were more open than their elders to alliances with Muslim religious forces against their authoritarian governments. But after the dictatorships were overthrown, the religious-secular divide roiled the transitions and played a role in North Africa and Egypt similar to that played by ethnic conflicts in the Balkans after the fall of communist Yugoslavia. This conflict was heightened by the shift among many young people, as demonstrated in polling, toward a less observant life.

As the elite born in the 1940s and 1950s, which had locked up the key political and economic institutions, attempted to move from socialism to a market-based system, they saw opportunities for self-enrichment and further entrenchment of their power. They could not imagine that increasingly desperate eighteen-year-olds were looking at them with a mixture of horror and disgust and that these youth were beginning to flex their organizational and ideological muscles.

2

The Republican Monarchs

$\mathcal{M}$illennials in the Arab republics were born into societies riven with profound contradictions between the proclaimed values of the state and the behavior of their politicians. They were raised with a set of expectations about governance and its relationship to the economy, which the historian E. P. Thompson referred to as a "moral economy."[1] I will use the phrase expansively to refer not just to a government's ability or willingness to ensure affordable food but also to its ability or willingness to live up to its stated larger social and economic commitments. This republican moral economy was being violated daily by the Arab states in the early twenty-first century. The youth were raised to see themselves as proud members of independent states that had attained their freedom both from European colonial domination and from local monarchs who had often collaborated with the occupiers in the first half of the twentieth century. Newspapers and television shows ridiculed or excoriated the old kings. The youth were raised to believe that the republics erected in the 1950s and 1960s by their parents' generation were dedicated to fostering the well-being of each Arab citizen. Socialist rhetoric spoke of the new Arab.

Most of the Middle East had been ruled by the Ottoman Empire, with its capital in Istanbul in what is now Turkey, from the early 1500s until

World War I. After the war, European powers carved up the empire into colonies; some were jointly ruled by the Europeans and by dynasties that had been Ottoman viceroys but were now recognized as monarchs in their own right, or (as in Iraq) by a dynasty created by the Europeans. During and after World War II, as the European powers were weakened, popular movements and young military officers conspired to create independent republics out of many of these colony-kingdoms. The monarchs often suffered in public opinion from having acquiesced to European rule. King Farouk of Egypt (r. 1936–52) was castigated in the Egyptian popular press as the "playboy king," whose corrupt government lost the 1948 war with Israel and whose courtiers oppressed peasants and laborers. In 1950 about 0.5 percent of the population owned 36 percent of all the cultivated land in Egypt, and the masses of peasant farmers often had only half an acre for themselves. (American farmers at that time had an average of sixty-five acres.) Worse, in 1942 his court had capitulated to the imperialists in London, as Britain reoccupied Egypt during World War II. (Britain ruled Egypt from 1882 to 1922, but even after that often interfered in its politics.) In the summer of 2011 I was living in Cairo on a houseboat near what was still called locally "Kit Kat Square" in the far north of the Agouza neighborhood, and Egyptian friends explained to me that in the 1940s it had been the site of the Kit Kat nightclub, a favorite haunt of King Farouk. Egyptian newspapers still ran scandalous stories about him. An obituary of the popular crooner Abd al-Ghani al-Sayyid (1912–2012) told of how he wooed and married the daughter of the minister of war in the 1940s. But King Farouk had his eye on the young woman and summarily issued a divorce decree for the couple only a week after their wedding. The hapless singer was forced to relinquish his bride to his sovereign. When the young officers, prominent among them Colonel Gamal Abdel Nasser, overthrew the feckless monarch in 1952, Farouk fled to Monaco, reportedly leaving behind a vast collection of pornography. The republic proclaimed on July 26, 1952, promised Egyptians that they henceforth were to be citizens, not subjects or playthings of a malevolent kleptomaniac.[2] In contrast to King Farouk, King Idris (r. 1951–69) of Libya had the reputation of having little interest in being a monarch, and therefore of being diffident and ineffectual.

The Arab republics also touted themselves as having rescued their citizens from the arbitrary and humiliating rule of foreigners. The French ruled Tunisia as a fiefdom from 1881 to 1956, and Syria from 1920 to 1946. The British ruled Egypt directly from 1882 to 1922, then again, as noted, in 1942–45 during World War II, and continued to exercise informal colonial domination until the Suez crisis of 1956. Italy took Libya in 1911 and ruled with special cruelty during the fascist period of Benito Mussolini. During and after World War II Libya became a British protectorate, until awarded independence by the United Nations in 1951 (though British and U.S. military bases continued to operate in the country, to the dismay of patriotic Libyans). Arab nationalists interpreted the implanting of Jewish settlers in Palestine during the British colonial rule of that territory (1920–48), their ethnic cleansing of hundreds of thousands of Palestinians in 1948, and the rise of an Israel backed by the West as a continuation of colonial tactics. (This Arab nationalist view of the rise of Israel ignores that most members of the Yishuv were refugees from a persecuting Europe and that they conducted a sort of anti-imperial revolution of their own against British Mandate authorities in the 1940s, but it is important to understand that the narrative of Israel as a colonial and imperial artifact is widespread in the Arab world.) Until the end of his presidency Hosni Mubarak (r. 1981–2011) boasted of his role as an air force commander protecting Egypt during the 1973 war with Israel and wore the action as a badge of anticolonial legitimacy. The tragedy for him was that by January 2011, most Egyptians had been born after 1973 and were not very interested in his old war stories, given their twenty-first-century travails. General Zine El Abidine Ben Ali (r. 1987–2011) claimed the mantle of Tunisian nationalist leader Habib Bourguiba, who campaigned for decades against French colonial rule, led his country to independence in 1956, and then became president for life.

The Arab republics lacked the legitimacy that derives from popular sovereignty. None of their leaders truly subjected themselves to free and fair electoral contests, though some engaged in a charade of polls or of referenda (which were easier to fake). Their legitimacy therefore derived from other sources. They claimed to have liberated the Arab masses from supercilious European proconsuls and from cruel and arbitrary kings who passed on their throne to debauched sons. They claimed to have created a modern economy, to have educated the people, to have erected infrastructure, to have developed the economy. They proclaimed their probity with public funds, unlike their crooked majesties. They offered new dignity and independence to a people formerly subjected to foreign rule. They pledged to improve standards of living and to pursue economic justice. They stood against continued plots and attacks against the nation by the European powers or one of the new superpowers, or by what they saw as a remnant of the age of settler colonialism, Israel.

While no state lived up to its ideals, the disjuncture between the politicians' and school textbooks' 1950s-style rhetoric of social welfare, nationalism, and republicanism and the sordid reality of neoliberal and nepotistic police states (often acting as enforcers for Washington and Paris) became increasingly obvious to Generation Y. Neoliberalism, a policy encouraged by Washington, London, and the Bretton Woods institutions (the World Bank and the International Monetary Fund), aggressively attempted to substitute an unregulated market for state institutions in many sectors of economic life, even in education; in reality, many countries found that the "markets" operated to distribute income upward to the hyperwealthy and their corporations and to reduce the share of national income of the bottom half of society.[3] The moral economy of the Arab republic had been contravened to the point where little was left of it save empty phrases in interminably long speeches given by presidents for life from their opulent palaces to unemployed or underemployed masses living in squalor. The gap between rhetoric and reality was all the easier for the millennials to see, given that a significant minority of them had access to the internet and a majority had access to satellite television. These media captured words and images and compared them across time and space. The new media aided a new generation of amateur investigative journalists both in their quest for evidence of corruption and torture and in their ability to disseminate the results.

Fathers and Sons

The genial, tousled-hair Egyptian sociologist and human rights activist Saad Eddin Ibrahim spent years in jail for a sardonic observation. I had studied with him at the University of California, Los Angeles, and was impressed with his quick smile, sharp wit, and keen sociological imagination. In a 2009 essay he told the story of how he became a global symbol of human rights and the freedom of speech.[4] "Let me begin this essay," he wrote, "by defining the term 'jumlukiyya.' It is a new term of opprobrium not found in our Arabic language or in any other language. I myself put it together from the two words *jumhuriyya* (republic) and *malakiyya* (monarchy)." He explained that *monarchy* refers to hereditary rule, and *republic* to a system in which the leader is elected every few years by the people. Both forms of government were widespread in the Arab world. "But what hadn't been known until that time (the year 2000) was for a regime to begin as a republic on paper, then to transform itself dishonestly, in reality, into a hereditary monarchy." He explained that the Orbit Showtime satellite television channel hired him to do a twelve-hour stint as commentator on the day of the funeral of Syrian dictator Hafez al-Assad, on June 13, 2000. The marathon appearance included telephone call-ins. A viewer in Paris asked Ibrahim who he thought would succeed the deceased president. Ibrahim replied that it would pretty surely be his son Bashar, given his prominent ceremonial role in the funeral, greeting the foreign dignitaries and relegating the vice president and foreign minister to lesser roles. Another viewer objected that the constitution required the president to be at least forty, whereas Bashar was only thirty-four. Ibrahim replied that constitutions can be changed and crowds can be sent into the streets to demand that "the cub succeed the lion" (*al-asad* in Arabic literally means "lion"). The Baath Party and its organs would then dutifully anoint the son as successor.

Another caller from Paris pressed him on whether, if Bashar did succeed his father, it would be an exceptional event or a precedent for the other authoritarian Arab republics. Ibrahim replied that essentially the same thing seemed likely to happen in Iraq, Yemen, and Libya. What, the caller asked, did those four republics have in common? Ibrahim recalled, "My reply was that in any country where the same leader rules for a decade or more, even if its form of government is the republic, he begins to feel that the country is his private property." In turn, private property is inherited by the heirs. If there is a son age thirty or more, Ibrahim asserted, he becomes president in his turn, and the rest of the inheritance is distributed among the brothers, sisters, aunts, and uncles.

Then came the dangerous turning point in this broadcast. The French Lebanese political scientist Ghassan Salamé, an acquaintance of Ibrahim's, called from Paris and pointed out that all the observations made about the other republics also applied to Egypt. Ibrahim, speaking from a studio in a police state, tried to duck the implications. He said on air, "Egypt is different in its size, history and in being a state made up of institutions."

Then, in a discussion that was becoming more heated by the minute, a caller from Tunis asked him, "Dr. Saad Eddin, what do you call this Arab practice of the inheritance of power in a republic?" It was then that Ibrahim came up with the humorous amalgam *jumlukiyya,* or monarpublicanism.

The next day his friend Abdul Rahman Al-Rashid, the editor of the London weekly *al-Majalla* (the Journal), called Ibrahim, having seen the broadcast, and proposed a special issue on sons succeeding fathers as presidents for life of the Arab republics. It came out the following week, with a picture on the cover of a general wearing a crown. It treated the rulers who had come to power in coups and then legitimated themselves with phony elections in which they won 99 percent of the vote, then purged their enemies, and then prepared for their son to succeed them. It treated Iraq, Syria, Yemen, Libya, and Egypt. Ibrahim maintains that when the magazine hit the stands in Egypt, it was quickly confiscated by the secret police and disappeared from the market.

As long as his argument was abstract and general, Ibrahim would probably not have been in danger. But, he explained to me, later that summer an aggressive radio anchor pressed him to say whether Egypt itself was part of the tendency to republican monarchy that he had identified. Ibrahim tried to duck the question, but in the end had to assent. Everyone believed that Hosni and Suzanne Mubarak were grooming their younger son, Gamal, to succeed his father. Hosni Mubarak, an air force general trained in Moscow during the cold war, became vice president of Egypt in the late 1970s under President Anwar El Sadat. When Sadat was assassinated by radical Muslim fundamentalists in 1981, Mubarak succeeded. After a brief period of greater political and press freedom, he cracked back down in the 1990s and into the twenty-first century. His National Democratic Party became a vehicle for rewarding political allies, dominated provincial and national government offices, and won almost complete dominance of Parliament in the occasional phony elections. For Gamal to succeed his father was an unprecedented move in the Egyptian republic, which had seen four unrelated military officers succeed one another since 1952. U.S. embassy officials noted that the Egyptian military was uncomfortable with these plans, in part because Gamal was a civilian: "Regarding succession, analysts highlight the armed forces' uneasiness with Gamal Mubarak, but largely agree that the military would support Gamal if President Mubarak resigns and installs him in the presidency, a scenario we view as unlikely. One professor opined that since 2003, the regime has tried to strengthen the economic elite close to Gamal at the expense of the military in an effort to weaken potential military opposition to Gamal's path to the presidency. Other analysts believe the regime is trying to co-opt the military through patronage into accepting Gamal and that despite tensions between the military and business, their relationship remains cooperative."[5]

Gamal's mother, Suzanne, had been Ibrahim's student in sociology classes at the American University in Cairo, and they knew each other socially. She may have been especially incensed that he had spoken out against the nonroyal succession she planned. Later in 2000 Ibrahim was arrested on trumped-up charges and tried for allegedly receiving undeclared European Union money to monitor elections. He won on appeal twice but remained in prison; he was finally acquitted and released in 2003. His health never recovered from the ravages of the Egyptian penitentiary to which he was consigned.[6] The cause of preventing a royal succession, however, was taken up by the new generation.

Family Cartels

Nepotism and corruption among the ruling elites in the Arab republics of the 1990s and the 2000s reached levels perhaps unparalleled in modern history. As the formerly socialist republics came under pressure from Washington, London, and institutions such as the World Bank and the

International Monetary Fund to privatize after the fall of the Soviet Union, opportunities for insider trading and family appropriation of public wealth proliferated. As a result, family cartels were formed that dominated the economy and rewarded cronies, creating a narrow, closed elite. Corruption probably took between one and three points a year off annual economic growth, discouraging both local entrepreneurs and international investment and creating persistent structural unemployment. Those left on the outside of these closed circles of wealth and power had little hope of moving up. If the ruling families were to pass power and wealth on to their children, the exclusions would become permanent.

From the point of view of a youth born in the early 1990s, the ruling families and their cliques were old and out of touch with the world. In his last year of rule, Mubarak was eighty-two and had been president since 1981, just after the first millennials were born. Gaddafi of Libya was sixty-eight in 2010, and all his plastic surgery could not disguise that he had been in power since 1969, when the Beatles' *Abbey Road* album was released. The hard-line prime minister of Bahrain, Khalifa bin Salman Al Khalifa, the power behind the throne, was seventy-five when the Pearl Roundabout protests broke out in 2011 and was the only prime minister the country had known, since independence in 1971, when Three Dog Night's "Joy to the World" topped the U.S. charts. Ali Abdullah Saleh of Yemen was sixty-eight in 2010 and had been in power since 1978, when the Bee Gees' disco hit "Stayin' Alive" ruled the world's airwaves. Ben Ali of Tunisia was seventy-four during the revolution and had ruled since 1987, when the Bangles' "Walk Like an Egyptian" was a one-hit wonder. Even the sons being primed to take over were no spring chickens.

Correctly or not, the public perceived the first generation of the Arab republics established after the colonial period as frugal and self-sacrificing. An Egyptian observed to me in Cairo in mid-May 2012 that Nasser, in power from 1954 to 1970, had not left any conspicuous wealth to his heirs. Nor did Nasser's family play any special role in Egyptian politics after his passing. In the minds of their people, the contrast of that first postcolonial generation of leaders with the neoliberal elites of the twenty-first century could not have been starker.

Egypt

In the 2000s youth discontent with the Mubarak government centered on a whole range of domestic and foreign policy issues. All of these grievances were amplified by the prospect that Mubarak would attempt to put his younger son, Gamal, in power after him, thus ensuring that an oppressive, inefficient, and grasping government would continue throughout the millennials' lifetime. The real value of wages was declining, and the government had fewer and fewer resources to devote to making the workers in the huge public sector happy. Although, after three decades of flat real economic performance, Egypt's annual growth rates ticked up to 5 and 6 percent in some years, the extra income appears to have gone mainly to the economic elite and did little for most young people. Youth unemployment remained higher than the national average, and unemployment among educated youth was at least twice that of the national rate. These problems were caused principally by the high population growth rate, declining government income, low rates of investment, and corrupt and authoritarian rule by Mubarak's National Democratic Party (NDP), which marginalized other parties and virtually monopolized real political power. The managed float of the Egyptian pound, a neoliberal measure implemented more thoroughly in the first decade of the twenty-first century, led to a fall in its value against world currencies and hurt Egyptian consumers who depended on imported goods (including food, since Egypt could no longer feed itself). The regime operated through a police state that was not as thorough or quite as absolute as those in the old Eastern Bloc but that cavalierly disregarded basic human rights and practiced torture. The revelation of torture through leaked videos by citizen journalists greatly harmed the regime's reputation. Government corruption lessened the willingness of both Egyptian and foreign investors to put large amounts of money into the economy, as they were fearful of having to pay expensive bribes or of having their successful enterprises subject to hostile takeovers by Mubarak cronies. In turn, this inadvertent discouragement of foreign investment probably took between 1 and 3 percent a year off economic growth. Foreign policy issues stemmed from the Egyptian government's decision in 1978 to make a peace treaty with Israel and to become a de facto American client, accepting $2 billion a year in foreign aid (which declined somewhat to $1.5 billion in the 2000s). This reorientation made Egypt a partner of Israel in dealing with the Palestinians, and enlisted Egyptian logistical and other help in imperial American adventures such as the invasion and occupation of Iraq in 2003.[7]

The issue of succession began to be pitched practically in 2002, when Gamal Mubarak was given an influential position in the ruling National Democratic Party.[8] There used to be a joke that the "Union of Soviet Socialist Republics" was "four lies." The name of Mubarak's organization was certainly three lies: it wasn't national, it wasn't democratic, and it wasn't really a party. It was an instrument of the president's and had no autonomy whatsoever. Parliamentary elections in the Mubarak regime, political scientists have concluded, were a way to reward and punish factions in the small elite at the top of society.[9] The emergence of Gamal and his cronies, then, threatened older, established factions, which feared being marginalized within the NDP. Since the elder Mubarak had appointed no vice president, questions of his successor had to be guessed at through such symbolic gestures. U.S. embassy officials observed that Mubarak's run for a sixth five-year term in 2005 only increased the speculation, since he was seventy-seven when he won, and though he was still vigorous the clock was obviously ticking. Suzanne Mubarak was generally thought to be pushing hard for her younger son. Gamal was establishing his own network of "new guard" political figures, and these began showing up in centers of power. In 2004 and 2005, officials at the U.S. embassy reported, "younger, ambitious technocrats, most with direct or indirect links to Gamal," began replacing the old guard in cabinet positions.[10] Then in 2006 Gamal was made assistant secretary-general of the ruling NDP, and some of his key allies were given high leadership positions in the party. He began staging photo ops, such as a March 2006 visit to the slum of Agouza al-Qadima in Giza to inaugurate new housing for the poor that had been built by his Future Generation Foundation. "Most political observers," U.S. embassy officials reported, "regard the foundation as a vehicle primarily intended for Gamal's public entrée onto the political stage." Gamal began appearing more frequently on state-owned television channels, promoting what he called "reform." Even his engagement to the twenty-four-year-old socialite Khadiga el-Gammal was viewed as an attempt by a forty-something playboy to make himself a more acceptable candidate in traditional Egyptian society. The choice of a beautiful, wealthy young socialite who dressed fashionably, however, was unlikely to increase his appeal to ordinary Egyptians. Dissident blogger Wael Abbas printed a photo of her looking like a runway model, without comment, on his blog. When Gamal and she married a year later, some bloggers mounted a satirical campaign they called "Khadiga, yes! Egypt, no!," suggesting the limits of what he could have, and said they wanted to hold their own wedding parties for the couple. (The Ministry of the Interior forbade it.) One young journalist, Khalid Elbalshy, wrote of the dissidents who had been jailed and mistreated, contrasting their estate with the opulent wedding. Bloggers referred to Gamal as "Jimmy Bey," giving him an English diminutive and an Ottoman feudal title to mark him as anachronistically aristocratic and putting on foreign airs all at once.[11] In 2009 activists in Egypt formed the Youth against Succession umbrella group consisting of leftist, liberal, and Muslim Brotherhood factions that would "work against the possible elevation of Gamal Mubarak to the presidency without a free and fair election."[12]

Regime critics saw Gamal and his circle as corrupt. In the late 1990s Gamal took an 18 percent stake in the private equity unit of the investment bank EFG Hermes. In 2007 he engineered the sale of one of its holdings, al-Watany Bank of Egypt, to the Bank of Kuwait. He and his brother, Alaa, along with some EFG Hermes officials, were accused of having violated investment rules by not conducting the sale transparently and of receiving kickbacks. (Gamal is alleged to have made $82 million on the deal. His trial on insider trading charges began in 2012.) Even at the time, the independent newspaper *al-Dustur* and dissident bloggers saw the deal as corrupt and as having harmed small investors. Gamal was rumored to use his high position in the NDP to award contracts to firms in which he had invested, and after the revolution investigators found evidence of massive amounts of unexplained money in his accounts.[13] Dissidents accused Gamal of having built a network of billionaire cronies, whom he rewarded with high party or government positions or with sweetheart deals from the government.[14] Among these was Ahmed Ezz, a steel magnate to whom the regime gave shares in the previously state-owned Dekheila Steel Company on extraordinarily favorable terms, and who then transferred funds and assets from it to his own Ezz Steel. In essence, critics alleged that he took over and looted his competition and cornered the market. U.S. embassy officials noted that in 2008 the government tried to please the many Egyptians engaged in building or extending their homes by cracking down on price fixing in the (largely foreign-owned) cement industry. Jaime Muguiro, president of Assiut Cement, a subsidiary of Mexico's Cemex, complained to U.S. diplomats that cement was on average only 8 percent of construction costs and that the real driver of building inflation was steel: "Steel is a sacred cow for the GOE [government of Egypt], as prominent NDP member Ahmed Ezz owns Egypt's largest steelmaker, Ezz Steel. The GOE will not take aggressive measures to control steel prices, Muguiro believes, even though steel constitutes around 30% of average construction costs."[15] A website dedicated to the discussion of corruption alleged in 2008 that Ezz had received some $725 million in unsecured loans from banks owned by or under the influence of the state to expand his steel business, thanks to Gamal Mubarak, who, it was alleged, had himself received tens of millions in kickbacks from the deals. After the revolution Ezz, accused of drawing from public coffers illegitimate gains worth $870 million between 2001 and 2011, was initially sentenced to ten years for licensing irregularities. In 2013 a retrial was ordered.[16] The story of the looting of the state Dekheila Steel Company by a new oligarch is typical of the more corrupt former socialist societies that moved to private ownership after the collapse of the Soviet model. Neoliberal theorists in Washington and London pushed for privatization of huge public sectors on the theory that these were inevitably inefficient and that the market would operate to the benefit of more people. They did not reckon on the problem of insider trading. The elites in control of the publicly owned factories knew when they were about to go on the block, and privatization was a means for them to turn formerly state-owned enterprises into piggy banks for themselves.

The stench of cronyism and corruption reached its height in 2008, when a murder case developed against Gamal's associate Hisham Talaat Moustafa, head of the Talaat Moustafa Group (TMG), an urban development conglomerate of twenty-three companies and three thousand employees worth $2 billion. Moustafa stood accused of paying $2 million to a security guard at the Sharm El Sheikh Four Seasons Hotel to slip into Dubai and murder his former girlfriend, the Lebanese pop singer Suzanne Tamim. Tamim had had a series of troubled flings and marriages and fled Beirut in fear of fraud and embezzlement charges. At the time of her murder she had been married for a year and a half to a British kick-boxer of Iraqi heritage and was living in the posh Palm Jumeira district of Dubai. On July 28, 2008, she was found in her apartment with her throat slit. The news of Moustafa's arrest sent the Egyptian stock market plummeting, though it recovered when the TMG issued assurances that the case would have no effect on the company and Moustafa's son Tarek stepped in. (TMG was 51 percent family-owned.) The Mubarak regime, which had thrown billions in construction contracts to the conglomerate, issued strict instructions to Egyptian media not to cover the story and jailed five journalists for breaching the decree. Satellite television and the internet, however, were consumed with the scandal, which reinforced the public's suspicion that the Egyptian business and government classes were highly corrupt, as officials at the U.S. embassy ruefully observed.[17] Moustafa's conviction and death sentence the following year were overturned on a technicality, and he was ultimately given fifteen years in prison. He is said to have escaped during the 2011 revolution.

In the run-up to the 2010 parliamentary elections and 2011 presidential election, the young journalist Umar al-Hadi explained why he was supporting Mohamed ElBaradei, the former head of the International Atomic Energy Agency, who returned to Egypt early in 2010 to explore a presidential run: "Our country deserves a president other than the current one, or the son, or our father [Gamal Abdel Nasser, whose mausoleum is] in Hada'iq al-Qubba." Al-Hadi wrote that Egypt deserved a political system that wasn't a "gang" that included Hisham Talaat Moustafa and Ahmed Ezz, along with other allegedly corrupt Mubarak officials.[18] Al-Hadi also named Hani Surour, a member of Parliament (who was accused of supplying hospitals with substandard equipment and contaminated blood and who was expelled from parliament in 2010 over the charges but acquitted when the case went to court), and Mamdouh Ismail, an appointed senator who was alleged to have used his position on the board of the Red Sea Port Authority to avoid inspections of ferry boats owned by a company in which he had shares. When one of the ferries sank in 2006, over a thousand persons drowned. He was convicted in 2009 but fled to London.[19]

The crescendo of corruption issuing from the Mubarak regime disillusioned more and more Egyptians, who used the internet to keep an accounting of charges of misbehavior in high places. Another blogger accused Gamal of developing a loyal cadre of Cairo University graduates beginning in the late 1990s, who were cultivated and trained as youth auxiliaries to the National Democratic Party but were loyal to Gamal. Emad Fawaz said that the new oligarchs close to Gamal, such as Moustafa, initially bankrolled six-month training institutes for these loyalist youth, including instruction in using computers and the internet and basic English. Eventually the NDP set an annual budget for the program. Over the course of eleven years, Fawaz wrote in 2009, some sixty-six thousand of these cadres had received training and were often successfully placed in jobs in government ministries, at a cost of about $33 million. These government jobs were denied to youth not close to the elite or lucky enough to be chosen as cadres, giving them the sense of being blocked and of having no future.[20] Even as activists worried about a dynastic succession, Gamal's growing prominence provoked consternation in Hosni Mubarak's circles, including the old guard politicians and the military.

Although the NDP was not exactly a Soviet-style one-party state or really even a party at all but rather a vehicle for the personal power of the Mubaraks, its top leaders did not brook much opposition, and when it was threatened it often enlisted the state security police in repressive tactics. The Egyptian lower house, about 450 members, often had no more than twenty or twenty-five opposition members. Essam Shiha, a member of the right-of-center Wafd Party favored by propertied classes and Coptic Christians not tied to the NDP, explained to the U.S. embassy the difficulties he faced in running in a parliamentary by-election. He wanted to run because there was a split in the NDP between an old guard candidate and a new guard candidate close to Gamal Mubarak. The Wafd Party, however, did not want to support Gamal's candidate, and it had apparently been discouraged from letting Shiha run by the state security, precisely because the rivalry within the NDP gave Shiha a chance of winning. Since the Wafd would not fund him, Shiha had to think about financing the campaign himself and through wealthy friends. Egypt's system was characterized by vote buying, as the political scientist Lisa Blaydes has explained.[21] Voters expected at least $20, and sometimes as much as $200, for their vote. Potential voters asked Shiha how much he would shell out rather than inquiring about his policies. He also had to bribe café owners to let him use their premises, given the "risk" they faced from state security police for letting a member of a party other than the NDP campaign there. "Shiha related how a personal childhood friend of his is now a 'big boss' in the Manial neighborhood, and told him he could provide 500 voters for him, but before doing so, he needed Shiha to get an officer from the State Security Investigative Services (SSIS) to call him to say that is permissible ('You understand, my friend, I just need to cover my own back')."[22]

In the provincial elections of spring 2008, the government discouraged Muslim Brothers and other oppositionists from contesting seats by stationing SSIS officers around the registration offices and not letting the candidates through and by arresting hundreds of people who had announced that they would run or help with opposition campaigns. The NDP itself was not a real political party but a façade centrally controlled by the Mubaraks, and increasingly by Gamal's new guard. The avenues for ordinary political contestation and opposition were firmly blocked off.[23]

Tunisia

Tunisia too had a problem with concentrated ruling-family power and wealth, though Ben Ali did not have a son. A former general, Ben Ali came to power in 1987 in a soft coup. He displaced Tunisia's first president, Habib Bourguiba, who had led the country to independence from France in 1956 and then ruled as president for life, pursuing authoritarian policies of state-led industrialization and favoring official secularism as his ideology. The Tunisian state grew more and more controlling through the 1990s and 2000s. Ben Ali's government used every method at its disposal to quell dissent or opposition. The government controlled key institutions: it threatened dissidents with losing their social security; it declined to give bank loans to small businessmen associated with the Muslim party, Renaissance, or with left-liberal critiques of the state. As in Egypt, the regime used the state banks as a personal piggy bank for close associates, awarding them unsecured loans, many of which were never paid back. Ben Ali was alleged to use European aid payments to restore capital to the banks thus gradually depleted. Businessmen from the family of the president or his circle were known to demand that successful businesses sell out to them, implying government reprisals if the owner refused.[24]

Had he not been overthrown, Ben Ali might have attempted to install his son-in-law Sakher El Materi in power, or his wife, Leila Trabelsi, might have made a play for the presidency à la Eva Peron in Argentina. U.S. embassy officials observed in early 2010, "Almost everyone in Tunisia believes Leila has presidential ambitions, which most Tunisians firmly reject. A hairdresser before meeting the married Ben Ali, many believe Leila—and her Trabelsi clan—represents the antithesis of Tunisia—uneducated, uncouth and nouveau riche. . . . Ben Ali showered economic opportunities on his wife and her ten brothers and sisters and gaggle of nephews and nieces." [25] Tunisia's nepotism and corruption were among the worst in the world.

A more plausible candidate from within the ruling family was El Materi, from a prominent business family, who married Ben Ali's daughter Nesrine. U.S. ambassador Gordon Gray observed, "Matri [sic] has significant business holdings in Tunisia and, reportedly, abroad. Often more active behind the scenes than publicly, Matri's star appeared to be rising in late 2007 when he was granted the license for a new Quranic radio station and was positioned next to Ben Ali at a major religious event in October and at the arrival ceremony for the late April 2008 state visit of French President Sarkozy." [26] A profile of El Materi appeared on the dissident website Nawaat (set up by young bloggers and activists) just before the revolution, detailing his vast wealth: "Zitouna Bank; an insurance company, Zitouna Takaful; a vehicle distribution company, Ennakl; investments in al-Tijari Bank (2.27%), Arab Tunisian Leasing (10.67%), two real estate companies, Les Hirondelles and Le Marchand; two tourism companies, Cruise Tours and Goulette Shipping Cruise; a marine shipping company, Goulette Shipping Services, three newspapers . . . a radio station." And, the journalist noted, the list was not exhaustive.[27] A comment appended by an anonymous reader on the website noted that El Materi's Princess Holding Company, which grouped these assets, had come from nowhere to such extravagant wealth in only a few years, and speculated that it was in part a front for the holdings of Ben Ali himself.

El Materi has the honor of having been described in among the more colorful State Department cables ever written.[28] Gray's predecessor, Robert Godec, had dinner with El Materi and Nesrine in midsummer 2009 at their sumptuous mansion, decorated with Greco-Roman antiques and sporting an infinity pool. Dinner "included perhaps a dozen dishes, including fish, steak, turkey, octopus, fish couscous and much more," and drinks that included exotic kiwi juice. "After dinner, he served ice cream and frozen yoghurt he brought in by plane from Saint Tropez." (The couple had just come back from a vacation there, by private jet piloted by an American in their employ.) The memorable passage, however, is this one: "El Materi has a large tiger ('Pasha') on his compound, living in a cage. He acquired it when it was a few weeks old. The tiger consumes four chickens a day. (Comment: The situation reminded the Ambassador of Uday Hussein's lion cage in Baghdad.) El Materi had staff everywhere. There were at least a dozen people, including a butler from Bangladesh and a nanny from South Africa. (NB. This is extraordinarily rare in Tunisia, and very expensive.)"

The Tunisian youth dissidents did not need to visit El Materi to form a poor opinion of him. In 2009 El Materi, then twenty-nine, made a move to buy a controlling interest in one of Tunisia's last semi-independent media companies, Dar al-Sabah, which published newspapers in Arabic and French. A blogger accused him of picking off the heirs one by one when the founder died, leaving each in turn less chance of controlling the company, and threatening to offer even less for outstanding shares if they did not quickly acquiesce.[29] El Materi hoped to outflank the Muslim Renaissance Party, establishing a radio station that broadcast readings from the Qur'an and then setting up a bank that operated on Islamic principles (offering investment shares rather than interest, which some Muslims consider usury). Godec says in the famous memo that when he pressed El Materi on press freedom in the country, El Materi actually used the way he had taken over and managed Dar al-Sabah as an example of a liberalizing move, because he had interviewed an older politician from outside the ruling Constitutional Democratic Rally.

As in Egypt, youth unemployment was high in Tunisia; the rates for educated youth were as high as 20 or 30 percent. Those who did work were often poorly paid, especially in provincial towns in the rural areas, and in 2008 the phosphate miners at a state-owned mine in Gafsa mounted a major labor action that galvanized progressives and critics of the government. Wealth in Tunisia was concentrated at the top, and the corruption of the regime was blocking opportunities for the youth. By the late 2000s half of them told pollsters that they wanted to emigrate abroad. (Nearly a tenth of Tunisia's population was already overseas throughout Europe, primarily in France.) El Materi's conspicuous consumption was an offense to many living permanently modest lives, and his pretensions to Muslim piety impressed few. A branch of his Zitouna Islamic Bank was among the first buildings torched when the revolution reached Tunis in January 2011.

It was the republican monarchies of Egypt, Tunisia, Libya, and Yemen that saw their presidents overthrown by vigorous youth protest movements in 2011–12, and Syria's regime too was besieged during the same period. The other Arab republics either were not tending toward a political dynasty or those plans were disrupted externally. For instance, Saad Eddin Ibrahim expected Iraq, another state ruled by the Baath Party, to have a dynastic transition, but that development was forestalled by the invasion and occupation of that country by the Bush administration. The problem of republican monarchy did not beset Algeria, where the population was already traumatized and weary from a civil war between secular and Muslim fundamentalist forces that had raged from 1992 until the early 2000s. Although President Abdelaziz Bouteflika came to power in 1999 and was the longest-serving Algerian head of state since independence, he ruled as part of a military and civilian oligarchy. The complaint against him in the thousands of youth demonstrations of 2011 was not that he intended to hand power to a relative, and those rallies petered out. By then the Algerian state was also practiced in confronting opposition because of the security services' long experience during the civil war. On February 12, 2011, some three thousand protesters assembled in downtown Algiers, but they were confronted by thirty thousand well-organized police and troops and eventually just went home.[30] Sudan's Omar al-Bashir, who came to power in 1989, was accused of authoritarianism, corruption, promoting his relatives, and even genocide. Yet he stood for election in 2010, and although there were questions about the process, he seems genuinely to have won many of the 68 percent of votes attributed to his followers. However, Sudan is much more rural than its peers and has a different social structure and set of divisions. Student protests that broke out in 2011 and again in the fall of 2013 were dealt with harshly. Like Algeria, Sudan is an oil state with the resources to quiet protest by grants of money if it so chooses. (Gaddafi in Libya made the mistake of refusing fully to share his oil income with the eastern provinces of his country, with whom he had a sort of feud.) Algeria and Sudan may experience political change, but it won't be linked to republican monarchy. Other Arab republics are either failed states or too small and rural (Djibouti, Mauritania) to participate in the same dynamics as the larger republics.

The budding republican monarchies for the most part had a large public sector in the socialist-inflected era of the 1950s and 1960s. They had pursued large-scale, state-led development, attempting to substitute local manufactures for international imports, to build infrastructure, and to educate and train their populations. In the 1990s, with the global collapse of the communist model, they turned to a greater reliance on the market, seeking to privatize at least some sectors of the economy. In part, they privatized under the pressure of Washington and the Western European countries, to which the Arab states often owed a good deal of money and so were vulnerable to such arm-twisting. This privatization created substantial opportunities for insider trading, since state officials still controlled much of the economy and knew when and where the opportunities for buying up former state enterprises would lie. They came to believe that what was good for them was good for the country. The rulers began making plans to bequeath their countries to their sons, as though they were feudal lords bequeathing estates and villages to their firstborns.

Forgotten were the egalitarian promises of the 1950s and 1960s, the project to raise up an independent and self-respecting Arab nation, that could by its productive energies galvanize all of Africa and Asia. This bad faith, this forgetting of the basis for the legitimacy of these unelected governments, led to a breach of the entire moral economy that had underpinned their earlier popularity, thus radically alienating the millennials. But the elites of the authoritarian republics had been in power for decades and had become skillful in shielding themselves from press scrutiny and demands for accountability, using censorship, arbitrary arrest, and even torture. They increasingly turned to nepotism and cronyism to bolster their wealth and hold on power. They employed tens of thousands of plainclothes informants and enforcers, making domestic surveillance a major national industry. Against this rigid structure of exploitation and degenerate selfishness on the part of the top elites lapped the waves of a new generation of young Arabs, waves that gradually swelled into a tsunami.

3

"Giants of Meat and Steel: I Come to You from Cyberspace!"

*I*n the 2000s and after, internet activism intersected in powerful ways with youth social movements. If we think of cyberspace as above all a virtual place, then it is simply another arena for the performance of the typical repertoires of social movements. Just as young people could paint a physical wall with graffiti ten feet high, so they could put graffiti on the "wall" of their blog or Facebook page. Just as they could gather for an intense political discussion in a café, so they could gather in chat rooms. Just as they could go door to door handing out pamphlets in meatspace, so they could pamphleteer by sending announcements in cyberspace. Just as they could show dissident films behind closed doors, they could post them to YouTube. Just as they could mount marches and sit-ins in the physical world, so they could create internet traffic and use their websites for protests and strikes. Virtual space is simply another social dimension in which activists can show solidarity, express common values, denounce political repression, celebrate martyrs, campaign for the freeing of prisoners, and generally engage in contentious politics. Moreover, the two spheres of protest, cyberspace and urban space, connect to and reinforce one another.[1]

The internet was not forbidden in the Arab world, given how useful it was, especially commercially, but it was limited in various ways and intensively monitored. Since the Arab millennials were early adopters of the internet, the more politically minded of them ran straight into the cyber police, and their struggles with regime web censors are an important part of the story of their generation. I spent some of May 2010 in Cairo, when Mubarak was still in power. One day I was downtown, near the old American University campus, visiting the bookstore. I walked up the increasingly dowdy Muhammad Mahmoud Street under a torrid May sun, and after passing a fruit vending stall and a ramshackle kiosk selling soft drinks, I found an internet café and decided to check my email. It was small and dimly lit, plaster coming off the grimy walls, with a bank of eight or nine dusty old desktop computers along the walls. I told the older, stubble-chinned man behind the desk what I wanted. To my astonishment, he leaned forward aggressively and demanded my passport. I pulled it out, and he carefully entered all my information in a bulky register. When I lived in Egypt again, in summer 2011, after the revolution, I was pleasantly surprised to find that the internet cafés no longer cared who I was or kept any record of who came and went. No one in Europe or the Americas, I think, can fully appreciate the sense of sheer liberation felt by young internet users now in the Arab world at being able to look up political news freely without taking any personal risks or facing the frustrations of having sites constantly blocked or having even personal email read and censored. How long this relative freedom will last is, of course, the big question.

In early May 2012 I was in Tunisia to give some talks at the Center for Maghrebi Studies in Tunis, one of a number of academic American research centers abroad. It was hosting a series on the Arab Spring and had gotten a small grant from the U.S. embassy to help pay for the speakers. I also spoke, in Arabic, at the Center for the Study of Islam and Democracy, a project of the Tunisian human rights worker Radwan Masmoudi, on Iran's policy toward the Arab Spring. In the old Islamic center of Kairouan, to the south of the capital, I addressed a university audience, also in Arabic, on President Obama's policies toward the upheavals in the Arab world. In between talks I had the opportunity to talk to and interview a wide range of Tunisians, including the leader of the Renaissance Party, Rashid al-Ghannushi. Word of my being in Tunis spread, and I got an email saying that some local internet activists wanted to take me to dinner. Would I be willing to meet them?

We gathered at a high-ceilinged restaurant with a spectacular view of the Mediterranean, in the upscale northern part of the city. One of the young activists who kindly came to meet me was Amira Yahyaoui, then in her late twenties and involved in a civil society effort to monitor the drafting of the country's new constitution and the working of its transitional Parliament. Her famed Twitter account, @Mira404, was well known to me for its incisive observations and invaluable linking of sources on developments in Tunis. The "404" refers to the extensive censorship of websites by the Ben Ali government, such that when you were searching for information you often got a "404 Not Found" error message. Dissidents personalized this censorship apparatus in Tunisia as "Ammar 404," as though it were a malicious person. In fact, after the revolution they demanded in vain that the Ministry of the Interior reveal the identity of the actual person behind the cyber censorship that had bedeviled them.

Amira is not herself so much a blogger as an organizer, but she was at the center of a network of bloggers and activists that played a key role in critiquing the old regime. Her father, Judge Mokhtar Yahyaoui, is a prominent judicial activist who was fired by Ben Ali. Her cousin, Zouhair Yahyaoui, founded among the more important dissident websites of the early 2000s. Amira saw those dramatic, and ultimately tragic, events unfold.

TUNeZINE

Zouhair Yahyaoui's site evolved out of interactions with anonymous internet activists with handles such as "Waterman" and "Foetus," the two who began a "cyber think tank" called Takriz (Tunisian slang for "busting my balls," though likely from a classical root having to do with hiding and seeking refuge).[2] During the revolution Foetus did an interview by Skype with the left-leaning *al-Safir* newspaper in Beirut:

What is "Takriz" and what is the nature of the role it plays in the Tunisian revolution? In 1998, the World Wide Web entered Tunisia, and since that time we have formed a group of internet activists to demand freedom of expression and to oppose censorship. When we began to form a threat to the regime, it began chasing us down and imprisoning us. We paid the price of it—some of us were exiled, and some were jailed. "Takriz" is youth power, and it has the ability to be positive and constructive, just as it can be negative and destructive. In other words we were forced by the regime, as a result of its repressive practices and its strangling of liberties, to harness this power to destroy the walls that Bin Ali built around us, and to target all of his cronies.[3]

Foetus began hacking because he could not afford the expensive internet rates, and he also wanted to avoid face-to-face meetings that would inevitably be infiltrated by Ben Ali's domestic spies, whom he referred to as "Stasi" (the East German equivalent from the days of the cold war). The hacktivists reached out beyond their own circles to ally with the Ultras (soccer hoodlums), who were politicized when the secret police was deployed to crack down on them. So they not only hated it when their team lost and were prone to violence when it did, but they also despised the regime and were happy to ally with and provide protection to the internet activists. By 2000 Ben Ali's internet police had shut down many of the Takriz sites and launched a cyberspace manhunt for members of the group.

Another early adopter of the internet, not necessarily in the Takriz group, who ran into trouble was Imen Derouiche, a young activist who told her story to journalist Pascale Egré.[4] Derouiche studied economics at the University of Tunis and was active in the General Union of Tunisian Students. She was arrested in March 1998, tortured, raped, and incarcerated. Her boyfriend, Noureddine Ben-Ticha, was suspected of belonging to the Communist Party of Tunisian Workers and was also arrested. Derouiche's guards taunted her that she would be in prison a long time: "By the time you get out, they'll be opening yoghurt boxes with a zipper." In fact, she was released in August 1999, after an international campaign on her behalf and that of Ben-Ticha. She was, however, forbidden to work and denied readmission to the University of Tunis. And she was kept under close police surveillance.

Once, while watching television in prison, she saw a show in which teenagers were surfing the web at internet cafés with incredible facility. She felt as though they had left her far behind (the World Wide Web came to Tunisia in 1998, while she was in jail), but she made up for lost time upon her release. She told Egré, "Using the Net was already a new sort of activism. . . . Getting access with one click to a [French] article . . . on Tunisia—when before it took hours to find, photocopy, and distribute it—was all at once untrammeled freedom and violative of prohibitions. At the same time, it conferred on us a new legitimacy from the point of view of the generation of the old activists, to whom we now ladled out information."[5]

The owner of the internet café near to where her parents lived was, unbeknownst to her, an agent of the Ben Ali regime. "I began in all naiveté talking about my story, and exchanging my views on the dictator in discussion forums. I also did searches so as to consult the sites of Amnesty International and other organizations defending human rights. I looked for the French dailies. Very quickly, [the café owner] came to me and asked me to stop." It turns out that both of the private internet service providers in Tunisia in the late 1990s, Planet and 3S Global Net, were in the hands of persons close to the president; one of them was his daughter, Nesrine, the wife of business magnate Sakher El Materi.[6]

Tunisia was a pioneer in expanding internet access to its citizens and in intensively monitoring and censoring it. I suspect that Ben Ali and the people around him saw internet commerce as yet another arena where they could use the state's monopolistic powers to make a killing. In 1999 a set of virtual stores was launched, "offering a wide range of Tunisian products, such as crafts, goods, clothing, foodstuffs, tourism packages and hotel reservations."[7] Ben Ali and his relatives and cronies had the opportunity to become the Amazon of the Middle East, if only they could expand and commercialize the internet while finding a way to blunt its political implications. Simply limiting internet access would not have served that purpose.

Tunisia benefited from having a good telephone network, so in the days of copper wire transmission, it was well situated to join the World Wide Web. The regime wanted to ensure that the new means of communication would not be used for political purposes, however, and took surveillance of it to extremes. Derouiche explained, "The internet police would attack first of all through your email, blocking your account. . . . You spend hours clicking on 'send,' hoping that the guy at the other end would finally take a cigarette break, so that your message could get through. As a second step, they go into your mailbox and read your correspondence before you even receive it. Sometimes, only 'hello' and 'goodbye' [are] left. Third, they change your password and you can't get into your mail at all."

At a Tunisian Amnesty International meeting in the summer of 2000, Derouiche and Ben-Ticha got the idea of holding a conference in Europe on torture. After a long wait she got a passport from the regime, but they denied one to Ben-Ticha. In protest he went on a hunger strike, for which he received hundreds of supportive emails from abroad, where a campaign was waged on his behalf. The regime relented and let him go. The two went on a speaking circuit that fall and ultimately decided to stay in France to pursue their education (an outcome the Ben Ali government may have been hoping for when it finally allowed them to leave). The two then became major internet human rights activists on behalf of Tunisia.

Zouhair Yahyaoui was among the early Takrizards who struck out on his own. A Marxist, he founded on the internet a "sort of Forum where he published caricatures" in 2000, when he was thirty-two, according to his cousin, Amira Yahyaoui, who was at his side at that time. In July 2001 Zouhair turned the forum into a dissident internet magazine, TUNeZINE.[8] Of the initial forum, Amira observed, "only the salmon color remains." In the beginning Zouhair, who was then unemployed, did not have a computer or internet access, so he went to the house of his uncle, the judge, to get online. Amira, then just a teenager, often sat beside him as he wrote and remarked on his points. She and her brother also often sat with their father, typing for him and serving as "his hands." Amira admits to occasionally using her father's account, Tunisiawatch, to post her own remarks. She was only one of several women associated with the site; the others were Hueida Anwar ("Antekrista"), Dalel Jegham, and Neila Charchour Hachicha ("NCH"). In addition to discussing authoritarian politics, some of them alerted the site's readers to problems, highlighted by organizations such as Amnesty International, of violence against women in Tunisian society.[9]

At length Zouhair found a job in an internet café and used its resources, publishing anonymously under the name "Ettounsi" (the Tunisian). His uncle Mokhtar, tired of constant pressure to rule on judicial cases as the regime desired, decided to wage a campaign for the independence of the judiciary. He wrote an open letter to President Ben Ali on July 6, 2001, warning, "Tunisian judges at every level are frustrated and exasperated by the obligation imposed on them to render the verdicts that are dictated to them by the political authority, and which are not susceptible of being made the object of any dispassionate reconsideration or critique. This way of proceeding has led to judgments which, most often, only reflect the interpretation that the executive branch wishes to place on the law."[10]

Zouhair published the letter on TUNeZINE. The judge was dismissed from his post, put under surveillance, and forbidden to leave the country. He created a foundation to work for the independence of the judiciary, and for a while maintained his own dissident site, Almizen.com ("the Balance"), with which Zouhair helped him. The judge was not reinstated until the spring of 2011, after the revolution.

At his webzine Zouhair covered the arrest in 2001 of a professor from the central east coast tourism center of Sousse, Moncef Marzouki, a human rights activist sentenced for allegedly spreading false news defaming the nation. His circle of internet collaborators grew. Amira recalls them as a diverse group: "There were militants of the Progressive Democratic Party, of al-Nahda [Renaissance], and of the Tunisian Communist Workers' Party at TUNeZINE; everyone was there, I think." Zouhair himself "was closer to the communists than anyone else; he was an idealist." Although the participants were diverse, Zouhair "hated the Muslim fundamentalists; he was profoundly secular and there were many conflicts at the site between him and them." Amira admits, however, that many of the Renaissance members were "most impressive." She thinks Zouhair may have gone to see one of them in Paris.

I was interested in what Amira and her friends were reading in their teenage years, what shaped their ideals. Since the revolution was relatively nonviolent, I wondered where that emphasis came from. She said that for her, nonviolence was practical, not philosophical. "Action must be nonviolent; you may defend yourself with arms, but never attack." I asked her if there were any famous Tunisian women or other Muslim women to whom she looked up. She was brutally frank: "There is no [observant] Muslim woman whom I admire." She does think well of the relatively secular-minded Iranian feminist and human rights attorney Shirin Ebadi.

A big influence on her was Etienne de la Boétie's 1548 essay denouncing tyranny and the oppression of religious minorities, "Discourse on Voluntary Servitude," which she encountered when she was fourteen and has reread perhaps thirty times. She was also haunted by Friedrich Nietzsche's indictment of the underman and much preferred being the superman. Beyond those works, her favorite author was the Polish playwright Slawomir Mrożek, whose 1964 *Tango* used absurdist techniques to condemn totalitarianism and who also wrote about exile in Paris and the ironies of revolution. Unlike her cousin Zouhair, she was not interested in Marxism. "I never believed in communism or in revolution in the destructive sense, against order, et cetera. I believe in the Tunisian revolution because it is a constructive revolution. We must create order, we must become responsible." The assemblage of influences she listed astonished me: an early modern French classicist concerned about the persecution of the Protestant Huguenots; Nietzsche; an Iranian human rights attorney; and an expatriate Polish absurdist. With the exception of Ebadi, there is nothing Middle Eastern about the list, nor do I think it would be the same in Cairo or Sanaa. Tunisia is perhaps the most determinedly French-speaking of France's former colonies, and its secular middle classes cite Paris as their primary intellectual home. Of course, an observant Muslim activist in Tunis would have looked to classical Muslim thinkers, to Egypt's Muslim Brotherhood, and perhaps to Turkish reformers such as the Justice and Development Party's foreign minister Ahmet Davutoğlu. Of all the Arab middle classes, those of Tunisia are the most impudently secular, and few would have any truck with Islamic thought.

Soon after the TUNeZINE site was created, a young French woman, Sophie Piekarec, discovered it while looking for information about Tunisia and joined in the discussions enthusiastically. She and Zouhair began an internet romance, and she flew to Tunis in December 2001 to meet him. Ultimately they became engaged. He even shared the password with her after the site suffered a denial-of-service attack. She later gave an interview on those days: "Having studied up on Tunisia, I knew the risks that Zouhair was taking and I was full of admiration for his courage, in addition to being seduced by his vivacious spirit and his irrepressible sense of humor. The site was divided into two parts, the magazine, which Zouhair put up on the page and which included announcements, information and the best contributions to the discussion forum, and then the forum itself, where we exchanged ideas directly. . . . His good humor was catching, and he gave a lot of hope to the readers, because he began to make them laugh at their own misfortune. Laughing at a Kafkaesque dictatorship makes one strong."[11] They sometimes talked privately about his ideals, the end of dictatorship, democracy and human rights.

Sophie was joined by other French friends, which caused tensions with Zouhair's Tunisian circle. Amira recalled, "I was very young at that time, but I know that there was a big problem between her and the rest of the people at TUNeZINE." She thought that one of the impetuses for the creation of Nawaat, a dissident site founded by Sami Ben Gharbia, an exiled activist based in the Netherlands, was the increasing dominance at the original blog by a set of French supporters. She alleged, "TUNeZINE was 'taken over by the French.' Sophie [and her friends] formed a clique, and many members of TUNeZINE left the group because of it." She added that Zouhair "was very much in love with Sophie, enormously so, and she as well with him. They made a nice couple, but she did not know how to fit in."

Ben Ali's internet police finally tracked down Zouhair. At 5 p.m. on June 4, 2002, six plainclothes policemen raided the internet café where he worked and took him to his apartment, where they confiscated his personal computer and files. He was subjected to brutal interrogation. Three times in the course of this questioning he was strung up by his wrists so that his feet barely touched the ground. During the third round of "suspension," he finally gave up the password to his site, which allowed the authorities to take it down temporarily. They also closed down the judge's Almizen site. They appear, however, not to have changed the password. Internet activist Sultan al-Qassemi of Dubai later explained at a conference that cyber activists typically shared their password with four or five trusted friends. If police picked up one of them, the others would change his password immediately so that police could not see his messages.[12]

Zouhair was tried with blinding speed and sentenced on July 10 to one year in prison for spreading false news and another year and a half for the fraudulent use of means of communication, because he secretly used the equipment at the internet café where he worked. Soon after his arrest

Sophie regained access to the site and reinstated the digital archives, which she had preserved, and Zouhair's circle kept it going. Amira recalls, "The internet was very often cut off. Every time, it was necessary to create a new account, using the names of friends or neighbors. Often Papa sent me to the cyber café to publish press releases on Zouhair's arrest. For me, it was an act of heroism to open a proxy in a cyber café in front of everyone! But I was banned by most of the cyber cafés in our district because in the end they all understood [what I was doing]."

Zouhair suffered in prison. According to his brother, Chokri, there were 120 inmates in a big hall, with "just one bathroom and hardly any water."[13] In the first half of 2003 he launched a hunger strike to demand his release. He ended it, and then began another. In the same period the Muslim fundamentalist journalist Hamadi Jebali of the Renaissance Party, also in jail, began his own hunger strike. The conditions of Zouhair's prison, the bad food, lack of water, and crowded cells, along with his hunger strikes, deeply damaged his health.

Zouhair's imprisonment caused a breach with his father, Said Yahyaoui, according to Amira. "The poor man never understood, and never accepted, what Zouhair had done." He could not reconcile himself to his son's having "defied the police" and getting arrested "and could never excuse it." He died while Zouhair was in prison, perhaps "of chagrin." She told me, "When Uncle Said died, we were called by my aunt to go to the house." They were all worried about Zouhair's reaction, since he "was already very feeble from his hunger strikes." Her aunt lamented, "Said is going to his grave without seeing Zouhair."

On the morning of the funeral, Amira's mother came to her room and cried out that Zouhair had been given permission to come home to pay his last respects to his father. The family hurried, still in pajamas, to the nearby house of Zouhair's deceased father:

> Day had barely broken, and when we arrived at my aunt's street, there were a dozen buses full of police, a camera truck, et cetera. We went into the house, and Zouhair was shackled at his wrists and his feet like a convict on death row. Because of his arrest, the majority of the family had not come to express their condolences to my aunt. The house had been empty, but

now it was completely full. There were at least thirty plainclothes men, the "great ones," there. One of the policemen walked over the corpse of my uncle, who was on the floor. I remember it well because my father wanted to kill him. He shouted, "Don't you have any shame, walking on a dead person?" Zouhair was sitting on the floor near his father and weeping. The whole family was in tears. It was horrible, and we were all disgusted to see the cops everywhere like that. But at the time we were happy that at least Zouhair would be able to attend his father's funeral. It was not to be. They just gave him half an hour; he did not have the right to go to the burial. He was sickened. After the funeral, the neighbors were convinced that a crew had been shooting a film in the neighborhood.

Zouhair weighed less than a hundred pounds on his release and suffered from dental abscesses and kidney problems. His family experienced reprisals, and the secret police warned employers not to hire his brothers. Amira remembers, "Zouhair completely changed after prison. He became very aggressive and insolent, as though he resented others who had not been arrested." Still, he resumed work on TUNeZINE. On March 13, 2005, he had a massive heart attack and died, at age thirty-seven. Activists believed that prison had destroyed his health and that he died as a martyr to internet dissidence.

After the revolution Marzouki, who had become the first elected president after the revolution, announced that the date would be commemorated as a national Internet Freedom Day. Jebali, who was hunger-fasting in jail at the same time as Zouhair, became Tunisia's first postrevolution prime minister. In the run-up to the revolution Zouhair's image was frequently painted on walls by dissident graffiti artists. In spring 2013 I interviewed a young Tunisian woman in her early twenties who had joined the protests that later overthrew Ben Ali and asked her whether she had read the dissident internet sites when she was growing up. She said she had been too young to be interested in TUNeZINE in its heyday but that she hungrily got into its archives when she came to political consciousness. The survival of dissident thought on the internet long after the first publication allowed a continuity of regime critique across the microgenerations of the millennials.

World Summit of the Information Society

For the Yahyaouis and other activists, the struggle was anything but over. The same year Zouhair died, the Ben Ali regime hosted the second meeting of a two-part World Summit of the Information Society (WSIS), sponsored by the United Nations International Telecommunications Union (comprising most UN member states and hundreds of private companies and organizations). The first meeting was held in Geneva in 2003 and produced a statement of principles that said, "We reaffirm, as an essential foundation of the Information Society, and as outlined in Article 19 of the Universal Declaration of Human Rights, that everyone has the right to freedom of opinion and expression; that this right includes freedom to hold opinions without interference and to seek, receive and impart information and ideas through any media and regardless of frontiers."[14] When the planning committee was criticized for meeting in Tunisia, they replied that they had hoped the summit would encourage the regime to open up. Instead, the government basked in the prestige of the meeting but ruthlessly deployed its usual techniques to silence dissent. A preparatory meeting for WSIS was held in Switzerland on February 17, 2005, and Reporters without Borders sent a delegation to attend, which included Zouhair Yahyaoui.[15] He was aware of the dangers, saying, "Maybe when I go back to Tunis I'll be arrested again. It's a risk, but I take it."[16] Afterward Zouhair gave an interview to the Inter Press Service slamming the world body's decision: "The censorship is implacable, the authorities close down any dissenting website. . . . The WSIS final phase being held in Tunisia is an unforgivable slap for Tunisian democrats."[17] It was his last major denunciation of the regime.

On March 3, 2005, Judge Mokhtar Yahyaoui circulated on internet forums a severe critique of Ben Ali's preparations for the conference, written by the correspondent Julien Pain, Zouhair's colleague at Reporters without Borders, who then also worked for the Internet Freedom Desk.[18] Pain pointed out that Tunisia had blocked access on March 1 to the website of the Progressive Democratic Party. It may be that the party's criticism of a planned visit to Tunis by Israeli prime minister Ariel Sharon was part of the reason for the filtering, but in general, Ben Ali tightened censorship ahead of the meeting. Reporters without Borders, in preparation for the summit, set up a website, Radionongrata, which, ironically, was itself blocked in Tunisia. The Internet Freedom Desk mentioned that the site carried an account by Zouhair Yahyaoui of his travails as an internet activist. (The essay was written only a couple of weeks before Zouhair's heart attack.) Pain noted, "Following the preparatory meeting, President Ben Ali accused human rights NGOs of carrying on 'trade in distorting Tunisia's image.' He also repeated that the holding of the WSIS in his country was a 'world of affirmation' of 'our choices and orientations.'" He appended a long list of sites that were blocked in Tunisia, including those of newspapers, NGOs, and political parties.

That fall the cyber activists created a website to protest the extreme censorship of the Tunisian web at a time when this prestigious international conference on the information society was being held in the country. It was immediately blocked. Activist Neila Charchour Hachicha, who organized the site, wrote on her blog, "Although most protesters are anonymous the regime censored the website in Tunisia the same day it was launched. If it proves something, it does prove that the regime is much more frightened than the 100 virtual protesters. So finally, who is more powerfull [sic]? Is it anonymous but free citizens claiming their right to be discontent or is it a frightened regime supposed to hold a strong legitimacy?"[19]

The regime pocketed the prestige of holding the UN meeting but shamelessly and brutally cracked down on dissent. Even Swiss journalists were attacked by Ministry of Interior goons at the meeting. A handful of internet activists fasted to protest the holding of the summit in Tunis, including Judge Yahyaoui. Those who did not go on a hunger strike, including Amira, decided to demonstrate on Bourguiba Avenue downtown: "There were many journalists, you couldn't miss that. My father was among the demonstrators and was afraid that I would attend. He had given me a stern talking to beforehand, saying 'You will not go, OK? Understood?'" Judge Yahyaoui often forbade his daughter to do more, saying that the family had already given enough to the cause. She went anyway, "and the cops recognized me. I was really beaten. They broke my glasses, and I couldn't see anything further, being punched in the stomach by cops who were several times my size. Above all, they tried to trap me on the rail of the tramway, and I thought I was going to die. Luckily, Mokhtar Trifi, then the president of the Tunisian League for the Defense of Human Rights, jumped in to save me. [The reaction to] that demonstration was particularly violent—everyone was beaten up and the cops went crazy." She went home and pleaded with her mother not to reveal what had happened; they decided to tell the judge that she was sick and to wait to see him only when the bruises on her face had healed. Some of the demonstrators, however, told the story, and her father ended up reading about it. He didn't speak to her for a while.

Amira's academic career was derailed by her family's dissidence. Despite top high school grades, she wasn't allowed into the University of Tunis. She went off to Paris and studied mathematics and information technology at the University of Paris VI. She was stuck in France, her passport revoked in 2006, more or less in exile and unable to travel, until the revolution. After a brief failed marriage in 2010, she was able to return to her country early in 2011. She married again, this time in the Casbah, or old city of Tunis, surrounded by all her friends from the dissident political network. She started a new life in a new Tunisia and has turned to monitoring politics and constitution writing. "I don't like writing all that much," she confessed. "I like to take action."

Zouhair's work was continued by a host of Tunisian internet activists, not least by many from the old Takriz network. Their audience burgeoned and therefore so did their political importance. The number of Tunisians online nearly doubled between 2006 and 2008, rising from 950,000 to 1.7 million. In 2009 the number of users doubled again, to 3.5 million, about a third of the country's 10.4 million people.[20] In addition, digital cell phone subscribers using the Global System for Mobile Communications protocol reached 9 million in 2008; almost everyone had a digital cell phone.[21] The change was noticed by U.S. embassy officials in Tunis in 2009, and they wrote a cable on Facebook use: "Some people use the site to engage in a frank political discussion and exchange of ideas that is singular for a public forum in Tunisia."[22] Journalists told the embassy officials that topics such as "unemployment, immigration, and cost of living" were off-limits in the newspapers. "Free speech in schools and university campuses is likewise strictly controlled; plainclothes police maintain a constant presence on campus and the national student union is harassed." Sizable Facebook pages such as I Have a Dream: A Democratic Tunisia had emerged, which then had 2,305 members, along with other pages, such as Facebook Alliance against Censorship, and other dissident groups with hundreds of "friends."

Prominent activists increasingly had popular Facebook pages, and these were harder for the regime to block than were conventional websites. Facebook groups were established to support the protests and strikes of mine workers in Gafsa in 2008 at a time when the Tunisian press was suppressing the news. Young people also went there to protest. U.S. embassy officials observed, "Demonstrators arrested in Gafsa for protesting hiring policies at a phosphate plant in 2008 were largely youths in their early 20s."[23] A newspaper closely tied to the Ministry of the Interior mounted a campaign against Facebook, accusing it of being a portal to sex, drugs, and violence and of opening readers to CIA monitoring. These efforts to discredit the platform, however, had little impact.

Social media were able to grow on the basis of this broad internet base. By early 2010 there were over a million Facebook users in Tunisia, predominantly millennials, and 40 percent of them were girls and women.[24] In summer of 2008 Ben Ali briefly attempted to ban Facebook, but even a repressed society such as Tunisia's protested so furiously that he backed off. Journalist and blogger Ziad El Hendi even dared to initiate a lawsuit against the Tunisian Internet Agency over the blocking of Facebook, in which he was joined by the Tunisian Union of Free Radio Stations and the Unionist Freedoms and Rights Observatory. (Predictably the suit was thrown out by the courts months later, but by then Ben Ali had already reversed his decision.)[25] Because of the way Facebook works, with individuals posting status reports to a circle of friends (usually fifty to two hundred persons), it was an excellent networking tool of which the activists made full use. Unlike newspapers (which were owned by regime cronies), the internet is interactive, and the dissidents started many vigorous discussions that could never have been held in meatspace. The internet's relative openness and transparency had the disadvantage of making it penetrable by the secret police, but the exponential increases in numbers of users overwhelmed them. Opacity was attained not by covert communication but by massive amounts of public comment, which Tunisian authorities could not effectively monitor or control.

Blogging also remained a key medium for dissidents. Another important blogger was Lina Ben Mhenni (b. 1983). She was in the United States in 2008 on a Fulbright exchange, teaching Arabic, and while there created a blog with a journalist colleague she met via Facebook. It was almost immediately blocked by Tunisian censors when she treated taboo political subjects. Enraged, she pounded out an anticensorship screed in half an hour. Sami Ben Gharbia suggested she publish it at Global Voices Online, a communal site for bloggers. She accepted immediately, and it was published in late August 2008, during the time the Tunisian government had briefly attempted to ban Facebook. She wrote, "Tunisian internet users are now very familiar with the error message '404 Not Found' and they went so far as to invent a virtual personality they named Ammar 404, armed with the scissors of censorship. When you are in Tunisia, just try to access YouTube or Dailymotion: you will abruptly receive the error message! Do you want to follow the news at Aljazeera or Alarabiya? The Tunisian Internet Agency regrets to inform you that they cannot furnish you with that service."[26] She noted that local Tunisian news sites, including Ben Gharbia's own Nawaat, were also blocked, as were a whole range of blogs, including her own. She joined in the successful campaign to bring back Facebook inside Tunisia.

In keeping with the themes of youth and their lifestyles, her blog was at first called Nightclubbeuse (Nightclubber). It then became Crazy Thoughts. After a meeting with Arab bloggers in Beirut in 2009 hosted by the Heinrich Böll Foundation, she retitled it A Tunisian Girl, in English, though the content was most often in Arabic or French.[27] She is distinctive in having refused to adopt a pseudonym, despite what had happened to Zouhair Yahyaoui. Indeed the regime's heavy-handed repression appears only to have emboldened each new internet generation, so that those born in the 1990s were more daring than their predecessors. In one of her entries, Ben Mhenni wrote a poem that epitomizes the young bloggers' impatience, saying "I long to commit a bookish crime / I yearn for my share in intellectual indecency."[28]

Ben Mhenni was back in Tunisia during the winter of 2008–9, when the Israelis attacked the Palestinians in Gaza. She was outraged, she said, that "hundreds of civilians were savagely killed during the raids, under aerial bombardment followed by a land offensive, [and] I participated in all the demonstrations staged in Tunis against this aggression." Even though the Ben Ali regime was not involved in that crisis, it tried to ban the rallies. She also wrote at her blog, denouncing "these crimes." Most of the activists who waged the revolutions of 2011–12 felt deeply about a range of issues on the left, from the plight of the Palestinians to crackdowns on workers' strikes. As will be seen in the next chapter, the Gaza protests were a major moment in youth protest and organization on the ground throughout the country.

Ben Mhenni continued to alert the international community when Ammar 404 became particularly intrusive. In the spring of 2009 she attacked Tunisian censors for having cracked down on a blog for reprinting an article from a Canadian newspaper on real estate purchases in that country by Ben Ali's corrupt son-in-law, multimillionaire Sakher El Materi.[29] She was frank about the difficulties in an interview with Voice of America: "Everything is blocked here. . . . I use a proxy to access my blog, my Facebook profile, and . . . they censored my Twitter account. It is not accessible in Tunisia."[30] She added, "In Tunisia you cannot express yourself." In May 2010 she joined internet activists Slim Amamou and Yassine Ayari to formally ask permission of the Interior Ministry to organize an anticensorship demonstration, "A Day against Ammar." The two young men were arrested, but were released on being informed that there would be no march. Instead, on May 22, bloggers in white T-shirts skipped from café to café on Habib Bourguiba Avenue, harassed by the police.[31]

In the period before the January 2011 revolution, Tunisian women bloggers such as Ben Mhenni were for the most part rugged individualists, not associated with any political party and seen as slightly scandalous. Typically they did not start out being determinedly political but were pushed in that direction by the regime's authoritarian tactics.[32]

In January 2011 Ben Mhenni traveled to hospitals in small cities and towns, taking photos of activists whom the regime's police had attacked and telling their stories, thus documenting a repressive apparatus that would otherwise have remained invisible. She and the other bloggers and Facebook and Twitter users, who had played cat-and-mouse with the Ben Ali regime for years, suddenly had the momentum on their side, and they were able to use their internet skills to help call into being flash mobs that effectively challenged the regime in ways that ultimately overwhelmed it. They were hardly alone, given the important role played by student, labor, kinship, and urban networks in setting up the relentless demonstrations, but their internet activism was among the more important megaphones addressing a restless Tunisian public. Slim Amamou observed of the revolution, "The great mass of Tunisians are on Facebook. They were enabled to launch appeals to demonstrate, to protest. Without the Net, the people would not have been informed, would not have been mobilized, and would not have made the government fall."[33]

Egyptian Bloggers: The Generation of 2005

In part under pressure from the U.S. government, which gave the Egyptian government nearly $2 billion a year in military and civilian aid, President Hosni Mubarak pledged to soften press restrictions in 2004. Despite promising to do so, however, the government did not actually amend the censorship laws, and it kept the 1981 state of emergency in place, which suspended civil liberties. On the eve of the revolution Human Rights Watch estimated that between five thousand and ten thousand prisoners of conscience were being held in prison by the Mubarak regime under this notorious provision, suffering arbitrary military trials and torture.[34] Some of these prisoners were internet activists.

As in Tunisia, the rise of the internet in Egypt created new virtual social spaces in which activists could meet and interact at a time when physical meetings of more than a few people attracted the attention of the secret police. Ahmad Gharbeia, an activist for open software, made a declaration of independence in the first entry in his blog in October 2005: "Governments of the industrial world, giants of meat and steel, I come to you from cyberspace, the new home of the mind. In the name of the future I ask you, who belong to the past, to leave us alone. You are not worthy, you have no easy solutions, and you have no power where we meet. We have no elected government and likely will never have a government. Therefore, I address you with a sovereignty that does not exceed that whereby liberty herself has sometimes spoken, to announce that the global social space that we are creating is by its nature independent of the tyranny that you attempt to impose on us. You have no legitimacy to rule over us, nor do you possess means to vanquish us of a sort that would merit our fear."[35]

It was not only the ability to meet and discuss beyond the ears of the secret police that the new dimension of cyberspace offered; it was also the ability to experience things directly. For the Arab baby boomers and Generation X who had no personal experience of it, torture was less visceral because it was only reported in rumors. Two key developments changed all that. First, smartphones began having video capabilities. The late 2004 Indian Ocean tsunami was the first time that most news footage of an event shown on television came from amateurs shooting on their mobile telephones. Second, some former employees of the internet money exchange company, PayPal, launched YouTube in 2005, and by 2006 dissidents in the Arab world had begun secretly recording videos of police torture and posting them to that site. Torture went from being a terrifying rumor in previous generations to being something the millennials saw routinely with their own eyes.

In 2006 Wael Abbas, an activist blogger, began posting graphic videos, taken surreptitiously, of police brutalizing their prisoners. One showed a bus driver being sodomized with a pole. The Egyptian public reacted with horror; people told Abbas the scene reminded them of American torture of Iraqis at Abu Ghraib prison. In late 2007 Google suspended Abbas's YouTube account, deleting one hundred video clips, including some twelve that depicted torture in police stations. Likely the internet giant moved against him because of the graphicness of the images, though the fact that many of the complaints lodged against him were false-flag operations of Egyptian intelligence should not be discounted. By then, however, Abbas had done significant damage to the reputation of the Mubarak regime.[36] By late 2006 the contribution of Egyptian bloggers to the revelation of torture was attracting recognition by international human rights organizations, and activist Amr Ezzat wrote humorously that he was proud that his colleagues were surging ahead of bloggers on torture in other countries.[37]

The work of Abbas and other bloggers on torture provoked the interest of the Al Jazeera Arabic journalist Howayda Taha Matwali, who reported for the Doha-based satellite channel on torture in Egyptian police stations. By January 2007 she had so provoked the Mubarak regime that its agents detained her briefly at the airport. She returned to Qatar, and a case was initiated against her in Egypt. On May 1 a Cairo court found her guilty in absentia of "falsely depicting events" and fined her 20,000 Egyptian pounds (then U.S.$3,600). Two years later officials at the U.S. embassy reported:

> At a public lecture in February following the screening of a documentary film about blogging, human rights lawyer Gamal Eid lauded Wael Abbas for posting an alleged police sodomy video a few days earlier, and for breaking the El-Kebir police brutality case. In November 2007, a court sentenced two polic[e] officers to three years in prison for assault and sodomizing bus driver Imad El-Kebir. The case gained notoriety after Abbas posted a cell phone video recording of the attack. Eid cited the "3,000 hits per day" on Abbas' blog as evidence of his influence, asserting that Abbas is more widely read than "Rose Al Youssef," the SSIS [State Security]–backed daily newspaper. Separately, a human rights lawyer specializing in torture at the Hisham Mubarak Law Center marveled at Abbas' power to expose police brutality on his blog.[38]

Rulers such as Mubarak went from being disliked to being hated. Secret police and torture were essential to maintaining the power of the republican monarchy, but they functioned best in the shadows. The millennials were adopting technology that would shine the light of day on them.

Whereas most Arab societies prefer gender segregation in public space, which is defined as predominantly male, and women have difficulty asserting themselves there, cyberspace was an arena where young Egyptian women could express themselves and even exercise leadership. Blogger Shahinaz Abdel Salam (b. 1978), from a wealthy family in Alexandria, explained that she gained political consciousness as a schoolgirl when she borrowed from the library at her Catholic private school a book co-authored by Simone de Beauvoir on the Algerian freedom fighter Djamila Boupacha, a woman who had been tried by French authorities on terrorism charges during the Algerian war of independence from France (1954–62), condemned to death, but then amnestied when France withdrew. Abdel Salam was also much influenced by the Egyptian feminist and dissident Nawal El Saadawi, who had been jailed by President Sadat. Abdel Salam described her upper-middle-class upbringing in Alexandria in her autobiography, complaining of the way her family became increasingly religiously conservative through the 1990s: "Many of my uncles and friends left in that era for Saudi Arabia or the Gulf emirates, and every time they returned on vacation, they brought with them the habits of the Wahhabi Islam that they practiced there."[39] She was gradually cut off from her Coptic Christian friends by the increasingly bigoted attitudes in her family, some of which she felt were imported from the Arabian peninsula and were alien to local Egyptian traditions. She once was horrified by a sermon at her local mosque, which painted a Hieronymus Bosch–like vision of women tortured in hell for having declined to wear the veil or for having sported décolletage, and she wrote a letter of protest to the preacher. Ultimately she was so distressed by this rising fundamentalism that she wholly abandoned belief in religion. She studied at Alexandria University and then, after a brief, disastrous marriage, went to work for a French telecom in Cairo. In 2005 she joined the youth wing of the Kefaya (Enough) movement and began her blog, which decried regime brutality toward dissidents and condemned Egyptian male chauvinism, whether secular or religious.[40] Many blogs, including those by male activists, took up the issue of sexual harassment.[41]

Some bloggers got into trouble for explicitly discussing explosive issues such as sectarian tensions between Muslims and Coptic Christians or for being critical of religion. Human Rights Watch reported, "Kareem Amer, a blogger whose real name is 'Abd al-Karim Nabil Suleiman, has been in Borg El Arab prison in Alexandria since November 7, 2006 for writing about sectarian tensions in Alexandria and criticizing President Hosni Mubarak and the Al-Azhar religious institution. Hany Nazeer, a blogger who voiced opinions critical of Christianity and Islam, has been in Borg El Arab since

October 3, 2008, and is denied visitors." In many ways the progressive youth movements of the early twenty-first century were attempts to bridge the divide between Muslim and Coptic Christian youth.

Young people who associated themselves with the Muslim Brotherhood, the equivalent of politically minded conservative evangelical youth in the United States, also took to the internet to blog. Their role in controversies in the movement was amplified in 2007, when the Muslim Brotherhood issued a divisive party platform. The move was in part a response to their having won eighty-eight seats in the lower house of Parliament in 2005 and in part a response to the subsequent government repression they faced. They were emerging as a political force rather than primarily a sectarian community, just as the Southern Baptists in the United States decided to become a force in the Republican Party from the mid-1970s forward, deserting their previous quietism. The platform, however, did not make clear whether there would be a separation between the Brotherhood itself and a political party that acted as a civil institution, as had happened in the most prominent fundamentalist movement in Morocco. One problem for the Brotherhood being in politics is that members must swear fealty to the Supreme Guide, which would limit their political independence. The draft covered many issues, including economic policy, but it provoked controversies around two main issues. It advocated the formation of a council of religious leaders that would advise the government on Islamic law, which sounded to many observers like a step toward theocracy. It also explicitly disallowed women and Christians from becoming president of the republic. Taken together these provisions projected an illiberal image and signaled aspirations for a right-wing religious society more closely resembling Iran than France.[42]

These provisions in the draft were controversial within the Muslim Brotherhood itself, with liberals like Abdel Moneim Aboul Fotouh and younger leaders like Essam el-Erian dissenting from them. Muslim Brotherhood youth, as Marc Lynch reported at the time, took to the internet to argue over the draft.[43] Lynch estimated that there were about 150 Brotherhood bloggers and that many of them had more in common with their liberal and leftist peers than with the older establishment of their own party. At the same time, Lynch observed, the fundamentalist youth of the Salafi movement, at that time largely a wing of the Brotherhood, attacked the document for being too liberal and demanded a more "Islamic" platform. The Salafis, often allergic to modern technology, mainly networked in meatspace, especially in some districts of Alexandria and in some Delta towns. Many Salafis had worked in or been influenced by Saudi Arabia, where the fundamentalist Wahhabi form of Islam predominates and where the government proclaims that there is no constitution save the Qur'an. The trenchant critiques of the draft were among the reasons for which the Brotherhood withdrew it in October 2007.

The draft party platform was only one of many controversies that exercised the Brotherhood blogosphere in this period, as German political scientist Ivesa Lübben explained.[44] Interestingly, many of the youth on the religious right spoke of a yearning for freedom and personal liberty—not the keywords of the older leadership. I find this in my own research as well. In 2009, when a movement was established to replace the controversial Muhammad Mahdi Akif as Supreme Guide, the young blogger Muhammad Hamza was provoked to a meditation on the movement. Akif got into trouble for seeming to claim that Osama Bin Laden was a holy warrior. (After a firestorm of protest he instead condemned Bin Laden.) But Hamza described Akif's leadership as marked by openness, inclusiveness, and group decision making within the organization and presciently feared a more controlling, authoritarian successor. He regretted what he saw as the Egyptian leadership's rigidity and unwillingness to experiment, compared to the Jordanians and Palestinians. He wondered about the impact of the change in Guides on Egypt itself, where, he said, the 1952 regime and its successors had created a misshapen politics and society. He pointed to the distortions in foreign policy, such as the Mubarak regime's policy of supporting Israel and the United States with respect to Hamas in Gaza. (He was writing just after the Gaza War.) On domestic policy he complained of "the extreme stagnation we experience in our political and social life. Simply put, it is not possible now for any of the youth to dream of a position of political or social leadership, based on personal expertise and self-discipline."[45] The only avenue open, he said, was the ruling National Democratic Party, and even there the potential role was carefully circumscribed. He admitted that a change in the leadership of the Brotherhood was highly unlikely to affect this distortion of Egyptian political and social life. Some of these youth bloggers later left the Brotherhood, deserting to liberal or leftist groups or joining the Muslim Wasat (Center) Party. Some of them later played a role in the 2011 revolution.

Internet Support for the El Mahalla El Kubra Strikes of 2006–2007

Many young bloggers and internet activists were leftists or, if on the religious right, so disdainful of the Mubarak government that they supported its class enemies, the workers and peasants. They used their electronic megaphones to publicize workers' and peasants' strikes and discontents. In the first decade of the century, the urban working class was exploring new tactics and identifying new issues on which to mobilize against the state, given privatization and the rising cost of food. A significant proportion of Egyptian factory and workshop laborers were themselves youth (not counting the 2 million children). Some 70 percent of the Egyptian population was under thirty. To get the word out about their grievances these young workers increasingly drew on the resources of the youth auxiliaries of left-wing parties and networks and of a sympathetic blogosphere. The new transparency of information about their activities made it more difficult for the government simply to tear-gas them, beat them, and arrest them en masse. Egyptian workers staged some three thousand strikes and other labor actions between 2004 and 2010, and in 2008–9 alone about a million workers participated in labor actions.[46] The workers, moreover, had the advantage of being organized and interested in their pay and working conditions, which were declining in real terms in the new century. In contrast, foreign policy controversies such as Palestine and the Iraq War were not ever-present in the minds of voters, and elections were infrequent and known to be rigged. The political activists therefore had difficulty maintaining their momentum. Factory workers led the way in showing the power of organized opposition in extracting concessions from the regime.

In the Sadat and Mubarak eras, from 1970 forward, the Muslim Brotherhood had increasing success in student union elections throughout Egypt.

In the 1990s and 2000s, however, a countervailing force grew up in the form of the Trotskyite Revolutionary Socialist Party, which had a strong youth component. Journalist Hossam el-Hamalawy, who also reported for the *Los Angeles Times*, emerged as an important blogger and member of that party. He and his leftist colleagues demonstrated in 2000 in sympathy with the Palestinian uprising, and again in 2003 against the Iraq War, for which he was briefly arrested. In 2005 he became a member of the reformist Kefaya movement. Workers and youth bloggers, who, for all their sympathy with one another, had few personal or social connections, were forming important alliances.

A Revolutionary Socialist Party website identified December 7, 2006, as a turning point in Egyptian labor activism.[47] The site explained that public sector workers (an enormous section of the working class) had been reluctant to engage in work stoppages in earlier decades because they considered their factory to belong to the people, whom they did not wish to harm. Disgruntled workers therefore tended to protest by occupying their factories, declining to go home at the end of the day but performing their ordinary tasks during working hours. The Revolutionary Socialists argued that government statistics suggested that factory productivity actually increased during worker occupations. By late 2006, however, workers in the vast industrial complexes of El Mahalla El Kubra, north of Cairo, had come to resent their corrupt managers and the declining real value of their salaries and bonuses so much that they decided to launch a work stoppage. The tradition of working-class deference to persons of high status, who filled management positions, was weakening.[48] Such strikes proliferated thereafter and posed great difficulties for the state, given its increasing commitment to privatization and inability to pay public sector workers what those in the growing private sector were earning.

While the U.S. embassy did not share the Egyptian Trotskyites' view that the 2006 strike represented a structural change in labor activism in the country, it agreed that this labor action was important. Embassy officials reported that on December 7 some seventeen thousand night-shift workers halted production at the government's Misr Spinning and Weaving Company's Ghazl al-Mahalla plant. They were protesting management's refusal to pay them their annual bonus (amounting to two months' salary), even though Prime Minister Ahmed Nazif had promised it. CEO Mahmoud El-Gibaly argued that the company had too much debt to pay the bonuses (which would have amounted to $4.5 million) and was not then profitable. The workers claimed in turn that the recently appointed El-Gibaly was personally corrupt. Fathi Naamatullah, the secretary-general of the Textile Union, insisted that the factory's production was increasing and that the firm's own records posted a profit of $12 million. On December 8, the U.S. ambassador, Francis Ricciardone, reported, the day-shift employees also stopped work and occupied the factory and the street on which it was located: "As the strike progressed, the number of workers involved grew to an estimated 27,000 to 54,000, including 4,000 women."[49] One labor activist described how, initially, the men asked their female colleagues not to occupy the building with them, but the women went up on the roof, and some threatened to commit suicide if they weren't allowed to join.[50] (Mixing of the sexes and overnight stays are unacceptable in conservative Egypt, and the regime often took advantage of any such cross-gender solidarity to dismiss protesters as unserious libertines looking for a good time.)

This labor action was clearly one of the largest and most threatening in recent Egyptian history, but apparently it took the government by surprise, and once it had been launched, it would have been difficult to deal with simply by sending in the state security police. The state cut off water and electricity to the factory. The Mubarak regime was pressured by a member of Parliament for El Mahalla El Kubra affiliated with the Muslim Brotherhood, Saad al-Husseini. The Muslim Brotherhood, despite its general lack of interest in working-class justice, took advantage of the workers' charges and discontent to slam the government for cronyism and corruption and to charge that management had swallowed the workers' bonuses. The NDP ministers of manpower and of investment were drawn into the negotiations. The government backed down on denying bonuses altogether and offered a twenty-one-day bonus. Ambassador Ricciardone wrote in a cable to Washington, "The workers refused the offer, however, citing the upcoming Eid Al-Adha holiday, rising food prices, and their dependence on the full bonuses to make ends meet."[51] The government countered by promising another half-month bonus in January, and the workers accepted the package, ending the strike on December 10 and going back to work. Encouraged by the success of their colleagues, four thousand workers at the al-Nasr Dye Company launched a sit-down strike in Gharbiya province, also asking for bonuses for the upcoming holy day. In the southern Cairo factory district of Helwan, 1,700 workers in the local cement factory struck to demand their bonuses and a salary increase.

Although the Muslim Brotherhood expressed sympathy with the strike as a way of slamming the Mubarak regime, the action came from the workers themselves and was promoted by leftist activists and young workers. The crisis was defused because at that point the Mubarak regime still had some elements of pluralism. The eighty-eight Parliament seats won by the Muslim Brotherhood the previous year had created some space for legitimate dissent. Even the state-authorized Textile Workers Union supported its members in this instance. Still, the very success of the strike and the startling willingness of workers to stop work provoked countermeasures by the regime in succeeding years. The Revolutionary Socialists may well have been right that a work stoppage on this scale indicated a major breakthrough in working-class consciousness, whereby they increasingly saw their factories not as public, socialist institutions but as private industry lite because of the corruption of the company's management.

Labor and human rights activist Atef Said wrote that although the El Mahalla El Kubra strike was unusual in its scale, it was typical of the new wave of Egyptian labor actions in 2006 and 2007. He wrote that one liberal daily "estimated that no fewer than 222 sit-in strikes, work stoppages, hunger strikes and demonstrations had occurred during 2006."[52] As 2007 unfolded, there was a new labor action every day. The government did not follow through on some of its pledges to the Misr textile workers, fomenting further discontent, which exploded on September 23, 2007, when twenty-four thousand workers walked off the job. The workers demanded unpaid bonuses as well as a raise in pay; they also wanted new company and union leadership. They occupied the Talaat Harb Square in front of the factory, camping out overnight, often joined by their families. U.S. embassy officials observed, "In addition to criticizing the National Democratic Party (NDP)-controlled trade unions as not representing worker interests, the workers are also voicing opposition to the Government of Egypt's (GOE's) overall privatization policies, chanting 'We will not be ruled by the World Bank! We will not be ruled by colonialism!'"[53] Workers at other factories joined in, such as the textile workers at the Ghazl Kafr al-Dawwar at another Delta mill town.

The intersection of labor action with political dissidence was underlined when, the U.S. chargé d'affaires reported, "opposition organization Kefaya's 'Workers for Change' group announced that it was mobilizing demonstrations of solidarity at the South Giza Grain Mills near Cairo." Leftist bloggers such as el-Hamalawy supported the workers with cyberspace broadsides and analysis. He wrote, "Virtually all the textile mills along the Nile Delta in the north went on strike from December through to the spring of 2007. The militancy spilled over to other sectors. The cement workers went on strike, followed by the railway drivers—who blocked the trains by sleeping on the rails. Cairo tube drivers lowered their train speed in solidarity. In all of these struggles the victory in El Mahalla El Kubra always resonated."[54] Although Muslim Brotherhood members of Parliament demanded that the government meet the strikers' demands, Brotherhood cadres were noticeably absent on the ground, according to the bloggers.

By October 1 the government had caved to key demands, including immediate payment of promised bonuses and a pay increase. Solidarity from trade unions abroad, including that of South Africa, may have helped. U.S. embassy officials sympathized that workers at the factory were paid only $71 a month and were facing high inflation costs for food, making it difficult for them to feed their families, and predicted that low factory productivity and wildcat strikes would continue until Egypt allowed the free formation of unions and formal collective bargaining.[55]

Labor historian Joel Beinin points out that textiles are Egypt's largest industry and that workers in that sector are paid substantially less than their counterparts in Pakistan and India (both of which have lower per capita income). Egypt's authoritarian government and the Mubarak clique's control of so much of the economy made it difficult for workers to get a fair wage compared to more open systems in South Asia. The El Mahalla El Kubra workers formed standing committees to attempt to remove their state-approved union leaders and to contradict government antiworker propaganda in the press.[56] The relatively successful textile strikes in an industry that employed 300,000 encouraged labor activism and protests not only among other industrial laborers but in other sectors of the economy as well. Both rural farmers and white-collar bureaucrats took the cue that they need not passively accept their declining standard of living, provoked by declining government resources.

It was not only urban workers who had grievances. Egypt still has an enormous rural sector, which was also restive. In the summer of 2007 the U.S. embassy reported, "Emboldened by successful strikes at textile factories, villagers throughout Egypt have held highly publicized demonstrations about water shortages."[57] The youth bulge in Egypt, which was produced by a doubling of the population in the thirty years from 1980 to 2010, discovered that not only were jobs scarce for them, but so were staples like water and food.

Although the ancient historian Herodotus was a notorious gossip and spinner of tall tales, he did get one thing right: Egypt is the gift of the Nile. The population map of Egypt looks like a long-stemmed lotus, its stem reaching up from the border with Sudan in the south and its petals ranged along the Mediterranean in the north, where the Nile flows into the branches through the delta. Egypt is so arid that most people live along the banks of the Nile. The flow of water reaching Egypt from points south in Africa, however, is no longer sufficient for its teeming masses. It was set at 55.5 billion cubic meters by a 1959 treaty with Sudan, at a time when the population was about 25 million and most people were farmers. By 2005 each Egyptian had access to an average of only 770 cubic meters of water a year, falling below the United Nations minimum of 1,000 cubic meters, the amount needed to avoid water scarcity. In the United States each person uses 10,000 cubic meters of water a year, and Europeans consume around 2,500. Climate change is also contributing to water problems for Egypt and Syria and was implicated in the 2011 revolutions in both countries.[58]

The crisis was especially acute in the countryside, where 80 percent of water is used for irrigation and the rest for drinking. The U.S. embassy claimed the shortage was exacerbated by poor management, deteriorating infrastructure, and population increases. Moreover, as with almost all social issues in Mubarak's Egypt, corruption made the situation worse. In Daqahliya water rationing to villages began in 2001. In August 2007 rural residents in that governorate protested a lack of drinking water. They alleged that the government had diverted their water to the Gamasah beach resort, where the wealthy disported themselves in the summer.[59] Farmers also staged protests in other governorates in the delta, as well as in Upper Egypt. When the U.S. embassy sent officials out to talk to the protesters in Daqahliya and Sharqiya, locals told them that "irrigation water does not meet the needs of local farmers, who are forced to use drainage water to irrigate fields." They also complained of the high salt content of the drainage water, which could not be used for any crops save rice, which was not as profitable as vegetables, corn, or cotton. They were upset that government officials were unresponsive to their requests.

The support for such rural water protests among urban dissidents could be seen on Egyptian internet bulletin boards of the time. A commenter wrote on Egypt Talk that he had heard on the radio that the residents of Burj al-Burulus in Kafr Sheikh had blocked the international coastal road along the Mediterranean to get through to officials that they had had no water for eleven days. Only then did officials, in this case the army, act. It was clear to the commenter that the Egyptian state "has gotten used to depending on thuggish repression and has come to refuse to acknowledge the problems, replying only with force." It had taken the rash of strikes, labor actions, and demonstrations to get its ear. "Really, the error is that of citizens, who patiently put up with the degradation inflicted on them by the government and do not act as the people of Burj Burulus did in making the government respond to them."[60] Even in Muqattam, in the hills above Cairo, a journalist for the newspaper *al-Misri al-Yawm* (Egypt Today), sympathetic with the people in Burj al-Burulus, wrote, "Every day for the last two weeks, water supply is cut off for hours and everyday also electricity is cut off for hours." In July the blogger Baheya printed photographs of people seeking water in Giza, a suburb of Cairo. The Egyptian Worker Blog published an exposé on a village near Samanoud in the Delta that had to spend all its money privately to bring electricity to the village because the government wouldn't run the lines, but then had no funds to bring in running water. Villagers had to walk a long way to bring water from another location.[61]

The following summer, in June 2008, 1,500 Burj al-Burulus residents mounted protests and blocked the road again, burning boats and tires in the street, allegedly inspired by the April 6 El Mahalla El Kubra textile strike. This time the issue was the cancelation of their allotment of subsidized flour, which the governor maintained they were selling on the black market and which he awarded to state bakeries instead. As fishermen, they maintained that they depended heavily on the subsidy. Their cause was taken up by the youth organization Revolutionary Socialists and other internet activists.[62]

Rural discontent with lack of water and urban dissatisfaction with poor wages and high inflation were much more pervasive and important social problems than those that preoccupied the fifty thousand political bloggers, most of them middle- or upper-middle-class urban youth. It was nevertheless important that the workers, farmers, and fishermen could now get the word out via the internet and social media and could attract the support of urban youth across the political spectrum. (Obviously leftists were most enthusiastic about the cause of the factory workers and peasants, but the Muslim Brotherhood also sometimes evinced empathy for their plight, and as a budding political party was looking for constituents for whom it could do favors in return for support at the ballot box.)

Gaza and the Crackdown on Blogging

The Gaza War of late 2008 and early 2009 drove a great deal of Egyptian internet activism and may well have been a turning point in the disgust of the youth with their government. Unlike Tunisia's Ben Ali, who was not explicitly tied to Israeli policy, Mubarak had a peace treaty with Israel, and Egyptian forces helped police Israel's blockade of Gaza. Some of the blogging on the issue was sentimental. The anonymous student blog Nothing Deserves That! published a touching music video about a little Palestinian girl, Maryam, who was celebrating her birthday in her refugee camp when she was killed by an Israeli bombing raid.[63] Diya' al-Din Gad, part of the

Egyptian Movement of the Enraged, who protested the Gaza War at his blog (The Angry Voice), insulted Mubarak as an agent of the West, complicit in the siege of Gaza, and hostile to Hizbullah, the Shiite resistance movement of Lebanon.[64] He was immediately arrested by state security police. The Arab Network for Human Rights Information alleged that Gad was put in solitary confinement, denied medical care, and threatened with being summarily killed.[65] The U.S. embassy reported that he was released in late March only after the state security police were satisfied that they had intimidated him into dropping the Palestine issue and ceasing any invective aimed at the president. (Judging from subsequent entries at his blog, the secret police were, to say the least, overconfident in their persuasive abilities.) A handful of other detained bloggers were also let go around this time. The releases, the embassy speculated, may have been a response to international pressure from the Committee to Protect Journalists and an article about Gad in the *New York Times*. My guess is that the releases instead reflected the regime's perception that the protests scheduled for April 9, 2009, posed little threat because there was no evidence that the activist youth were succeeding in mobilizing the public the way they had for the April 2008 attempted strike by textile workers.

By 2009 officials at the U.S. embassy were becoming increasingly interested in the role of bloggers in Egyptian politics and estimated that by spring of that year there existed 160,000 blogs in the country.[66] They were a prime manifestation of Egypt's youth movements. An NGO estimated that "a solid majority of bloggers" were between twenty and twenty-five years old and that about a third of the blogs concentrated on politics. An embassy cable reported, "Hossam Bahgat of the Egyptian Initiative for Personal Rights told us that blogging allows Egyptian youth to air their views about social and political issues in ways that were 'unimaginable five years ago.' He said that blog debates currently cover formerly 'taboo' topics, such as Christian-Muslim tensions and the military's potential role in succession." Bloggers interviewed by the embassy were convinced that their anonymity was relatively secure and were delighted finally to have an outlet for their frustrations over issues such as religious hypocrisy, torture, censorship, and government ineptitude. An American academic, Lawrence Pintak, argued that the bloggers had put pressure on the independent press to take up issues such as sexual assault and had created space for the satellite television channels to become more daring. Prominent blogger and activist Amr Ezzat told me that the founding of the independent-minded newspaper *al-Misri al-Yawm* in 2004 created a three-way nexus of information exchange, among reformers publishing studies of critical human rights issues, bloggers, and some journalists.[67] U.S. ambassador Margaret Scobey emphasized that bloggers were taking up a wide range of issues and gave as an example Tamer Mabrouk, who accused a chemical company of "dumping toxic waste into the Suez canal and a nearby lake" and as a result was fined for libeling the firm. Researcher Merlyna Li showed that in Egypt "54 out of 70 recorded street protests from 2004 to 2011 substantially involved online activism."[68]

In the summer of 2009, as the state began revving up for the parliamentary elections scheduled for 2010, the U.S. embassy in Cairo sent a cable to Washington with alarming reports of a crackdown on commentators, journalists, and bloggers.[69] Embassy officials reported that "a recent series of selective GOE [Government of Egypt] actions against journalists, bloggers and even an amateur poet illustrates the variety of methods available to the GOE to suppress critical opinion, including an array of investigative authorities and public and private legal actions." The officials noted that a government clerk who had written unpublished poetry critical of Mubarak narrowly escaped prison. The state had jailed three Muslim Brotherhood bloggers who "criticized trials of MB members in military courts and have voiced support for MB detainees. . . . Our contacts have asserted that the GOE fears young, tech-savvy MB-affiliated bloggers because of their ability to generate mass support for the Brotherhood and organize rallies and other events via the internet." Another tactic used by the regime was to have members of Mubarak's National Democratic Party bring defamation charges against regime critics (a practice that postrevolutionary regimes later continued, even after 2011). Human Rights Watch concurred with the U.S. embassy, writing that in 2009 there was a palpable increase "in the harassment of human rights activists at Cairo airport." Among those detained were bloggers, including Wael Abbas, and "human rights activists such as Kamal Abbas from the Center for Trade Union and Workers Services."[70] Wael Abbas had been attacked by a policeman and lost a tooth; when he sued, the courts took the policeman's side and sentenced Abbas to six months in prison. He appealed successfully that time, but was in and out of the courts again in 2009 and until the 2011 revolution.

Early in 2010 the internet activists in Egypt gained new energy from the prospect of parliamentary elections later that year, to be followed by presidential elections scheduled for fall of 2011. Mohamed ElBaradei, former head of the International Atomic Energy Agency, returned to Egypt and became a favorite to challenge Mubarak for the presidency. Many in the April 6 group of youth activists gravitated to him. An ElBaradei for President Facebook page was established, which garnered 250,000 supporters. ElBaradei has an international reputation and is a liberal but probably could not have won an election in Egypt. Still, his popularity with the left-liberal youth created important synergies between them and the older generation of reformists.[71]

Youth grievances, from unemployment to political repression and torture, abounded in Tunisia and Egypt in the first decade of the century. Grievances in and of themselves, however, only sometimes produce social movements. Social and political entrepreneurs have to point out the grievances, develop a language that unites a group in opposition to them, and offer solutions. This project of gathering and mobilizing people requires communication strategies that reach the target audience and create a sort of publicity mirror in which people see themselves.[72] The internet activists in Tunisia and Egypt played this role for a segment of the youth population. For a relatively small section of engaged youth, figures such as Lina Ben Mhenni, Sami Ben Gharbia, Wael Abbas, Shahinaz Abdel Salam, and Amr Ezzat became the "cool kids," the peer group that many youth wanted to join. The rise of social media allowed their citizen journalism to function not just as one more inert contribution of information but as a nexus of lively discussion among a community formed around it. The sense of connection and interaction fostered by the internet was important to the activists' ability to bring their audience to see themselves in the dissident program, creating an "online civil society."[73]

The reach and impact of the internet was amplified from about 2005 forward by the ability of bloggers to share sound and video files. These could be sent to youth far less literate than the blogging community, and their impact could be quite visceral (as in the case of evidence of police torture).[74] The ability of the internet activists to attract the interest of both old and new media also intensified their impact. Wael Abbas's crucial work on police torture was taken up by the satellite television station Al Jazeera, which had millions of viewers in Egypt and throughout the Arab world, catapulting him into a prominence that was recognized when CNN named him the "Middle East Person of the Year" in 2007. In 2008 Abbas turned down an invitation to meet President George W. Bush. Likewise the studies done by the Egyptian Initiative for Personal Freedom, spread by bloggers and Facebook users, were cited by independent-minded newspapers such as *al-Misri al-Yawm*. This synergy was more muted in Tunisia, where there was no independent press. The findings and reports of human rights groups were also sometimes amplified by satellite channels independent of the Tunisian and Egyptian governments such as Al Jazeera. Tunisian dissidents often gained the notice of the French and European media, which then were rebroadcast back into Tunisia via You-Tube and other internet channels. Internet activism was virtually the only outlet for youth of a political bent in Tunisia, given the Ben Ali regime's close control of physical spaces (party headquarters, public buildings, and university campuses) and intensive police surveillance of suspected dissidents. While speaking up online courted danger, the massive and rapid expansion of the blogosphere clearly overwhelmed the cyber police assigned to monitor it.

Much of the activity of the internet activists was empathetic, driven either by a left-of-center political ideology or a moralistic Muslim one. They took up the causes of others, whether a bus driver sodomized by sadistic police, workers arbitrarily denied their annual bonus, or villagers whose water had been diverted to swanky resorts. This informational activity on behalf of groups outside the urban youth who had grievances against the regime allowed them to combine social resources over time. The workers became important to the big demonstrations that the internet activists were later able to help orchestrate, going on strike to free up members to attend and using union channels of information to get the word out. How much sympathy there was across these social barriers for what the bloggers were writing was not immediately apparent in the mid-2000s, and only in January 2011 did it really begin paying dividends. In Egypt organizational opportunities, however limited by police repression, were far more extensive than in Tunisia. Youth created a whole range of NGOs, organizations, and associations.

The New Left

$\mathcal{T}$he Arab New Left burst on the scene as a huge new force in the years leading up to the 2011 upheavals. It differed from the Old Left parties of the 1960s in important ways, on the level not only of ideas but also of organization. The Old Left was prone to cults of personality, hence Nasserism (an assemblage of vaguely socialist and nationalist ideas championed by Egyptian leader Gamal Abdel Nasser, who died in 1970). Although the Baath Party was initially more of a classic cadre party, it too fell victim to the Great Leader syndrome, captured in Syria by Hafez al-Assad and in Iraq by Saddam Hussein. The New Left did not lack for leaders, nor did it discount their importance, but its members preferred less hierarchical forms of organization and tended to engage in lateral networking rather than establishing party lines of command and disciplined cadres. As a result, women played a more prominent role, especially in cyberspace, than was common in the old leftist parties, though they were often scathing about the male chauvinism with which they had to contend.

The Old Left in the Arab world almost everywhere adopted the Leninist theory that the progressive working classes needed a vanguard of intellectuals and state bureaucrats to champion their cause. While some of its members or constituent movements could occasionally be drawn into parliamentary frameworks, on the whole they preferred the authoritarian one-party model. The New Left could not be less interested in Leninism and instead believed in the possibility of democratically mobilizing workers and the people. The shift is stark and reminds me of a scene in Soviet dissident author Alexander Solzhenitsyn's novel *The Gulag Archipelago.* One of his characters, imprisoned by Stalin, comes into contact with an Estonian dissident passionate about Western liberties and confesses, "I had never expected to become interested in Estonia, much less bourgeois democracy."[1] Unlike their elders in the 1960s, the Arab New Left was for the most part committed to free, fair, and transparent elections as the norm of the new Arab politics. They wanted more than just elected leaders, of course, insisting on deploying demonstrations and petitions to deepen democratic action. They did not give up their generally socialist commitments, continuing to work for a higher minimum wage, rights to unionize and strike, and better working conditions for factory workers and peasants. (As with the American New Left of the 1960s, though, sometimes the youth and workers had a dispute over who was more important to the movement.) Their experience with the Leninist vanguard was that it too easily metamorphosed into corrupt bureaucrats and billionaire cronies and could not be trusted in the absence of the checks and balances provided by democratic action in society.

Many were probably from families that had belonged to leftist parties, but as the state shrank opportunities for those organizations, the next generation chose a different path. A canny Egyptian observer wrote, "Given the inability of these parties to . . . recruit new members . . . a large number of youth with leftist tendencies, who had lost confidence in the old parties, departed from the organizational framework."[2] They tended to join nongovernmental organizations or to network rather than be party members, and they innovated new forms of political action and more open, dynamic ideologies, as well as simply preferring pragmatic action to strict ideology. Some of what I am calling New Left movements, as with the youth around the Nobel Peace Prize winner Mohamed ElBaradei, might more properly be seen as liberals, but in an Egyptian context most of what are called liberals look like European socialist democrats rather than, say, the American Democratic Party.

The New Left continued to be strongly pro-Palestinian and generally hostile to Israel and often had contempt for U.S. foreign policy, which it viewed as heavy-handed and excessively pro-market. Many of its members, however, declined to make anti-Americanism their hallmark. Some were willing to explore contacts with the United States and to see it as an ambiguous force in the region rather than uniformly negative. Indeed from 2004 forward important segments of the New Left felt it was necessary to convince the United States to cease giving knee-jerk support to dictatorship. They developed this position even as they announced a determination to see the United States pushed out of Iraq. Ironically the pragmatism and flexibility of the Obama administration, which showed a willingness to work with movements of political Islam that came to power in Tunisia and Egypt in late 2011, often angered the progressive youth, who felt as though the older fundamentalist politicians were acting in authoritarian and high-handed ways reminiscent of the Ben Ali and Mubarak parties and wanted the United States to criticize them (or, as in Egypt in June–July 2013, to give its blessing to their overthrow). Despite their advocacy for workers, the left-of-center youth were not necessarily hostile to business, and some were involved in internet start-ups. Of course, I have painted with a very broad brush, and some of the New Left movements differ from others in their exact emphases. (Some are far more anti-American than others, for example, and some less interested in parliamentary democracy than the mainstream of their peers, while some shade over into elite liberal rather than Marxist commitments.) These New Left currents faced competition in the spring and summer of 2013 from the Rebellion Movement, which was far more pro-military and was disappointed to find that democratic procedure can produce "ballotocracy" (elective dictatorship, where leaders came to power in elections but then ruled in an authoritarian way until the next one). For most of the period covered in this book, however, the main competition for the New Left leaders was the older political parties and the youth wings of political Islam.

Egypt

Kefaya

In colloquial Egyptian Arabic, the way you say "Enough, already!" is "Kefaya, ba'!" The word *enough* came to stand for criticism of the long-lived and increasingly corrupt government of Hosni Mubarak.[3] The leading activists behind Kefaya, or the Egyptian Movement for Change, whether on the left or the religious right, had engaged in dialogue with one another throughout the 1990s and early 2000s. They came together for political action for the first time around support for the second Palestinian uprising (the Intifada) that began in the fall of 2000. These street demonstrations were the first for some time in Mubarak's Egypt. The clear signs in early 2003 that the Bush administration intended to invade Iraq produced some of Egypt's largest demonstrations. One rally filled a stadium with 100,000 protesters, and demonstrations were also held in Tahrir Square in downtown Cairo. These two moments of protest created links and networks among a diverse group of leftist and Muslim fundamentalist organizations.

In November 2003 Abul Ela Madi, a left-of-center Muslim activist who helped found the liberal Muslim Wasat Party as a rival to the conservative Muslim Brotherhood, hosted a dinner to which he invited many of the thinkers who later formed Kefaya. They included Marxist, Nasserite, Islamist, and liberal veteran activists.[4] They agreed on the need to bridge the gap between intellectuals and the person on the street. But the organization took firmer shape with the issuance of a manifesto in summer 2004 and in meetings among anti-Mubarak activists that September, which produced another joint declaration of principles: "We believe there are two grave dangers which beset our nation today. They are two sides of the same coin, each nourishing the other, and neither curable alone. First, the odious assault on Arab native soil. . . . Second, the repressive despotism that pervades all aspects of the Egyptian political system."[5] The organization centered on two threats: foreign domination and domestic tyranny. The foreign problems were the Israeli occupation of Palestine and the Bush administration's occupation of Iraq, which Kefaya leaders saw as the beginning of a wave of neo-imperialism that threatened Egypt itself. The domestic threat was the continuation of Mubarak's authoritarian and corrupt government, which harmed workers and intellectuals. A founding member, Kamal Khalil, of the Trotskyite Revolutionary Socialists explained to researcher Rabab al-Mahdi that with economic mingled with foreign-policy discontent: "The regime's authoritarianism could not be tolerated any more. Not only is it an economic failure pushing forward neoliberal impoverishing economic policies but also it is 'friends with the U.S.' that occupied another Arab country. . . . Being their servant in the region, it could not play a role even as an American agent to stop atrocities in Palestine and Iraq. The American invasion of Iraq would not have been possible without Mubarak's help."[6]

They called on the president not to run for a fifth term and to give up his plan to turn the government over to his son Gamal. Kefaya launched its first attempted demonstration in front of a court building late that fall. The organization innovated in protesting both domestic and foreign policy, whereas in the recent past street rallies had always been focused on foreign policy. A U.S. embassy official recalled, "The demonstration, though small, was the first time Kifaya's distinctive yellow and red placards, banners, and stickers, with simple slogans such as 'Enough hypocrisy,' 'Enough corruption,' and 'Enough oppression,' were displayed in public. Local and international journalists immediately took note of the group's simple, direct, and bold approach, and of the diversity of those gathered under the Kifaya banner."[7]

U.S. embassy analysts immediately understood that Kefaya was not a political party but a network, saying, "It lacks both a cohesive political program and even a discernible organizational structure beyond a loosely-knit and apparently erratic leadership."[8] The embassy's political and economic counselor, Michael Corbin, characterized Kefaya as an umbrella movement made up of elements from a highly diverse set of opposition parties and organizations: "Communists, 'revolutionary socialists,' Nasserists, liberals, and Islamists have all identified themselves as Kifaya members." All that united them was a conviction that "Egypt has had 'enough' of the Mubarak regime and its vices." Their most prominent spokesman, a retired Catholic teacher, George Ishaq, held meetings in his downtown apartment. Another prominent spokesman for the group, the editor of *al-Arabi,* Abdel Halim Qandil, had been "abducted, beaten, and left naked on a desert highway in an obviously political incident in November 2004." His newspaper was Nasserist (leftist, anti-imperial) in tone. Other spokesmen were also on the left, some of them with academic training. The wealthy businessman Hany Anan was widely thought to be funding the group. They emphasized networks, demonstrations, and liaising with unions and syndicates as a way of sidestepping the small number of recognized political parties, which had not been able to function as a genuine opposition to the regime because they accepted regime limits and were often themselves run in a top-down fashion by the secretary-general.[9]

In February 2005 Mubarak proposed a constitutional amendment changing the way the president was selected, probably because of American pressure to liberalize. Instead of holding a referendum on a single candidate (who could not lose), there would now be a multiparty election in which the sitting president would have to compete against other candidates. The grudging way that Mubarak formulated the change, ensuring that any such election would be a mere kabuki play and that he would always win, galvanized the opposition.

Kefaya joined other political forces such as the Muslim Brotherhood and the National Progressive Unionist Party (Tagammu') in calling for a boycott of the referendum scheduled for May 25, 2005, on the new Article 76 of the constitution, on the grounds that it stipulated that candidates could not run for office unless large numbers of sitting parliamentarians endorsed them. Parliament was solidly dominated by the ruling National Democratic Party, which could thus block any turn to political pluralism. The academic wing of Kefaya, Professors for Change, held demonstrations on April 19 at universities in Cairo, Asyut, and Minya against the police state's careful control of campuses and the state security's manipulation of student union elections. The U.S. embassy reported, "During the April 19 protest, organized by a group known as 'Professors for Change,' dozens of faculty members on the three campuses donned black academic robes and stood silently in front of university administration buildings for an hour, carrying banners with slogans such as 'No to security interference in universities'; 'Yes to free and independent universities'; and 'No future for

Egyptian students without freedom.'"[10] The writer added that the "prominent intellectual and Shura Council member Usama Ghazaly Harb" told the embassy that the protests against the state security police were "'very important' because they had 'shattered the fearful silence' of professors and openly expressed views widely held among Egyptian academics."

When the day of the referendum came, in late May, Kefaya protesters took to the streets. The U.S. embassy reported, "Young men apparently affiliated with the ruling NDP assaulted several protesters from the Kefaya (Enough) movement in several locations, most notably in front of Cairo's Saad Zaghlul Monument and next to the Press Syndicate building. Police officials at the scene failed to intervene to prevent the attacks."[11] Women protesters and journalists were groped by Mubarak's goons. In the aftermath of the beatings at the May 25 demonstrations, the blogger and Kefaya activist Alia Mosallam spoke of the experience of waking up the next day, surprised at still being bruised and sore. She remembered her terror, the hatred in the eyes of the thugs, her sorrow that the regime had suborned other civilians to do its dirty work, people who should be on the same side. She was relieved that the international press was filming the violence, and wondered how they had become the source of justice.[12] Prominent blogger Alaa Abd El-Fattah reported that the NDP goons also attacked him, breaking a bone in his foot, smashing his glasses, and stealing his laptop and other equipment, a loss of some $2,000.[13] Wael Abbas took the official newspaper *al-Ahram* to task for reporting that a woman had protested by provocatively stripping off her clothes, when in fact she was a reporter attacked by NDP thugs, who tore her dress.[14]

Kefaya's youth section, Youth for Change, formed five rotating committees (culture, art, communications, media, and outreach), each of them run by a five-person steering committee. Wael Abbas, a member at the time, told me of the struggles of Youth for Change to maintain independence from the parties making up the Kefaya coalition, whose older leaders wanted to use the young people for their own purposes and who were factional and hostile to one another.[15] Unlike their more cautious elders, they spread their networks via laptops and mobile phones, "from coffee shops to university halls to unions and syndicates throughout the city. . . . Youth for Change's strategy is almost guerrilla-style in relation to some of the more conservative tactics of Kefaya."[16] The youth developed an interest in inserting themselves into the physical geography of the city, using the internet to plan impromptu occupations of public space otherwise typically controlled by the regime. In mid-June bloggers assembled at the popular shrine to the granddaughter of the Prophet Muhammad in Cairo, al-Sayyida Zaynab, where they gave speeches in favor of political change and protesting police brutality. They were piggy-backing on an annual ritual, the "sweeping of the tomb," when devotees gather to clean the shrine's floors. State security officers showed up to prevent the bloggers from continuing, so they moved inside the shrine. They gave out pamphlets with the message "We're a group of youth protesting the current conditions of no health, no education, no work, no housing, no freedom. That's why we decided that it's necessary to change all that. We're sure you too feel as we do, let's think together and act together so we can have better living conditions."[17] Some were arrested for handing out these pamphlets. The youth decided to do an event every Wednesday in one of the city's densely populated working-class neighborhoods rather than always gathering in front of the Press Syndicate. The pamphlets they distributed included the URLs of their blogs and websites.

By mid-June Kefaya was riven with policy disputes, especially over how closely to cooperate with the Muslim Brotherhood. Corbin argued that the "split was particularly clear along generational lines, with youthful members strongly in favor of cooperation with the MB while the older generation, reportedly including Qandil and Ishaq, adamantly [*sic*] opposed. These Kifaya leaders pointedly and publicly declined the MB's late May invitation to join its own 'Coalition for Change and Reform.'"[18] Blogger Amr Ezzat explained to me that he had joined Kefaya in 2005 after several years of experimenting with the Muslim Brotherhood and Salafism as an undergraduate, when he was studying engineering and philosophy. He gradually became disillusioned with political Islam, founded a blog, and became active in Youth for Change. He said that the youth's willingness to cooperate with their Muslim Brotherhood counterparts posed a problem for the Brotherhood, whose leaders worried that their youth might become infected by ideas from Kefaya. Although the Brotherhood often bused in activists from Delta villages for Kefaya meetings, the leaders were not enthusiastic about young Cairene brothers participating. Most of the prominent youth bloggers for the Brotherhood in that period later abandoned political Islam, he said, finding it ideologically hidebound.[19]

There was also a conflict over how close to get to the long-time liberal politician and activist Ayman Nour, who headed the Tomorrow Party, given that many Kefaya leaders saw Nour as a lightweight and a self-promoter. Nevertheless, Corbin admitted, many young Tomorrow supporters protesting their leader's trial on charges of having forged the papers used to create his party carried Kefaya posters, and Nour himself put a Kefaya sticker behind him in his courtroom cage during the trial. The millennials' eclectic instincts, perhaps shaped in part by the unbounded character of internet reading and interactions, made them willing to include both the Brotherhood and a wide range of center-left movements. A further dispute broke out over the value of demonstrations. One of the Kefaya leaders, Muhammad Sayyid Said, proposed an alternative: "We need to rebuild democratic institutions in villages and cities. . . . We need to reactivate trade unions, labor unions and local assemblies . . . until Egypt becomes a workshop for democratic change."[20]

On July 30, 2005, George Ishaq led a small demonstration in downtown Cairo against Mubarak's announcement of his candidacy in the fall elections. As with the May 25 rallies, NDP thugs swooped in to beat up the protesters, preventing them from reaching Tahrir Square. Two protesters were sent to the hospital and thirty-one were arrested, then released three days later.[21] A few days later the U.S. chargé d'affaires, Stuart Jones, met with the notorious interior minister Habib Al-Adly to protest the heavy-handedness of the crackdown: "With regard to the July 30 protests in Tahrir Square, whose aggressive suppression by police was broadcast world-wide on satellite television, Chargé asserted that the broadcasts of Egyptian police violently quelling a protest were highly negative for Egypt."[22] Al-Adly defended the steps he had taken to close down the protest, asserting that the protesters "attacked the police with stones" and that any country would move to prevent the closing off of a main thoroughfare, characterizing the demonstration as a "riot." Jones pushed back against Al-Adly's dry proceduralism, suggesting that other countries did care how the world perceived them. In any case, Al-Adly questioned the significance of the young protesters: "Regarding the emergence of multi-party elections and new democratic movements, El Adly attempted to differentiate between what he called 'legal opposition' and movements, such as Kefaya, which he called 'a cocktail of different parties.' He said the movements aren't necessarily 'real' and very small in membership."[23]

The Fall 2005 "Elections"

Mubarak arranged to win his just-for-show presidential election in September with 88 percent of the vote. Ayman Nour was allowed to get 7 percent. Having been trotted out as a putative rival in the presidential race for Washington's benefit, he was sentenced to five years in prison later that year. On October 8 the opposition parties, both recognized and unrecognized, announced a National Front coalition to contest the parliamentary elections to be held in three rounds in late November and early December. The licensed parties, all of them small and ineffectual, were the right-of-center Wafd, the (Old Left) Progressive Unionist Party, the Nasserist Party, and the Muslim fundamentalist Labor Party. The Wafd Party blocked Nour's Tomorrow Party from joining because of the long-running feud of its head, Nu'man Gum'ah, with the liberal politician. According to the U.S. embassy, the leftist Hussein Abdel Razek, secretary-general of the Progressive Unionist Party, had wanted to keep out the Muslim Brotherhood but apparently was persuaded to back down on that issue, which had delayed the announcement of the National Front for several months.

Young intellectuals from smaller groups such as the Revolutionary Socialists had argued that the Old Left's antipathy to the Brotherhood was misplaced; they appealed to Trotsky's principle of the united front and claimed that an alliance of progressives with the religious activists against the regime could be effective. Small unlicensed parties such as Hamdeen Sabahi's Karama (left-wing Nasserist) and the Wasat Party (liberal Muslim) also were included. The Muslim Brotherhood and Kefaya, both of them arguably movements rather than parties (and neither of which the government recognized), rounded out the roster. The Brotherhood's willingness to be part of this coalition, no less than the coalition's willingness to partner with it, marked another sea change in the rise of the new Egyptian opposition to Mubarak.[24]

The National Democratic Party won just over a two-thirds majority, enough to legislate unilaterally and even to amend the constitution, but significantly less than in previous elections. Dissidents charged that the NDP used dirty tricks and ballot stuffing to achieve even this tepid win. Shahinaz Abdel Salam alleged that Kefaya's candidate, Mona Ahmed, who ran as an independent from the southern conservative town of Sohag, was gotten out of the way by the expediency of falsely accusing her of having sex with her aged chauffeur in the car. She was let go with a warning, but her reputation suffered.[25]

The regime permitted many more members of the Muslim Brotherhood to win seats than usual.[26] Brothers running as independents won eighty-eight seats, a gain of five times over their previous showing, and other unregistered parties took another twenty-four independent seats. The Progressive Unionist Party, Tomorrow, and the Wafd together took just nine, underlining the greater popularity of the unrecognized parties fielding candidates as independents over the small registered opposition parties, which were forced to play by the regime's rules. The U.S. embassy saw the election as a loss for Gamal Mubarak and the younger, more technocratic and reform-minded members of the NDP, since most of those elected were old warhorses enabled by corruption and voter intimidation. Chargé d'Affaires Stuart Jones saw the election as marking a sea change in Egyptian politics, in part because the Muslim Brotherhood did so well and in part because the public was showing greater political courage. "The fear barrier has been shattered, and deference to the regime is ebbing," he observed.[27] He also pointed out that electoral abuses were "widely reported and discussed." He argued, "Egyptian civil society, including a small but hardened core of democratic advocacy groups has solidified its position on the political landscape, and an emboldened independent media continues to push ever farther its coverage of sensitive issues and its criticism of the senior political leadership. The new and passionate debate about liberal democracy versus political Islam and authoritarian alternatives to either may be the most significant advance in Egyptian politics of 2005, and it is that which lends the most promise of further advances in 2006." Jones was referring in part to the frank and extensive discussions on satellite television, especially Al Jazeera. But he was also referring to the lively blogosphere and to Kefaya and its various activist components.

Kefaya's Decline

With the election season behind them, the activists struggled to find an issue that would catch on with the public. They tried supporting the judges seeking more independence, and they invoked anti-imperial themes. They tried to find new forms of public contention to draw attention to the regime's continued authoritarianism. The dissidents innovated on March 16 and 17, 2006, by calling for not just a demonstration but an all-night sit-in at Tahrir Square in support of Egyptian judges demanding more independence from the government. (Two judges were charged by the state for alleging corruption in the 2005 elections.) The square is one of the few large, central, open spaces in downtown Cairo, and it has a circular traffic island in the middle good for pitching tents. The youth protesters couched their appeal in the language of romance, calling it "a night for the love of Egypt" and describing it as "an evening of chit chat [*lailat al-samar*]."[28] For unrelated young people of both sexes to spend the night together in a public place violated Egyptian conservatives' values of gender segregation and propriety. The sit-in was the first major such action at Tahrir Square since a large student protest in 1972, though considerably smaller.

Three days later, on March 20, as many as two thousand protesters drawn from opposition parties and movements, along with members of professional syndicates, gathered in Tahrir Square to mark the third anniversary of the U.S. invasion of Iraq and to protest the continued U.S. occupation of that country. Photographs published on dissident blogs included a banner declaring, "No to American Terrorism!" Protesters insisted that the Arab and Muslim worlds support the Iraqi resistance, which they lauded for inflicting heavy damage on the United States. They also insisted on support for the Palestinian resistance "until the independent Palestinian state is declared with Jerusalem as its capital."[29] In April activists staged two more sit-ins, this time in front of the Press Syndicate, in favor of judges demanding judicial reform. Although many judges were dismissed before and after the revolution as corrupt Mubarak appointees, in fact many others defied the regime from time to time. Jurists and attorneys were often carriers of Egypt's liberal tradition of belief in pluralist politics that went back before the 1952 revolution.[30]

Kefaya and its allies staged demonstrations in May on university campuses and in front of official buildings over the arrest of judges who had impugned the probity of the 2005 elections. On May 25 they reprised the demonstrations that had ended in vicious violence the previous year. U.S. embassy officials observed, "The center of the action on May 25 will be in the area just south of Ramses Street and a few blocks east of the Nile in central Cairo, where contacts advise us that the Ghad [Tomorrow] Party, the unlicensed Karamah Party, and the student groups Youth for Change and the 9th of March Movement plan to gather at the Bar Syndicate at 1 pm."[31] The mention of the two youth groups points to the emergence of the millennials as a key component of Kefaya. In fact, at the end of the commemorative May 25 demonstration, two Youth for Change activists, Muhammad al-Sharqawi and Kamal al-Shaer, were arrested. The U.S. embassy reported that the police allegedly "battered and sexually assaulted Sharqawy at the Qasr Al-Nil police station, in the Garden City district of Cairo. Shaer was reportedly beaten but not sexually assaulted."[32] The dissident blogosphere burned red hot with the news of al-Sharqawi's rape and the beating of the two men. Undeterred, on June 8 Kefaya held a demonstration jointly with the Muslim Brotherhood and the Tomorrow Party of about six hundred in front of the Lawyers Syndicate, pushing again for judicial independence and demanding the release of protesters who had been arrested.[33]

During the summer of 2006, after Israel attacked Lebanon and especially its Hizbullah party-militia, dissidents mounted numerous demonstrations, including one of ten thousand in the al-Husayn district near al-Azhar Seminary, a hotbed of Muslim politics. The leftists and liberals were able to get out only much smaller crowds. Despite their secular commitments, they often waved placards celebrating Hizbullah leader Hassan Nasrallah and denouncing the United States, Israel, and Mubarak. A demonstration of about a thousand protesters was held in Tahrir Square on July 26, the anniversary of the 1956 nationalization of the Suez Canal. The rally was called for, a U.S. embassy official said, "by the protest group Kefaya in collaboration with the Wafd, Nasserite, Ghad [Tomorrow], Tagamma and Labor parties and the Youth for Change movement."[34] The official observed that "online blog postings for the protest asked those attending to bring Lebanese and Palestinian flags" and that the bloggers addressed Arab leaders who had abandoned little Lebanon to the Israeli assault by saying, "[I] spit on you!" The demonstration in support of the Shiite Hizbullah was mainly attended by secularists, with light representation from the (Sunni) Muslim Brotherhood.

By the end of 2006 the government had managed to repress most Kefaya street demonstrations and had arrested many activists, though typically they were ultimately released. The organization had difficulty maintaining a fruitful relationship with the much bigger and better organized Muslim Brotherhood, which, after winning eighty-eight seats in late 2005, focused on parliamentary politics. Youth for Change remained the most active of the Kefaya organizations, and many of its most vigorous members migrated to the internet as the most fruitful arena for their activities. The Egyptian government pursued them there, making the first arrest of a blogger for the content of his blog in late 2006. The following year the activists strove to continue their momentum, but in the absence of big national issues such as an election, they lost steam.

April 6

In the spring of 2008 Egypt was roiled by a conjunction of economic and political issues. The regime planned local elections for April 8, mobilizing the NDP but also its rivals, the Muslim Brotherhood and smaller opposition parties. At the same time, an international spike in wheat prices had produced a scarcity of flour, a scarcity of subsidized bread, and increased prices for unsubsidized bread. In addition, Egyptian labor continued to flex its muscles, launching strikes and planning a general strike two days before the local elections.

The wheat crisis had caused bread prices to shoot up beyond the reach of the poor. Subsidized bread in government bakeries still cost only 5 piasters (then about 1 U.S. cent), but the U.S. ambassador alleged that "public

bakeries have only been using part of their subsidized flour quota to produce bread, selling the rest of the flour on the black market" because of the
high price it was bringing, causing shortages.[35] By mid-March fifteen poor
Egyptians had died in stampedes while standing in line for a dwindling
supply of crusts; they were dubbed "martyrs for bread." Egyptian pundits
berated the government for not dealing with this problem before it became
a crisis, since the Food and Agriculture Organization of the United Nations
had been warning of high wheat prices since early 2007.[36] The global price
increase was caused in part by a spike in petroleum prices, which in turn
increased the cost of fertilizer. Growing world population had increased the
demand for meat, which requires large amounts of feed, including grains
taken off the market for human consumption. Droughts and crop failures
had reduced wheat supply and created uncertainty about the yields in 2008,
causing speculation, which also increased prices. The wheat shortage added
200 million people to the 800 million afflicted by chronic hunger in the
world, before it eased in the second half of 2008.[37]

In March 2008 labor movements and the New Left continued to demand a higher minimum wage, a goal made all the more urgent by the rising food prices. Since the 1980s the minimum wage for unskilled workers
had been only 40 Egyptian pounds (about U.S.$7.20 in 2008) per month.
Pay for public sector workers had not kept up with inflation since the
1980s, and the Egyptian state, which employed about a third of the workforce, found it increasingly difficult to pay them well or on time. Its major
sources of income, including U.S. aid, a bit of petroleum pumped from the
Sinai, Suez Canal tolls, and cotton, had all declined, and despite institut-
ing a retail sales tax, the government had not found a way to tax the new
class of wealthy entrepreneurs, leaving the state much less able to satisfy its
constituency among public sector workers than had been the case twenty-
five years earlier.[38] It did not help that inflation rose to 10 percent a year in
2006 and 2007, hurting public sector workers who were on fixed salaries.
According to a cable by U.S. ambassador Francis Ricciardone, physicians
and university professors staged sit-ins and a strike on March 23, calling
for pay raises. In El Mahalla El Kubra textile workers built on their earlier
successful labor actions of 2006 and 2007, which many young bloggers had
supported, by planning a wildcat strike on April 6 and 7, insisting on a new

monthly minimum salary of 1,200 pounds (U.S.$218). Some of the discontent, Ambassador Ricciardone argued, derived from a sense that workers in the growing private sector ("construction, telecoms, banking, tourism, manufacturing and oil and gas") were seeing regular increases in wages, unlike government employees. The teachers and physicians were also inspired by the office workers in one of the government tax-collection agencies, who had successfully struck for higher wages in late 2007. Physicians in public hospitals, making only the equivalent of U.S.$63 a month, wanted a threefold increase, and the Physicians Syndicate planned a sit-in at Parliament. The left-wing Progressive Unionist Party, Ricciardone said, was pointing to the disaffection of even medical doctors and college teachers as a sign of the declining legitimacy of the regime. The El Mahalla El Kubra spinners and textile workers, who had struck without the government's permission in both of the two previous years, asked the entire Egyptian public to support their planned strike in April. The Kefaya political movement called on workers to strike on May Day and to act independently of the National Democratic Party's official union.[39]

As March unfolded, tempers ran high. Early in the month Israel's strike at Gaza killed fifty-four on a single day and was condemned as "disproportionate force" by the UN secretary-general. Thousands of Egyptian students demonstrated on campuses. (As noted earlier, the Mubarak government's own complicity in the Israeli blockade of Gaza was a sore point for many Egyptian youth.) On March 24 a U.S. Navy ship in the Suez Canal fired warning shots at a small approaching vessel, killing an Egyptian civilian and provoking anger against Mubarak for not standing up to the Americans.[40] Activists associated with Kefaya, the U.S. ambassador said, "have called for a nationwide strike to demand higher wages, a fair judiciary, and better education, transportation, and health care, calling for 'freedom and dignity.' "[41] Ahmed Maher of the Youth Movement for Change called the planned general strike on April 6 a "Day of Rage." Israa Abdel Fattah, a young woman who belonged both to Ayman Nour's Tomorrow Party and to the Youth Movement for Change, put up a Facebook group in support of the planned textile workers' strike. It was an act of bravery, since most accounts were not anonymous, so posting the page and joining it were a way of volunteering to be subject to surveillance by the secret police. Abdel Fattah would come to regret her audaciousness. Ambassador Ricciardone observed, "One Facebook group organizing around the theme has collected 20,000 members, including 5,000 who say they will turn out to protest." He said that the Kefaya protests were intended to "complement" the planned El Mahalla El Kubra textile factory strike for a higher minimum wage. In his cable to Washington on the last day of March Ricciardone missed a chance to be prescient, writing, "As one blogger acknowledged, when the revolution comes, it will not be on the Internet—Facebook is not a viable means for turning the Egyptian masses out into the street."

Ricciardone pointed out that on April 4 the Muslim Brotherhood had abruptly announced that it would not join the demonstrations, despite being generally sympathetic with the grievances that had provoked them. Wael Abbas complained that the Brotherhood said on April 5 that it had changed its mind and would participate, but then did not show up. Muslim Brotherhood youth blogger Abd al-Rahman Rashwan was visibly disappointed in the leadership's decision. He pointed out that the date for this demonstration had been set by the people themselves and that the movement had welled up from the workers. High inflation, he said, was something all Egyptians suffered from and was the target of the strike. He noted that the Brotherhood remained committed to contesting the provincial elections and asked rhetorically which had the better chance of shaking the government: a mass protest or winning some provincial seats? "Perhaps," he wrote, "change will come from an unexpected quarter; perhaps change in our country will begin with the workers and not with us."[42]

When April 6 came, the call for a general strike had a fair amount of success. Blogger Wael Abbas posted his phone and Twitter messages from activists that day.[43] They began with alerts that bloggers and activists were being arrested and hauled off to jail as a precautionary measure, including Israa Abdel Fattah, who had put up the Facebook page calling for the sympathy strike. At just before noon he got reports of a gathering of fifty demonstrators in front of the Hardees off Tahrir Square. The police, which were alleged to have nine hundred vehicles on the streets downtown, dispersed or arrested them. Women students at the American University in Cairo were arrested. Abbas also put up pictures taken in Cairo by the activist Shahinaz Abdel Salam, whose camera the police had wanted to confiscate, but she managed to elude them. They show a middle-class demonstration of hundreds in front of the Lawyers Guild building, which then moved to its roof. Many university students cut classes, and some school exams were postponed because teachers stayed home in sympathy. U.S. embassy officials were worried: "Cairo's streets were noticeably emptier than usual."[44] Traffic was extraordinarily light in both Cairo and Alexandria. Abbas published a photograph of the usually gridlocked Talaat Harb Square completely deserted. Many shops and minibus stations were closed in the capital, in Alexandria, and in Mansoura, Abbas was told. (When transportation workers join a general strike, whether out of solidarity or out of fear of trouble, they aid it greatly, since even those who want to go to work cannot.) A small demonstration was held in the northwestern Delta depot town of Damanhour. Still, the plans for a big demonstration downtown at Tahrir Square were not realized. Without the Brotherhood's proven vast organizational abilities, the remaining, mostly secular groups around Kefaya were unable to draw really large crowds in Cairo, though Abbas's video suggests the demonstrations at the Lawyers Syndicate and Press Syndicate buildings were hardly minor, and there appears to have been widespread passive participation by people just staying home.

In El Mahalla El Kubra itself on April 6 and 7 there was substantially more public turmoil. Abbas got news of a big demonstration in the city's main square in the early afternoon. Later he was given a video (which he posted and which was then rebroadcast on the Al Jazeera satellite news channel) of a huge crowd, mostly youth, chanting against the regime. In the center of the square stood a pole, atop which was a large photo of Mubarak, as though on a giant cereal box. The video shows a young man clambering up and slashing the photo; the crowd begins rocking the steel pole holding up the icon and finally topples it.[45] No one who sees this video can fail to conclude that it is a genuine and spontaneous version of the U.S.-staged toppling of a statue of Saddam Hussein in Baghdad in April 2003. A hated tyrant had been symbolically brought down.

The government had had ample warning. Security police in riot gear kept the Ghazl al-Mahalla textile factory open and forced the workers to man the equipment, snuffing out the threatened factory strike. When the 4 p.m. shift ended and workers departed into the streets, many seem to have joined the demonstration already in progress. The police then cracked down on the protesters who had assembled in the main square and had brought down Mubarak's icon. Abbas got a frantic text message that police had directed live fire toward the crowds, sending some protesters to the hospital. The U.S. ambassador subsequently interviewed several activists who were present, and reported, "Protestors hurled rocks at riot police who according to several activists responded with live fire and tear gas." At least two were killed, a twenty-one-year-old man and a boy of nine. Others were injured, some in the eyes, by rubber bullets. The government charged that angry crowds in El Mahalla El Kubra later looted shops and set them afire, as well as blowing up a gas station, though local activists denied that there was much vandalism and blamed what did occur on government agents provocateurs. The U.S. embassy reported that thousands of youth battled "riot police in the streets of the Nile Delta mill-town."[46] Abbas got a message that the police had blocked all the roads into El Mahalla El Kubra from surrounding towns, then that a curfew had been imposed with warnings that those contravening it would be shot on sight.

Ambassador Ricciardone's staff discovered that class politics was alive and well in Egypt. In their interviews after the strike, they found that lower-income Egyptians were "ecstatic" about the disturbances, believing that the government deserved it. The rapid rise in the price of food that winter was widely thought to underlie some of the discontent, with food inflation pegged at 22 percent in March 2008. Ricciardone argued that the high food prices undermined the moral economy of the Egyptian state, which demanded obedience from citizens in return for providing them with a minimal standard of living. One worker told embassy officials, "It is the people's right (to strike), if their government lies to them, tells them that food prices are stable, but then we go try to buy oil or bread, and cannot afford it." Other severe discontent centered on the regime's corruption and its good relations with Israel and the United States. The elite, Ricciardone reported, were nervous, and many did not send their children to school on April 6. The small, precarious middle class, he thought, was on the fence. The regime sent Prime Minister Ahmed Nazif to El Mahalla El Kubra to pay bonuses to the factory workers and to praise those who did not join the demonstrations. The ambassador concluded that the El Mahalla El Kubra demonstrations were important: "The violent protests demonstrated that it is possible to tear down a poster of Mubarak and stomp on it, to shout obscene anti-regime slogans, to burn a minibus and hurl rocks at riot police." He also perceived that the alliance of disgruntled workers and unemployed youth with the largely middle-class Youth Movement for Change, with its seventy thousand Facebook friends, was new and significant: "The nexus of the upper and middle-class Facebook users, and their poorer counterparts in the factories of Mahalla, created a new dynamic." The ambassador regretted that the events likely would derail further reductions of government subsidies and slow any further steps toward privatization, and would make the Mubarak regime especially touchy about U.S. criticisms of its human rights record.

On April 16 a coalition of nongovernmental organizations held a meeting at the Hisham Mubarak Law Center in Cairo, where they screened a short documentary by Wael Abbas on the killing of a fifteen-year-old at El Mahalla El Kubra, then conducted a discussion of the government's repressive tactics.[47] Wounded demonstrators from the mill town were brought to the capital to talk about the regime's tactics, and they denied the charges of vandalism launched by the regime to justify its brutality. They pointed out that government buildings were well protected by the state security police and maintained that only a few private establishments were attacked. Journalists also testified to having been arrested en masse, to having the memory cards pulled out of their cameras, and to having been detained for hours without water. The official Journalists Syndicate had declined to defend anyone who was not a registered journalist, pointing to the special jeopardy for bloggers and citizen journalists.

The Hisham Mubarak Law Center had been founded by the socialist activist and attorney Ahmed Seif El-Islam Hamad and some like-minded colleagues in 1999 and was dedicated to defending dissidents. Egypt's courts, while often under regime influence, sometimes retained a modicum of independence and sometimes could be persuaded to buck the state prosecutor or at least hand out a lighter sentence than the government wanted. The center was one of a latticework of Egyptian NGOs that mounted small acts of defiance against the regime. The list of the many groups that joined it in defending the El Mahalla El Kubra demonstrators, despite each being small and having a limited impact, suggests the extent of the loose dissident organizational network: the al-Nadim Center, al-Hilal Association for Lawyers Freedoms, al-Hilali Association for Freedoms, Foundation for Freedom of Thought and Expression, the Egyptian Association for Participating in Society, Syndicate and Workers' Services Center, Human Rights Association to Help Prisoners, Arab Center for Independent Judges and Lawyers, Children of the Earth Foundation, Coordinating Committee for the Trade Union and Worker Rights and Liberties, Ansar al-Adala Association, the Progressive Unionist Party Freedoms Committee, Arab Organization for Penal Reform, Arab Foundation to Support the Civil Community, the Human Rights Committee for Mahalla Lawyers, and the Center for Egyptian Women's Issues. Many of these NGOs had youth wings or employed interns and election observers from among the millennial generation, giving them experience in organizing.

April 6 Seeks Momentum

As in the aftermath of the 2005 elections, when Kefaya found it difficult to keep public interest, so the passing of the local elections in April 2008 created a challenge for the newly networked and energized April 6 organization. Incoming U.S. ambassador Margaret Scobey did what she could to help the April 6 activists arrested by the state security police. She worried that although Israa Abdel Fattah had been ordered released by the courts, state security had abruptly rearrested her under the Emergency Law, and so she was subject to indefinite detention.[48] She was allegedly tortured while in custody, and when at length released, she withdrew from politics and broke with her former dissident colleagues. Ahmed Maher and Ahmed Saleh, both secular, left-of-center young men, emerged as among the more important leaders of the Youth Movement for Change, which increasingly became known as "April 6" in honor of its first relatively successful attempt at mobilizing the youth. Maher was briefly arrested in May and badly beaten while in jail. According to journalist David Wolman, Maher had been a bookish adolescent and a fan of science fiction, comic books, and video games. He did not score well enough on his exams to get into medical school and decided to become an engineer instead, devoting himself to mathematics even though it did not come easy to him. In 2004 he joined the nascent Kefaya movement. He played online games under the name "Ghosty" and began exploring the internet, reading and following prominent blogs like those of Wael Abbas and Shahinaz Abdel Salam. In 2008, Sherif Mansour of Freedom House observed, "he made the bridge from online to offline organizing."[49]

The April 6 network continued to attempt to stage demonstrations, including on May 4, Mubarak's birthday. On July 23 (the anniversary of the 1952 young officers' coup) the U.S. embassy reported that "security forces in Alexandria arrested 26 members of a Facebook social networking group known as the '6th of April Youth.'" Fourteen of them were briefly jailed and investigated for disrupting traffic, attempting to foment street riots, and possessing subversive printed materials. Ahmed Maher was among those taken in. The Alexandria Court of Appeals, however, released them all without charges a few days later.[50]

That fall Ambassador Scobey decided she wanted Ahmed Saleh to attend the Alliance of Youth Movements Summit in New York in December, and she telephoned him in November. He confessed to thinking at first that the call was a trick by the secret police, and he insisted on coming to the embassy in person. In her cable Scobey reported, "Saleh described how he lives on the run from State Security, using 3 or 4 different phones to make GOE surveillance efforts more difficult and rarely sleeping at his home. To earn a living, he works as a 'fixer' for international media companies, setting up appointments and interviews for journalists, and doing translations. Saleh recounted how he and his colleagues in the 'Youth Movement for Change' speak on the phone in coded messages and hold informal meetings in remote restaurants where they do not believe State Security will look for them. Saleh characterized the movement as currently 'under siege' by state security."[51]

Saleh told Scobey that the state security police had just arrested an April 6 member with Muslim Brotherhood affiliations, Muhammad Adel. (Adel, like many April 6 members, opposed the Israeli blockade on the civilian population of the Gaza Strip and had made numerous visits to Gaza that fall in order to organize aid campaigns. The Egyptian government then trumped up charges against him of being a member of Hamas, the militant

Gaza party-militia. In fact, Adel was moving away from political Islam toward a secular outlook typical of most April 6 members.)[52] Saleh wanted a guarantee that there would be no press around his meetings in the United States, fearing that he would be jailed on his return.

Speaking in late November 2008, Saleh described the incoming Obama administration "as 'the last hope' for effecting democratic change in Egypt." He pointed out that although the Bush administration had orally urged democratization, Mubarak was still in power. He then went on to describe the Youth Movement for Change, which he said was also called "April 6." It had eight hundred active core members and another seventy thousand supporters on Facebook. It had alliances with other groups, such as the youth wing of the liberal Tomorrow Party of Ayman Nour, but he was not close to them. The core members of April 6 were subject to arrest and harassment, even for innocuous events such as celebrating a "Day of Love" in a park in Cairo. He said that female members were especially targeted by police as a means of terrorizing youth into quiescence and noted that "police arrested one female member of the group as she was returning home from Cairo to Tanta (a Delta town approximately 75 miles north of Cairo), and then 'stripped and sexually molested her' causing her subsequently to suffer a nervous breakdown."[53]

Saleh was able to take the trip to the United States in December 2008. He attended the Alliance of Youth Movements Summit in New York, as Scobey had hoped, and then went to Washington to meet with concerned members of Congress and think tanks, lobbying them to permit regime change in Egypt. He urged members of the U.S. government to give up hope that Mubarak would ever accept reform and to view him as worse than Zimbabwe's incorrigible dictator, Robert Mugabe. He said that the U.S. government surely had information on Mubarak's offshore accounts and should threaten to reveal it or even just freeze them. He was arrested on his return at Cairo's airport, and his notes from his trip were confiscated by state security. After his release he told the U.S. embassy that the Egyptian regime "will never accept democratic reform." He also somewhat bitterly and undiplomatically pointed out that "Mubarak derives his legitimacy from U.S. support, and therefore charged the U.S. with 'being responsible' for Mubarak's 'crimes.'" NGOs working on incremental reform, he said, were living in a "fantasy world." Mubarak, "the head of the snake," would have to step down if there was ever to be democracy.

The April 6 leader then went on to reveal something that the U.S. ambassador found completely incredible, but which in retrospect seems likely to have been true: "Saleh claimed that several opposition forces—including the Wafd, Nasserite, Karama and Tagammu [Progressive Unionist] parties, and the Muslim Brotherhood, Kifaya, and Revolutionary Socialist movements—have agreed to support an unwritten plan for a transition to a parliamentary democracy, involving a weakened presidency and an empowered prime minister and parliament, before the scheduled 2011 presidential elections. . . . According to Saleh, the opposition is interested in receiving support from the army and the police for a transitional government prior to the 2011 elections. Saleh asserted that this plan is so sensitive it cannot be written down."[54] Saleh's description of a wide-ranging plot to overthrow Mubarak may have been too concrete and baldly put to fit the reality, but he reflected the increasingly desperate and revolutionary thinking of his generation. As for those conspiracy theorists who point to Scobey's contacts with April 6 as evidence that the United States was behind the overthrow of Mubarak, they should reread the cable: Scobey found Saleh's plans completely unrealistic and implausible.

In March 2009, April 6 began organizing alongside the remnants of the Kefaya movement for a commemorative set of rallies and demonstrations on the one-year anniversary of their relatively successful protest the year before. By that time the April 6 Facebook page had seventy thousand members, about 7 percent of all Facebook users in the country. The call for a strike on the web was phrased in the terms of a youth movement. One notice said, "General Protest by the People of Egypt—6 April 2009: It is the right of our generation to try. . . . Either it will succeed . . . or will gain experience that will benefit the other generations—The Youth of April 6, youth who love Egypt. Strike 6."[55] This time, however, Ahmed Saleh told the U.S. embassy that he was pessimistic about the chance of success. From without, state security would certainly interfere with pamphleteering and organizing. It was already actively torturing members who had been arrested and had recently managed to convince one young woman to become an informer. From within, the movement had developed a strong secular-Muslim divide. Members wrangled over whether to adopt an anti-Western stance and whether to accept the indictment by the International Criminal Court of Sudanese dictator Omar al-Bashir for crimes against humanity in Darfur. Saleh insisted that these foreign policy issues were a distraction and that the movement "should be focusing on internal Egyptian issues."[56] Saleh himself was ill, suffering from kidney stones, and unemployed. Many other prominent members, he said, were on the verge of going underground to avoid arrest. His codirector of the organization, Ahmed Maher, was employed as an engineer and had more resources and intended to remain in the open so as to organize the strike. Maher was arrested in early March for photographing "civil servants taking bribes at a government traffic office," and the pictures were deleted from his camera.

On March 10, April 6 activist Mohammed Adel, who had been arrested for his aid trips to Gaza, was released from prison after months of brutal imprisonment. He alleged that "police tortured him with electric shocks during his approximately 4-month detention." He was kept in a tiny cell. A physician was allegedly present during the torture to instruct state security officers how to avoid leaving permanent marks on his body. After his release he contacted an attorney about suing the Interior Ministry.[57] Police harassment and torture as an everyday practice in Egypt's neighborhoods left many young people feeling constantly humiliated.[58]

In the lead-up to the anniversary, Sara Rizq and Omnia Taha, two young women activists from April 6, were arrested for distributing pamphlets at the university in Kafr Sheikh, a town in the Delta with a strong Nasserist and leftist tradition. The organization maintained that they were beaten severely while in custody. When April 6 then staged a protest at the courthouse in that Delta city, demanding their release, between ten and thirty-seven of the protesters were allegedly violently beaten and arrested. The young women were let out on bail on April 5. That same day police broke into the homes of April 6 workers in Fayoum and Port Said and hauled them away for having posted announcements calling for the anniversary strike. The organization's members in Alexandria were also targeted for arrest, and some were seized; others had gone underground, as planned, afraid of being arrested.[59]

On April 6, 2009, although some protesters did show up, especially on campuses and in Cairo, the effort at commemorative street politics generally flopped. The movement's leaders had announced their goals as a new constitution that would put bounds on presidential prerogatives, increasing the political rights of citizens, a higher minimum wage, and the cancelation of a sweetheart natural gas deal with Israel whereby Mubarak provided the fuel at substantially below-market prices. Some 250 protesters from several organizations and parties gathered in front of the Press Syndicate in downtown Cairo. Students at Cairo University held a rally, and at Ain Shams and Helwan universities police cracked down, leading to clashes and the arrest of three students and a press photographer at Ain Shams. Activists attempted to gather at the Egyptian Trade Union Federation in the center of the capital, but police dispersed them. The Reform and Development Party, led by Anwar Essmat Sadat, the nephew of the late president, and backed by billionaire and sometime parliamentarian Rami "Raymond" Lakah, joined in the call for a demonstration but could rally only about fifty supporters. In Mansoura, a depot city in the Delta, and at Aswan in Upper Egypt small April 6 demonstrations were also held. In general, however, shopkeepers and street crowds ignored the day. The Progressive Unionist Party refused to join the strike, and the Old Left leaders dismissed the young activists as "amateurs." The Muslim Brotherhood again showed little interest, though its eighty-eight members of Parliament boycotted a speech of the prime minister on economic achievements. U.S. embassy officials noted, "Egyptian Initiative for Personal Rights Director Hossam Bahgat characterized the demonstrations as 'small, elite pockets of protest,' which he termed as much less effective than recent labor protests by pharmacists and truckers."[60]

The conjuncture in 2008 of the El Mahalla El Kubra textile workers' call for a general strike, the demonstrations in that city, the political mobilization around the local elections, and the Facebook activism of the New Left youth in solidarity with the workers produced an important political moment on April 6. The failure of the attempt to commemorate it a year later showed the limits of youth activism and internet campaigns. This time the workers and the crowds were absent. The failure of the strike may have encouraged the secret police to crack down on the young activists. On April 9 in Alexandria, Wael Abbas and his mother were allegedly assaulted by two police officers, who beat him and broke a tooth. He was arrested, ordered to reconcile with his attackers, then threatened with being charged as the assailant and with incurring a 1,000 pound (roughly U.S.$150) fine. Abbas was able to describe his ordeal on Twitter and attracted national and international attention, including an article in *BBC Arabic*, after which he was abruptly released.[61] Likewise April 6 member Asmaa Mahfouz went public a few weeks later with the story of how the secret police had put pressure on her through her family. First they called her father and asked him to come downtown to be questioned about the activities of his daughter. (He refused, claiming there were no legal grounds for this harassment.) Then they bothered her brothers. She figured that among her brothers, sisters, nephews, nieces, and cousins the Mahfouz clan comprised some four hundred individuals, all of whom, it seemed to her, the regime was determined to punish for her activism. Wael Abbas published her open letter on his widely read blog.[62]

Purging the Fundamentalists, Cooperating with the Brotherhood

The lack of public response to the strike call may have caused long knives to come out inside the organization's leadership. A loosely networked organization such as April 6 is difficult to keep together, and the ad hoc leadership faced constant challenges. Joiners with other ideological commitments than the New Left premises of the founders attempted to shift its emphases. A little over a year after its founding, April 6 was roiled by internal fighting provoked by the alleged ties of Ahmed Saleh and Ahmed Maher to the U.S.-based NGOs Freedom House and Voices for a Democratic Egypt.

Dia Isawi, a Labor Party figure and Muslim fundamentalist who viewed Freedom House as a Zionist organization, allegedly slammed the two Ahmeds after he discovered documents indicating that Freedom House planned to fund some of their activities. He and other Muslim fundamentalist members "held a mock trial of Ahmed Maher for 'treason' into the early morning hours of April 22."[63] Youth activists in the Tomorrow Party also lambasted the two for treason. According to the U.S. embassy, blogger Wael Abbas was also angry at Maher and Saleh over the charges of American funding and threatened to post the Freedom House documents on his blog.

(He did not.) He complained that Maher was weak and the group disorganized. Saleh, dejected, considered establishing an underground, secular wing of April 6. He also was making plans to testify to a committee of the U.S. Congress about the need for democratization in Egypt, allegedly convinced that behind the scenes Saad Eddin Ibrahim was paying for his airplane ticket via Voices for a Democratic Egypt.

In July 2009 the power struggle within the organization came to a head. According to Saleh as reported by the U.S. embassy, "the group ejected 13 Islamist and Nasserist members the previous day in an attempt to consolidate its secular, western orientation."[64] Saleh said that these individuals had "tried to hijack 'April 6,' and turn it into a Islamist movement opposing the west and rejecting Egypt's peace treaty with Israel." In the aftermath of this struggle, he expected the organization to be more harmonious, though also vilified by the expelled elements. He hoped that April 6 would be able to add members in the thousands now that its political line was clarified.

Saleh and Maher were committed to nonviolence, to fair elections and government accountability, to an end to torture, and to good relations with Western Europe and the United States. One suspects that they would have been at home in the left wing of the British Labour Party or the far left wing of the U.S. Democratic Party. They had foiled an attempt to turn the group in a different direction. It cannot be ruled out that some of those working in that direction were triple agents, actually attempting to sow discord on behalf of the State Security Investigative Services. (Saleh himself suspected as much.) In the aftermath the organization elected a general coordinator, four lieutenants, and a steering committee and set up other committees based on specialization or on which governorate they were active in. By that summer the organization had about two thousand active members in twelve governorates, not counting its Facebook friends.[65]

By the fall of 2009 Saleh and Maher were exploring new forms of activism beyond strikes and demonstrations, which had been easily deflected by the secret police. In the Delta town of Kafr Sheikh, they worked with local residents to find victims of police torture and connect them to organizations offering legal aid. Some of their new efforts seem humble on the surface, but they did address important discontent. In the lower-middle-class Muslim neighborhood of Embaba and in the largely Coptic Christian neighborhood of Ain Shams, the youth had helped residents put pressure on their local councils to collect the trash. In Ain Shams they threatened a sit-in.[66]

From October 30 through November 1, 2009, as the annual National Democratic Party conference was unfolding in a luxurious setting, April 6 held its own event. The first two days consisted of an online conference, including interviews with dissidents such as the liberal Tomorrow Party leader Ayman Nour and the Supreme Guide of the Muslim Brotherhood, Muhammad Mahdi Akif. During these two days the April 6 website was targeted by the State Security Division of the Ministry of the Interior for a denial-of-service attack (using automatic programs to send so much traffic to the server that it is slowed down or made unavailable). The site's availability was reduced by 90 percent. Then, on the third day, about four hundred activists gathered at the headquarters of the Democratic Front Party. The headliners included Nour; the head of the Kefaya movement, George Ishaq; Muslim Brotherhood officials; and NGO leaders. The point of their speeches was to dispute the overly rosy claims at the NDP convention about the regime's meeting of its goals and to denounce any move to install Gamal Mubarak in power by fiat. The leftists of April 6 had agonized over whether to invite the Muslim Brotherhood but in the end decided to include them. The socialist Progressive Unionist Party was not invited, nor was the centrist Wafd Party. (Both had been willing to function in Parliament under NDP dominance and so were seen as insufficiently committed to change. Moreover, the Progressive Unionists would not have shared a roster with the Muslim Brotherhood, nor the Wafd with Nour.)[67]

The alternative conference was one of the more successful public activities since April 6 was founded in 2008. A series of attempted demonstrations were broken up by the secret police. Even a patriotic sing-along in Alexandria was not allowed, nor was a "Day of Love" in the capital. The attempt in 2008 to have an alternative meeting coinciding with the ruling party's meeting had been foiled because it was scheduled for the Press Syndicate premises, a government-controlled entity that simply canceled it. By fall of 2009 the organization's leaders were expanding their efforts to recruit on campuses more aggressively, though a member was arrested in October for handing out pamphlets on campus. They also began gearing up to monitor the fall 2010 parliamentary elections and to coordinate with Nour on another possible campaign for the presidency in 2011.[68] Later Ahmed Maher in particular became interested in the possible candidacy of Mohamed ElBaradei.

The April 6 organization was again unable to get large numbers of the public to support its now-annual rally on April 6, 2010. They demanded more open elections and the abrogation of the 1981 Emergency Law. The Voice of America reported, "Witnesses say Egyptian police broke up the protest by beating the activists and dragging them away." Ninety-one were arrested.[69] It was almost as if the Egyptian public was waiting to see how the regime would deal with the fall elections. In the end, the regime openly stole the elections, and suddenly there was again a bull market in the protest sector. Everything April 6 and the other youth groups had learned about using the internet to call for demonstrations and to network with labor unions and with the Muslim Brotherhood, and about challenging the regime's claims to legitimacy, would again come in handy.

Tunisia and the Student Movement

Among the important youth organizations in Tunisia was the left-leaning General Union of Tunisian Students (UGET), which had been founded in 1952. Some revolutionaries viewed it with suspicion since it was recognized by the Tunisian state and so in some ways co-opted by the regime. On the other hand, it was an organizational alternative to the student union of the ruling Constitutional Democratic Rally. At some points, either the government allowed the UGET to blow off steam or young members deployed its organizational resources for demonstrations and other purposes that went substantially beyond what the regime desired. As in several semi-independent Tunisian organizations, the leadership tended to be closer to the government than the rank and file, but sometimes even leaders with a reputation for being close to power broke with the government when it attempted to marginalize them. There were fewer truly independent youth organizations in Tunisia than in Egypt because the Ben Ali regime was even more controlling than that of Mubarak.

In 2010, out of a population of about 10.5 million, some 370,000 students attended thirteen state-funded and thirty-two private colleges and universities throughout the country. That came to over a third of the population age nineteen to twenty-four. Some Tunisian intellectuals believed that Ben Ali had established new, provincial campuses in order to divide the students and better control them but then proved unable to fund either the old or the new institutions at an adequate level. The training in many of these institutions was third-rate, and they often did not produce what the labor market was looking for. Students were assigned majors by the government, and many were shunted into fields where jobs were scarce.[70] In Tunisia university students typically remained without work for eighteen months after graduation, and the overall unemployment rate in this stratum was as high as 40 percent. The U.S. embassy noted, "Unemployment among young graduates has even spurred the organic development of an [unrecognized] independent union for unemployed graduates, which now has branches throughout the country."[71] The Ben Ali government, alarmed by the obvious ennui in the next generation, held meetings all over the country in what they called a "Dialogue with Youth" and promised hundreds of thousands of new jobs.[72] But there was little prospect of talking the problems away, and it may be that in calling youth together for these dialogues throughout the country the regime mainly managed to introduce the discontented to one another.

The regime was especially afraid of campus activism. The U.S. embassy reported that the government forbade the few recognized opposition political parties from coming on campus. Parties other than the ruling Democratic Constitutional Rally (Rassemblement Constitutionnel Démocratique, RCD) that attempted to hold student events off-campus were most often blocked by security forces. Police monitored students and warned the parents of those seen visiting party headquarters. Demonstrations were desultory and staccato affairs, most often centering on discontent with campus housing or the small student stipends. Professors were often denied offices on campus and were prevented from meeting with colleagues there or elsewhere. Political activism increasingly migrated to the internet, as we have seen.[73]

U.S. embassy officials noted that youth complained of the lack of cultural events in Tunisia and of the crushing boredom of a carefully managed police state. Those who stayed put their energies into café life or various underground subcultures. A furtive music scene of hip-hop cheekiness or Joan Baez–style folk protest was kept going. Folk singer Emel Mathlouthi did fundraising concerts for the UGET before her music was banned in 2008, forcing her into exile in France. (Her protest lyrics later became anthems of the 2011 revolution.) El Général (Hamada Ben Amor of Sfax) produced raw rap and touching ballads, leading to his arrest at home by a phalanx of thirty policemen in January 2011. There was even a reggae band, Nouveau Système, which turned to explicit political satire after the revolution and whom I once heard play at a culture center in the medina (old city) of Tunis. Others devoted themselves to following soccer obsessively. Some of the working-class soccer fanatics, known as Ultras, were dedicated to a rowdy lifestyle that brought them into frequent confrontations with the police and made them allies of disgruntled workers and dissident students. As in Egypt, the regime probably benefited from the emigration abroad of educated youth in search of work, which functioned as a safety valve and removed people from the scene who might otherwise have mounted an opposition. By the summer of 2008 nearly half of young people wanted to go abroad. The fall 2008 global economic crash closed off this safety valve for the regime. After that it became harder to escape the injustices and economic stagnation of the regime through emigration.

In November 2008, as the new, even more depressing economic reality was beginning to sink in, President Ben Ali finally signed his "Pact with the Youth," the culmination of the year of dialogue, bringing thousands to Tunis for the ceremony. U.S. ambassador Godec reported, "The agreement was signed by young people representing various political parties, members of domestic organizations and NGOs, and young expatriate Tunisians."[74] The document spoke in an empty way of the rule of law, human rights, justice, and women's rights. Since many Tunisian "nongovernmental organizations" were actually secretly government organs and many others were infiltrated by double agents of the ruling RCD, this event was an intra-regime celebration rather than a genuine attempt to reach out.[75]

Gaza

Almost immediately after the pact with the youth was signed, the young people mounted one of the biggest rallies seen in Tunisia since the 1991 Gulf War, provoked by the Israeli attack on Gaza. An undertone of dissatisfaction with the Ben Ali regime was visible in these demonstrations, in part because of Ben Ali's close relations with France and the United States, supporters of Tel Aviv. In the coastal industrial city of Sfax, the country's second largest city, an estimated twenty thousand students came out on January 6 and 7, 2009. One local activist, Fathi al-Hamami, wrote that labor unions and the whole spectrum of political organizations began organizing in Sfax for demonstrations in solidarity with the Palestinians of Gaza right from December 27, 2008, when the war began. A peaceful march was attempted but was stopped by the security police. In the following days further attempts to stage demonstrations were mounted by the labor syndicates and civil society organizations against the mounting death toll among Gaza's residents. Every time, the security police surrounded the activists, blocking them with a human wall and stopping them in their tracks. Faced with the people's determination to express themselves, the city authorities from Ben Ali's party finally allowed the opposition parties and worker and professional associations to conduct a march on January 2. A good number of people gathered in front of the union building instead of at the RCD headquarters, as the authorities had stipulated. This was their way of avoiding marching in unity with the representatives of the ruling party and of being used by them politically. "This was apparent," al-Hamami wrote, "in their placards and slogans, and was a victory as well for the right to freely and independently demonstrate, which had been denied to them in past days."[76] Likewise on January 2 secondary schools and universities canceled classes. On January 3 the attorneys demonstrated, leading to a clash when the security forces attempted to box them in. The attorneys rallied and found a way to break through the police line, successfully completing their march. As images of the dead and wounded of Gaza flooded into Tunisia from old and new media, the streets became tense.

Student leaders and their elected representatives then decided to mount a youth demonstration. Al-Hamami expressed approval, believing it would transcend their earlier, unorganized efforts, get the youth used to working in concert with one another, and teach them the meaning of solidarity. It would also challenge the sad spectacle of security police swarming the streets and preventing citizens from freely expressing their views.[77]

According to another local account of subsequent events, the regional secondary teachers' union in Sfax called for a big demonstration on January 6. By this time the local security police and RCD officials appeared to have given up on attempting to keep a lid on the situation. Thousands of students and teachers assembled in front of the workers' union headquarters, coming from all the schools and institutes of the province. Arabic press reports spoke of there being as many as thirty thousand participants; even if this figure is an exaggeration, in Tunisian terms these were enormous rallies. The students and their teachers denounced not only Israel and its imperial backers but also the reactionary Arab regimes that acquiesced in the attack on Gaza. Leaders of the secondary teachers' union and the workers' union gave enthusiastic speeches condemning American state terrorism and the treason of "some Arab organizations." Then the massive crowds surged into the city's thoroughfares, chanting slogans and pledging aid and medicine to Gaza's victims.[78]

Ambassador Godec reported, "There has been an uptick in the number of demonstrations, especially by students, with some high schools closing as a result. Police have allowed some peaceful demonstrations to take place. Some activists have used the Gaza demonstrations to protest GOT [Government of Tunisia] policies; if this trend continues, a GOT crackdown is likely."[79] An American resident in the southern coastal city of Sousse told the U.S. embassy that a series of demonstrations had begun in that city on January 8 and were getting bigger and bigger. "She said that the main street in Sousse was completely full of demonstrators at midday, with adults having joined the youth. She described high school and college-aged students as becoming more aggressive—climbing on top of cars and shouting slogans against the United States and Israel." Godec noted, "Meanwhile, many other student demonstrations have been reported in the last two days in the Governorates of Ben Arous, Rades, Ariana, Bizerte, Jendouba, Monastir and Kairouan."[80]

The organizational energies and the contacts made and repertoires of protest learned in January 2009 as a result of the Gaza protests would prove useful to the youth two years later, when many of them joined in the effort to overthrow Ben Ali. The regime may have miscalculated badly in allowing the demonstrations, believing that the lack of involvement of Tunisia in the issues of Israel and Palestine, and Ben Ali's pro forma denunciations of Tel Aviv, would protect the state from any spillover of the passions on the street. The recognized status of the General Union of Tunisian Students, like that of the General Union of Tunisian Workers, made it a double-edged sword: it was open to infiltration, artificially induced divisions, and influence by the regime, but it also had a freedom of organization and action that allowed it occasionally to push the envelope. In late 2008 the government appears to have decided that the UGET was too independent, for it then attempted to replace it with the student union of its own party, the RCD.

Campus Issues

Some issues preoccupying youth grew out of their own struggles with the regime over poor schooling and lack of jobs for graduates. Five students who were expelled for protesting from their campuses (and thereby denied the right to finish their degrees and become professionals) staged a two-month-long hunger strike in front of the national UGET headquarters beginning in February 2009. They also faced prison for terms of up to eighteen months. They maintained that they had been disciplined simply for student union activities, which were protected under the Tunisian constitution, and for protesting poor school and university facilities. Physicians who examined them worried that their health had badly deteriorated, but the Ministry of Higher Education declined to reconsider its decision, despite the publicity their hunger strike garnered. Police had the striking students under surveillance and intervened to prevent sympathetic students from visiting them. U.S. embassy officials observed, "In a sign of how Tunisians are circumventing this type of GOT action, a group of 158 Tunisians and others used Facebook to organize and publicize a one-day hunger strike March 26 in solidarity with the students."[81] The students finally called off the hunger strike on April 9.

The UGET itself had been agitating to be allowed to hold its twenty-fifth National Congress that spring and had initially received permission to do so on April 11–12 in Bizerte. (The previous national meeting had been held in 2003.) The Ministry of Higher Education, however, abruptly withdrew permission for the gathering. Ezzedine Zaatour, the secretary-general of the UGET, attempted to hold the congress in Tunis at the organization's own facilities, but, the U.S. embassy reported, "police blocked participation, physically harassed several of the union leaders and prevented the union from holding the congress."[82] In the aftermath the UGET headquarters was closed by the authorities, and Zaatour maintained that he was being followed by the police. He discovered in February that he had been secretly sentenced in absentia to six months in prison. He complained that "government harassment of UGET members is a continual problem making it difficult for him to even stay in contact with UGET organizers in other towns. He said seven or eight UGET activists are in prison for periods ranging from five months to four years. The government reduced its funding for the union in 2008 and has not provided any funding for 2009."[83]

After the uproar over the Gaza War died down when that struggle abruptly ended in January 2009, rural labor issues, such as the Gafsa miners' strike and other similar expressions of small-town discontent, attracted the sympathies of the inchoate Tunisian New Left. Youth wings of the small leftist parties such as the Progressive Democratic Party (PDP) and the Communist Workers' Party played an important role in protest and exposure of injustice, as did the youth wing of the Muslim Renaissance Party. For instance, in 2009 Zouhaïer Makhlouf, an activist with the barely tolerated PDP, was sentenced to three months in jail by a provincial court for having interviewed people in a provincial industrial region and putting their complaints on the web. All along, leftist intellectuals sympathetic with workers were specially targeted by the regime. The authorities maintained that Makhlouf had failed to obtain the consent of the people he filmed (a charge that is obviously not true, say those who have seen the video) or to acquire permission to film in an industrial area (no such law was on the books).[84]

The government campaign against activist youth and student organizers intensified. By February 2010 U.S. Ambassador Gordon Gray became concerned enough to write a general cable on the issue.[85] He reported UGET's insistence that most of its activities were not even political per se but involved protests against inadequate classrooms, libraries, and computer equipment, as well as poorly trained teachers. Of course, another of its emphases was the need for more freedom of speech, a profound challenge to the regime's philosophy of governance. In September 2009 five student members of the UGET were brought before a judge on charges of "damaging property" and "aggression against a government employee." In October 2009 one student activist, Muhammad Sudani (one of the hunger strikers of the previous spring), was interviewed on the France 24 satellite television channel on the presidential elections of that fall. Afterward he was charged with public inebriation and "disorderly and immoral conduct" and served two months of a six-month sentence. Students who staged a sit-in at Manouba University near the capital to demand more student housing, including for female students, were arrested in early November; eleven of them were sentenced to between one and two years for damaging government property. They maintained that they were tortured in prison. In early January 2010 students at the University of Tunis marched to demand the release of their Manouba colleagues, but the police attacked the procession and dispersed the students, arresting one of the organizers.

Then the high school students got into the act. In early January 2010 some rallied outside their school in the town of Jebeniana in Sfax governorate, alarming the police, who deployed tear gas to disperse them. Some of the students and teachers were said to have been wounded. Then on January 8 other high schools in the area staged a two-hour sympathy strike with those who had been attacked. On January 11, Ambassador Gray reported, "several teachers unions, textile unions, and employees from the national power company and the municipality of Jebeniana staged a two-hour strike in solidarity with the teachers and students of Jebeniana." It is worth noting that Sfax was where as many as thirty thousand youth had rallied exactly one year before for Gaza, and that Jebeniana was also the scene of such activism then. Also in early January police dragged off four UGET activists who protested in front of the prime minister's office in the capital. On February 18 a dissident website reported that 90 percent of the student body struck in Gafsa to complain about police harassment. There is plenty of support on the internet for Gray's report of discontent and crackdowns. In 2010 the website Militantuniv.maktoobblog printed a series of impudent letters by its members to the minister of higher education, complaining about everything from food, housing, and instruction in universities to the oppressive atmosphere created by regime heavy-handedness and the lack of freedom of thought and speech. In May, one letter writer commented sarcastically on a new policy to forbid smoking on campus: "Tunisian Students to the Ministry of Higher Education: In the absence of our Liberties, Rights and Capabilities, what Good does it Do to Forbid Smoking?"[86]

Many of the themes I've discussed came together in the fall of 2010 in explosive ways. Both rural labor discontent and concern for justice in Palestine were topics in a postrevolution interview given by Al-Amin al-Bu'azizi, a cultural anthropologist and union activist in the small town of Sidi Bouzid, in the center of the country.[87] He observed, "The revolution was brought about by new activists, that is, by the youth, not by the working class and not by the 'vanguard.'" He said that "the youth" had challenged "traditional political thought" and described how, in spring of 2010, youth in Sidi Bouzid had chanted slogans calling for the fall of the "fascist, collaborationist and comprador regime," in support of the Gaza relief flotilla that had been attacked by Israeli commandos that May. The Israeli assault on the *Mavi Marmara* proved that "the best way to support our people in Gaza would be to break the neck of this [Tunisian] regime and other such subdued regimes, and that it was necessary to make a connection between the national struggle and the local, social struggle. We pointed to the importance in this regard of the various headquarters of the General Union of Tunisian Workers, the sole national organization that was semi-liberated." He said that the offices of the Union générale tunisienne du travail (UGTT, General Union of Tunisian Workers) in Sidi Bouzid were the one place where activists could hold meetings and make plans.

In the summer of 2010 there was a local protest by some twenty families of farmers from Erregueb, a small town of seven thousand near Sidi Bouzid, because the banks were foreclosing on the land they had been encouraged to buy early in the century. They complained of high interest rates, of requirements that they also borrow to buy farm equipment, and of not being informed they were in arrears before the foreclosures. They staged angry demonstrations in Sidi Bouzid and even tussled with police.[88] A thousand farmers in Meknassi in the same province staged a protest against the expropriation of their land by the state. Al-Bu'azizi compared them to the Palestinians, insofar as Ottoman absolutism, French colonialism, and that day's arbitrary regime had similarly rendered Tunisian farmers insecure in their property. Likewise, from the beginning of the 2010–11 school year a group of fifty student activists staged almost daily sit-ins at the high school in Meknassi, demanding the rights of union workers and protesting the sexual harassment of young women working for family welfare. This local discontent, he affirmed, paved the way for the outbreak of concerted demonstrations in December.

The New Left in Egypt and Tunisia conceived of the youth and students as a generational power base, a stratum that could challenge the entrenched Mubarak and Ben Ali elites. Somewhat like the Students for a Democratic Society in the 1960s in the United States, they saw the urban, middle-class youth as a political vanguard that could play a revolutionary role of which blue-collar workers alone did not seem capable. Unlike the U.S. situation, however, the New Left and the workers succeeded in forging an alliance against the establishment. Although the April 6, 2008, labor action in El Mahalla El Kubra failed as a strike, it succeeded as an exercise in political organizing. The regime likely would have buried accounts of what happened there by forbidding the official press to report them or would have succeeded in its calumny that El Mahalla El Kubra devolved into mere mob violence, if it had not been for the youth activists. Their ability to spread videos and eyewitness reports on their blogs and Facebook pages created a counternarrative of the strike, which indicted the regime for heavy-handedness and for the first time showed crowds of youth publicly disrespecting an icon of Mubarak. Likewise the Tunisian youth activists' support of the Gafsa mining strike and other labor actions in the triangle of poverty in the center of the country amplified the voice of those workers.

These youth organizations had an armory of resources, which they sought to mobilize. Their base was disproportionately unemployed or in school and unencumbered by family obligations and so had some free time on its hands. They were "biographically available" for meetings, internet communications, and small demonstrations. The deployment of folk festi-

vals like that at Sayyida Zaynab in Cairo for the purpose of pamphleteering and the resort to the diverse urban geography of the growing cities as
unexpected spaces for publicizing their cause to working-class and poor
youth showed their determination to build a cross-class alliance against the
oligarchs. In Egypt, unlike in Tunisia, there were a few public spaces not
under government control, such as the Hisham Mubarak Law Center and a
few other NGOs, where informational meetings could be held. Those who
were engineers or programmers were internet-savvy and could develop ways
of foiling the cyber police and of innovating in interactive forms of connectivity. Activists in Egypt in 2008 for the first time discovered the power of
Facebook to create branching networks of political allies and to publicize a
major political campaign around a key issue.

Egyptian youth also innovated in seeking alliances across the ideological spectrum, attempting to unite for their political and social campaigns
everyone from the Trotskyites to the Muslim Brothers, a tactic with which
older Kefaya leaders like George Ishaq were not comfortable. Sometimes
they failed to get the mainstream of the Brotherhood elite on board, since it
was now interested in seeing what power could be gained by being a junior
partner in the Mubarak system rather than acting as perpetual outsiders. At
other times the activist youth were able to hold joint meetings with their
counterparts among devotees of political Islam or gain their support for
demands such as payment of worker bonuses, though each group attempted
to seal itself off from the other internally. As of 2010 the youth had not
yet found a way to gather really large crowds for their demonstrations and
had not yet found a set of issues that could reliably capture the interest of
the broader public. In Egypt, the high bread prices of 2008 subsided, the
provincial elections were over, and the textile workers were forestalled from
striking by the security police. In Tunisia, the youth outrage over the Israeli
attack on the Gaza Strip, which brought out tens of thousands of protesters, could not be sustained when that war abruptly ended. The gradual
radicalization of the UGET and its alienation from the Ben Ali regime had
created an organizational vehicle of some importance, but its successes were
occasional and discontinuous.

The youth had learned, however, how to network, both in the streets
and in cyberspace. The resort to fasts was a claim on the sympathy and iden-

tification of other youth rather than a hope that the regime might develop a conscience. They had developed address lists and databases of potential supporters; Facebook alone served as a huge informal database of connections (those who had joined the April 6 page, those who "liked" it and its announcements, those who were in the circle of pro–April 6 friends). In 2000 youth who wanted to work in opposition to the regimes had few vehicles for dissent outside of some small political parties dominated by middle-aged or elderly politicians, in which young people had little voice or autonomy. These parties often despised one another and had little prospect of working together. Ten years later a whole range of youth organizations had sprung up actually led by youth, which had developed new repertoires of social and political action and pursued alliances across ideological divides. The New Left leaders attempted to show how youth and student discontent derived from regime policies. Many millennials admired and identified with the engaged leaders of these organizations. They were primed.

From Bouazizi to Tahrir

The strands of youth discontent came together in an unexpected way beginning in December 2011 in Tunisia and spread from there throughout the Arab world, though the impact was most dramatic in the republican monarchies.[1] Boiling resentments included bad working conditions for young laborers in state-owned factories; high unemployment, especially among youth and among educated youth in particular; rural water and electricity shortages and farmer indebtedness; the resentments of police regimentation by soccer fanatics and political activists; religious Muslim resentments of curbs on political participation; and general middle-class distaste for arbitrary arrest, torture, censorship, nepotism, corruption, and the predatory business practices of the republican princes.

On the surface 2010 looked little different from 2009 in the Arab world, an era of political and economic stagnation in which hated regimes unaccountably muddled through. Underneath, the social compact had been irretrievably breached by thousands of small regime betrayals and a handful of large ones. The 2008 international economic downturn contributed to the misery in a big way, reducing tourism and its income, reducing industrial exports, and threatening the ability of the hundreds of thousands of Tunisians in Europe and Egyptians in the Gulf to retain their jobs and send remittances home. The effects of climate change were beginning to be felt among young farmers in the form of frequent droughts. High school and college students and recent graduates were among the boldest and best-organized challengers of the old order. For all its appearance of spontaneity, the severe social and political struggle that broke out in late 2010 was waged by urban youth organizations that had existed and strategized ways of provoking change for some time. What was different about this time?

Tunisia

Self-Immolation

The despondency produced among many ordinary Tunisians by Ben Ali's combination of police state, corruption, and plutocracy created a new social phenomenon of self-immolation. Suicide rates are relatively low in most of the Muslim world, and the act is forbidden in Islamic law, as in Catholicism. Still, people made depressed by their circumstances and feeling they have no other escape take their lives all over the world. Blogger Lina Ben Mhenni noted that in April 2010, Abdesselem Trimeche of Monastir self-immolated, provoking a demonstration in the city on the day of his funeral in which protesters "expressed their anger and indignation in the face of the government's indifference to the fate of its citizens."[2] In Metlaoui in Gafsa province, Shams al-Din El Hani burned himself in mid-November 2010 out of despair at being unemployed after his applications for jobs were repeatedly rejected. Ben Mhenni pointed out that the newspapers owned by the government or by Sakher El Materi, the son-in-law in chief, did not typically report on these dramatic suicides, but social media such as Facebook and Twitter spread the news.

The unlikely spark for the upheavals was yet another suicide, of a vegetable and fruit vendor in the small town of Sidi Bouzid on December 17, 2010. Tarek Bouazizi, later known as Mohamed, was born in 1984, a typical Arab millennial in some respects. His father was a construction worker who went to Libya to work and died of a heart attack. His mother married her brother-in-law, who also had health problems and could not support the family's seven children. Although it was said of Bouazizi at the time that he was a college graduate, his sister clarified that he did not even finish high school, having been forced to go to work as a teenager to help support the family.[3] What is important is that educated Tunisian youth believed he was one of their own. On December 15 he borrowed $200 to buy fruit and vegetables to sell from his cart. The next day local police, who often bullied and harassed him, confiscated his cart as a way of demanding a bribe. Instead, he went to see a municipal official, who was most unhelpful; when he argued with her, she is said to have confiscated his electronic scale and slapped him. (She claimed it was security guards who slapped him.) He stormed off to city hall, where he doused himself with gasoline and set himself alight, suffering burns over 90 percent of his body.

Bouazizi's act of despair set off local demonstrations in Sidi Bouzid and other rural towns, where the secret police were not as numerous or in control as they were in the large urban centers. (The government had eighty thousand secret police in one branch of the service or another.) The regime was forced to pull antiriot police (Brigades of Public Order) out of Gafsa, where they had been stationed after the mining strikes of 2008, and send them north to Sidi Bouzid. This move, however, simply encouraged the people in Gafsa to protest more freely. There were not enough government security assets in the center and west of the country to crush the demonstrations. One YouTube video uploaded three days later, on December 20, shows young men throwing stones at police gathered around an armored vehicle, and the sound of gunshots rings out as the police deploy live fire against the youth. Another, uploaded on the same day, shows a crowd of young men after they have taken control of the street and set a car on fire. (At one point its gas tank explodes.) Such videos garnered thousands of views. The following week the demonstrations spread to surrounding towns. In Menzel Bouzaiane, some sixty kilometers south of Sidi Bouzid, on Friday December 24, a week of rallies culminated in clashes with the police, who opened live fire on the youth. An unemployed high school graduate, Muhammad Amari, was killed by a bullet to the chest, creating yet another martyr.[4]

The story that circulated about Tarek Bouazizi—that he was a college graduate employed as a menial and that police and government officials had maliciously deprived him of both his livelihood and his dignity—struck a nerve with Tunisian and Arab youth. At some point in the internet discussion, he became confused with a Facebook user named Mohamed Bouazizi, and so that is how he came to be known. The reformist Nawaat cooperative published an Arabic-language article by a local intellectual explaining the roots of rage in Sidi Bouzid, particularly the corruption that led to underpayment of local farmers for their produce and the failure of the state to develop tertiary industries in the area such as tourism, leaving educated youth with little prospect of employment.[5] The Nawaat youth were at that time heavily involved in translating and interpreting the U.S. State Department cables on the Ben Ali regime released by Wikileaks that fall, which confirmed their worst suspicions about the regime's corruption, torture, and "mafia-like" tendencies. They may have initially considered the demonstrations in Sidi Bouzid a regional story, and it is significant that they published their first major analysis of it in Arabic, not cosmopolitan French. Other internet activists, such as Pirate Party activist Slim Amamou, however, took a keen interest in the aftermath of Bouazizi's self-immolation in the small towns of the center, where protests were repressed. "I went down to Sidi Bouzid with a few colleagues, and we made our own videos of the events in Sidi Bouzid, Kasserine, and other areas," he told researcher Alcinda Honwana. "We placed our information on the web, which was immediately picked up by people all over the country and by the international media."[6]

The President of the Country

Five days after Bouazizi's dramatic suicide attempt went viral, a twenty-one-year-old rapper named Hamada Ben Amor, who went by "El Général," released his second major video, "Tunis Is Our Country," on Facebook and YouTube. The chorus goes, "Tunisia is our country, with politics or with blood! / Tunisia is our country and her men will never surrender! / Tunisia is our country, the whole people hand-in-hand! / Tunisia is our country and today we must find the solution!"[7] Two days later secret police took him from his parents' house on the outskirts of Sfax to solitary confinement. The secret police were not aware of his enormous popularity and were surprised when subsequent street demonstrations demanded his release. The government hastily backed off and released him on a pledge to stop rapping politics. It was not a pledge he was to keep. Unlike the majority of activist youth, El Général is a Muslim fundamentalist.

The song was a sequel to his searing "President of the Country" ("Ra'is li Bilad"), addressing Ben Ali, which he had posted to Facebook on November 7, the anniversary of Ben Ali's 1987 soft coup against Bourguiba. "President of the country," he rapped, "the day has come to talk with you in my name and the name of the people, and of all who live in torment / 2011: the one who is dying of hunger wants to work and live, but his voice is not heard. / Go out on the street and see how the people have become like beasts / See the governor with his gavel, tap, tap—he doesn't care." Friends told him the video, which begins by showing Ben Ali trying to talk to a terrified and weeping schoolboy, was more or less a suicide note, but he was undeterred. "I wanted to make a strong song and make it reach the president, for him to know what's happening in our country," he told a journalist. "I expected it might get me in trouble."[8]

Ben Amor claimed to have been influenced by the American rapper Tupac Shakur (d. 1996). His ideological commitments, however, were closer to the Renaissance Party and Muslim fundamentalism. His third video to be released that winter was entitled "The Standard of Islam over Tunisia," which shows scenes of holy warriors riding to battle and involves shouts of "God is great" along with fist salutes like those of the Black Power movement.[9] Most Western journalistic accounts of El Général missed his religious commitment and that of many of the revolutionaries. While Muslim religious activists were a minority of those who made the revolution in the major cities, in the small provincial towns distant from the capital, the ideals of political Islam likely helped animate the youth. They did not have the help of an organized party, since the Renaissance Party had been effectively destroyed by Ben Ali's secret police, but many had read the books and pamphlets of the Egyptian Muslim Brotherhood and of the Tunisian writer Rashid al-Ghannushi. Attorney Ferida Labidi, a Renaissance member who had been imprisoned as a student activist early in Ben Ali's reign, told me that she had never paid much attention to the internet or Facebook; her revolutionary fervor was fueled by being steeped in the literature of political Islam and by her own circle of friends with Renaissance commitments.[10] From the old Muslim center of Kairouan, southwest of the capital, she was typical of provincial revolutionaries in being more oriented to the mosque and Muslim norms than to the left-of-center currents in the industrial cities of the coast. These provincial Muslims were likely the target audience for El Général's militant third video.

The demonstrations became daily affairs and spread from small rural towns in the center of the country to the big urban centers along the Mediterranean. The Algerian newspaper *al-Khabar* reported that demonstrations were held on December 27 in the mining town of Gafsa in the south, in Kasserine in the west near Algeria, in the central coastal industrial city of Sfax, and, most ominously, even if on a small scale, in the capital of Tunis itself.[11] The geography of protest had a history. Gafsa mine workers had been striking since 2008; Kasserine is one of the more economically neglected provinces in Tunisia; and, as we saw, Sfax, a city of some 300,000 with many schools, erupted in demonstrations estimated to be as large as twenty thousand during Israel's attack on Gaza only two years before, organized by the teacher, student, and labor unions.

As for the December 27 demonstration in Tunis, the *al-Khabar* sources in that city described police clustered at every intersection in the capital and plainclothes police at every corner. Hundreds of activists gathered, complaining about the brutal repression of the rallies in Sidi Bouzid and nearby towns during the past week and the thousands of unemployed in the capital. Thus, young people in the capital protested in sympathy not only with Bouazizi but with his townspeople, and they employed the common themes of repression and lack of gainful employment to bind urban to rural populations. Slim Amamou's colleague, Azyz Amami (then twenty-eight), helped organize the Tunis protests and made videos of them with his cell phone, sharing them with Arab satellite television for rebroadcast.[12]

The Tunis crowd, a thousand strong, was described as "union workers, publicists, human rights activists, and university students." They had assembled in response to calls by the teachers' unions (especially that of the secondary school teachers), the Social Security Workers Union, and other labor organizations. Police formed a phalanx to prevent them from marching from Muhammad Ali Place to Habib Bourguiba Avenue, the main artery of downtown Tunis. Police also accosted journalists and attempted to keep them from covering the protest. The crowds' chanting centered on a demand for the return to Tunisians of their dignity and an end to coercion in politics and union life. Protester Hussein Ben Tayyib warned the authorities, "We saw how a policeman's slapping of Muhammad Bouazizi . . . and the refusal of the local authorities to listen to him provoked naked fury." Newspaper reporters talked to the protesters, who expressed solidarity with college graduates who could not find work and who therefore were forced to turn to menial labor incommensurate with their abilities. One interviewee boasted of the demonstrations breaking out among Tunisians working abroad, in front of their embassies, as well as in small towns such as Siliana, Ariana, and Jandouba. The article noted that the Tunisian League for Human Rights had condemned the state for using live ammunition on the protesters and for tactics such as "home invasions, arson against shops, and arbitrary arrest of citizens." The Al Jazeera satellite channel aired a long report on the demonstration (immediately posted to YouTube), with footage of the chanting and police repression, asking if it heralded further turmoil in the Tunisian capital.[13]

Alarmed, Ben Ali returned from the Persian Gulf and attempted to get out ahead of the building story of government harassment and youth martyrdom. In one of the worst-considered public relations campaigns in modern history, on December 28 Ben Ali staged a photo opportunity at Bouazizi's hospital bedside. The photo of the president in his expensive business suit looming over the completely bandaged young working-class burn patient, a look of thinly disguised disgust on his face, only fanned the flames of protest. At the same time Ben Ali warned against continued rallies to protest unemployment, saying they besmirched the image of the country, and he menaced the youth with severe punishment if they continued. The youth lampooned the president as a buffoon, using an acronym of his name and calling him ZABA. One cartoon showed the dictator angrily shouting into his telephone, "There is nothing going on in Sidi Bouzid, just some idiot playing with his lighter!" Contemporary observers remember that date as the day Tunisians on the social networks stopped censoring themselves and flooded the internet with videos of protests and acerbic comments about the president and his circle.[14]

Tunisian youth were deadly serious about their despair. The same day Ben Ali spoke, a fourth young man, Ayman al-Numayri, twenty-five, from a small town near Sidi Bouzid, set himself afire to protest unemployment. In the evening activists in Sidi Bouzid thronged the streets, raising placards that demanded liberties and dignity. At the same time, the security perimeter around the area was lightened and the government suddenly accepted 1,300 applications for civil service employment from the city. In Gafsa a sympathy demonstration with Sidi Bouzid organized by the UGTT labor union was repressed. At that point three were dead and ten wounded in the protests throughout the country.[15] In Tunis the Lawyers' Union staged a small rally in front of the Court of First Instance. Two were arrested, including the leftist leader Chokri Belaid. Then, on December 31, blogger Lina Ben Mhenni described how the lawyers rallied in small groups in cities all over the country, protesting the use of live ammunition to repress demonstrations. Their movements were restricted by the secret police, however, who sometimes assaulted them. Ben Mhenni reported, "Some lawyers such as: Leila Ben Debba and Samia Abbou were badly beaten with truncheons."[16] The protests were covered by Al Jazeera, which supposedly was not available by satellite in Tunisia but which youth accessed online via proxy servers and to which Tunisians were sending footage of the protests.

Attempts at Repression

On January 3 the government cyber police hacked into the accounts of several prominent internet activists, including Lina Ben Mhenni, Azyz Amami, and Sofiene Chourabi, attempting to erase files and cancel multiple sites. Ben Mhenni maintained the Tunisian website for folk singer Emel Mathlouthi, who had translated Joan Baez's 1971 "Here's to You" into Arabic and repurposed it as a ballad commemorating Mohamed Bouazizi. "Here's to You" had memorialized the Italian American communist anarchists Sacco and Vanzetti, who were likely victims of a fraudulent prosecution in the 1920s alleging that they had killed a guard during a bank robbery. Sacco and Vanzetti and the American 1960s New Left still resonated with young Tunisians attempting to understand Bouazizi's sacrifice in the twenty-first century.

January 3 was also the day that both high school and college students began returning to campus for the new semester. Now the ability of the youth to gather, plan, and stage demonstrations formed a potent challenge to the regime. On January 4 high school students throughout the country staged public marches in sympathy with Sidi Bouzid. In Thala, in the western Kasserine province, students were said to have deliberately provoked the police with a march, receiving tear gas in response. They burned tires in the street and threw stones at the police, then they burned down the headquarters of the ruling RCD. In Redeyef, in Gafsa province in the center of the country, the students marched and chanted slogans demanding dignity and improved conditions. In Sfax students of several private educational institutes also marched. The government in Sidi Bouzid was by now wary of tangling with the students, so there were no clashes or arrests at their procession.[17] The countrywide high school student marches of January 4 were probably coordinated by local branches of the UGET via Facebook. On the same day, in what turned out to be very bad news for President Ben Ali, Mohamed Bouazizi died of his burn wounds. Five thousand attended his funeral the next day.

On January 6 the lawyers held a general strike throughout the country. They said it was in protest at the widespread attacks on them by police on December 31, when they had rallied in sympathy with the people of Sidi Bouzid. In Tunis they staged a demonstration at the courthouse. Ben Mhenni was told that the strike was successful in several parts of the country. The French press reported that 95 percent of the country's attorneys took part, though in some cases they appear to have come to court and then remained idle.[18] On the same day clashes between students and police were reported in the al-Habib district of Sfax and the al-Riyad neighborhood of Sousse. In the west, in the agricultural depot town of Tajerouine, students confronted the police. Schools were closed in Sidi Bouzid.[19]

Also on January 6 the rapper El Général was arrested again, provoking uproar among his fan base. The early-morning raid seemed ominous to him. "I thought I'd probably be killed," he recalled later to a journalist.[20] In addition, blogger Azyz Amami and his colleague Slim Amamou were arrested and held at the Interior Ministry. It was, Ben Mhenni remarked on her blog, a black day for youth activists. "I am really sick at heart," she wrote, "at seeing youth arrested just for having expressed their opinions."[21] Amami and Amamou, however, had gone further than simply expressing their views. They had formed the Pirate Party (such parties in Europe are dedicated to the free sharing of information, open access to the internet, direct democracy, and human rights) and had probably cooperated behind the scenes with the international hacking cooperative Anonymous, which had briefly taken over Tunisian government websites. They were active in sharing videos and reports on suicide cases and police brutality in Sidi Bouzid and surrounding towns and getting around the official media blackout on the protests. One contemporary squib at a pro-Pirate site noted, "The Party is also distributing in Tunisian universities and schools USB Keys and CD ROMs with installation of the TOR Software needed to circumvent the major wave of cyber censorship happening on the Tunisian Internet and to protect Tunisian Internet users from the hacking."[22] The next day the secret police kidnapped off the street Wissem Sghaier, a member of the national secretariat of the youth wing of the Progressive Democratic Party, confirming the importance of even the small oppositionist leftist parties in organizing student protests.[23]

On January 8 the regime arrested several student leaders from the General Union of Tunisian Students. Some of those detained, including Rima al-Saghrouni and Nadia Bousta, were young women, underlining their important role in student leadership and revolutionary activities. Tunisian women were crucial to the revolution and well represented in the union movement. They have a relatively high literacy rate (71 percent), represent more than 20 percent of the country's wage earners, and make up 43 percent of the nearly half-million members of eighteen local unions. Most of these unionized women work in the education, textile, health, city services, and tourism industries. The police began compiling lists of the teachers of the student troublemakers with the intention of pressuring them to rein in the students, but the Union of Secondary Teachers pushed back, roundly condemning police interference in their schools. Likewise in small towns of the center and west, students continued to agitate, and sometimes their teachers struck.[24]

Journalist Marie Kostrz interviewed a student at the University of Sousse, a two-hour drive south from Tunis: "After the resumption of classes at the beginning of January, the college and high school students took part in the revolt that has been shaking the country for several weeks. Visibly afraid of street demonstrations, the Tunisian regime surrounded the universities and high schools with anti-riot police. It forbade any demonstration in public places and any gathering in the streets."[25] The student explained that on January 8 police assaulted students at the Faculty of Letters at Sousse. They had gathered after a morning exam and wanted to stage a sit-in to protest the arrest of two student leaders of the local chapter of the UGET. The security forces stopped them from leaving the school to demonstrate in the streets. Trapped, the students attempted to break through the police barricades, which led to a violent confrontation. Police then fired tear gas and broke into the campus, chasing students down in exam halls, offices, even the infirmary. "Several dozen among them were injured, not to mention those who inhaled too much tear gas." Professors who attempted to intervene were attacked, and one was knocked out. Local branches of the UGET appear to have become increasingly radicalized since 2009, especially after the demonstrations began on December 17, 2010, and they likely played a significant role in mobilizing the youth. The assault on the University of Sousse fueled a wave of indignation and provoked a plan for a national general strike in the universities.

If the blood of martyrs waters the church, so too does it fuel revolutions. The regime presented the opposition with a whole batch of them on January 9, when its troops opened fire on protesters in Kasserine and Thala, appearing to aim high, at chests and heads. Others were killed in Erregueb in Sidi Bouzid province. Security forces were apparently angry about attacks on police stations, many of which had been burned down, in the center of the country. The number of dead was controversial; opposition websites claimed thirty-five or more killed, while the government reported fourteen dead in the three towns. [26] YouTube video surfaced of the army hunting protesters as though they were game. It was widely perceived as a massacre, and one YouTube poster referred to it as the "Falluja of Tunisia," a reference to the Bush administration's brutal reduction of an Iraqi city in 2004. Opposition leaders charged that security forces were also sniping at the funeral processions. Lina Ben Mhenni wrote, "Tonight, I went to Erregueb after hearing about clashes between demonstrators and the police and the death of several people killed shot by the police. Today 5 people were killed."[27] She named them, including a mother of three. Then she posted pictures of the cadavers and of security vehicles. Her ability as a blogger to share her citizen journalism and the gruesome photos on the internet, along with the YouTube videos uploaded by youth from the affected towns, made the massacre of Black Sunday real for the public. That same day, responding to calls from the UGTT and the UGET, thousands came out to demonstrate in the central city of Kairouan.[28]

No Jobs without Liberty

On January 10 the mood of the country was grim. The national leadership of the UGTT broke with Ben Ali and called a meeting of regional labor leaders to consider a national strike. In recent years some branches of the union, such as that grouping the university teachers and the Tunisian Labor Party, had played a more oppositional role; now the rest of the UGTT was joining them. Despite the glacial slowness with which the national organization committed to change, local UGTT activists had joined the youth protests and shared their organizing and political experience right from December. A Tunisian observer wrote, "Certainly, the local unions—notably those in the regions of Sidi Bouzid and Kasserine—and certain national unions—such as those of primary and secondary teachers, where one finds a strong presence of far-left activists—were present from the first days and attempted to give support to the young demonstrators."[29] The local branch of the UGTT called a general strike in the city of Sfax in protest against the indiscriminate use of live fire by troops in Kasserine, Thala, Erregueb, and Sidi Bouzid. Likewise Erregueb announced a general strike. Thala and Kasserine were ghost towns, the shops closed, but clashes broke out again in Kasserine, and five were said to have been shot dead by security forces, which also made arrests at the regional offices of the UGTT. Physicians there demonstrated outside the hospitals over the lack of equipment and medicine to deal with dozens of injured. A big crowd of girls and young women massed in downtown Kasserine and then marched into tear gas, confronting the security forces and daring them to open fire. It was speculated that they were the sisters, fiancées, and wives of the young men who had been killed or injured on Sunday and Monday.[30]

Also on January 10 a huge crowd marched to the RCD headquarters in Kairouan, attacking it. In Bizerte, the northernmost city in Africa and a tourist destination known for its beaches, massive student protests were held that morning in front of the Farhat Hached High School. The Progressive Democratic Party insisted that "the present government has completely lost the confidence of the people" and called for a national unity government to prepare the way for a transition to democratic elections. That evening Ben Ali went on television and promised not to run for another term as president, saying he would step down in 2014 and that Tunisia had no "president for life." He told the public, "I have understood you." He said he had issued orders to the security forces not to use live ammunition on demonstrators, and he promised an enormous jobs package. But he also castigated the protesters as terrorists and looters, angering his audience yet again.[31]

The situation continued to unravel on January 11. People were chanting, "The people want the fall of the regime." The powerful slogan references an anticolonial poem by Aboul-Qacem Echebbi (d. 1934), one of the authors of the Tunisian national anthem, which begins, "If one day the people were to want life, it would be necessary to answer fate / and it would be incumbent on night to shine and on the chains to shatter."[32] Although working-class youth from the poor quarters were the most numerous participants in the ongoing urban demonstrations, a realization had set in among many Tunisians that what had begun as a jobs protest would falter if it did not go all the way. One informant told researcher Alcinda Honwana that he had concluded that it would be no good to have "jobs and food without freedom."[33] Peaceful crowds were giving way to armed resistance fighters now that the regime had taken off the gloves. In Meknessi, in the province of Sidi Bouzid, a fierce firefight broke out between townspeople and the Brigades of Public Order. Reports of looting proliferated, as well as of false-flag sabotage and sniping by the secret police. Rumors circulated that members of the ruling family were leaving the country. In many cities that had witnessed violence, the secret police and Brigades of Public Order were withdrawn from the streets in favor of the army. It was said that the army chief of staff, Rachid Ammar, refused to allow the regular army to fire on demonstrators, for which he was in danger of being dismissed.[34] The Tunisian army was only about thirty-five thousand strong and was likely kept small by Ben Ali out of fear that it could become a political base for another ambitious officer to lead the kind of coup he himself had led. Clearly it was inadequate to restore order in a country of 10.5 million, when many of the cities were now engaged in an armed insurrection. In Paris the French minister of defense Michele Alliot-Marie offered Ben Ali help with training his police, in keeping with the general policy of the government of Nicolas Sarkozy of supporting authoritarian states in the former French colonial sphere in the name of stability.[35] As a result Alliot-Marie suffered a firestorm of protest and was ultimately sacked.

On January 12 an estimated thirty thousand protesters gathered in the center of Sfax amid a general strike. Some assembled outside the UGTT headquarters, where the local secretary-general of the union, Muhammad Sha'ban, addressed them. Security forces failed to prevent them from reaching the RCD headquarters and burning part of it. They then made themselves scarce. Observers spoke of Sfax as having the air of a "liberated city." Likewise union members in Tunis were gathered at Muhammad Ali Place and at the UGTT building, where they were under attack by police. Clashes between protesters and police went on into the night in the capital. Crowds began burning down local RCD buildings and police stations and attacking and looting mansions belonging to the Trabelsis and Ben Alis, including a branch of El Materi's so-called Islamic bank. The disturbances had spread to every corner of the country, even in southern cities such as Degache, where virtually the whole town was marching, and to Duz, known as the gateway to the Sahara. In small towns like Fériana, near Kasserine, youth burned down police stations. In Erregueb a big crowd of protesters was attacked by the secret police and ran into army lines around government buildings. The troops intervened against the police, who were firing live ammunition. The military menaced their police colleagues with their weapons and made them back off. In the capital Ben Ali fired his interior minister and his army chief of staff.[36] It was, one young man from Kasserine told a researcher, "too little too late." Washington finally spoke up, calling on Ben Ali to avoid excessive use of force.[37]

By January 13 the country was in a state of full-fledged uprising. Le Kram, a town in the west along the shore near Tunis, witnessed "an unprecedented state of violence," including attacks on the fancy homes of the elite. A few months later I was sitting in a pizzeria in Tunis, talking with the young man behind the counter. He was from Le Kram and told me about joining crowds in the streets, some of whom attacked RCD buildings. Another young man spoke to me proudly of the excitement in being in the street crowds in the capital and making history on that day, showing me how he had puffed out his chest and locked hands with other youth. He knew young people who were felled by bullets just yards away: "You never knew when it would be your turn." Some thirty-eight people died in the clashes on January 13, fourteen of them in Tunis. At last even the capital was stirring. In the far southeast, in Médenine, enraged crowds marched in mourning for Narjis Nuwayra, a slain female protester and elementary school teacher. They were protected by the army, which received verbal abuse from the police.[38]

On January 14 tens of thousands gathered in front of the Interior Ministry, responding to calls from UGTT, demanding the departure of Ben Ali. They chanted in French, *"Dégage!"* (Get out!) There were similarly huge crowds in the streets of Sousse and Sfax. The revolution had come to the capital three days before, but the appearance of masses on Habib Bourguiba Avenue and the movement on the Interior Ministry were decisive. The crowds were too large to shoot down, even if the army had wanted to take that risk, which it did not. The masses could physically endanger the officers of the state and could even surround and trap the security forces. The attack by more militant youth on a high-security prison and their release of its inmates signaled another danger. The conflict was becoming militarized, and there was danger that protesters turned guerrillas would now attack military bases and loot them for weapons, starting a civil war. That evening the army and the old political class put Ben Ali on a plane, which ended up in Jedda, Saudi Arabia, reportedly because France's president Sarkozy feared popular disturbances from Tunisian French if the deposed dictator were granted asylum in Paris.[39]

The tactics of the young protesters began with simple rallies and marches, primarily in the rural belt in the center and far west of the country. As police attempted to repress these activities, more and more of the population joined the protests. The provincial unions helped organize people. However much their top leaders might have been co-opted by the Ben Ali regime, the younger members of the rank and file quickly joined the revolution and used UGTT networks and buildings for their cause. Local branches of the Union of Secondary School Teachers and the General Union of Tunisian Students, already alienated from the government, also appear to have quickly become radicalized and to have deployed their organizational resources and access to buildings on campus for the purposes of the revolt. Lawyers and other professionals played a role in the protests, and artists and nongovernmental organizations joined in. With massive repression by the Brigades of Public Order, the protesters began fighting back by throwing stones and Molotov cocktails. Attacking buildings linked to the ruling party or the police became common, and many were burned down. The secret police appear to have retaliated against this violence by engaging in sabotage, burning down the businesses of supporters of the revolution or turning to sniping as a means of raising the cost of public dissent. (Demonstrators could never know whether a government sniper's sights might fall on them.) As order broke down and food became scarce, looting and burglary became common, and security deteriorated.

The use of live fire to kill over a dozen people at Kasserine and vicinity on January 9 appears to have rung the death knell of the regime, inspiring nationwide outrage and still more general strikes, rallies, and antigovernment violence. Dissidents deployed all the tools of youth culture to delegitimize the regime, from protest songs and YouTube videos to internet manifestoes and hilarious caricatures of the dictator. Even just assiduously reporting on the repression and publishing in the blogosphere and placing pictures of the wounded on social media stoked public indignation and steeled the youth in their growing determination to see Ben Ali gone. The movement had evolved from a rural protest against unemployment and government neglect to an urban demand for liberties and, thence, to a nationwide revolution. The constant turmoil split the Tunisian elite, with the army largely declaring neutrality or even coming into conflict with the secret police, and members of the old Bourguiba clique who had been marginalized by Ben Ali deciding that he had to go. The youth got their wish.

Egypt

I asked the veteran Egyptian human rights activist Saad Eddin Ibrahim what kind of impact the Tunisian revolution had on subsequent events in Egypt. "We never thought that it could be done. That a dictator could be chased out," he answered. "Tunisia demonstrated for us that it was possible." Likewise in an Al Jazeera interview on January 21, Egyptian blogger Wael Abbas, despite his skepticism that Egyptians could unite to effect real change, admitted that the overthrow of Ben Ali had given him renewed hope.[40] The question was the viability of a strong push for change. The grievances had piled up to the point where the Mubarak government was deeply unpopular across a wide swath of the public. Egypt, then a country of 83 million, presented challenges for mobilization very different from those that had confronted the youth in Tunisia, a much smaller country geographically with a population of only 10.5 million.

As 2010 began, the issues of police brutality and social justice continued to exercise the youth, whether working-class Ultras at the soccer stadiums or middle-class activists. In January Asmaa Mahfouz (b. 1985), cofounder of April 6, posted heartrending images of prisoners being tortured and called for a demonstration on Police Day, January 25, the day that the government had designated to honor the officers of the law. Her call went unheeded for the second year in a row. The poor and lower middle class suffered then from high bread prices, caused in part by a freak drought in Russia the previous summer that led to an export ban on that crop. The renewed hardship recalled the bread martyrs of 2008. Mixed-gender teams went regularly to bakeries to pamphleteer and to plead with them to keep bread prices affordable for the poor. "Bread, liberty and social justice" became their slogan.[41] That summer a major riot broke out between soccer fanatics and police in Cairo. The Ultra movement in Egypt, modeled on that in Italy, had taken root among youth around 2007. When police stepped into the middle of a fight between fans of rival teams, the Ultras clashed with the police, leaving several on each side wounded. Ultras had begun forming a very negative view of the Mubarak regime.[42]

Just as the suicide of Mohamed Bouazizi played a key symbolic role for Tunisian youth, those in Egypt were galvanized by the case of Khaled Said. His father had died when Said was young, and as a teenager he became very interested in computers and music, studying for a while in the United States. He was arrested in an internet café in Alexandria on June 6, 2011, and beaten to death outside. Rumors swirled that he had a damaging file on his flash drive on police corruption, perhaps video of a drug sale, though some researchers doubted this. In some ways it is a more lugubrious story if he did not, for that would make him the victim of mindless police brutality. The authorities attempted to spread the rumor that he had not died from the beating but from choking on a packet of drugs he was trying to swallow, hiding the evidence, but the picture of his battered face that later emerged left little room for doubt as to what had happened. For Egyptian youth, the important point was that he had done nothing to deserve being killed and had been given no judicial process. His treatment was, in their view, made possible by the Draconian Emergency Law of 1981, put into effect by Mubarak after the assassination of Sadat, which suspended the few civil liberties in the constitution. The outpouring of grief also reflected the everyday practices of police surveillance and brutality toward young people in Egypt's urban quarters. On the family's visit to the morgue, his brother took a picture of Said's battered face and posted it to the internet.[43]

The dissident internet activists across the political spectrum took up Khaled Said's cause. The framework for understanding his death as a result of the quotidian practices of Mubarak's police had been made familiar by the work of Wael Abbas, Nael Atef, and other bloggers who exposed prison torture. Some youth made Said's battered death mask their Facebook profile photo. A Google marketing manager then in Dubai who had Muslim religious commitments, Wael Ghonim (b. 1980), created the Facebook page "We are all Khaled Said" on June 10, which attracted tens of thousands of "likes." As with Mohamed Bouazizi in Tunisia, Khaled Said served as an important symbol for the youth of the ways the regime repressed them and blocked their aspirations.

Ghonim's background at Google gave him advantages in managing the Said page. He assembled a team of three other administrators: a prominent young blogger who earlier had been a member of the Muslim Brotherhood, Abdel Rahman Mansour; an Egyptian American activist, Nadine Wahab; and a liberal blogger, Mustafa Al Najjar. The latter two were connected to presidential aspirant Mohamed ElBaradei. They ran the site as an arena where followers could get to know and network with one another. This interactivity distinguished it from the relatively static blog sites of earlier years. Ghonim also gave the Facebook page a clear and consistent practical focus on ending torture and police brutality, as well as protesting corruption and unemployment. The page demanded the abrogation of the 1981 Emergency Law, the removal of the minister of the interior, limiting presidential terms to two, and a war on poverty. Ghonim attempted to keep the tone nonpolitical and did not want the page used as a vehicle for attacking Mubarak as opposed to achieving the more abstract policy goals on which he was focusing.[44]

By late 2010 there were some 4 million Facebook users in Egypt (the company had begun facilitating Arabic-language pages in 2009), and the ease with which items could be shared and promoted or "liked" made it an ideal networking tool for urban, literate youth. Dissident Facebook pages acted as a clearinghouse for contact information, including telephone numbers of activists. Forms of e-government emerged, with members sometimes voting on issues.[45]

The democratic character of discussions on the Said page allowed suggestions to bubble up from the grassroots and sometimes pushed the administrators in new directions. Commenters suggested that the site could be used to stage demonstrations in the real world or to call for a flash mob (when social media are used to assemble people on short notice in a public place), something that had not occurred to the administrators. A careful trial run was conducted in late June along the Alexandria sea road (Corniche), where the one hundred participants were instructed to keep five feet away from one another so as not to fall into the legal category of an illicit public gathering.[46]

The administrators wanted to avoid sectarian politics, and although they had warm relations with the April 6 youth movement and the ElBaradei campaign, they initially wanted to avoid being branded as merely political. Over time, however, Ghonim acted jointly with the other dissidents to make political statements. On November 26, 2010, the day of the parliamentary elections, all three groups jointly called for demonstrations and asked for their supporters to write in "Khaled Said" on their ballots. The protest call had only a limited response, but the exercise was good practice in coordination between the cyber activists and the grassroots organizations. The outcome of these elections was widely seen as an announcement that the government would do as it pleased without the slightest regard for public opinion. The fixed ballots came back overwhelmingly for the National Democratic Party, virtually erasing the gains of the Muslim Brotherhood and the small parties linked to Kefaya in 2005. Video of police stuffing the ballots went viral on the internet. 'Abd al-Rahman Yusuf (b. 1970) is the third son of the Muslim Brotherhood televangelist Yusuf al-Qaradawi (who has a perch on Al Jazeera), but he broke with his father and became a liberal, working for Mohamed ElBaradei. He wrote in his memoir of the revolution that the aftermath of the fixed election was the low point for activists, the moment of "deepest despair, that is, when the majority of activists and perhaps the majority of Egyptians felt that there was no hope for change or reform in the near term."[47] The message—that authoritarianism was being reinforced and that any earlier movement toward pluralism was a mirage—was received loud and clear by the public.

The year 2011 began badly for the Mubarak regime. On New Year's Day, as the faithful were issuing from the Saint's Church in Alexandria after a special Saturday service, an enormous car bomb went off that killed twenty-four and injured nearly a hundred. Christians immediately gathered to protest, and more demonstrations were held on Sunday in Alexandria, Cairo, Asyut, and elsewhere. Some Coptic Christians and leftists believed that the bombing was a false-flag operation of the state security forces to justify the regime's continued harsh police state. At the very least Christians felt that the Mubarak state was not exerting itself to protect them. Four thousand Christian demonstrators rallied in the slum of Shubra, where over half the population is Christian, with some marching to downtown Cairo. They were joined by supportive Muslims and some politicians. The crowds demanded the removal of Interior Minister Habib Al-Adly, either for not having done his job in forestalling the bombing or for being implicated in it.[48] Hostility to Al-Adly united poor and middle-class Christians with the New Left dissidents, who then aligned, ironically enough, with the Muslim Brotherhood. Copts, some 10 percent of the Egyptian population, had for the most part been neutral toward or supportive of the Mubarak government because they feared the Brotherhood, whose members openly called for making Egypt's Christians second-class citizens. However, the Mubarak regime's attempts to mollify the Brotherhood by making gradual nods to Muslim law and practice, and its inability or unwillingness to protect Copts began to sour relations as the century unfolded. Coptic youth, like Egyptian youth more generally, were shocked by the evidence of systematic police torture posted to the internet by activists such as Wael Abbas. Some Copts, moreover, were ideologically on the left and joined the dissident human rights networks. Kefaya itself had been founded by an Egyptian Christian.

Asmaa Mahfouz of April 6 again promoted the idea of a demonstration on Police Day, January 25, against torture practices, and this time the ElBaradei campaign and the Khaled Said Facebook administrators were onboard. Not only was the date symbolic, but that police were excused from work on that day made it a protester's ideal moment to come out. On January 19 Mahfouz uploaded to her Facebook page and to YouTube an impassioned plea for all those who cared about the human dignity of Egyptians to come out on the 25th.[49] She noted that Egyptian youth were now setting themselves on fire and that the Tunisians had showed the way forward. Egypt could also "be a country of liberty, a country in which there is justice, and a country in which there is dignity." She tried to shame her audience, pointing out that she was able to get only three others to come to an earlier demonstration, and the four of them were quickly surrounded by the state security police and taken off to be intimidated. She urged Egyptians to put away their fear and to take to the streets with their family and friends. She even appealed to the manhood of the young, saying that they should come to protect her and other young women from government thugs. It was not important, she allowed, that everyone come downtown. It would be enough to come out on the streets anywhere and tell others about the government practices of repression. The powerful video went viral. Cyberspace was enabling female leadership, since there were few public spaces where Mahfouz could have gotten a similar hearing. (Both in Egypt and

Tunisia about a third of Twitter conversations about the revolutions were by women.)[50]

The call was supported by the "We are all Khaled Said" Facebook page administrators, Kefaya, the Tomorrow Party, the youth wing of the liberal Democratic Front Party, the Freedom and Justice Movement of the Muslim Brotherhood, the leftist Popular Democratic Movement for Change (Hashd), the Free People's Front, two campaigns supporting the liberal ElBaradei, and the Nasserist Hamdeen Sabahi's Karam Party youth wing. Whereas the Muslim Brotherhood's top leadership was more or less neutral, the hard-line fundamentalist Salafis firmly rejected the idea of participating.

Although many in the military establishment supported a conspiracy theory that the Brotherhood had been behind the revolution, and liberals later tried to attribute it to semi-establishment figures such as ElBaradei, the fact is that the revolution was a loose network of youth activists, and no one would be in control of the resulting grassroots process.[51]

The thirty-year-old Ahmed Maher of April 6 explained that the Tunisian success inspired the youth to demonstrate on Police Day rather than simply ridiculing the police for their repressive tactics. Their initial goal was the resignation of Interior Minister Habib Al-Adly. Although a whole range of Facebook pages and blogs supported the plan for a January 25 rally, including Ghonim and the "We are all Khaled Said" group, the tradition of face-to-face meetings and street campaigning was more important. April 6 distributed twenty thousand leaflets summoning people to Tahrir Square, and also made sure to tell as many taxi drivers as possible, since they functioned as key spreaders of information. Coffee shops and soccer stadiums were also employed as information exchanges, and the Muslim religious activists used mosques. Kefaya and the ElBaradei campaign used their mailing lists from activists who had gone door to door and kept records of which residents had welcomed them. These street resources were now deployed in an attempt to ensure that the protest did not fizzle out. According to Ziyad Alimi, a member of ElBaradei's youth campaign, on January 23 and 24 the activists fanned out through neighborhoods such as Bulaq and al-Abbasia, distributing thousands of pamphlets urging people to assemble on Tuesday morning and then march to Tahrir Square.[52]

January 25

Crowds in Tahrir Square began small on January 25.[53] A young person who was there told me that at midmorning she was worried that the event would fall short. Then, shortly before noon, a large procession of youth from the Shubra slum crossed the bridge and headed for the square. She remembered seeing the crosses around the throats of some of the young women glinting in the sun, signaling that some of the Christians of Shubra were joining the revolution. Four or five hundred youth came from al-Haith Mosque, loudly chanting slogans as they proceeded. "Their role," a Muslim Brotherhood youth leader later explained, "was not only to call out slogans but also to talk with people and to encourage them to join the demonstration."[54] One of the April 6 activists told me that shouting slogans, which were then picked up and passed on to others, was much more important to the revolution than social media. The activists had sent messages they knew would be intercepted by state security police, directing them to the wrong parts of town. In accordance with a plan put forward by Ahmed Maher of April 6, people also initially gathered in several different lower-middle- and working-class parts of the city and launched marches so that the police could not stop them by closing one or two major arteries. Wael Ghonim texted Maher that he feared many activists had gotten lost, and Maher replied that if they were lost, so were the security police.[55]

The youth wing of the ElBaradei campaign gathered at coffeehouses, where they received instructions to assemble in front of the Physicians Guild building, where they eventually numbered in the hundreds—almost all very young. The police tried to throw up a cordon around them, but the youth broke through it, suffering some casualties and meeting more police resistance before streaming successfully into Tahrir Square. The throng there burgeoned to perhaps ten thousand. People went wild with each new wave of entrants, and those who arrived wept at seeing the enormous turnout. 'Abd al-Rahman Yusuf of the ElBaradei campaign marveled at the class diversity, with students, workers, and peasants all mingling. He began arranging for loudspeakers, since the first-time demonstrators had no idea what to do next and needed instructions. Crowds chanted, "Mubarak, Mubarak, Saudi Arabia awaits you!" in reference to the exile of Tunisia's

Ben Ali. Thousands ominously chanted, "The people want the fall of the regime." They demanded the dissolution of Parliament, given that the November 26 election had been a fraud. They demanded an end to hunger, poverty, unemployment, inflation, rising rents, and the looting of public wealth. They intoned the mantra of the movement: "Bread, liberty and social justice!" Hundreds pitched tents or rolled out sleeping bags, determined to stay in the square all night.

The police responded with heavy use of tear gas, pushing most of the protesters out of the square onto side streets after midnight. Activists reported that "the youth took out jars of vinegar, and onions, and open cans of Pepsi," having been told by Tunisian internet activists that these were ways of fighting the effects of the tear gas. As they retreated in the middle of the night, the youth continued to chant loudly, shaming their neighbors for not joining them and calling on them to come to the next demonstration.[56]

Another demonstration was held at Nahda Square in Giza. Mustafa Rizq (b. 1984), an Arabic literature major, recalled, "Spontaneously, we formed lines: Lines to treat those coming from the front, lines to wash faces burned by smoke with vinegar and cola, lines successively confronting police administering beatings, and lines on Giza bridge. The war lasted more than three hours of continuous tear gas volleys, but in the end we took the square."[57] Less-reported and much smaller protests were also held in Alexandria, Suez, Ismailia, El Mahalla El Kubra, Asyut, and other towns, despite Ahmed Maher's decision to focus solely on Cairo. In Alexandria, Ahmad 'Ali remembered getting up the courage to demonstrate by watching the film *V for Vendetta* for a second time. (The 2005 film tells the story of a futuristic revolutionary in London.) In Alexandria thousands of protesters marched to a city square demanding the fall of the regime. They walked at sunset to Khalid b. Walid Avenue, despite the futile attempt of police to stop them. In the Delta city of Mansoura three thousand young protesters went to Mash'al Square and demanded that Interior Minister Al-Adly be put on trial and that Mubarak leave. The activists in the crowd chanted, "Peacefully, peacefully," despite the passions against the state.[58] In Suez activist circles sent news to a website in liberated Tunisia that a big crowd in the central square clashed with police, who used tear gas and rubber bullets to chase them into side streets. The report said one young person, Mustafa Ragab Mahmoud, was killed, the first martyr of the revolution, and about one hundred were wounded and dozens arrested.[59]

The April 6, ElBaradei, and youth Muslim Brotherhood street networks were more effective than the internet in getting people to assemble: a poll done soon after the revolution of 1,200 participants in Cairo's Tahrir Square found that about half of them first heard of the rally through face-to-face interactions with other youth.[60] Another eighth or so found out by telephone. About a quarter said they first heard about the protest via Facebook. The mean age of participants was twenty-nine; women were on average a few years younger than men (likely because women older than twenty-six were most often married and with young children, and the teenagers and early twenty-somethings had more freedom of movement). About a quarter of the protesters were women. Youth of both sexes who came out for the demonstrations were disproportionately well-educated, with 70 percent having at least a bachelor's degree (10 percent had higher degrees). About 80 percent of the protesters had internet connections at home; the women were even more wired than the men. In another study, of a representative sample of 3,500 Egyptians, Mansoor Moaddel found that those who said they participated in demonstrations against Mubarak most actively were newspaper readers, lived in cities, and used the internet a great deal. They were disproportionately likely to consider themselves not very religious.[61] Tahrir was in the main the work of recent college graduates who were unemployed or otherwise stymied by Mubarak's policies. It functioned as a sort of "mother square," a demonstration project emulated in city squares all over the country by provincial youth who were sometimes quite different from the activists in the center of the capital—more tied to the opposition parties, including the Muslim Brotherhood, and less oriented toward the internet.

The Ministry of the Interior mobilized in downtown Cairo to clear the square near midnight, deploying water cannons and tear gas, and security forces attempted to chase away the crowds into Wednesday morning. Hundreds were arrested. Demonstrations continued on a smaller scale throughout the country on Wednesday and Thursday, with some activists attacking police stations. The military responded to large demonstrations in Suez, where six protesters had been killed, by cordoning off the city and cutting off its roads and communications.[62] A coordinating committee of the major youth groups met daily and called for another big demonstration on Friday, which they termed a "Day of Wrath." Ahmed Maher explained, "There was a daily meeting of the ten-person committee formed by the coalition to discuss means of escalating the protests and alerting those participating in the sit-in of our decisions, via broadcast by the revolutionary youth and our activists spread around the square."[63] In Washington an alarmed vice president Joe Biden told *PBS NewsHour* that he wouldn't refer to Mubarak as a dictator and that Egypt's protests were not like those in Eastern Europe before 1989, showing the reluctance of the Obama administration to let go of a regime key to the American Middle East policy of security for Israel and for oil and gas exports.

For mosque-going Muslims, Fridays are prime days for demonstrations since, after the prayer ceremony, the big crowds are available to assemble for other purposes. The youth attempted to capitalize on mosque attendance by calling on worshippers to go to the streets after the ceremony. The Mubarak regime wanted to prevent the Friday protests from being effective, and that morning it cut off wireless telephone and internet service. Activists told me when I was in Egypt a few months later that the move backfired on the regime. Those supportive youth who ordinarily would have followed the demonstrations on the internet or via SMS messages from friends suddenly could not find out what was happening. Many of them became concerned about the welfare of friends or relatives; they went to Tahrir Square and other rally venues in order to see the unfolding events with their own eyes. As a result the mass of protesters swelled beyond what had been achieved the previous Tuesday. Muslim Brotherhood youth interpreted their leadership's neutrality on the issue as permission to go to the square, thus increasing the numbers from that quarter. Ahmad Rami, a Muslim Brotherhood youth, later told the press that the Brothers "were not participating as a group and had no explicit instructions from the leadership."[64] He said that no more than 15 percent of those in the square identified with the organization but that "the Brotherhood has generally become more open to the society in the recent period," leading to a decline in the number of Muslim Brothers in Egypt.

The youth leaders were committed to using peaceful tactics. Despite the regime's brutal response, killing over nine hundred protesters during the course of the revolution, the crowds remained relatively nonviolent, except when responding to police attacks. Some demonstrators did attack buildings, setting fire to police stations and the headquarters of the National Democratic Party, and rank-and-file protesters sometimes turned violent. 'Abd al-Rahman Yusuf described an incident in which dissidents started throwing stones at police; other protesters inserted themselves in front of them, forming a human wall and chanting "Peacefully, peacefully!" The sources of the commitment to nonviolence seem to have been more practical than ideological. Nonviolent opposition is an appeal for public support and deprives the regime of key tactical and ideological advantages, making it absurd to call the dissidents "terrorists" and depriving security forces of the opportunity to deploy formal counterterrorism techniques. (Remember too that al-Gama'a al-Islamiyya and al-Qaeda had delegitimized for most Egyptians the use of violence and terrorism in what they viewed as a just cause.) For some, peace was a commitment. Wael Ghonim was influenced by Gandhi's writings on nonviolent noncooperation and says that many commentators at the "We are all Khaled Said" Facebook page quoted the Indian activist. His circle encouraged people to watch the 1982 film *Gandhi*. Others distributed two thousand copies of Dalia Ziadeh's translation of a comic book about Martin Luther King Jr. or spontaneously translated some of his speeches in an appeal to the success of the civil rights movement in the United States in the 1960s. Some activists had also read the democracy theorist Gene Sharp on pacific popular revolutions and were aware of the trap of being forced by the regime into military confrontation. I asked Ahmed Maher about the origins of this commitment to peace. He pointed to indigenous traditions, saying that the youth learned from history (for instance, the 1919 Wafd rallies against British colonial rule) and from older activists who had been involved in earlier protest movements, such as the 1972 student movement, that peaceful methods were more effective.[65]

At the end of the day, Interior Minister Al-Adly ordered the police to use deadly force to disperse the youth, despite their commitment to nonviolence. The activists fought them off at Qasr al-Nil Bridge and on the side streets leading into Tahrir Square, abandoning for the moment their commitment to peace. When the smoke cleared, the massive crowd decisively controlled the public space of Tahrir and did not surrender it until Mubarak was gone.[66]

There were other sites of protest in the capital on that Friday as well; crowds were protesting in the street in al-Abbasia, Ramsis, Bulaq, and elsewhere. In the al-Husayn district of Cairo near al-Azhar Seminary, crowds spilled onto the street after Friday prayers, chanting for the fall of the regime and demanding revenge for the martyrs who had fallen in Suez. They likely included many Muslim Brotherhood youth who ignored the numerous clerical authorities who had declared the protests illicit and asked them to obey the duly constituted authority. As in Tahrir, those marching at al-Husayn were subjected to tear-gas barrages by the police. Mubarak ordered the army into the streets and declared a curfew from 6 p.m. until 7 a.m. Nevertheless many youth activists defiantly pitched tents in Tahrir Square, creating a protest village that persisted through time. In a blow to the revolution, Wael Ghonim was tracked down and arrested and kept incommunicado for over a week.[67]

For understandable reasons, many accounts of the events in Egypt focus on Tahrir Square in Cairo, but the revolution unfolded in midsize and small cities up and down the Nile, and the cumulative effect of the regime's gradual loss of control in such economically crucial centers contributed to its success. Official radio stations assured their listeners that there was only a small crowd in downtown Cairo and that most of the country was unaffected. In reality, in Alexandria, the country's second-largest city, tens of thousands poured into the streets and prominent squares, chanting against torture and fighting with the security forces, which failed to disperse them. The pro-Mubarak elements in Alexandria were a small minority, and the city more or less threw them off, despite occasional later clashes or futile attempts at reassertion. In Suez the demonstrations began in the morning, with participants assembled by opposition parties. After Friday prayers the dissidents marched to the governor's headquarters and clashed with police, who tried to deploy armored vehicles against them. The crowd burned many of these vehicles. Some then attacked and set fire to police stations. Ultimately the police withdrew to the outskirts of the city, which the activists declared "liberated." An estimated twenty-five thousand demonstrated in

Port Said, many after Friday prayers, tearing down large posters of Mubarak and chanting, "The people want the fall of the regime." At the head of the march were two former members of Parliament from the Muslim Brotherhood. Aside from a small military base in the Canal Zone, that area of northeast Egypt became virtually an independent republic. In Mansoura in the Delta the April 6 youth and the Muslim Brotherhood, among other groups, organized protests in front of the provincial governor's offices. Police attacked with tear gas and rubber bullets, and the crowd responded by throwing stones. Dozens were injured. Similar scenes were enacted in Delta cities such as Tanta and Damietta. In al-Qawsiya, in Asyut province, a former Muslim Brotherhood member of Parliament led chanting crowds after Friday prayers. In downtown Cairo an angry crowd torched the headquarters of the National Democratic Party near the Egyptian National Museum, its burned-out hulk thereafter looming ominously over Tahrir Square. The same fate overtook the party headquarters in the Mediterranean city of Damietta. Crowds attacked the party centers in several cities that day. The situation was spinning out of control.[68]

The next day Mubarak fired his prime minister and brought in Aviation Minister Ahmed Shafiq, a former air force general, as the new head of government. He also appointed General Omar Suleiman, the former head of military intelligence, as his vice president. Suleiman had led the opposition within the officer corps to Gamal Mubarak's succeeding his father, and the president may have been attempting to rally the army behind the regime by indicating that another officer would come to power after him. Men whom the activists believed were regime thugs fanned out to engage in looting and violence, attacking a number of malls. The theory was that the government was attempting to signal to the propertied classes that they should support Mubarak or risk expropriation.

That weekend oppositionists freed prisoners at Wadi Natroun, including Muslim Brotherhood leaders such as Mohamed Morsi, Essam el-Erian, and Saad al-Katatni and three dozen others. El-Erian was the leader of the reform youth wing of the Brotherhood and favored participation in the demonstrations.[69] Also over the weekend the ElBaradei camp issued pamphlets calling for rallies on Friday, February 4, which they termed the "Friday of Departure" for the president, and also asked the military to declare its position on the protests. On the last day of January, Army Chief of Staff Sami Anan went on television and declared that the army would never use violence on the Egyptian people.[70]

The youth had called for Tuesday, February 1, to be the first million-person rally in Tahrir Square and throughout the country, demanding that Mubarak step down. The sound of the 1960s pop singer Shadia's hit, "Egypt My Love," blared from automobiles, and young women painted the Egyptian flag on their faces. Crowds waved the flag. Internet access was restored. People in downtown Cairo stood in long lines to get past the informal security checkpoints the popular committees and the Ultra soccer enthusiasts had set up with volunteers around Tahrir and other squares. The crowd in Tahrir was so enormous it was hard to move around. Soldiers supporting the crowd changed into civvies or into the uniforms of the Special Forces to mark themselves out from pro-Mubarak infiltrators, and the crowd chanted, "The people and the army are one hand!" The popular actor Khalid al-Nabawi (b. 1966) climbed a parapet and led the crowd in the chant "We're not leaving, he should leave!" A culture of sharing and conviviality developed among the youth who had begun living in the square, sleeping on sidewalks or in pup tents, sharing small meals provided by taking up collections or by wealthy supporters of the demonstrators. The poetry readings, music, and impassioned speeches from the impromptu stages contributed to keeping the crowds energized. It was in some ways a much more serious and entirely urban version of the 1969 Woodstock festival that came to symbolize the 1960s counterculture in the United States.[71]

In Alexandria the crowds were even larger than in Cairo. It may have been the biggest set of national demonstrations to that date in the country's history. The independent press showed greater and greater courage in reporting the events without much self-censorship, even as the pro-Mubarak official press became more and more strident in insisting that masses were rallying *for* the president and that the youth in Tahrir Square had mainly come down for Kentucky Fried Chicken. (The one KFC outlet there was closed for the duration.) As Ben Ali had done in Tunisia, that evening Mubarak pledged not to run for another term.[72] A counterdemonstration by his supporters was held in the upscale Mohandiseen neighborhood, which later allegedly turned violent. It was a harbinger of tragedy to come.

The Day of the Camel

Mubarak's offer to step down split the country even more sharply, since some of the less committed protesters felt that enough had been achieved to allow them to go home. At the same time, the success of the million-person demonstration, just after the withdrawal of the army from the fray, seems clearly to have struck terror in the hearts of the Mubarak clique. The next morning, February 2, a pro-Mubarak crowd set off from Mohandiseen, intending to walk to Tahrir Square, with all the potential for a clash implied in that plan. Employees of public companies were forced to stage pro-Mubarak rallies. The activists got frantic messages on their phones from loved ones pleading with them to accept their partial victory and depart, but the youth in the square were adamant that they would remain until the president had resigned. Mubarak backers and hired thugs arrived at length at Tahrir, some of them transported in minivans, and mounted an attack on the young demonstrators, aided by angry, unemployed tour guides from the Pyramids whose tourist trade had collapsed. Some brought their camels and rode into the crowd, trampling the demonstrators, in what became known as the "Day of the Camel." The youth organized themselves for self-defense, in which the Ultras played an important role. They were also helped by old-timers from the Muslim Brotherhood experienced in standing up to Mubarak's police, who instructed some to form rock-throwing vanguards while others gathered the rocks or guarded the flanks. The two sides also deployed Molotov cocktails against one another. What were essentially field clinics were set up around the square to treat the wounded. Around 6 p.m. snipers on rooftops started firing into the crowd, killing three or four activists. Nevertheless youth streamed defiantly into the square that evening, assembling in huge numbers. The fighting in the streets was mirrored on the restored internet, with flame wars on Facebook between pro- and anti-Mubarak citizens. The military declined to side with the thugs and, indeed, helped curb them. At length the revolutionaries in the square prevailed.[73]

In Alexandria some thirty thousand demonstrators came out in solidarity with the youth in Tahrir Square and chanted for Mubarak to be tried for the deaths and injuries there, which were being broadcast on satellite television stations and on the internet. The regime's plans for a pro-Mubarak counterdemonstration fizzled in that city, which was no longer in the hands of the government.[74] Similar routs were staged in some provincial cities, such as Zaqaziq in al-Sharqiya in the Delta, where thousands rallied in the central square against the regime, forcing the handful of pro-regime protesters and police to leave the scene.[75]

On Thursday, February 3, it became clear that the thuggish tactics had failed to cow the people as activists streamed to Tahrir Square in preparation for a planned Friday mass event in which various factions would join in afternoon prayers. Organized youth groups continued to be important to the demonstrations. Several of the youth leaders met with Mohamed ElBaradei in Giza that afternoon, including those from April 6 and representatives of the far left and the Muslim Brotherhood. Since for decades the Mubarak clique had attempted to make the case that there was no alternative to him, latent presidential candidates such as ElBaradei and former foreign minister and Arab League secretary-general Amr Moussa played an important role in shattering that illusion. The ElBaradei campaigner 'Abd al-Rahman Yusuf reported that one of the socialists claimed that they dominated the Square. Indeed each of the factions claimed leadership and a majority following. Yusuf spoke last, insisting that the crowds in Tahrir had no leadership and were not ideologically united. He advocated keeping up the pressure but saw nothing wrong with talking to the regime if it might help usher Mubarak out. After the meeting the regime arrested six of the April 6 representatives. April 6 was exploring ways of taking the protests to the next level, including long-lasting occupations of big city squares all around the country, promoting widespread civil disobedience, and encouraging general strikes by labor. Ahmed Maher explained, "We stayed in contact with many labor sectors, who had protested earlier, to encourage them to join the sit-in in their factories. We had no authority over them, but we wanted to apply some more pressure." Oddly enough, Maher later denied that the workers had played a central role in the revolution, perhaps eager to ensure that the credit for it remained with the youth organizations.[76]

Nor were the masses in downtown Cairo Mubarak's only headache. In Alexandria there were dueling demonstrations by supporters of the National Democratic Party in some parts of the city and by oppositionist Muslim Brothers at Qaed Ibrahim Square. While the crowds in Tahrir were disproportionately secular, in the provinces the Muslim Brotherhood played an important role. In Kafr Sheikh in the north, Muslim Brotherhood demonstrators clashed with pro-Mubarak groups. Anti-Mubarak demonstrations continued on Thursday in Mansoura in the Delta, where five thousand dissidents and Muslim Brothers came out for rallies. In Suez three thousand oppositionists, including Muslim Brothers, joined the protests. In Asyut in Upper Egypt, four thousand persons demonstrated, as did a similar number in El Minya. Thousands also came out in El Arish, in the northern Sinai. About a hundred pro-Mubarak forces attempted to attack the demonstrators in El Arish, but the army stopped them.[77]

On February 4 tens of thousands gathered at Tahrir Square for the "Friday of Departure." Protesters prayed Friday prayers and even ordinary prayers jointly. Since worshippers are vulnerable while prostrating for prayer, Coptic Christian youth organized to protect their Muslim colleagues. Thousands of demonstrators had been camping out in the square at night in tents to avoid giving police an opening to clear it. They were protected by squads of Ultras, who manned barricades around the square. There were large demonstrations all over the country on February 4, especially in Alexandria. By this time Alexandria had chased away the security police and was a liberated city, and the gatherings along the seaside road were for the most part celebratory and supportive rather than contentious.

That weekend Muslims and Christians gathered in Tahrir Square to pray for the martyrs. Each group performed the rites of their own religion, but members of both stayed throughout in a show of unity. President Obama put public pressure on Mubarak to make an orderly transition, which appears not to have been very effective, although anti-American rhetoric and graffiti in Tahrir Square were reduced.[78] On Sunday the demonstrators expanded and formalized the coalition organization representing the youth of the January 25 revolution. They comprised April 6, the youth wing of Freedom and Justice (the Muslim Brotherhood civil party), members of the ElBaradei campaign, the youth of the leftist Democratic Front Party, as well as independents. They formed a steering committee with twenty members, each representing one of the youth organizations, and demanded that former cabinet members and high officials (many of whom Mubarak had dropped with alacrity by then) be tried and their accounts frozen. They also insisted on a massive jobs program for the young people. The demonstrators in downtown Cairo were still amounting to tens of thousands a day, many of them living in that postmodern village.[79]

By Monday the country was teetering on the edge of civil war, and security had deeply deteriorated. Looting had broken out, and hundreds were dead. Many Egyptians, tired of the disruptions and satisfied with the changes Mubarak had made and the ones he was promising, were losing their enthusiasm. The Muslim Brotherhood was negotiating with the regime. In contrast, activists in Tahrir raised a banner declaring, "No negotiation, no representation, until after [Mubarak's] departure; no rulers, no Muslim Brotherhood—that's the demand in the Square!"[80] On the evening of February 7 the popular channel Dream TV hosted Wael Ghonim, just released from prison (where he had been beaten and abused), on its 10 p.m. magazine show hosted by Mona Shazly. Shazly allowed him to tell his story and to argue that the accusations against him, of being a spy and a traitor, were outrageous.[81] However, the director of the show abruptly put up a slide show of youth killed in the rebellion and told Shazly to ask Ghonim if it had been worth their lives. Ghonim had been in prison during the most violent days of repression and had not absorbed the magnitude of the hundreds of young victims lost. The faces, mostly of college students full of promise, had audiences weeping. Ghonim himself broke down and fled the set. Doubts beset the movement.

The next morning, having recovered his nerve, Ghonim went to Tahrir Square. Khaled Said's mother was there, and she hugged him and told him, "My son did not die. You are my son Khaled." He then mounted one of the stages at the square. The crowd chanted his name, but he asked them not to, in keeping with the youth movement's stress on egalitarian networking rather than leaders. The Interior Ministry had pressured him before they released him to give up the demand that Mubarak go, and some in the square were fearful he might abandon them, as some of the country seemed to be doing. He did not. Ghonim affirmed that his demands were those of Tahrir Square and that the president must step down. After his uncertain performance on television, Ahmed Maher had begged him to insist on the dictator's departure.[82]

If there had been any question after Ghonim's moment of doubt that the youth would show up for yet another big rally on Tuesday, February 8, it was soon answered. Journalist Muhammad al-Shamma', an eyewitness, wrote, "That day was the fourth million-person gathering, and I believe that the numbers exceeded a million. All the roads leading to Tahrir Square were jammed with demonstrators." It did not seem to him that the regime would get away with just making some concessions.[83] Elsewhere in Cairo demonstrators massed in front of Parliament and other official buildings and shut down the government. Workers' strikes spread. The newly established Egyptian Federation of Independent Trade Unions called a general strike. One newspaper estimated that by that Tuesday some 300,000 workers had mounted protests in sixty work sites in nine of Egypt's governorates. There were fifteen strikes in Suez, eleven in Alexandria, and thirty-five in factories and companies in Cairo. Rail workers had brought rail traffic to a halt. Hospital workers were on strike in a number of medical facilities throughout the country. Ismailia's longshoremen were on strike. Workers were staging sit-ins at factories in Suez and Alexandria. Most of these workers had announced their solidarity with the "Revolution of Wrath," which was demanding better wages, trials of corrupt officials, stable employment, and better health care. It should be remembered that about a fifth of these wage earners were women, and some women took the lead on calling strikes and walkouts. The workers pledged to continue their labor actions until the revolution's demands were met.[84] In Port Said three thousand oppositionists attacked the governor's limousine and set fire to his offices. An estimated fifty thousand demonstrators marched in circles through downtown Mansoura that evening, organized by the civil parties and the Muslim Brotherhood. They demanded Mubarak's resignation and bore placards saying, "Yes to freedom!" In the south of the country, hundreds gathered at Culture Square in Sohag to declare their solidarity with the youth at Tahrir. In Cairo the youth launched an appeal for each Egyptian to buy shares worth 100 pounds (about U.S. $20) in the stock market to prevent its collapse.[85]

On Wednesday, February 9, demonstrations continued in Cairo and broke out in a wide range of provincial cities and towns. In Tahrir Square the youth called for a 10-million-strong nationwide rally on Friday. Thousands of medical students from all over the country gathered at the Qasr al-

'Ayni Medical School near the square and then marched to Parliament in a carefully planned and orchestrated intervention on behalf of the protesters. In general it is difficult to find evidence that student unions played the kind of role in Egypt that the UGET did in Tunisia, but this massive rally and procession clearly show organization at a national level. At Cairo University five thousand adjuncts demonstrated at al-Shahid Square in front of the campus, demanding permanent positions and better pay and reminding the country of the underemployment and unemployment of educated youth.[86] Thousands of members of the Cinema Guild demonstrated at Talaat Harb Square, a few blocks from Tahrir, in support of the demands of the youth, especially Mubarak's resignation. (Cinema people were mostly leftists and pro-revolution, while television news people had been carefully vetted by the regime and to the last reported sympathetically on Mubarak.)[87] In the port of Ismailia along the Suez Canal, Youth for Change founded the January 25 Revolution Coalition, which included members of April 6, youth wings of opposition parties, the Muslim Brotherhood, and the National Association for Change. They declined negotiations with any government official and stood firm behind the demands that the regime must fall, Mubarak must go, and Parliament must be dissolved. They complained that the Mubarak-appointed governor of Ismailia was attempting to defame their movement and to divide and rule them. The model of a broad coalition of youth organizations was spreading to provincial cities.[88]

Also on Wednesday petroleum and gasoline workers demonstrated for the third day in front of their ministry, insisting that they be given regularized positions and that the minister of petroleum, Samih Fahmi, step down. They threatened to "go to Tahrir" if their demands were not met.[89] The workers at the steel factory in Suez had occupied their facilities and gone on strike as early as January 29, and all along the blue-collar workers had shown support to the youth. Now they demanded raises and better working conditions, just as many of the youth had called for. Journalists rebelled against the head of their syndicate, Makram Muhammad Ahmad, over his denunciation of the protest movement, staging a demonstration at the Journalists Syndicate building. Youth working for the state-owned *al-Ahram* newspaper issued their own "Youth of Tahrir" supplement, rejecting the editorial line of their editor in chief. In the Delta town of Kafr Sheikh, thousands attacked the governor's offices and burned the latter down along with the government labor offices.[90]

In Asyut, in the south, the governor had unwisely promised increased numbers of jobs in state factories, which did not materialize, provoking unemployed youth to demonstrate in the provincial capital and small towns all around. As in Tunisia, many of the rallies were about unemployment rather than politics per se. Bread shortages led villagers of Bani Shuqayr in Manfalut to blockade the expressway between Cairo and Upper Egypt. Villagers cut down palm trees and set them on fire, or piled up donkey carts and other barriers. For the south, jobs and bread were the issues that caused many residents to call for Mubarak's resignation. In Upper Egypt, April 6 had only recently established a toehold, and most political demonstrations were organized by the Muslim Brotherhood.[91]

On Thursday, January 10, rumors were rife that Mubarak would step down that day. The nation, and the world, awaited his speech that evening. Turning up the pressure, some twenty-four thousand textile workers in El Mahalla El Kubra announced a work stoppage and demanded a wage increase—a moment of revenge for the failed strike of April 6, 2008, when the regime had been strong enough to repress them.[92] Forty-five thousand workers in the transportation sector went on strike, demanding higher fares and better pensions.[93]

The revolutionary youth had already put thought into the post-Mubarak period, proposing that they send a delegation to negotiate with the military about the need to transition to a civilian government. Ahmed Maher said that they demanded "the formation of a temporary presidential council made up of civilians and officers and a government of national unity comprising all the major parties to facilitate the affairs of the country during a transitional period."[94] A delegation of youth from Tahrir Square met with Prime Minister Ahmed Shafiq and Interior Minister Mahmoud Wagdy on Thursday afternoon. They included Wael Ghonim and others from the ElBaradei campaign. They complained about the continued repression to Wagdy's face. Their suggestion of a presidential council appears not to have been taken seriously.

That Thursday, although the president did address the public, he did not announce his resignation. Mubarak said he would transfer most of his power to his vice president and, in one of the more desperate gestures in modern history, went on to praise the youth in the streets as the representatives of the next generation and to pledge that their martyrs would not go unavenged. Many protesters dispersed in preparation for a big push the next day. But three thousand were so furious that they headed toward the presidential palace, where they staged a demonstration.[95] Another ten thousand struck out toward the television station, which they surrounded in what was clearly the threat of a people's coup. I was at a panel on the Egyptian revolution that evening at Columbia University, and MSNBC anchor Rachel Maddow brought me on her show at 9:30 p.m. I said I thought that Mubarak's bait-and-switch tactic was very dangerous, since the crowds the next day could march straight to the presidential palace, provoking a potentially deadly confrontation. In fact, the next morning the Egyptian military put the old man on a plane to Sharm El Sheikh, at the tip of the Sinai Peninsula (far away from Egyptian population centers), and Omar Suleiman went on television to announce the president's resignation. Field Marshal Hussein Tantawi, the head of the Supreme Council for the Armed Forces, became the de facto president. The youth had accomplished far more than just forcing out the interior minister, their initial goal. But now they had a new problem: they had inadvertently provoked a military coup, when most of them had aimed instead at moving to a left-liberal civilian government.

April 6, Kefaya, and other New Left groups put tens of thousands and sometimes hundreds of thousands of demonstrators in city squares, making specific, achievable demands and using a range of communications technologies to mobilize for crowd action. They used accessible symbols such as Mohamed Bouazizi and Khaled Said to create a common feeling of oppression and blocked opportunities among members of their generation. The Egyptians innovated with mass occupations, pitching tents in city centers and refusing to leave until their demands were met. They created a youth culture in those public spaces, with chanting, poetry, and popular music. Their methods of mobilization included not only social media such as Facebook and Twitter but instant messaging, SMS, sharing videos on smartphones, and using interviews on Arab satellite stations to promote their message and encourage demonstrations. The youth also deployed old media, including wall graffiti, chanting in streets and from balconies in densely populated neighborhoods, and pamphleteering. An emphasis on secular youth martyrs to the revolution and the use of self-immolation and hunger strikes touched the hearts of the people.

In both Tunisia and Egypt the youth movements resorted to the flash mob, marches, and other forms of the occupation of public space to make a claim on public attention for their grievances and their righteous alternatives and to disrupt the economy and ordinary life. The Ultras provided specialists in crowd violence and self-defense, skills lacking among the initially somewhat naïve college students. Youth in provincial cities played starring roles in starting up the protests, as in the province of Sidi Bouzid, and in liberating economically important cities. The youth in Tahrir Square saw it as a model for similar protests in dozens of cities. In Upper Egypt and elsewhere in the countryside, the Muslim Brotherhood youth took the lead, whereas in the large urban centers they tended to be junior partners of the New Left. The widespread misery caused by worldwide high wheat prices in 2010–11 created large numbers of disgruntled allies among ordinary Tunisians and Egyptians. The progressive youth activists' support for and ties to blue-collar and white-collar unions gave them further tools of mobilization, including calling for national strikes that freed up workers to come to rallies. Both in Tunisia and in Egypt the labor unions decisively joined the revolution only in its last week, and in both countries that youth-labor alliance was likely decisive in convincing the elites that the dictator could not survive. Unions in cities outside the capital often had greater opportunities for defiance as the ruling cliques weakened.

In Egypt the regime's loss of the key port of Alexandria and the dissidents' strength in Suez and Ismailia, ports on the crucially important Suez Canal, also likely convinced the army and the wealthy that Mubarak had to go. In Tunisia the regime's increasing weakness in the key industrial city of Sfax and the vulnerability of central government buildings to the masses in downtown Tunis were decisive. Raids on police arms depots by revolutionaries in Tunisia also raised the specter of guerrilla war if the uprising were not brought to a quick conclusion. The importance of political Islam in organizing protests in provincial cities in the countryside likely also alarmed the militaries of both countries, which had devoted significant resources to keeping those movements weak.

The youth made it impossible for the elite to conduct business as usual, for the oligarchs to make money, for the office workers to get to their offices and the shopkeepers to sell handicrafts to tourists. They undermined the legitimacy of the regimes simply by demonstrating that they could be defied. They presented the security forces with the choice of cracking down hard and risking massacres that would further destabilize the state or backing off and accepting a new political reality. They thus provoked a split between the secret police and the army. The secret police were creatures of the president; without him and his system they lacked a clear future. They were therefore willing to use deadly force, as at Kasserine and in Cairo on the Day of the Camel. In contrast, the officer corps could live without the president and perhaps even improve their prospects for wealth and power without him. In Tunisia the army was small and could not plausibly take on the hundreds of thousands in the street on January 14. In Egypt the army was large but mostly made up of youth conscripts, many of whom sympathized with the activist youth and their aims and who could not be trusted to crush the demonstration if ordered to do so. In both cases the youth crowd actions provoked a deep split in the ruling elite. In Tunisia the chief of staff and the older Bourguiba political class acted jointly, producing a civilian interim government. In Egypt the powerful officer corps staged a coup and came to power in their own right. That the youth of Tunisia provoked a civilian transition, and those in Egypt a praetorian one, would be fateful for the subsequent unfolding of the revolution in the two countries.

6

Tunisia: "Leave My Creators Alone!"

*C*ountries that begin moving toward democracy are said by political scientists to be in "transition." They may or may not succeed. If they do, they enter a phase of "consolidation," when key democratic practices become normalized and regular. Two democratically elected leaders in a row and a general agreement on the rules of the political game are the signs of consolidation. Why some countries that begin this path succeed and others fall back into dictatorship is a matter of lively debate. It appears to help to have a relatively high per capita income, perhaps because strong working, middle, and business classes can then offset the considerable wealth and power of the central government. In contrast, declining economic growth during the attempted transition is significantly associated with a return to authoritarianism. While some countries move relatively smoothly from authoritarian forms of government to a consolidated democracy (for example, Poland), others become partial democracies or bounce between elected governments and a return to dictatorship. Tunisia's transition, however bumpy, was fairly successful among the revolutionary Arab states, helped by its educated and relatively well-off population. Threats of a return to authoritarian practices, whether on the part of the police or the newly powerful Muslim religious party, were met with resistance by the mobilized youth.[1]

Despite its relatively high per capita income, Tunisia's economy did poorly in the years after the revolution, which is a high hurdle for a budding democracy to overcome. The youth movements in Tunisia and Egypt, having succeeded in removing the dictators, continued to agitate in the period of transition for more democratic practices and for an end to the abuses of the old regime. They did not accomplish all or even most of their goals by 2014, and in some ways the continued power of old elites and the rise of illiberal politics of the religious right after the fall of the secular police states threatened to reduce some liberties. Still, the engaged youth continued their struggle. They tended to be sidelined by the return of parliamentary politics after the end of the dictatorships, inasmuch as that sort of politics favored an older and more established kind of politician. Yet their techniques of street campaigning, demonstrations, sit-ins, social media campaigns, and coordination with a broad spectrum of groups for the attainment of their goals allowed them to continue to influence developments, though they also met with significant defeats. If successful transitions and consolidation do occur in Tunisia and Egypt, it will be in part owing to the efforts of the young.

Courts in Tunisia declared Parliament speaker Fouad Mebazaa president after the fall of Ben Ali, in accordance with the 1959 constitution, and he presided over the country's transition. The revolutionary youth were dismayed that old regime warhorses came to power after Ben Ali's flight. To be fair, Mebazaa was a member of the older Bourguiba elite and was not a Ben Ali insider. Prime Minister Mohamed Ghannouchi, a technocrat, tried to continue in office but was widely called "Monsieur 'Oui, Oui'" (Mister "Yes, Yes") on the street because of his obsequiousness toward the fallen dictator, though he was not suspected of personal corruption and had no blood on his hands. He attempted to deal with these objections by resigning from the RCD and forming a government of national unity. Appealing to the youth active on the internet, he got rid of the infamous Ammar 404, abolishing the Ministry of Information that had been in charge of censorship and announcing "the total freedom of information." He retained the ministers of defense, interior, and finance and three others from the last Ben Ali government. He was able to persuade the oppositionist Mustapha Ben Jafar of the Democratic Forum for Work and Liberty (Ettakattul) to join his government, along with Ahmed Najib Chebbi of the Progressive Democratic Party. He also brought in a member of the communist Renewal Party. Three members of the UGTT labor union were appointed. Pirate Party activist and blogger Slim Amamou, who had been in prison the previous week, was made undersecretary for youth and sports in the Ministry of Youth.[2]

The revolutionaries immediately staged a demonstration against these arrangements, which police broke up. One student, Ahmad al-Haji, told the Arabic press, "The new government is a trick. It is an affront to the revolution, in which people died and blood was shed."[3] Another complained to a Western anthropologist, "We cut off the head of the beast, but the beast is still very much alive."[4] After only a day, popular rallies and a backlash from their own organizations forced the three UGTT members and Ben Jafar to resign. Several hundred activists again demonstrated in downtown Tunis against the retention of the old cabinet members, shouting, "Get out, Ghannouchi!," just as they had shouted at Ben Ali, before being dispersed by aggressive police with tear gas. Five thousand demonstrators belatedly got around to burning down the RCD headquarters in Sfax, and thousands also rallied in Sidi Bouzid. The administrative council of the UGTT voted not to recognize the new government. The PDP and Amamou decided to remain; Chebbi said it would be irresponsible to destabilize the interim government.[5]

At the dissident website Nawaat the anonymous blogger Alyssa declared, "The transitional government formed by Mohammed Ghannouchi is a big fat farce. Thereby, the RCD seeks to maintain its control over the country so as to protect their privileges through commandeering the key posts—nothing could be more normal for them."[6] She worried in particular about RCD control of coercive ministries such as Interior and Defense. She warned, "We will occupy the street peacefully until our message is understood and translated into strong, concrete acts." As she vowed, the protests continued, with youth gathering at Government Square in the Casbah for five days in a row, culminating in a big rally on January 26, 2011, where many announced that they would go on a hunger strike until Ghannouchi's government resigned. Young activists streamed to the square from all over the country. The student union, the UGET, helped rally supporters, some of whom tried to tear down police barricades. Some of the youth marched through streets in silent protest. Their use of the sit-in in a big public space thus preceded the similar occupation strategy of the youth at Tahrir Square in Cairo.

On January 27 Ghannouchi attempted to defuse tensions by firing his cabinet ministers and bringing in technocrats.[7] It turned out, however, that the problem, from the point of view of the youth activists, was Ghannouchi himself. They went on campaigning for dissolution of his government. On January 28 police forcibly cleared the square with tear gas and baton charges, dispersing the youth for the moment.

Then another shoe dropped. Rashid al-Ghannushi, the leader of the Muslim religious party, Renaissance, returned from exile in London on January 30 and was greeted at the airport by thousands of joyous followers.[8] The devotee of political Islam joined the revolutionary youth in demanding that all former Ben Ali high officials resign from government. He also spoke about the ability of his form of political Islam to engage in parliamentary, pluralist politics. Al-Ghannushi (b. 1941) was from Gabes and was educated in Arabic, which French colonial administrators had demoted to a less prestigious language. He was not initially a proponent of political Islam but rather supported Nasser's militant pan-Arab nationalism, which was feared by the government of the Tunisian nationalist Habib Bourguiba, who had come to power in 1956 on the French departure. Since al-Ghannushi did not know French, he could not hope to rise high in the still very Francophone Tunisian establishment. After teaching high school for two years at Gafsa, he went to study in Egypt in 1964. At Bourguiba's request, Egypt expelled Tunisian students from the country soon thereafter. (Bourguiba feared dissident youth beyond his reach after his rift with another nationalist politician that year.) After traveling in Europe and toying with becoming a communist and going to Albania to study, al-Ghannushi instead went to another hotbed of Arab nationalism, Syria, where he pursued a Ph.D. in philosophy at Damascus University. There, disillusioned by the conflicts among Baathists, Nasserists, and other leftist nationalists, he turned to political Islam in 1966, having encountered the Syrian branch of the Muslim Brotherhood and deciding it was a more authentic expression of Arabism.

He then studied at the Sorbonne in Paris, where he joined the Indian Muslim organization the Tablighi Jamaat. His family in Tunisia, worried about his turn to fundamentalism, brought him home after only a couple of years. In 1981 he founded the Islamic Tendency Movement, which had political ambitions, but immediately met repression from Bourguiba's secular government. After two rounds of imprisonment in the 1980s, al-Ghannushi went into exile in London in 1988. There he rejected Islamic dictatorship and emerged as an important theorist of the compatibility of democracy and political Islam, and he received support for his ideas from the success of the Justice and Development Party in Turkey beginning in 2002.[9]

Tunisian youth wanted a genuine change in government, including Prime Minister Mohamed Ghannouchi's resignation and the abolition of the Brigades of Public Order secret police. A set of demonstrations was called by activist youth on Facebook for February 20, with a big gathering at Government Square before the Casbah in Tunis and marches through the streets. Following on the success of late January, when they made several ministers resign, the youth called this movement "Casbah 2." The protesters at the square were joined by university and institute students. They demanded Ghannouchi's resignation, the dissolution of the ruling party (the RCD) and Parliament, the firing of Ben Ali's cronies from the ministries, complete judicial independence, and the election of a transitional legislature. The demonstrations at the square continued in the following days. In addition to this peaceful gathering, however, some of the youth engaged in more disturbing actions. A video posted to Facebook at the time showed students calling on others to go to Habib Bourguiba Avenue at the city center and "paralyze the economic life of the country." Some one hundred of them attacked and burned shops along the upscale esplanade, attracting the condemnation of internet activists and police intervention; five people were killed. Even some of the demonstrators turned to coercive tactics, with UGET members pressuring other students to join protests. On February 27, a month and a half after the fall of the government, Monsieur "Oui, Oui" resigned, saying he did not want to be the cause of more bloodshed. The turn to violence clearly influenced his decision, but that development disturbed many of the revolutionaries themselves. As for the peaceful demonstrations at the Casbah, blogger Emna El Hammi wrote, "The new prime

minister will nevertheless remain in the eye of a part of the Tunisian population. The Casbah is still, to this day, occupied by numerous demonstrators.
This pressure maintained by the people on the government is necessary and
indispensable."[10]

With the fall of the transitional government, the country teetered on the
brink. The legions of secret police, their fates yet to be determined, often
turned to sabotage. On March 3 President Mebazaa attempted to calm the
situation by calling elections for a constituent assembly for mid-July, one of
the key demands of the youth. This constituent assembly would double as a
constitution-drafting body as well as a transitional parliament. He opened
the political system by licensing a hundred parties, including the Renaissance Party, to participate in elections. The announcement convinced the
youth occupying the Casbah and their counterparts in Sfax and elsewhere
to suspend their protest, to the relief of the shopkeepers and workers who
had been idled by it. The youth pledged to reassemble, however, if any of
the Ben Ali elites returned to high office.[11]

The new prime minister, the octogenarian Beji Caid Essebsi (b. 1926),
who, like Mebazaa, had been close to Habib Bourguiba, had never been
an intimate of Ben Ali. On March 7 Essebsi announced a cabinet full of
technocrats, some of them continuing from the second Ghannouchi government but none of whom had served Ben Ali. He also announced that the
secret police would be dissolved. (The personnel were apparently integrated
into the regular police, and the extensive apparatus of domestic surveillance
was largely mothballed, with many Stasi-like files on individuals burned or
hidden away.) Many youth continued to be suspicious of the transitional
government. At a cultural center in the medina in the capital, I later heard
the Tunisian reggae band Nouveau Système sing their angry, sardonic, Bob
Marley–style hit from that era, "Baba Essebsi," which included the lyrics
"Baba Essebsi, where are we going / With an illegitimate government?"[12]
Aisha, twenty-four, of Nabeul asked the anthropologist Alcinda Honwana,
"Where is the youth in this transition process? What I see is the absence of
the young generation in the interim government." She complained that the
millennials, having made the revolution, had been "set aside."[13]

The hopes of some revolutionaries that they could continue to deploy
street power to shape postrevolutionary Tunisia proved largely forlorn in

2011. Essebsi's urbane eloquence and deft, experienced conduct of public affairs and diplomacy won over many Tunisians (including the upper middle classes, who had had their doubts about the revolution and were afraid of political Islam). On April 11 the government announced that some fourteen thousand former members of the RCD who had served in high positions under Ben Ali during the previous ten years would be banned from running for the Constituent Assembly, thus reassuring the revolutionaries that the old regime would not come back in that way. While some observers worried that the step was undemocratic, it probably contributed to Tunisia's relative stability in the run-up to the parliamentary elections and their immediate aftermath. In contrast, many bureaucrats beneath the level of cabinet minister remained in their posts, and some maintained the same mind-set they had in the Ben Ali years. The new prime minister was able to improve the security situation. Far-left groups and Muslim religious forces unhappy with a Bourguibist prime minister attempted to launch a "Casbah 3" protest movement at Government Square in April, but the turnout was small and the effort fizzled out. Another such attempt, in mid-July, fared no better and was harmed by suspicions among secular youth that it was a stalking horse for the religious Renaissance Party.[14]

On May 5 Farhat Rajhi, who had served briefly as minister of the interior in February and March, gave an interview that went viral on Facebook in which he said that the Essebsi government was still being manipulated by a powerful figure from the Ben Ali era. He also alleged that army chief of staff General Rachid Ammar had a contingency plan to stage a military coup if the Muslim Renaissance Party came to power. Revolutionary young people were outraged and demonstrated over the next few days along Habib Bourguiba Avenue, demanding that the government respond to the charges. Instead, the state deployed the police. Blogger Lina Ben Mhenni was disheartened by how little the techniques of policing had changed: "The government used the same old methods of the previous regime to repress the peaceful demonstrators: tear gas and live ammunition were in the rendezvous." She alleged that "several journalists and bloggers were kidnapped, beaten and tortured, to be later on released in an awful state," and she had heard of deaths from police using live ammunition on the protesters. She wrote that whether or not what Rajhi had charged was true, people had the right to protest. In response to the police crackdown, Pirate Party activist Slim Amamou resigned his post in the Ministry of Youth.[15] Also in May three hundred youth in Kasserine staged a rally to complain that the government had still not done anything to improve the lot of youth who were unemployed and had not responded to submissions of project proposals. "Four months had passed," one said, "since the fall of Ben Ali and the governorate had not lifted a finger to help the unemployed graduates."[16]

In early June the government announced that elections would be postponed until October 23, 2011. I arrived in Tunisia toward the end of June, eager to experience a postrevolutionary Arab state. The walls were still plastered with calls to rallies and meetings and with graffiti. The Socialist Party of the Left, according to one faded wall poster, called people to a meeting at 2 p.m. on May 21 at the convention center in the capital for a rally in favor of the elected Constituent Assembly as a guarantor of a democratic transition.

Walking around the capital, I came upon a number of picket lines and workers' strikes. Much of Tunis seemed to me run down, and the summer sun unforgivingly revealed its blemishes. Away from downtown, the blindingly white older buildings were pockmarked with worn stones and crumbling stucco, as though in the midst of a slow-motion collapse. The low skyline in some areas resembled a row of drunk's teeth. It did not seem like a place where there had been 5 percent a year economic growth for fifteen years in a row, as Ben Ali had mendaciously reported to the World Bank. (For the real thing, try walking around Ankara in Turkey or Taipei in Taiwan.) In the summer of 2011 many people were still concerned about security, and most shops closed before dark. As for political life, some two thousand nongovernmental organizations sprang up after the revolution, and over a hundred new political parties had been founded. Ben Ali had allowed only eight.

One Saturday afternoon I went to the town of Kélibia, an assemblage of white buildings along the beach, overlooked by an antique fortress, on the Cap Bon peninsula. It is about an hour and a half drive east from the capital. I wanted to attend a rally there of the Modern Democratic Axis, a coalition of four small leftist and centrist parties and some citizen initiatives. Kélibia is a fishing village that also has a school for training fishermen and vineyards which produce a well-regarded white wine, Muscat de Kélibia. It is clearly dominated by the Renaissance Party of the religious right, and the mosque plays a big role in its civic life. The rally was held in a Roman-style amphitheater with uncomfortable stone benches, surrounded on one side by coppices of cypress, eucalyptus, and palm trees. I was greeted, like other attendees, by young activists at tables distributing pamphlets. The Renewal (al-Tajdid) Party was there, and the Socialist Party of the Left in Nabeul governorate, which proclaimed, "Citizenship is one of the foundations of the Republic."

Before the event began, I chatted with some of the teenage party workers. One complained, "Renaissance is well-heeled, but we lack money. It was hard even just to raise the funds to get out here from Tunis. . . . The artists and college teachers are with us, but the schoolteachers are divided." He described Kélibia as politically diverse, despite the obvious strength of Renaissance, since so many townspeople work in Tunis or abroad and so had become politically cosmopolitan. He also took hope from his party's support for the workers.

Amid the parade of aspiring members of Parliament, we heard some loud noises and shouts coming from the street outside the amphitheater. My driver ordered me to stay put and went to have a look, along with about a third of the audience. When at length he returned, he explained that a crowd of Muslim religious activists had shown up outside the event and begun chanting against the leftists. Then the local army commander and his troops appeared. He accosted the leader of the counterdemonstration, saying that while Kélibia was not a big place, there were lots of other areas where a rally could be held, and they were to take theirs elsewhere and leave the leftists alone. The religious group then marched off to their mosque. The third of the audience that left when the disruption began never came back, and I was told that some of them actually joined the fundamentalists as they marched away. The Renaissance Party supporters clearly felt that the Modern Progressive Axis had invaded their territory and were not happy about it. The confrontation suggested that Tunisian pluralism had a ways to go. The authorities handled the potential confrontation well, but I wondered what would happen when the military went back to their barracks. When I got back to my hotel that night, around 11, my driver told me he was so happy he could just go home and go to bed. "What else would you do?" I asked. He explained that just a few months previously, he would have had to write a long report about me and my activities for the Interior Ministry.

On June 26 there was a showing of the film *Ni maître, ni Allah* (Neither Master nor God), about secularism in Tunisia, by Nadia El Fani at the AfricArt Cinema in the capital. It was sponsored in part by the Reunion Coalition (Lamm al-Shaml), founded after the revolution and encompassing fifty-three associations and organizations, which supported the separation of religion and state, gender equality, and freedom of expression. The event was part of their "Leave my creators alone!" campaign, which supported artistic freedom. After the film commenced, according to press reports, a group of bearded young Salafis appeared and started chanting "God is most Great!" and "Get out!" and throwing stones. The militant crowd grew from twenty to about a hundred; then they broke the plate-glass window, flooded into the movie theater, and started beating up the spectators and demanding the death penalty. Some in the audience tried to exit, but the doors were locked. Then young men from Reunion started fighting with the Salafis and telling people not to be intimidated. About an hour into these events, the police finally showed up and hauled the Salafis away. The projectionist finished showing the film, and then another film was screened.[17]

The incident struck fear deep in the hearts of the capital's secular middle class. Some Tunisians alleged to me that the police deliberately delayed their response in order to support the Salafis. The Reunion Coalition, which included student groups, announced on Facebook a series of meetings to discuss what steps they should take. They were held at the El Theatro in Tunis, in a wing of the fancy Golden Tulip El Mechtel Hotel, which towers like a chalky ziggurat above the two-story storefronts around it. I went to a couple of those meetings, talking to people before they began and then just being a fly on the wall and listening to the discussions. Outside, a young member of a teachers union assured me that security problems in Tunisia were being exaggerated by the international press and that the difficulties between various groups, including Muslims and Jews, would be resolved. "For fifty years," he complained, "Tunisians have been prevented from having a national conversation with one another. Now we have to learn democracy."

The two hundred attendees were clearly middle and upper-middle class, many of them young, and they were determined to push back against the fundamentalists. Their discourse was one of tolerance for all; some spoke of women's rights, others of the rights of Jews attending synagogues in Djerba. One man stood up and said that the Salafi attacks had "targeted thinkers, writers, and artists, who are the eyes of the nation." A young woman read a poem, in which she alternated the pious phrase "in the name of God" with "in the name of art" and "in the name of liberty." She drew thunderous applause, though the religious right would have found her language objectionable. An activist in the teachers union complained about Facebook campaigns against blasphemy and atheism that were thinly veiled attacks on Reunion and said that the struggle should be defined as the right to create and innovate (*al-ibda'*), not as a struggle between belief and unbelief. Another young man said that the Salafis viewed artists as the weak link, easily isolated and cut off from society. Many in the audience deplored the reaction of Renaissance Party leader Rashid al-Ghannushi, who had blamed the violence in part on the "provocation" of the secular filmmakers. They realized that acceptance of his accusation would hand the Salafis a veto on public discourse. A woman stood up and summarized the action items agreed upon: they had decided to stage a rally and to march on Muhammad V Avenue. The discussion did not have a leader, and a wide range of views were expressed, with a sort of consensus emerging around the course of action. Thereafter, Reunion mounted several counterdemonstrations against Salafi intolerance.[18]

The Salafi hard-line fundamentalists are a tiny minority in Tunisia, with footholds in the slums of the capital such as al-Tadhamen and in provincial cities such as Kairouan. They are very different in ideology and style from the Renaissance Party cadres, who have declared for parliamentary democracy and pluralism while championing Muslim values. The Salafis, influenced by Saudi Wahhabism and by the jihad movements in Afghanistan, Bosnia, and Algeria in the 1990s and after, have a far more authoritarian vision. Most of them do not consider Tunisia to be a realm of conflict (Dar al-Harb) where violence is permitted, but some are willing to launch attacks. At one end of the Salafi spectrum, members might support the Renaissance Party. At the other end, they might belong to the Ansar al-Sharia terrorist group, founded in the spring of 2011 by Abu Ayadh, a former fighter in Afghanistan, which rejects parliamentary democracy. Despite their tiny numbers, the Salafis are very good at drawing media attention to themselves, often by deploying brownshirt tactics of attacking public events such as film screenings and art exhibits. This strategy makes them seem far more important than they are.

The elections of October 23, 2011, were hailed by observers as free and fair. The majority of the 217 seats was taken by small leftist and centrist parties. Unfortunately for the secular left, they were extremely fractured, and each party received only a small number of seats. Longtime liberal human rights campaigner Moncef Marzouki's Congress for the Republic did best among them, winning about 8 percent of seats. Mustapha Ben Jafar's Democratic Forum for Labor and Liberties, which champions social democracy, came in at 7 percent. The secular conservative Popular Petition group, a vehicle for media mogul Mohamed Hechmi Hamdi, got about 6 percent. Voters punished the Progressive Democratic Party for being willing to serve under Mohamed Ghannouchi; it gained only sixteen seats. The Modern Democratic Axis coalition, whose performance I critiqued at Kélibia, managed to secure a mere five seats. Many other small leftist parties won between one and three seats, including the Tunisian Communist Workers Party, the Movement of Socialist Democrats, and the People's Movement. Some of the youth activists, such as Amira Yahyaoui, were unsuccessful, lacking a grassroots organization or campaign structure. Her colleague, Imen Braham, who blogs at Moongirl, ran on the Independent Voice ticket, pledging to work to protect the natural environment. She wrote on her blog, "I am convinced that we have an interest in seeing independents in the Assembly." She admitted that she had no chance of being elected.[19]

The right-wing religious Renaissance Party, despite having been virtually uprooted by Ben Ali, surprised many observers by reorganizing and establishing a nationwide campaign apparatus in less than a year; it became the single largest party in the Constituent Assembly.[20] It won 37 percent of the vote, but because of the electoral formula used, that victory ultimately translated into 42 percent of the seats. About 25 percent of the seats went to women, and most of those were members of Renaissance. Still, the Muslim religious party lacked a majority and would need to join a parliamentary coalition in order to form a government. The disciplined Renaissance Party, unlike its fractious left-liberal rivals, could put together a majority by allying with only two or three of the small secular parties, whereas a secular coalition of many small parties would have been unwieldy and unstable. Marzouki's Congress for the Republic and Ben Jafar's Democratic Forum were willing to give Renaissance a chance to prove its assertion of dedication to parliamentary norms. Marzouki, a physician and, as mentioned, human rights campaigner and longtime exile in France once jailed by Ben Ali, was elected president with an overwhelming 155 votes. Ben Jafar, also a physician by training, became speaker of the assembly. Renaissance took the prime ministership, which went to the photovoltaic engineer and journalist Hamadi Jebali, who had suffered fifteen years of harsh imprisonment under the old regime for his alleged role in a 1992 coup plot by the Renaissance Party, which he denied. The Tunisian press dubbed the three politicians "the Troika." The Renaissance Party also acquired most of the key cabinet posts. Some observers saw this Renaissance-dominated coalition as an "Islamic Winter" succeeding the "Arab Spring." Given the actual composition of Parliament and the choices of the majority of voters, however, this characterization is flawed. The Renaissance Party's ascendancy was in part a quirk of the way parliamentary coalitions work, not a sign that the electorate was right of center. Many Tunisians told me the following spring that they suspected Qatar of having bankrolled the Renaissance campaign.

Leftists lamented the disarray and fragmentation in the ranks of the progressive parties, which had prevented them from forming a government even though they had done well in the aggregate. The youth movement was now split between the left and the religious right. The significant constituency among activist youth for political Islam tended to be absorbed by the Renaissance Party, though some turned out to be to the right of that party. The celebrated rapper El Général (Hamada Ben Amor) came out for sharia law (Muslim canon law) in the place of civil statute. The Renaissance victory showed the importance of Islamic norms for many voters, putting pressure on the Tunisian far left. The Tunisian Communist Workers Party, with only three seats in Parliament and a disproportionate base in university students and urban intellectuals, decided after the election to drop *Communist* from its name to attract more members.[21]

Those youth activists most interested in human rights issues had their work cut out for them. The Ministry of Justice, along with the Ministry of the Interior and other bureaucracies, was now headed by conservative Renaissance Party functionaries, some of them determined to roll back the largely secular and unrestrained forms of public discourse that emerged after the revolution. Persons close to the Renaissance Party were appointed to head the media, and new, Muslim-themed media were licensed. The main arena in which battles over the limits of discourse were fought was morality, blasphemy, and pornography. In the spring of 2012 two youths were sentenced to seven years in jail for posting caricatures of the Prophet Muhammad on their Facebook pages. The director of *Attounissia* magazine tested the limits of the new liberties by reprinting in Tunisia a salacious cover from the German *GQ* magazine showing Tunisian German soccer star Sami Khedira (who plays for Real Madrid) using his hands to cover his otherwise unclothed German model girlfriend, Lena Gercke. He and two editors were arrested, jailed for a week, and ultimately fined $665 by a local court. Another controversy ensued when the privately owned Nessma television channel showed the French film *Persepolis*, based on the graphic novel by Marjane Satrapi, in the fall of 2011. The film, a critique of the Islamic revolution in Iran by a secular young woman forced into exile, contains a scene showing God as a white-haired old man, and Muslim religious groups objected that depicting God is forbidden in Muslim law. Nessma's owner, Nabil Karoui, who had opposed the Renaissance Party and interviewed former regime figures on his channel, was fined $1,700. A year later, two prominent rappers were sentenced to nineteen months in jail for defamation of civil servants (the police). Weld El 15 was initially sentenced for a video he made against police brutality (he was ultimately acquitted). The police maintained that he had called for people to kill them and had defamed them as public servants, contravening Tunisian penal law. Many youth activists noted these prosecutions and fines with extreme concern, worried that the Renaissance government was putting in place new restrictions on the freedom of speech, though some pointed out that the prosecutors, judges, and police were mostly leftovers of the old regime and not necessarily acting at the behest of political Islam.[22]

Amira Yahyaoui and her colleagues formed an organization, Bawsala, to monitor the drafting of the new constitution, which began in the Constituent Assembly in the winter of 2012 and the completion of which was a prerequisite for electing a regular parliament. The Constituent Assembly was a transitional body, and the government was an ungainly combination of constitutional convention and ordinary national legislature. The drafting process took much longer than was initially envisaged, prolonging the transitional period and delaying new elections. The shaky coalition of secular parties and Renaissance spent the first months of 2012 wrangling about the place of Islam in the new constitution. Devotees of political Islam wanted an explicit statement that Islamic law was the source of legislation. Secularists vigorously opposed this step. These positions were expressed in street demonstrations, which sometimes turned into violent clashes between the two factions, and led to a ban on rallies on Habib Bourguiba Avenue. In late March Renaissance leader Rashid al-Ghannushi announced that his party would abandon any quest to change the first article of the old 1959 constitution, which simply asserted that Tunisia is an Arabic-speaking state, the religion of which is Islam. He was pledging that sharia statutes and clerical, scholastic methods of their interpretation would not be enshrined in the constitution, showing pragmatism and willingness to compromise. It was a hard sell to many rank-and-file members, and not only to those with Salafi tendencies. The announcement provoked a demonstration by Renaissance youth members in front of the party's Tunis headquarters, protesting the seeming abandonment of this goal.[23] From the other side, leftist youth and workers mounted demonstrations on April 9, 2012, in continued opposition to the policies of the Renaissance government. The police deployed brutal tactics to shut them down. Demonstrations on Habib Bourguiba Avenue were still forbidden but were theoretically permitted on the side streets. In fact, peaceful demonstrators came away beaten and bruised, as blogger Lina Ben Mhenni demonstrated with photographs at her blog. She also suspected police of break-ins at the offices of opposition activists and wondered if they were returning to the practices of Ben Ali's time.[24]

I visited Tunisia again soon thereafter, in May 2012. The country had already made strides toward normality. The shops were open later, and shiny new consumer outlets had opened. The walls were plastered with posters advertising music concerts, not political events. Many newspapers no longer seemed to carry that useful list of the day's political and cultural events. There were still a lot of economic and security problems. I spoke at Kairouan University in the center of the country, where a policeman had been murdered by persons unknown and the public was rallying to insist that the government do better on the security front.

On this trip I had the opportunity to talk to Rashid al-Ghannushi, the Renaissance leader, in Tunis. I was interested in his willingness to accept a civil constitution that did not specify the implementation of Islamic law, for decades a key demand of the Muslim Brotherhood and other proponents of political Islam in the Arab world. I hold that fundamentalist movements are reactions to the impact of the Enlightenment, with its ideals of democracy and popular sovereignty. If the people ruled, many Muslim religious thinkers feared, they could theoretically pass laws at variance with Islam. Muslim fundamentalist regimes either made no place for democracy (the Taliban in Afghanistan) or imposed some form of clerical oversight over the people (as in Iran). Arguably it was in Turkey that proponents of political Islam first began making their peace with the Enlightenment. The Justice and Development Party (AKP), which came to power in 2002, had philosophical problems with Turkey's secular tradition and ruled as a center-right party. As it became more powerful and the secular military establishment was weakened, it did institute legislation restricting abortion and banning some alcohol sales after 10 p.m., and its politicians began peppering speeches with Islamic references. That sort of political behavior, however, is analogous to that of evangelical Republicans in the U.S. South. Crucially the AKP did not attempt to curb the popular will by installing a form of dual sovereignty, with clerics as minders of the people or possessing powers of legislative review. It seemed to me that the Renaissance Party in Tunisia had just taken a similar fateful step.

"Have you," I asked al-Ghannushi, "accepted the principle of popular sovereignty?"

"Yes," he answered. "Why should we be afraid of the will of the Tunisian people, more especially since the vast majority of them is Muslim?"[25]

Many among the leftist students and workers and the secular middle and upper classes in Tunisia did not trust al-Ghannushi when he spoke this way. While I was there in May 2012, leftist youth insisted to me that the Renaissance Party had a secret agenda of imposing a theocracy on the country. They tended to blame the excesses of the Salafis, which Renaissance leaders deplored, on al-Ghannushi and his colleagues, suggesting darkly that the latter secretly use the Salafis as shock troops for party purposes. I did not believe that this allegation was true. That spring a video was posted to the internet showing al-Ghannushi advising Salafis to be patient and avoid provocations, lest they provoke the still-dominant Tunisian military, police, and secular elite to act as the Algerians did in 1992, when they staged a coup against a Muslim party that won Parliament. He said that religious Muslims' goals could be reached by founding media and institutions and through democratic gradualism. He also slammed those secularists who spoke well of Islam but deplored Islamic law, probably a swipe at Mohamed Talbi, a prominent intellectual who proclaimed himself a believer but said that much of sharia derives from the Jewish Talmud and is the worst thing that ever befell Islam. Critics took al-Ghannushi to be saying that he secretly shared the Salafis' hopes for a theocracy in the long term, but they ignored that he was clearly counseling democratic action and gradualism.[26] Dissatisfaction with Renaissance rule led Essebsi in the summer of 2012 to launch the Nida' (Call) Party, which represented the secular-minded middle and upper-middle classes. Although some caricatured it as the revenge of the Ben Ali Remnants, it was broader than that characterization implied. Its potential electoral strength could not be measured until new parliamentary elections in 2014.

The failure of the Renaissance government to confront the increasingly bold Salafis, when it did not actively run interference for them, continued to alarm left-liberals. In the summer of 2012 a network of Egyptian Coptic Christians and right-wing Islamophobes based in the United States released on the internet what they purported to be a U.S.-made film defaming the Prophet Muhammad. They finally succeeded in drawing attention to it among Egyptian Salafis, provoking anti-U.S. demonstrations throughout the Muslim world. It is likely they hoped the turmoil would hurt Barack Obama's reelection campaign. On September 14, as a result of the film, hundreds of Salafis rode in minibuses to the U.S. embassy in Tunis. Unable to get into the main building, they damaged and looted an annex and set fire to a nearby international school. U.S. embassy staff in Tunis later told me that they had warned the Renaissance Party of the possibility of such an action and had asked for increased security but received none. Government forces were slow to intervene, and when they did there were violent clashes that left four dead and forty-nine wounded.[27] Lina Ben Mhenni, who had taught Arabic in the United States for a year, wrote, "I understand that young people feel annoyed, attacked and harmed in their sacred beliefs, but I do not understand at all those who push them to react violently in a country where peaceful youth overthrew a dictator."[28] She added, "I am astonished at the passivity and incapacity of the security forces to control the situation despite their awareness of the possibility of such events in advance. Why didn't they cut off the access to the area?" In contrast, the Nawaat group published only a short squib on the incident, and the comments by youth activists were distinctly unsympathetic to the United States. One blamed Washington for "seeding the region" with Muslim fundamentalist regimes after the 2011 revolutions and said it was now paying the price.[29] Obviously Washington had not in fact deliberately put fundamentalist governments in place; it would have much preferred that relatively secular dictators such as Ben Ali and Mubarak continue in office, but had simply made peace with the victors of the 2011 elections in Egypt and Tunisia.

The attack on the embassy put al-Ghannushi in a difficult position because his party had fairly good relations with the United States, and he warned that it would tarnish Tunisia's image and harm Tunisia-U.S. ties. However, he probably did not want to be seen as cracking down hard on other Muslims in defense of the United States. In revenge for government passivity over this incident, the U.S. State Department slapped a travel advisory on Tunisia and reduced its embassy staff to a skeleton crew, limiting Washington's engagement with the country during the crucial transitional period. It was like cutting off your nose to spite your face.

Three factors accelerated the growing dread of the left-liberal youth activists about the Renaissance Party's plans for the country in 2013. The first was the continued prosecution of activists and dissidents for nonviolent speech, as with the prosecution of rapper Weld El 15 for a video slamming police brutality. The second was the draft constitution, which initially contained language that explicitly subordinated women to men and restored the Ministry of Information, which activists took to be a threat to resuscitate the practices of political censorship. (The final text of the constitution enshrined gender equality and freedom of belief.) Despite the occasional prosecutions of media companies and individuals for violating Islamic religious norms or for political libel, and despite continued police brutality at demonstrations, the range of acceptable political critique in newspapers and on television and the internet had vastly expanded, but the youth revolutionaries clearly worried that Ammar 404 could be resurrected.

The third source of angst was brutal political assassinations on February 6 and July 25, 2013. Both targeted leftists. In February the progressive firebrand Chokri Belaid was shot in his automobile outside his home as he was heading to the offices of the Popular Front. He had been active in 2008 in defense of the Gafsa mine workers and had been a fiery orator during the 2010–11 revolution. He led the Democratic Patriot Movement, which in October 2012 had joined in a coalition with eleven other small left-wing parties, termed the Popular Front. Thousands of leftists attended the first Popular Front congress that fall, chanting, "The people want the fall of the regime."[30] Belaid complained openly about the continued role of the neighborhood militias that had grown up during the revolution and never been demobilized. He was unusually public and blunt in expressing his biting criticism of the Renaissance Party, its right-wing religious and economic policies, and its alleged intolerance of opposition. He also lambasted the Salafis for their bigotry and violence. The government put forward a theory that Belaid was assassinated by the al-Qaeda–linked Ansar al-Sharia (Helpers of Islamic Law). However, Belaid's widow, and many among the secular middle classes, blamed the Renaissance Party itself, an extremely dangerous accusation for Tunisian social peace. If the sitting government had begun rubbing out leftist opponents, the country was headed for massive turmoil. It was not a plausible accusation but was widely believed in the upscale neighborhoods of northeastern Tunis. Experts in constitutional law immediately called for the Renaissance prime minister, Hamadi Jebali, to step down in favor of a government of technocrats, given that he had lost public confidence.[31]

On the next day, a Wednesday, students, workers, lawyers, and others gathered in Tunis to protest Belaid's murder. They also assembled in provincial cities such as Gafsa and Sfax. The mine workers, who were not much better off than they had been under Ben Ali, remembered their champion. In industrial Sfax the event unleashed violent passions against the status quo, which deteriorated into looting downtown. On Friday, February 8, Tunisia was shaken by huge demonstrations in many cities, accompanying Belaid's funeral. Young bloggers I met in Tunis in the spring told me that the crowds were far larger than any that had assembled during the revolution itself. The General Union of Tunisian Students organized demonstrations in favor of Belaid and against the Renaissance Party on numerous campuses throughout the country, considering him a martyr to freedom of speech. Ben Mhenni wrote a fiery column eulogizing Belaid's role in the revolution and declared herself an "unbeliever" in any God that caused his assassins to have such a blatant disregard for the value of human life.[32]

Prime Minister Jebali dealt with the crisis by urging that the Renaissance Party relinquish cabinet posts and establish a government of national unity. The party rejected this approach, however, forcing him to resign. The Renaissance interior minister, Ali Larayedh, became prime minister, and the Renaissance Party toughed it out that winter and spring, remaining in control of all but a few key ministries, which it ceded to independents for the sake of calming political nerves in the country. I heard Larayedh speak in Tunis about a month later, and the critics who say he lacks charisma are certainly correct. His delivery was tentative and dry. Many secular Tunisians felt that he had coddled the Salafis as interior minister and so bore some of the blame for Belaid's death; they saw it as ironic that he should be rewarded with the prime ministership. There doesn't seem to be any doubt that the party suffered a serious loss of popularity and confidence as a result both of the assassination and of the sectarian way it handled the aftermath.[33]

In March 2013, on 120 college and institute campuses nationwide, elections were held for student representatives for university councils. The positions were contested by the leftist UGET and its conservative, religious-right rival, the Union générale tunisienne des étudiants (UGTE, General Union of Tunisian Students), which was close to the Renaissance Party. The secular progressives won 250 seats; the religious right gained only thirty-four. The elections tolled the death knell of the progressive-conservative youth alliance of January 2011 against the dictatorship. It also showed a massive shift in opinion among the twenty-somethings against Muslim fundamentalism. Moreover, since so many Tunisian youth go on to some form of higher education, these results are probably indicative of attitudes at least among the young urban population, the vast majority. The leftists may also have crushed their fundamentalist rivals in part because of revulsion at the assassination of Belaid. When the victory became known, students flooded into downtown Tunis, where they celebrated with banners, national flags, and revolutionary chants in front of the municipal theater. The leftist parties and civil society organizations addressed the UGET with congratulatory messages.[34]

The Renaissance government had long had a Salafi problem. When, for instance, in the winter of 2013, Salafis attacked students on campuses who were filming themselves doing the internet dance craze "Harlem Shake," the minister of education actually took the side of the Salafis and spoke of expelling the students.[35] By the middle of spring, however, Larayedh appears to have decided that he had to risk a split in the religious right, which he led, by cracking down at last on extremists. When the terrorist group Ansar al-Sharia attempted to hold a national convention at Kairouan in May 2013, Larayedh forbade it. Police blocked roads and engaged in clashes with adherents or with sympathetic Salafis in the slums of Tunis.[36] An observer at Nawaat wrote, "In choosing preventative repression, the party in power belatedly permitted the state to recover its prestige, but Ennahdha [Renaissance] lost some feathers from its right wing, and even among numerous democrats who, in the name of freedom of expression, are unhappy with this prohibition."[37]

The struggle over the small Salafi minority was only one of the secular-religious divides that afflicted the Tunisian transition. When, on July 3, 2013, a coalition of millions of youth activists and the Egyptian military overthrew the Muslim Brotherhood president of Egypt, Mohamed Morsi, the crisis echoed throughout Tunisia. The Call Party, led by the old Bourguibist warhorse Beji Caid Essebsi, demanded the dissolution of the elected Tunisian Constituent Assembly, dominated by the Renaissance Party. But President Marzouki insisted that Egypt's agony would not derail Tunisia's much less troubled transition, and he denounced what he called the military coup in Cairo.[38]

Soon thereafter, on July 25, 2013, Tunisia was shaken by the assassination of yet another Popular Front leader, indeed the coalition's founder, Mohamed Brahmi. It was a sure sign that the Muslim extremist far right was determined to weaken and intimidate the country's small leftist coalition. The Renaissance interior minister fingered Boubaker al-Hakim, a French-born extremist of Tunisian heritage, who had escaped from prison in France. He had been jailed for running a recruitment ring that sent French Muslims to fight the U.S. Army in Iraq, and he himself had battlefield experience there.[39]

As news of the assassination spread, large crowds assembled on Habib Bourguiba Avenue in the capital and in city squares throughout the country, demanding the fall of the government. The powerful nationwide General Union of Tunisian Workers (UGTT) responded by calling for a general strike that Friday. Brahmi had represented Sidi Bouzid, the small town in the center of the country where the Tunisian revolution was launched in late 2010 by the self-immolation of Mohamed Bouazizi. Sidi Bouzid erupted in anger, and a crowd invaded the Renaissance Party headquarters and set it on fire. Renaissance offices were also attacked elsewhere in the country, though most often police used heavy tear gas to disperse the crowds before they could damage the buildings. Secular and leftist critics of the religiously tinged government accused it of coddling the hard-line Salafis and of declining to confront al-Qaeda offshoots such as Ansar al-Sharia. Secular oppositionists argued that some Renaissance officials had said inflammatory things against secularists, and blamed them indirectly for the assassination. Three members of Parliament resigned in protest over the government's inability to provide security, and over fifty more threatened to step down or freeze their activities, putting pressure on the transitional government to step down.[40]

Renaissance Party leaders were clearly extremely anxious. Although they had the legitimacy of having been elected and of gaining a plurality of Parliament, they were aware that the Egyptian masses had come out against Muslim Brotherhood president Morsi, giving the military there the pretext to intervene and detain him. Tunisian youth formed the Rebellion

(Tamarrud) Movement on the model of the one in Egypt, mounting an internet campaign aimed at dissolving the religious-right government, proroguing Parliament, and holding new elections immediately. Renaissance Party leader al-Ghannushi initially warned against any such move, asserting, "We are not in a position of weakness." In the months after Brahmi's assassination, the January 2011 alliance of left-liberal youth organizations and the more progressive elements in the General Union of Tunisian Workers revived, staging large protests and sit-ins throughout the country and especially in front of the Parliament building at Bardo in the capital. They wanted the government to resign in favor of a new caretaker cabinet and prime minister that would preside over new elections and not attempt to influence them. Under the pressure of the youth demonstrators and of a very determined and outspoken UGTT, the ruling Renaissance Party agreed in late 2013 to step down in favor of a neutral interim prime minister and a cabinet of technocrats once the constitution was approved by parliament early in 2014. The interim government would then oversee the holding of new parliamentary elections. Had the youth movements not reactivated in summer–fall 2013, the Renaissance government might have tried to remain in power in the run-up to elections, which would have weakened faith in democracy. It was a reminder that the youth groups, however marginalized they had seemed, could still flex their muscles when they felt the political moment was propitious.

The Tunisian youth movements accomplished a number of important achievements in the years after the revolution. They went beyond their staccato protests of January 2011 to the new "Tahrir" method of longer-term sit-ins. They forced a genuine transition away from the Ben Ali cabinet and ensured that the Democratic Constitutional Rally, the old one-party state, was dissolved and its high- and midlevel officials banned from mounting a counterrevolution. They sidelined thousands of high RCD officials from a role in politics in succeeding years, though Ben Ali's bureaucracy often managed to remain in place. With that one exception, they successfully pushed for political pluralism, so that a multitude of parties was formed and could freely run for office. Even the Remnants ultimately got a party they could support, in the form of Essebsi's Call Party. They ensured a relatively quick transition to an elected government, making clear that they would not put up with years of what Nouveau Système called "illegitimate government."

As a result of the youth movements' efforts, political speech became freer than under Ben Ali, even if there were occasional miscarriages of justice, and even if censorship on the grounds of public morals was still common. Internet censorship was formally abolished and Ammar 404 ushered from the stage. Despite the despair expressed by bloggers such as Lina Ben Mhenni about the return of police brutality at demonstrations, the press and the bloggers criticized Renaissance prime ministers Hamadi Jebali and Ali Larayedh in trenchant terms that would have been unthinkable if aimed at the Ben Ali government before 2011. The progressive youth also pushed the elected Renaissance government into taking a harder line against Muslim extremists after the assassination of Chokri Belaid. It seems unlikely that Larayedh would have prevented the Ansar al-Sharia congress in Kairouan in May 2013 had it not been for the massive crowds assembled after Belaid's murder or for the evidence given by the UGET election results that public opinion was shifting against the proponents of political Islam.

As for the millennials' demands for jobs and a thriving economy, these goals will take time to achieve. After the revolution, there was an economic contraction. But 2013 saw growth of over 2 percent, and the interim government projected a doubling of that rate in coming years. A more open system could well emerge that allows genuine growth. Although some signs of the consolidation of a new order could be seen, three years after the revolution the political system still had not become regularized. In the summer and fall of 2013 the crisis provoked by the assassination of a prominent leftist brought the youth back out in force and forced the Larayedh government from office, showing that the millennials' repertoire of collective and internet action was still consequential for the political evolution of the new Tunisia.

Egypt: From April 6 to Rebellion

*U*nlike the young activists in Tunisia, those in Egypt retained their momentum after the initial revolution and deployed shifting political alliances to have a continued impact on politics and the shape of the state. The military executive, headed by Field Marshal Hussein Tantawi, ruled from Mubarak's fall until the June 2012 elections but was continually bedeviled by youth demonstrations, graffiti, and other challenges to its legitimacy. In that period the youth often allied with the Muslim Brotherhood against the Supreme Council of the Armed Forces. Mohamed Morsi's presidency, from June 30, 2012, until his overthrow on July 3, 2013, was likewise subject to powerful challenges in the streets by a whole range of left-liberal youth movements. Morsi's dictatorial tendencies, recalling some of the abuses of Mubarak's style of rule, were ultimately checked by youth who allied against him with officers such as General Abdel Fattah al-Sisi, even though the youth and the military had a history of animosity. How did the postrevolutionary youth movements end the careers of several prime ministers and yet another presidency and shape Egypt's society and politics?[1]

Struggles with the Supreme Council of the Armed Forces

In the aftermath of the overthrow of Hosni Mubarak in February 2011, the officer corps staged a coup, and the Supreme Council of the Armed Forces (SCAF), headed by Field Marshal Tantawi, became a sort of collective presidency that appointed interim prime ministers and shepherded the political process toward parliamentary elections in fall 2011 and presidential elections in 2012. The military in Egypt owns factories and land and is a major economic force in its own right, and its leaders were clearly attempting to salvage as much of their wealth and power as they could. In the first eighteen months after the revolution, Egypt's youth groups mobilized to send the military back to its barracks.

Ahmed Shafiq, the former air force general whom Mubarak had attempted to install as his successor, sought to remain as prime minister. The revolutionary youth went back to the city squares, demonstrating and demanding that he step down. On March 3 the SCAF acquiesced in the continued unrest by dismissing their colleague. The revolutionaries in Tahrir Square were not mollified, insisting that the deposed prime minister be put on trial. They alleged that he had had a hand in the infamous crackdown on protesters on the Day of the Camel. Their demand, however, was ignored.

The officers then brought in as the new prime minister Essam Sharaf, a reformist politician who had briefly served in a 2004 cabinet as transportation minister but who had broken with the regime and joined the Tahrir protests in January. Sharaf immediately consulted with the youth movement leaders about his proposed cabinet. Mustafa Shawqi of the Muslim Brotherhood's Youth Movement for Justice and Freedom reported that the activists expressed their concerns about some of his candidates. The young people also made suggestions as to how to revive Egyptian industry and tourism, a key earner of foreign exchange, which had been hurt by the turmoil of the revolution. The willingness of a sitting prime minister to take suggestions about the shape of his cabinet from twenty-somethings was a remarkable development in Egypt's hierarchical society. Sharaf then went to Tahrir Square after Friday prayers the next day to greet the crowds, who welcomed him enthusiastically.[2] In mid-March U.S. secretary of state Hillary Clinton visited the new government and sought a meeting with the coalition of six youth movements that had been at the center of the revolution. The January 25 Youth Coalition announced, "There was an invitation for members of the coalition to meet Secretary of State Hillary Clinton but based on her negative position from the beginning of the revolution and the position of the U.S. administration in the Middle East, we reject this invitation."[3]

With the 1971 constitution suspended after the revolution, SCAF moved to propose key constitutional provisions, limiting the president to two terms and specifying the procedures and framework for moving to parliamentary and presidential elections. Youth movements on the left protested in Tahrir Square against these amendments, on the grounds that they did nothing to reduce the dictatorial powers of a future president and did not abrogate the 1981 Emergency Law. Many leftists and liberals opposed them because they implied a relatively quick march to elections, which would disadvantage the disorganized leftists and liberals and benefit the Muslim Brotherhood and remnants from the old regime, which had extensive experience in running political campaigns. They also felt that a constitution should be drafted before elections were held, to ensure civil and human rights. The country could have saved itself a lot of turmoil by listening to these wise suggestions. Instead, on March 19, with a turnout of 77 percent and a victory of two-thirds for the amendments, the public gave the SCAF plan a vote of confidence in a national referendum.[4]

A few days later the military council attempted to outlaw labor strikes and demonstrations that harmed the economy, a move that drew howls of outrage from the youth organizations. Shady Ghozali, a member of the Youth Revolution Coalition, protested that the legislation would contravene the human rights for which the revolution had been waged: "Peaceful demonstrations are among the basic human rights." Ironically, in the aftermath of the revolution the military arrested thousands of protesters in 2011, subjecting many of the young women to humiliating virginity tests. These arrests were a form of shaming, suggesting that the women's motive in joining the sit-ins was to engage in illicit sex in the Tahrir tents, and they functioned as an implicit means for older men of the establishment to silence young female activists. The military continued to try civilians, often in summary, ten-minute "trials." Despite the wave of arrests and the proposal of Draconian new laws, however, protests and strikes continued, and the officer corps was not always able to suppress them. At a big rally at Tahrir Square on April 1, Ahmed Maher, the leader of the April 6 youth movement, told journalist Patrick Cockburn, "I am worried that there are so many forces against the revolution, mainly in the army. By demonstrating, we are showing our anger at what is happening." He was confident that the revolutionary youth could effectively pressure SCAF: "They don't want a clash with us."[5]

One of the wedge issues deployed by the youth in their continued demonstrations that spring and early summer was their demand that the officers expeditiously put Mubarak and his two sons on trial for corruption and for the ex-president's alleged role in ordering the deaths of hundreds of protesters. Every Friday they would hold mock trials, which were extremely popular and often televised. In early April they assembled tens of thousands of protesters in Tahrir Square and elsewhere for this demand. SCAF attempted to deal with the continued unrest among the youth in two ways. It tried to raise the cost of protest, forcibly clearing Tahrir Square of tents and risking violence with protesters. (One blogger was jailed for three years for defaming the military.) And it sought to mollify the revolutionaries, finally arresting Mubarak and his sons and disbanding the National Democratic Party. Feared and hated former interior minister Habib Al-Adly was quickly tried and sentenced to twelve years for corruption, then sentenced to life for his part in killing protesters (in 2013 a retrial was ordered on the latter charges). Unlike the case in Tunisia, however, prominent NDP figures not charged with lawbreaking were not excluded from running for office. This fateful decision would cause Egypt far more turmoil in the transitional era than was experienced in Tunisia.

April 6 and other youth movements became suspicious that the military was still protecting Mubarak and some of his colleagues, and they were upset at the lack of prosecutions of police for the more than nine hundred deaths during the revolution. They also wanted provincial governors appointed who supported the goals of the revolution. They staged a protest at Tahrir Square in late May but had trouble getting national traction, as other Egyptians supported the military or the Muslim Brotherhood and yearned for a return to stability. The Brotherhood, busy holding rallies in the provinces in preparation for elections, largely ceased supporting or participating in the Tahrir events. Demonstrators in late June gathered at Tahrir to express outrage at rallies that had broken out to protest the defamation of prominent Egyptians of the old regime. Families of the martyrs joined them and demanded trials of the police responsible for killing their children. When some began chanting for the fall of Field Marshal Tantawi, clashes broke out between them and police.[6]

Tahrir 2.0: "The People Want the Trial of Mubarak!"

The progressive youth called for another series of demonstrations beginning on July 8, 2011, which lasted throughout the month. I had just returned to Egypt and was eager to get to Tahrir Square to see what it was like. I had to walk in, since the protesters had blocked off the streets to traffic (a major headache for motorists, given its centrality as a thoroughfare for the capital). The youth had called for volunteers to man checkpoints. They patted me down and checked my passport, then waved me through. The barricades were manned by Ultras, who provided security to the square. There I was, hanging out in a Tahrir Square familiar from nearly forty years of visiting and living in Egypt, transformed into a revolutionary Disney World. (Disney was present in the graffiti, with an image of Snow White carrying a machine gun, suggesting that the youth were not as innocent as they looked.) I copied the lists of demands, photographed the caricatured wanted posters of former officials, and talked to activists. A bewildering bazaar of youth organizations—April 6, Kefaya, the Coalition of Revolutionary Youth, Libyan Revolutionary Youth, the Wafd Party, the Wasat (Center) Party, and many other groups and political parties—erected tents in the center of the busy roundabout. Red tents, blue tents, white tents fluttered in the languid breeze.

"The people," one enormous banner proclaimed, "want the trial of Mubarak." One tent was erected around the theme "Stop the trial of civilians by military courts forever!" They wanted the secret police and members of other security forces who fired on and killed demonstrators in January and February tried for murder. They wanted a more rapid transition away from the corrupt former regime, with crooked or time-serving bureaucrats fired. They wanted some sign that there really had been a revolution, not just a palace coup. Graffiti showed Mubarak hanged and alleged that Tantawi, the de facto president of Egypt, was "the protector and servant of Mubarak." Some posters insisted that the military go back to their barracks immediately and allow the civilian interim government to rule. Demands were made that the state-controlled workers' and professional unions be dissolved and new, independent unions be allowed to form. They wanted payments given to the families of the martyrs of the revolution. Some insisted on a political ban on high-level members of the old ruling party. Others wanted parliamentary elections postponed yet again to give the left-liberal revolutionaries more time to prepare for them. A young man sat outside his tent in 115 degree heat with a sign saying, "I am fasting until our demands are met."

Often the really big gatherings took place at night, with supporters streaming into Tahrir Square after midnight. On the evening of Friday, July 15, I walked around the square, listening to the speeches, poetry readings, and chanting. I saw an extremely diverse crowd of young people and their elders, men in traditional gallabiya robes and youth in jeans and polo shirts, others in a kind of business casual. The women ran the gamut from Islamic chic to lower-middle-class scarves, a few wearing black face coverings, others bareheaded in tight jeans and Western blouses. A strange assortment of university intellectuals, mosque activists, lower-middle-class families, workers, and idiosyncratic cranks swirled through the square kaleidoscopically. Women were a minority, but their numbers were hardly small, despite the well-known dangers of sexual harassment and assault in the square. The atmosphere was that of a country fair. Hawkers touted revolutionary memorabilia—caps, T-shirts, flags—the way they would ordinarily press pharaonic mementos on the tourists. Vendors sold hibiscus tea, grilled corn on the cob, and tropical fruit. There were several stages with sound systems. When one became active, with speakers working the microphone, crowds surged before it, joining in the chants or shouting approval of the slogans. The bright lights of the square completely obscured the stars above and made it seem almost like daylight.

The giant Mugamma, a hulking Interior Ministry administrative building in gray Soviet style, loomed over the square, closed by the protesters.

The Muslim Brotherhood and the Salafis boycotted the sit-in for a couple of weeks after the initial July 8 demonstration, ensuring that the crowds were much thinner subsequently. The religious parties seem to have felt that the leftist youth had upstaged them. The stalwarts were disproportionately leftists—hence their distrust of the establishment returning under a new guise and their alliance with the workers who had formed unofficial wildcat unions. One evening I heard a young dissident on one of the stages explain that the three branches of government, the executive, legislative, and judicial, needed to be separate and that military rule was objectionable because it inevitably combined those functions in itself. Tahrir Square was haunted by the specter of the Baron de Montesquieu.

The new Tahrir movement was divided over whether to challenge the military council that, behind the scenes, ultimately ruled the country. Some of the protesters demanded that Prime Minister Essam Sharaf resign, others that military men in his cabinet be replaced by civilians. Some at Tahrir, especially the more vocal April 6 leaders, insisted that the military council itself be dissolved. Others feared that these demands risked destabilizing the country. One activist at Tahrir Square, a young woman, told me, "The army is our army." Others could not see the point of trading Sharaf for someone who might be very much like him, when elections were scheduled for only two months later anyway. April 6 was insistent on change. It put pressure on Sharaf's interim reform government to dismiss cabinet ministers they felt had been too close to the Mubarak regime and to appoint reformists in their place. These demands were popular with a significant proportion of the Egyptian public, which clearly felt that the military was dragging its feet on making real changes and was continuing to protect Mubarak and his more venal and brutal colleagues. "Tahrir Square Part 2" was clearly engineered and led by the New Left groups, prominently including April 6.

The July movement was an unparalleled success, accomplishing several of its most urgent objectives. Egyptian investigators charged the former speaker of the Parliament Safwat El-Sharif and some of his associates with being behind the notorious "camel attack" on demonstrators in Tahrir Square, on one of the bloodiest days of the popular revolt. Some six hundred policemen were dismissed for their alleged part in planning or carrying out violence against the protesters. The military council announced in mid-

July that elections would be postponed to "October or November." Sharaf shuffled his cabinet, dismissing about half of the ministers to whom the revolutionary youth objected and appointing more acceptable members.[7] He even appointed some revolutionaries; for instance, a physician who had led other medical personnel in demonstrations against the state physicians' guild during the revolution was made minister of health.

On the day of the cabinet changes, I had Turkish coffee off Tahrir Square with some of the young activists who had brought about these changes. We met in the stately old Groppi teahouse, on the bottom floor of a triangular building dark with decades of soot and automobile exhaust. Its ceilings are high in the way only an early twentieth-century architect could have imagined. You enter through square columns that support a second-story balcony and are met with a large, run-down, sparsely furnished room with a few tables and chairs on one side and a smorgasbord of fancy French pastries behind glass cases on the other. Waiters in starched shirts stand at attention and arch their eyebrows in solicitude. An interior room, now sporting a flat-screen television often tuned to political news, is cozier, with more tables and chairs, some of them lined up against storefront windows to aid in people-watching. The back mauve wall is adorned with an incongruous moose head.

Founded by Giacomo Groppi in the 1920s, the teahouse has been the scene of generations of political intrigue and literary debate, and in 2011 new, vigorous conspiracies were hatched there that shook the foundations of the state. When I was a student in Cairo thirty-five years before, the Nobel Prize–winning novelist Naguib Mahfouz read his morning newspaper there. The high society that once partook of its French-style strawberry tarts and lemon cake was liquidated by land reform in the 1950s, and its republican successors more recently fled to the upscale suburbs of New Cairo and Nasr City, with their megamalls and Beverly Hills–like mansions. Now Groppi's clientele is humbler, more bohemian—a mixture of tourists, local students, and respectable families committed to living in the increasingly dowdy old downtown.

The advantage of Groppi's for revolutionaries is its proximity to Tahrir Square, the symbolic political center of Cairo's 20 million inhabitants. When I met with the April 6 activists, we ordered Turkish coffee "correct" (with no extra sugar). The muscular, taciturn young engineer Ahmed Maher, now a household name in Egypt, sported a blue polo shirt. An earnest and articulate female scientist was veiled in the Egyptian way, covering her hair but not her face and wearing a long-sleeved, modest blouse. Her husband, confident and animated, is also an engineer.

Despite their unassuming appearance, they were one pole of power in the new Egypt, in part responsible for Mubarak's overthrow. This time they wanted more than a change in the man at the top; they demanded genuine transformation of the regime. Other activists were supposed to join us, but in the end they declined to meet an American. (The United States had staunchly supported Mubarak for three decades, and there were sore feelings in some quarters.) I shrugged off the snub and asked the ones who showed up, in Egyptian Arabic, if they were happy with the fifteen new cabinet ministers whose appointment they had done so much to force. They nodded in satisfaction. "Most of them," they said, "are good. But not the one proposed for the ministry of higher education." They briefly spoke among themselves, one saying that the prime minister had been apprised of their displeasure in that regard. These energetic young people in their late twenties or early thirties were attempting to guide the transitional government. I had a sense of what it would have been like if President Obama, who won Iowa because of the youth vote, had taken seriously his debt to the young people.

I pressed them on their preparations for the elections scheduled for that fall. They seemed puzzled. I asked them if they were canvassing neighborhoods and lining up votes for candidates they supported. They shook their heads in consternation. "No," the engineer said. "That would be something for a political party [to do]." I was alarmed. They did not seem to realize that putting crowds in Tahrir Square made them a one-trick pony and that the next stage of politics would require getting their supporters to the polls. In contrast, the Muslim Brotherhood's civil party, Freedom and Justice, knew exactly what would be needed and had marshaled an army of campaign workers.

The Muslim political forces were not enthusiastic about the new Sharaf cabinet because it contained secularists. The success of the leftists in reshaping the government provoked threats from the Muslim right to hold its own million-person demonstration on July 29. The al-Gama'a al-Islamiyya, formerly a terrorist organization that had become a civil political party, denounced the April 6 youth as "agents" and "infidels." Field Marshal Tantawi, angered at the calls from Tahrir for the military council to step down, piled on, intimating that April 6 was getting outside (implying American) money.

The very success of the secular left led the right wing to mobilize to forestall what they saw as a leftist coup. Leaders of the secular and Muslim religious youth movements attempted to avoid a clash and end the polarization by holding a joint demonstration on July 29 for commonly agreed-upon demands such as punishment of corrupt or murderous former officials and police. The Muslim Brotherhood erected a huge stage in anticipation. The Salafi fundamentalists had decided to announce their arrival as a public political force, and they bused in thousands from the countryside. (You ordinarily don't see that many Salafis, who dress distinctively, in Cairo.) Later that day I saw a group of them outside Groppi's, dressed in white robes and wearing beards without moustaches, Saudi style, being picked back up by a minivan to return to their village. There were severe divisions at the square, with secular and fundamentalist groups chanting opposing slogans, and around noon the secularists withdrew and went home. What was left looked like a sea of beards. The Muslim Brotherhood called from their stage for the implementation of Islamic law as the law of the land. The other political forces considered the Salafis rude for chanting slogans condemning their rivals as infidels and using triumphalist language suggesting that they had a monopoly on the true Islam. Their personal demeanor, however, was peaceful and polite. My son was with me, shooting a film, and they came up to him and offered him dates as refreshment. This moment of secular-religious tension passed, thanks to the general dissatisfaction with military rule and the continued prominence of the old Mubarak elite, against which both groups continued to mobilize. But it turned out to be prophetic of a coming clash that would turn Egypt upside down again.[8] The following Monday the state security police mobilized to invade and clear Tahrir Square, the Ultras banging desperate warnings with plastic water bottles on the metal barricades, calling for street reinforcements that never came. My family and I barely managed to avoid getting caught in the middle of that battle. By the end of the day the tents were flattened, the placards and banners torn down, and the taxi drivers delirious with joy that they could drive through the square again.

The biggest accomplishment of the July rallies was surely the agreement of the SCAF at the end of that month to proceed with a trial of the deposed dictator Hosni Mubarak.[9] This announcement took a great deal of the wind out of the sails of the protesters. At the beginning of September, after Ramadan, Egyptians were mesmerized by the spectacle of Mubarak, rather dramatically lying in a bed in court because of alleged health problems, behind the bars of the cage in which Egyptian courts place defendants, listening to opening arguments in his trial and that of his two sons and six associates. The youth activist movements were proving that they could still shape the country's politics in key ways, could still challenge an establishment that had hoped sacrificing the doddering, confused dictator would propitiate the gods of change and that enough would be enough.

"May the Military Government Fall!"

In the meantime SCAF nursed sore feelings about the victories in public opinion of April 6 and took out their frustrations on one of its prominent leaders. Asmaa Mahfouz of April 6 gave an interview to the media on July 23 in which she slammed the military for not protecting protesters when they faced violence from opponents of the revolution.[10] On August 10 she wrote on Facebook and Twitter, "If the courts don't protect our rights, no one should be angered if armed groups appear and carry out a series of assassinations; as long as there is no law and no courts, no one should be angry about anything at all."[11] She was clearly warning against a descent into chaos if arbitrary government continued and there was no rule of law. In response Mahfouz was arrested and had to post a 20,000 pound bail (then over U.S.$3,000).[12] During the preliminary hearing, as though she had become a character in a Kafka novel, she was charged with defaming the military and advocating the assassination of officers.[13] Angry protesters retweeted her offending message over and over again and began a Facebook page for her to which thousands subscribed. The military blinked and abruptly released her two days later, perhaps thinking they had delivered a message to April 6 about the boundaries of what would be tolerated. But as soon as she was out of jail, Mahfouz tweeted, "May the military government fall!"[14]

The reputation of the military was further tainted in October, when Coptic Christian youth protested near the television station in the Maspero district against Salafi attacks on Christians in Upper Egypt, where a storefront church had been burned. Egyptian troops were ordered to open fire on the youth with live ammunition, killing twenty-four. The Maspero massacre strengthened the bonds between Copts United and other Christian youth groups and the New Left, turning them decisively against SCAF (which had squandered an opportunity to shore up its legitimacy by championing minority rights).[15]

In the fall Egypt prepared for and carried out parliamentary elections. The April 6 youth movement started a "white circle, black circle" campaign to expose candidates with close ties to the Mubarak regime and his National Democratic Party, distributing lists of their names to potential voters. Whether or not the campaign was significant to the outcome, few Mubarak holdovers won seats. Instead, the Muslim fundamentalist forces scored their expected victory, though with some unforeseen twists. The Muslim Brotherhood's Freedom and Justice Party won 37 percent of the vote, but because of the electoral formula used and because some seats are appointed, that victory translated into 41 percent of the seats in the lower house. The Nur Party of the hard-line Salafi movement, virtually unknown in that form a decade before and previously political quietists, unexpectedly won 24 percent of the vote and some 20 percent of seats. A court later determined that the Muslim religious parties did so overwhelmingly well because they cheated. A third of seats were set aside for independents, but the Freedom and Justice Party and Nur nevertheless ran candidates in many of those constituencies, who handily won against unknowns.[16]

Some young members of the New Left ran for seats, and all but three were defeated. Even the old-style leftist party, the Progressive Unionists (Tagammu'), got four seats. Although the left-liberal parties were defeated, they did garner 39 percent of the seats in the lower house if one includes Muslim liberals and appointees, despite long years in the wilderness, when most of them were not recognized or allowed to run for office. (However, they won only about 30 percent of elected seats, and the purely secular parties won only about 22 percent on their own.) Egypt's newly invigorated labor movement was mostly sidelined in these elections; the victors tended to represent the small and large business classes that had been forced to operate outside Mubarak's public sector because their commitment to political Islam had made them taboo. The victory of the Muslim Brotherhood did not, however, translate directly into much political power. The Egyptian constitution provided for the president to appoint the prime minister without regard for which party had the majority, and SCAF continued to act as a collective presidency.[17]

Women went virtually unrepresented in the election results, and many middle- and upper-class women were worried about their rights, given the patriarchal emphasis of the all-male religious right, which now controlled the legislature. The Mubarak regime had posed as a champion of women's rights with a project of "state feminism." Having autocratic elderly males of the old order bestow limited rights on women while ruling with an iron fist, however, was always an unsatisfactory resolution to the real problems of inequality that women face in Egypt. Many young women played key roles in April 6 and other organizations, as well as in NGOs such as the Ibn Khaldun Center, and they participated in the demonstrations and campaigns of the revolution in large numbers. I could find no sign of specifically feminist literature produced in that milieu in 2011. I was told that Suzanne Mubarak and her upper-middle-class state feminism had sucked all the oxygen out of that particular room and had associated feminist discourse in the minds of the public with the leftovers of the old regime (*fulul*). Young women were as much as a third of activists and protesters, playing a central role in the revolution and transition, but they did so as members of their youth groups rather than as separate feminist organizations. Despite the pressure on women's rights from the religious right, young women I interviewed insisted that there had never been as much dynamism in the Egyptian women's movement as there was after the fall of Mubarak, when they became free to organize and publish. The political openings created new spaces for women's NGOs and civil society organizations, and the internet and new media were places where women's voices could be heard. A coalition of eighteen women's organizations continued to press for women's rights to be enshrined in the constitution.[18]

The Muslim Brotherhood chafed under the secular Sharaf government. In November they staged demonstrations against Sharaf and against a memorandum issued by his vice premier, Ali al-Salmi, that sought to constrain the drafters of the new constitution in a secular framework.[19] These guidelines, the "Salmi Document," would have kept the military budget secret, allowed the military to appoint four-fifths of the members of the Constituent Assembly that was to write the constitution, and permitted the officers to veto any articles of the constitution with which they disagreed before it went to a national referendum. Leftists were outraged by the prospect of heavy-handed military intervention in governance. Muslim fundamentalists were upset because they suspected that the military would use its veto to keep Egypt a relatively secular state. When the Muslim Brotherhood, Salafis, and leftist youth mounted another demonstration in Tahrir Square in mid-November, the police replied with violent attacks, and several days of rioting ensued.[20] Sharaf, unable to rein in the police, was forced to resign. The military then appointed as prime minister Kamal al-Ganzuri (b. 1933), a former Mubarak prime minister from the 1990s, in what was obviously a slap in the face of the revolutionaries and the Muslim Brotherhood. Still, the alliance of left-liberal youth and the Muslim Brotherhood sank the Salmi document's proposals.

On December 16 the leftists made another attempt at a big demonstration in Tahrir Square, still pushing for the military to withdraw. They returned the next day on the side street of Qasr al-Aini but unexpectedly met extreme violence at the hands of the police, who used tear gas and live ammunition against them, leaving ten dead and five hundred wounded. The police and soldiers particularly attacked women protesters, beating them and in some cases tearing off their clothes. One young woman who was beaten viciously and stomped on, her blue bra exposed to public view, became iconic of the brutality of the military junta that controlled Egypt and sparked worldwide outrage. Undeterred, women demonstrators chanted, "The girls of Egypt can't be humiliated!"[21]

That Sunday the revolutionaries were back out in force, demanding that SCAF immediately step down. They also insisted that al-Ganzuri resign.

The demonstrators wanted presidential elections held in January rather than June, so that Egypt could move as soon as possible to civilian government. The Brotherhood was not a prominent part of these rallies in Cairo. Instead, the New Left was joined by women's groups; some ten thousand women were said to have demonstrated. At one point a phalanx of women volunteers sought to form a buffer between police and demonstrators. Demonstrations were also held in provincial cities, sponsored by the Muslim Brotherhood or the Salafis. In Alexandria both the Muslim Brotherhood and the Coptic Church demanded that compensation be paid to the victims of police brutality. On Tuesday, December 20, thousands of women protested in Tahrir Square against the assault on their honor the previous Saturday.[22] Some demanded the execution of the soldiers who tore off the women's clothes and beat them. The Supreme Council of Military Affairs, sensing that public opinion was turning against them, called a press conference and apologized for the violence against women. Most women activists and women's groups rejected the apology as insufficient.[23]

On December 23 activists and parties called another million-person march in Tahrir Square to protest the military's violence against the demonstrators and to demand that it sack the appointed government of Kamal al-Ganzuri. They especially came out against "violent practices by Army forces against female protesters" and demanded that the perpetrators be brought to justice.[24] Both Muslim and Coptic funeral services for the deceased were scheduled for Friday afternoon. The march to "regain the honor of women" was spearheaded by April 6, Kefaya, and the Revolution Youth Coalition and was joined by several small leftist and centrist parties, including Wasat (moderate Muslims), Tagammu' (the Old Left), the Egyptian Social Democratic Party, the Justice Party, the Free Egyptians Party, and the Current Party. Two of the presidential candidates, Abdel Moneim Aboul Fotouh and Hamdeen Sabahi, announced their participation. The Muslim Brotherhood's Freedom and Justice Party and the Islamic Group boycotted these demonstrations, again pointing to a severe fissure in values between the New Left and the religious right that would become more consequential the following year.

On January 25, 2012, the anniversary of the beginning of the revolution, 100,000 Egyptians assembled in Tahrir Square. There was also a huge crowd in Alexandria. The gatherings were not, however, simply a commemoration. The revolutionary youth used the occasion to put more pressure on the Egyptian military to step down and hand over power to the elected Parliament and its speaker. The leftist youth were not at that time concerned that the civilian Parliament was heavily dominated by right-wing religious deputies from the Muslim Brotherhood and the Salafi Nur Party. They believed that nothing could be accomplished in the new Egypt unless military rule was ended. Their stance was institutional, not ideological. Under this pressure Field Marshal Tantawi offered to partially lift the 1981 Emergency Law, under which Egyptian civil liberties guaranteed in the 1971 constitution and in statutes had been set aside by the authorities, and under which the military could arrest and try civilians. Tantawi exempted acts of "thuggery," which he maintained still fell under military jurisdiction. The youth activists were not satisfied, recalling that Mubarak too had sometimes offered to restrict the application of the law. Hossam Bahgat, director of the Egyptian Initiative for Personal Rights, told the *Christian Science Monitor*, "For us the state of emergency has not been lifted. . . . Police were not deprived of wide-ranging powers to stop, search, and detain anyone without a judicial warrant. On the ground, this will mean very little."[25]

The established parties, such as the Muslim Brotherhood's Freedom and Justice Party and the secular middle-class Wafd Party, also participated that day in Tahrir Square. The revolutionary youth vowed to set up tents and stay in the square, in preparation for more rallies on Thursday and Friday, January 26 and 27. The Muslim Brotherhood, in contrast, went home Wednesday night.[26] The role of the periodic mass rallies at Tahrir and elsewhere in shepherding the revolution toward democracy was approved even by older, established politicians. Muhammad Abd al-Alim Da'ud, who was elected to Parliament on the liberal Wafd ticket, urged the protesters to keep a close eye on and to pressure their elected representatives, and to work to unseat them if they betrayed the ideals of the revolution. Da'ud was describing an almost Jeffersonian ideal of democracy, wherein there are constant revolutions or pressures from revolutionaries.

On February 1 a tragedy at a soccer stadium in Port Said reinvigorated the revolutionaries.[27] After the game, played by al-Ahli of Cairo and al-Misri of Port Said, soccer hoodlums and thugs attacked the al-Ahli players and fans with knives, staves, and other weapons, and threw some from the stands. The gates on the al-Ahli side had been locked, and some fans trying to escape were crushed by the panicked crowd. Seventy-nine persons were killed, and about a thousand were wounded. Al-Ahli fans and Ultras had played an important role in the January–February 2011 revolution at Tahrir Square, functioning as security guards and shock troops for the protesters. Ultras had often fought police after games, and they used that experience during the revolution. Those in Egypt's dissident movement already predisposed to see the military and police as holdovers of the Mubarak regime darkly suspected that police in Port Said had their own thugs target al-Ahli Ultras in an act of revenge; they saw the massacre not as an unfortunate brawl but as a counterrevolutionary act.[28]

The revolutionary youth, including April 6, reacted angrily to this perceived provocation and to the danger that the military might attempt to take advantage of a manifestation of public disorder to tighten their control. A big rally was held on February 3 at the Interior Ministry building in Cairo, the headquarters of the state security police and a center of torture and arbitrary imprisonment under the old regime.[29] There were also demonstrations in Alexandria and elsewhere, and large numbers of protesters were injured or sickened by military-grade tear gas deployed by police and security forces. One protester and an officer were said to have been killed. In the port city of Suez crowds threw stones at the offices of the security police, and two persons were reported killed.

Encouraged by the nationwide demonstrations against police inaction at the stadium in Port Said, the April 6 movement and other revolutionaries called for a general strike on February 11—the anniversary of Mubarak's fall. The Supreme Council for Military Affairs conducted a campaign against this plan on its Facebook page. It charged on February 6 that the call for a general strike "was an attempt to 'blow up' society from within, to spread chaos, and to throw the Egyptian economy into a pit."[30] April 6 replied at its own page that "the millions who chanted for the fall of the Military Council, and chose to carry out civil disobedience until power is surrendered to civilians, have the constitutional right to do so." The youth complained about the "language of threat" and vowed that it would not be successful. They charged the SCAF with being "a natural extension of the former president," thus grouping the officers with the hated dictator. It was, they said, the noble citizens of Egypt and the best of its youth who paid the price for their opposition to Mubarak. "The parliament is one of the accomplishments of the revolution in our view and we will continue demanding that power be surrendered to it." SCAF, they said, was responsible for the massacres at the Port Said soccer stadium and the killing of "our brethren" before the Maspero building, in front of the Parliament, and on Muhammad Mahmoud Street. While April 6 may have won the argument, they lost the street action on this occasion. The degree of actual participation in the February 11 general strike was generally viewed as disappointing, especially after the success of the week before.[31]

The country returned to politicking. Among the major dissatisfactions of many political factions was the formation of the Constituent Assembly that would draft the constitution. Gradually the Muslim Brotherhood–dominated Parliament had asserted its right to shape the assembly, provoking other political forces to withdraw in disgust. Speaker of Parliament Saad al-Katatni decided that half of the one hundred assembly members would be from Parliament, which was dominated by the Muslim Brotherhood and the hard-line Salafi fundamentalists, a procedure that would guarantee a fundamentalist majority. Both the Coptic Christians and the Muslim al-Azhar Seminary dissociated themselves from the process. On April 10 the Egyptian judiciary intervened.[32] The court found that the Muslim Brotherhood's Freedom and Justice Party was seeking to pack the assembly with members or sympathizers, excluding large numbers of Egyptians from representation. The court ordered that the appointment process be started anew, forbidding sitting parliamentarians from serving on the Constituent Assembly.

In the lead-in to the presidential elections, the first round of which was scheduled for mid-May, nearly two dozen candidates threw their hats into the ring. The Brotherhood went back on its earlier promise not to put up a candidate for president (by which they had intended to reassure the public they were not seeking a one-party state). SCAF responded by putting up their own candidates, former officers. The revolutionary youth movements found it absolutely insupportable that former officers tied intimately to Mubarak should be allowed to run for president and pledged that they would return to the streets in another million-person march to stop it. "We'll either be in the maydan [Tahrir Square], they announced, or in prison [*al-liman*]."[33] The revolutionary youth called for participation in the march under the slogan "The people want the fall of the remnants" (the remnants of the old regime). They set April 20 as the date of this new campaign and aimed for countrywide rallies to protest the candidacies of Omar Suleiman (former vice president and head of military intelligence), Ahmed Shafiq (former prime minister, aviation minister, and air force general), and Amr Moussa (who last served on a Mubarak cabinet in 2000).

On the evening of April 15 Egypt's Electoral Commission issued a ruling making ten of Egypt's twenty-three presidential candidates ineligible to run. Those excluded included Suleiman, for not having gathered the required number of names in his provincial petitions, and Muslim Brotherhood candidate Khairat al-Shater, for corruption convictions. Hazem Abu Ismail, favored by the hard-line Salafi Nur Party, was disqualified because his mother had taken American citizenship, making him the son of an American and violating the constitutional provision that the president must be the scion of an Egyptian family. The exclusions left five major candidates: Amr Moussa, Ahmed Shafiq, Abdel Moneim Aboul Fotouh (a Muslim reformist and liberal who broke away from the Muslim Brotherhood), Hamdeen Sabahi (a left-labor activist), and Mohamed Morsi (another Muslim Brotherhood leader, a materials engineer trained at the University of Southern California). The revolutionary youth tended to support Aboul Fotouh, both because he had begun speaking like a liberal and on the pragmatic grounds that he had a chance of winning. (In interviews in May 2012 in Cairo, some told me that while they liked Sabahi, they felt voting for him would be a waste of their vote.)

The planned April 20 demonstration gained another motivation. After the disqualifications SCAF began making demands to speed the drafting of the new constitution and to establish a "presidential council," which would dilute the elected civilian president's powers in a sea of khaki. Many Egyptian activists, including April 6, were alarmed.[34] In response, April 6 reinstated its call for a demonstration by a broad range of political forces on April 20, this time to protest continued military rule and interference in the political process.[35] Ahmed Maher distributed 122,000 leaflets calling on people to participate, and a splinter group, April 6—The Democratic Front, distributed over 100,000.

Tens of thousands of Egyptian activists arrived in Tahrir Square for the Day of Reviving the Revolution.[36] Some thirty political parties participated, including the Muslim Brotherhood and the Salafis, as did major New Left youth movements, including April 6 and the Movement of Revolutionary Youth. They demanded that the military stick to its promise to return to its barracks by June 30. They also wanted transparent presidential elections, held on time. April 6 had scored yet another impressive victory in mobilizing a broad range of Egyptian political forces against SCAF's foot-dragging.

In response to Abu Ismail's disqualification, the Salafi Nur Party turned to street protests and provoked a new round of violence in early May, just weeks before the presidential elections were scheduled. The Salafis assembled before the Ministry of Defense in al-Abbasia, to the dismay of the military, which preferred that rallies be held in Tahrir Square, far from their bases and facilities. The five hundred demonstrators included a handful of New Left activists who supported the demands of the Salafis that the full roster of presidential candidates be restored. It was also rumored that Muhammad al-Zawahiri, brother of the notorious al-Qaeda leader Ayman al-Zawahiri, was there, reinforcing the officers' suspicions that at one end of the spectrum the Muslim religious parties shaded off into violent extremism. At dawn on May 2 unidentified assailants attacked the demonstrators, leaving eight dead. The violence was renewed on May 4, when police cracked down on the protesters. One soldier was said to have been killed, and the spokesman for the junta warned that if soldiers were attacked, they would defend themselves. Even the relatively isolated officers heading SCAF must have felt the weight of popular opinion turning against them. They finally allowed the 1981 Emergency Law to lapse on May 31, meeting a key demand of the revolutionary youth.[37]

I was in Egypt in mid-May 2012 for the first round of the presidential elections and found the atmosphere exhilarating. There was an outbreak of pluralism like I had never seen before. I played the game of asking everyone within earshot who they supported among the remaining thirteen candidates. I seldom got the same answer twice. An older Muslim Brother told me, "NASA needed Dr. Morsi. How would Egypt not need Dr. Morsi?"

(Morsi had worked on a NASA project when he was an assistant professor at Cal State Northridge.) I was near Tahrir Square one morning when a convoy of two hundred automobiles came up Talaat Harb Street. These were campaign vehicles for the leftist labor organizer Hamdeen Sabahi, an ideological holdover from the Nasserist period. Cairo's traffic is in a constant state of gridlock, but the campaigners used the slow going to their advantage, passing out pamphlets and posters from their car windows. I saw many women in headscarves occupying the ambiguous space between the privacy of their automobiles and the public arena of the streets, stretching out their arms to neighboring vehicles to pass out Sabahi materials. The upscale areas of Cairo were blanketed with posters for Ahmed Shafiq, who had become the great hope of the remnants (fulul) of the Mubarak regime and who hoped to slow if not reverse the wave of revolutionary change.

The youth activists I met at the Ibn Khaldun Center expressed lively optimism about the future. Finally, they said, they had a shot at political liberty and a decent life. I stayed up late at coffeehouses off Talaat Harb, talking politics with activists, journalists, and intellectuals. An Egyptian journalist who worked for a wire service pointed out that of all the possible outcomes of the first round, the most dangerous would be a run-off between Shafiq and Morsi. The standard-bearer of the old regime and the representative of the sectarian Brotherhood would split the country, he worried. On the first day of the elections, my friend and fellow historian Samir Fadel took me to polling stations in various parts of Cairo. The turnout seemed respectable but not overwhelming. (Later, turnout was estimated at 43 percent, showing election fatigue, since Egyptians had just gone to the polls the previous fall to vote for members of Parliament.) The polling stations had one line for men and one for women, and the women standing in line demonstrated a startling diversity of dress. Some were bareheaded and in jeans; some were wearing headscarves and colorful tunics; some were dressed Salafi-style, in the full black costume called niqab, their faces entirely covered. The style of dress was no sure guide to their voting preferences; some women wearing the niqab supported the leftist candidate, according to my journalist friends who did some informal exit polling.

The five front-runners split most of the votes among them. The three secular candidates (former regime figures Shafiq and Moussa and leftist oppositionist Sabahi) together won over 55 percent of the votes. If one includes the religious liberal Aboul Fotouh, nearly 73 percent of votes went to a liberal nonfundamentalist. The candidate who did best, however, was the illiberal Muslim Brotherhood standard-bearer, Mohamed Morsi, with nearly 25 percent of the votes. In second place was Shafiq, with over 23 percent, who had done himself no favors by saying publicly that Mubarak had been like a father to him. In third place, with 20 percent of the votes, was Sabahi, the leftist, who got the support of many Egyptians in the middle classes and the labor unions and managed to defeat the Muslim religious parties in their stronghold of Alexandria. This outcome contradicted the results of the parliamentary polls held only a few months before, in which Muslim religious candidates won a supermajority of the elected seats. Analysts who read the commitments of the electorate from one election erred badly. Secular and leftist currents were still lively and powerful in Egypt and, indeed, accounted for the majority of votes cast in May.

The second round of the presidential election, held in June, was between the two candidates with the highest vote tally: Shafiq and Morsi. The polarizing disaster foreseen by my journalist friend had come to pass. On the eve of the contest the Supreme Constitutional Court yet again intervened forcefully, dissolving the lower house of Parliament because of widespread electoral fraud on the part of the Brotherhood and the Salafis, who had put up party candidates for seats reserved for independents. The public was now focused on the presidential election. Faced with a choice between a man of the old regime who spoke of Mubarak nostalgically and a right-wing Muslim Brother, many of the revolutionary youth sat out the presidential election. Morsi barely eked out a victory, gaining 53 percent of the votes. It was not an impressive victory in a revolutionary country against the overthrown dictator's last vice president. Still, the thousands of demonstrators in Tahrir Square objecting to the high-handed attempts of Tantawi and SCAF to remain in control went wild when Morsi's victory was announced on June 24, and the square celebrated with fireworks.[38]

SCAF supported the court-ordered dissolution of the elected Parliament and maintained that the officer corps would function as the legislative branch until a new Parliament could be elected. It also attempted to circumscribe the drafting of a new constitution. Neither the youth activists nor the new president accepted that role for the officer corps, however, which that summer seemed to gradually give up their various claims to continued civil power. It seemed as though Morsi initially avoided confrontation with Field Marshal Tantawi and Army Chief of Staff Anan. Behind the scenes, however, the military was alarmed and appalled by Morsi's governing style.

In the president's first major speech in Tahrir Square, he called on the United States to release from prison Omar Abdel Rahman, the "blind sheikh" and a former leader of the al-Gama'a al-Islamiyya terrorist organization who had been found guilty of involvement in the first attempted bombing of the World Trade Center in 1993.[39] Morsi went on to pardon dozens of former militants, whom the military believed then went to the deserts of the Sinai Peninsula (Egypt's no-man's-land) to join other extremists in attacks on soldiers. The Egyptian military had expended a great deal of blood and treasure in fighting the Muslim extremists, and Morsi's behavior seemed criminal to the officers. AP reporter Hamza Hendawi interviewed officers and heard a telling anecdote: Morsi brought along a group of fellow Muslim Brothers who lacked security clearances to his first national security briefing. The general giving the briefing objected, but Morsi replied, "Come on, general, there are no strangers here."[40] The officer gave the briefing without sharing classified information and was soon dismissed.

On August 12 Morsi more or less staged his own coup against the senior officers. He declared SCAF subordinate to the president's authority and abruptly retired Tantawi and Anan. There was no more talk of SCAF being the temporary legislature or interfering in the drafting of the constitution. In their stead he promoted Major-General Sidqi Subhi as army chief of staff. General Abdel Fattah al-Sisi, Morsi's minister of defense, also emerged as powerful. It turns out that, faced with a president who had won a popular mandate, the military had decided to bide its time. But according to Hendawi, the officers put Morsi under electronic surveillance, recording his conversations, and began building a case against him of running interference for Muslim extremists. If Morsi thought a decree and a couple of retirements had put him in charge of the Egyptian military, he was mistaken.

Morsi deeply distrusted the judiciary. He saw most of the judges as secular Mubarak appointees who had an animus against the Muslim Brotherhood. This view was unfair, since some judges had fought back against

Mubarak's interference in the judiciary and had held strikes and protests against him. Shafiq sued to contest the outcome of the election, and Morsi could not be sure that the hostile courts would uphold his victory. He appears to have been apprehensive that the judiciary might strike down his August decree placing himself above the military. He also feared that the courts would strike down the reconstituted Constituent Assembly, still dominated by the Brotherhood, which was drafting the new constitution. With the legislature in abeyance, it was possible for secular Mubarak appointees in the judiciary and their counterparts in the military to move against an isolated president with a base in only half the country. Morsi was vulnerable.

The politics inside the hundred-member Constituent Assembly, which had been reconstituted after the spring 2012 court judgment striking down the inclusion of parliamentarians, still favored the Muslim Brotherhood and the Salafis. They wanted a paragraph in the new constitution that would put the interpretation of any Egyptian law drawn from Islamic law in the hands of the al-Azhar Seminary, Egypt's foremost religious authority. Opponents saw this language as an opening to theocracy on the Iranian model, since so much law in Egypt has at least something to do with the Islamic legal heritage. President Morsi had promised that the constitution-making process would be consensual, but the few liberal, women, and Christian assembly members felt consistently outmaneuvered and outvoted. On November 15 the representatives of the Coptic Church announced their resignation, starting an avalanche of resignations. Ahmed Maher of April 6 soon followed suit, as did Amr Moussa and members of the journalists' syndicate. The resignations threatened a constitutional crisis. Although Morsi was able to maintain a quorum by appointing members to fill the seats of some of those who resigned, the forty who withdrew from the process were a powerful argument for the body's illegitimacy, a matter that went before the Supreme Constitutional Court.[41]

Morsi and his circle appear to have feared that this constitutional crisis would become an opening for a judicial-military coup. If the president could be overruled with regard to the Constituent Assembly and the constitution he wanted, his subordination of the military and his rejection of a legislative or constitutional role for the officers could also be undone. In what looked like a preemptive strike against any such coup, Morsi went on television on November 22 and issued a constitutional decree, a sort of presidential executive order, declaring that the courts had no authority to challenge presidential decisions until such time as the new constitution was in place.[42] In so doing he gave the appearance of putting himself above the law in a way all too reminiscent of Hosni Mubarak (or, for that matter, Richard M. Nixon). He was backed by Muslim Brotherhood cadres in the provinces and parts of Cairo, but the opposition parties and left and liberal youth movements were outraged and immediately began staging nationwide demonstrations.

The withdrawal of Ahmed Maher from the constitution-making process marked the end of the long alliance between the progressive youth and the Brotherhood against the military. Maher complained that the Constituent Assembly was not being run in a consensual way. He held that "making the decisions of the president and the constituent assembly unassailable is the beginning of a new dictatorship. For that reason, the decisions are rejected and must be abrogated."[43] Asmaa Mahfouz of April 6 tweeted that Morsi was taking the country to civil war. Even some youth leaders with religious commitments, such as Wael Ghonim, broke with the president over these decrees. Ghonim was quoted as saying, "The revolution was not made in search of another dictator."[44]

April 6 and the revolutionary youth revived the demonstrations at Tahrir Square in Cairo and Caid Ibrahim Square in Alexandria in late November and throughout December and rallied in front of the presidential palace in Heliopolis. Protesters breached the walls on December 4, and Morsi had to flee in a limousine. The next day he defiantly returned. On the evening of December 6 Muslim Brotherhood cadres mounted an attack on the protesters outside the presidential palace that reminded the youth of the tactics of the plainclothes thugs employed by Mubarak in the old days. The Brotherhood enforcers used police as cover, hiding behind them during counterattacks. The leftist youth movements were convinced that Morsi and the Brotherhood leadership, angered by the president's forced flight two days before, had organized a deliberate militia attack. Six youth were killed in the clashes, and 450 persons were wounded. That the elected president should use what the revolutionary youth saw as his private gangs to kill and maim them was the last straw. The April 6 youth organization rallied the people to the presidential palace "to protect the revolution" and to "bring down the Brotherhood gang." It warned that all the liberties and sacrifices of the January 25 revolution would otherwise be lost. Apostrophizing Morsi, the youth declared, "Our demands are no longer only that you retract your unconstitutional declaration [of being above the courts] and your counterfeit constitution, rather our fundamental demand is that you personally fall from power."[45] In the provinces violent clashes broke out between leftists or former NDP members and the Muslim Brothers, and some Brotherhood or Freedom and Justice Party headquarters were torched. There were brawls in places like Suez between Ultras and Muslim Brothers. The stock market plunged, costing investors billions.

With the country in flames, Morsi reneged on his earlier pledge that the constitution would be a consensual document. He had the rump Constituent Assembly hastily pass their draft (the same one that had provoked the raft of resignations by secularists, Christians, and women). Then he announced a national referendum on the text in two rounds in December. The political opposition, grouped in the National Salvation Front, objected that the draft was sectarian, not consensual, and that the public would not have time to understand its implications in such a short period. The judges, who by law were supposed to oversee the polling stations and certify the security of the ballot boxes, for the most part went on strike. Morsi called on law school professors, many of them Muslim Brothers, to fill in for them. The youth movements and the left-liberal opposition coalition were split on whether to boycott the referendum or to assemble their troops and defeat the proposed constitution. In the end, the referendum got only a 33 percent turnout. In the first round, when the opposition had hopes of defeating it, it passed by only 56 percent. Overall it was approved by 63 percent of those who bothered to vote. Moreover, the referendum did not meet international standards for elections. Many polling stations were not properly overseen, given the judges' strike, making an opening for fraud. The left charged that Brotherhood cadres chased away some secular voters. The document was roundly defeated in Cairo. As it was, the highly controversial constitution was passed by only about 20 percent of the Egyptian electorate.

Ironically the preamble of the new constitution (for the most part modeled on that of the French Fifth Republic, with an Islamic overlay) paid ample respect to the youth revolutionaries who largely rejected its text: "Our Constitution, the document of the 25th of January revolution, which was started by our youth, embraced by our people, supported by our Armed Forces; Having rejected, in Tahrir Square and all over the country all forms of injustice, oppression, tyranny, despotism, exclusion, plunder and monopoly; Proclaimed our full rights to 'bread, freedom, social justice, and human dignity,' paid for by the blood of our martyrs, the pain of our injured, the dreams of our children, the strife of our men and women." Its more theocratic passages, however, remained unacceptable to most politically active Egyptians. It oddly forced all workers in a particular industry into a single union, which the workers themselves completely rejected. Morsi's attempt to shoehorn the constitution through the voting process created a chasm in the body politic that would not soon be bridged. His opponents among the activist youth and workers and among the old Mubarak elites were determined to undo what he had done.[46]

After the enactment of the new constitution, Morsi attempted to defuse the crisis that his November 22 decree had provoked. First, he declared that the decree was no longer in effect, since the constitution was now in place. Then he appointed a raft of new members to the upper house of Parliament, which had not been dissolved by the courts when they struck down the lower house. He declared that until new elections could be held, the upper house would function as the legislature, even though only 7 percent of its members had been elected and it was disproportionately made up of politicians from the religious right. Morsi now had the presidency and Parliament. One of the measures the Brotherhood-dominated Parliament proposed was reducing the retirement age of judges from seventy to sixty, which would have forced about a fourth of them to step down, allowing Morsi to insert Muslim Brotherhood jurists in their place. The judges' protest slowed but showed no signs of halting this plan, which alarmed all the political forces worried about a creeping one-party coup.[47] In early June 2013 the Supreme Constitutional Court struck down the upper house as having been illegitimately set up under Morsi, though it did not dissolve that body, nor did it strike down any laws it passed. (Morsi's constitution protected the body from those steps.)[48] The same court also impugned the legitimacy of the Constituent Assembly that produced the constitution, though it did not attempt to strike down the constitution. When I was in Egypt that June I asked blogger and human rights activist Amr Ezzat what the point of these judicial decisions was, since they did not seem to have any practical effect. He said that the court was likely attempting to undermine the legitimacy of these institutions to prepare the way for more effective legal and political challenges to them. He was prescient.

Morsi's arrogant ruling style and dependence on a small circle of advisers from among the high officials of the Muslim Brotherhood was the opposite of what the youth had been hoping for. He increasingly mistreated the Brotherhood's former political allies in the New Left, showing a level of ingratitude and sectarianism that frightened them. They did not forget the attack on them of December 6 by what they considered Brotherhood enforcers, which gave them another six martyrs. To them, it seemed as though Mubarak was back, only with a different ideology and different patronage network.

Despite the deep polarization of the public, Morsi continued to resist sharing power and in the spring of 2013 appointed nine Muslim Brothers to key cabinet posts and seventeen as provincial governors. Showing how tone-deaf he was, he appointed a member of the al-Gama'a al-Islamiyya, the former terrorist group, as governor of Luxor, where in 1997 Muslim radicals had shot down sixty-two persons, mostly tourists. Local youth organized demonstrations and sit-ins, preventing the appointee from entering the governor's offices, and he eventually resigned. Morsi closed television stations, prosecuted Ahmed Maher and other members of April 6 for demonstrating, and brought charges against critical bloggers and Facebook administrators. He or his supporters initiated political libel suits against journalists, just as Mubarak and the old National Democratic Party had done. He even charged the wildly popular comedian Bassem Youssef for ridiculing the president. Youssef responded by appearing on Comedy Central's *The Daily Show with Jon Stewart*, and then bringing Stewart into his studios in Cairo, where Stewart said, "If your regime is not strong enough to handle a joke, then you don't have a regime." Morsi even toyed with making Cairo's night-owl populace go to bed early by closing shops and coffeehouses in late evening.[49]

Perhaps more consequentially Morsi and his clique were extremely poor stewards of the economy. The number-two man in the Muslim Brotherhood, Khairat al-Shater, held no government position but was extremely influential with the president. Egyptian politicians who broke with the Brotherhood's Freedom and Justice Party accused him of being a narrow-minded free-marketer who insisted on imposing neoliberal, pro-market policies on the country. Since half the workforce is in the public sector, he was alienating a lot of people. Although tourism revived somewhat in the spring of 2013, it brought in less money per tourist than before because hotel and other prices had fallen. Moreover, it had become enclave tourism, with most vacationers going to resorts on the Red Sea, far from the demonstrations and political turbulence. The pharaonic circuit of the Pyramids of Giza and Luxor, which had supported the hotel industry and handicrafts in Cairo and Upper Egypt, languished. The Brotherhood did not make Western tourism their highest priority, since, after all, it involves bikinis, alcohol, and generally a style of life of which they disapprove. Morsi's cabinet did not arrange for enough wheat to be purchased from abroad, raising the price of bread (always a mistake in Egypt). With less tourist money and little foreign investment coming in, foreign currency reserves plummeted further, having already been eroded by the revolution, to a low of $15 billion from a high in 2010 of $36 billion. (Things would have been even worse if Morsi had not received massive aid from Qatar, which supported the Muslim Brotherhood throughout the region.) As a result, the Egyptian National Bank did not have the ability to defend the Egyptian pound in world currency markets, and it fell by 10 percent in early 2013 alone, hurting ordinary Egyptians who purchased many staples from abroad (including wheat and building materials). Morsi represented the business classes of the Muslim Brotherhood who had been excluded from the public sector by Mubarak's discrimination. His economic policies therefore had a neoliberal shape, friendly to business but advocating austerity for workers. This position was reinforced by his negotiations with the International Monetary Fund. Workers were so angered by his economic policies that the number of strikes and economically motivated protests during the year of his presidency doubled from the previous year, to 3,817.[50] The disgruntlement of progressive youth over the return of censorship, the imposition of puritan mores, and challenges to human rights norms might not have sunk Morsi by itself, but his economic policies were angering large numbers of poor and working-class Egyptians.[51]

In late April 2013 outraged youth launched the Rebellion (Tamarrud) Movement. They spread around a one-page petition demanding a recall election. Long-standing youth movements such as April 6, the Revolutionary Socialists, and others joined the campaign, lending it their organizational experience, social media followers, and databases. When I was in Egypt in early June, I was repeatedly given this petition by Egyptians from all walks of life and urged to sign it myself. (I took it as a compliment that they made me an honorary Egyptian.) Even just being seen with the petition in my hand was enough to bring a smile to people's lips and an expression of thanks for supporting them. The resort to a one-page photocopy was not such a departure from previous tactics as it might sound, since pamphleteering had all along probably been more important than Facebook. Still, one wag called the petition "a defeat of Facebook and Mark Zuckerberg and a thunderous triumph for Xerox!"[52]

The premise of the movement was that Morsi had reneged on his promise of consensual government and had behaved dictatorially, and even killed demonstrators, and should therefore be recalled or made to defend his record in another run-off. The youth were undeterred by the unconstitutionality of their demands, since they objected to Morsi's constitution as well. Rebellion was on the lips of most of the Egyptians I talked to, and it was clearly popular with working-class people as well as with middle-class elites. The textile workers of El Mahalla El Kubra signed onto the campaign, and one who was interviewed said that the entire city would sign because Morsi had not achieved any of the aims of the revolution. This working-class disaffection created a crucial ally for Rebellion.

Rebellion sought to collect 15 million signatures on its petition. That number was chosen because Morsi had won about 13 million in his contest against Shafiq, so 15 million would demonstrate buyer's remorse even among some who had voted for him. Rebellion's leaders claimed to have 15 million signatures by mid-June, and by the end of the month they said they had 22 million.[53] Doubts have been raised as to whether this number is plausible, but I believe they are unfounded: it doesn't take long to sign a petition, and people circulated them to friends and friends of friends, who put down their names and national ID numbers, then handed them in to a movement organizer. It was the paper equivalent of an internet meme going viral. It has also been charged that the youth were cat's paws of old regime figures, an allegation that seems to me unlikely if we consider the whole movement. April 6 and the Revolutionary Socialists were a key part of the new youth movement and hardly on good terms with the former elite.[54] (Remnants of the Mubarak regime were no doubt also plotting the overthrow of Morsi, but then most Egyptians were pretty unhappy by that point.)

Morsi's authoritarian and sectarian actions clearly took a large toll. A Gallup poll found that the favorability rating of the Brotherhood's Freedom and Justice Party plummeted from about 50 percent to only 19 percent between April 2012 and early June 2013. Perhaps more worrying, the public quickly became convinced that the electoral process was corrupt. On the first anniversary of the revolution, January 2012, about 89 percent of Egyptians said that they believed the elections were fair. At the time of Morsi's constitutional fiasco in December 2012, that number fell to 60 percent. By early June 2013 only 34 percent had confidence in the elections. (Egyptians' most recent experience with the ballot box, the hasty constitutional referendum on the constitution, which was deeply flawed procedurally, likely went a long way toward fueling this new cynicism.) The people did not like their ruling party at all two and a half years after the overthrow of Mubarak, and they despaired of the probity of any subsequent elections. It was a recipe for another revolution.[55]

On June 30, only one year into the four-year term of President Morsi, millions of Egyptians demonstrated to demand early presidential elections. According to the military, the nationwide rallies were the largest in Egyptian history: 500,000 in Tahrir Square in Cairo and 100,000 in downtown Alexandria demanding that Morsi "depart."[56] The streets were so packed that late arrivers could not reach the square. Tens of thousands of protesters marched from Tahrir to the Ittihadiya presidential palace, chanting, "The people want the fall of the regime" and slogans against the Muslim Brotherhood and calling for the fall of the Supreme Guide, Muhammad Badie, whom they considered Morsi's puppeteer.

Demonstrations were also held in provincial towns and cities all over the country. Crowds at Damietta chanted in reference to Muslim Brotherhood politicians, "Katatni and el-Erian: Egypt won't become Iran." Activists on Twitter in Ismailia declared the city a Muslim Brotherhood–free zone. Brotherhood centers were attacked or burned in some provincial towns. In the Muqattam Hills above Cairo crowds set fire to the headquarters of the Freedom and Justice Party. The army estimated that twenty thousand supporters demonstrated for Morsi in the square in front of the Rabi'a al-'Adawiya Mosque in Nasr City, about five kilometers from the Ittihadiya presidential palace.

On July 1, Brigadier General Abdel Fattah al-Sisi, Morsi's minister of defense, gave the government two days to reach a political settlement with the revolutionary youth in the streets, saying that he would not allow Egypt to slide into civil war. It later emerged that al-Sisi had been giving Morsi fruitless ultimatums all spring, extremely distressed at the president's polarization of the country and what the officers saw as a tendency to be soft on Muslim extremists. He had pushed the president to come to an accommodation with his liberal and leftist rivals, but to no avail. Morsi replied the next day with a brief, defiant speech, in which he repeatedly insisted on the legitimacy of his presidency, based on the free and fair election of the previous year.

On July 3 al-Sisi launched a military coup, to the delight of the Rebellion Movement youth, who partied in Tahrir late into the night and put on an epic fireworks show. The action set off a vehement argument about whether what had happened was a coup (with the implication that it was illegitimate) or a revolution, in which case it was a manifestation of popular will. There certainly was a popular revolutionary element to the events, with millions of protesters coming out on July 7 and after, in the biggest demonstrations in Egyptian history. It was not merely a coup d'état from above by a handful of officers, though there certainly was a coup, with the military moving armored vehicles into place and the president and several other high officials taken into custody.

Al-Sisi announced that the disputed constitution rushed into law by Morsi would be suspended, and a balanced Constituent Assembly would be formed to revise it. He also pledged new presidential and parliamentary elections, which were scheduled for 2014. He announced an interim president, Adly Mansour, who had been the acting chief justice of the Supreme Constitutional Court, asserting that it was the crowds at Tahrir Square who insisted Mansour head the transition. Al-Sisi initially played to the progressive youth, promising that a mechanism would be established to allow them to be partners in policy decisions. Sharing the podium with the military was a young Rebellion spokesman, Mahmoud Badr, looking like a nervous undergraduate amid a roster of notables that included senior officers, the Coptic pope, and the rector of al-Azhar Seminary. The scene underscored the centrality of the millennials to Egypt's ongoing political turmoil, though it also raised the question of whether they were allowing wily baby boomers to manipulate them. Al-Sisi revealed that the officer corps had been in dialogue with the various political parties and forces since the crisis of November 2012. He said that all the political actors had shown a willingness to compromise to end the crisis except Morsi, who refused to show any flexibility. Since the Egyptian army is a sort of corporate holding company, with vast economic interests, one suspects that Morsi's poor economic record was one motive for the coup, quite apart from ideology.

In the end, the revolution and the coup worked in tandem, as a "revocouption." Such a conjunction is not unusual in history. There is a sense in which the 1952 Egyptian revolution, the young officers' coup, was made possible only by months of popular unrest during which parts of downtown Cairo were burned. The initial split personality of the July 3 revocouption was apparent in the contrary positions taken by the opposition. On one hand, many of the youth organizations called for pluralism and for allowing the Freedom and Justice Party to participate in politics. Those activists saw Morsi, not his party, as the problem. On the other hand, many of the military officers (and a section of the youth movement) frankly despised the Muslim Brotherhood as a manipulative and grasping cult that used dishonest tactics to grab power and subject others. Some even viewed it as a stealth terrorist organization. These anti-Brotherhood figures pointed to the attempt to prosecute the popular comedian Bassem Youssef for criticizing Morsi as typical of the Brotherhood's intrinsic intolerance, and they suggested there were dark conspiracies to free extremists from prison and allow them to gather in the Sinai. A legal case was prepared against Morsi, Khairat al-Shater, and Supreme Guide Muhammad Badie, charging them with ordering goons to kill protesters in front of the presidential palace on December 6, 2012.

Al-Sisi called for, and got, massive crowds on July 26 supporting his request for power to pursue a "war on terror" (to repress the Muslim Brotherhood). The Rebellion Movement warmly embraced his call and organized processions to Tahrir Square that day from seven other city squares. Sixty-eight political parties also deployed their campaign organizations to bring out members and sympathizers. Across the country millions demonstrated in favor of a mandate for the military. The main labor federation said it would try to assemble 5 million factory and office workers.[57] Al-Sisi got his extremely divisive mandate, in part because of his new popularity with the millennials, who were scarred by their bad experience with procedural democracy, of which they felt Morsi had taken illicit advantage.

April 6 and the Revolutionary Socialists, now somewhat eclipsed by the Rebellion Movement, objected to this creep toward military reassertion. They demonstrated at a "Third Square," forced to cede Tahrir to Rebellion, whose leaders were somewhat younger than Ahmed Maher, then in his early thirties. Unlike the long-standing New Left organizations, Rebellion was nothing but an ad hoc network and lacked the long-honed principles of the former. Many of its leaders had first become politicized by the January 25, 2011 revolution and lacked the long history of political cooperation across party lines characteristic of Kefaya and its successors. The New Left was glad enough to see Morsi's increasingly authoritarian rule end (some of them had been prosecuted for demonstrating against him), but they were uneasy with the direction things were taking. Having spent most of 2011 and 2012 struggling to return the military to its barracks and transition to civilian government, the progressive youth movements were unhappy about al-Sisi's signs of grandiosity.[58]

The Muslim Brotherhood initially responded to the coup by attempting to use the Tahrir method of occupying city squares and calling for waves of demonstrations, in hopes of mobilizing the country against the military. However, they were unable to attract the millions that Rebellion assembled. Instead, a few tens of thousands gathered at select sites, such as the square in front of the Rabi'a al-'Adawiyya Mosque in Cairo, the central square at Giza, and a few squares in other cities. The military and the National Salvation

Front parties accused them of kidnapping and torturing secularists and of plotting a campaign of terrorism. Likewise the officers and the secular politicians charged that Muslim Brother cadres attacked or even burned churches in several parts of the country. Some of the charges may have been true, but most of the demonstrators at Rabi'a al-'Adawiyya and Giza were peaceful.

In mid-August the military moved against these massive sit-ins, killing hundreds. The military-backed appointed government declared a state of emergency, bringing back for several months an authoritarian tool of governance against which the revolutionaries had protested for the preceding decade. Elements in the government of interim president Adly Mansour wanted to ban the Muslim Brotherhood, whose major leaders were rounded up and treated as conspirators or would-be terrorists. Al Jazeera Egypt and other media were suppressed and some reporters were arrested. The New Left and liberal youth movements protested vigorously against this retreat from the civil liberties for which they had worked so long and hard, girding themselves for what seemed likely to be many more years of struggle and risk. Disturbingly, Rebellion youth leaders such as Mahmoud Badr supported the Draconian crackdown on the Muslim Brotherhood by the military and by elements of the old Mubarak elite. Egypt's path to democratization, never smooth, had just become strewn with new obstacles.

In the fall of 2013, the fiction of a civilian elite increasingly fell away as the officer corps became more repressive. The interim government of Hazem el-Beblawi passed a Draconian law against demonstrating without receiving prior approval from the Interior Ministry. Veteran blogger Alaa Abdel Fattah was arrested for violating this statute, as were Ahmad Maher and other members of April 6. Maher was initially sentenced to three years of hard labor. Abdel Fattah was given a one-year suspended sentence but threatened with jail time if he was arrested again. In December 2013, the security directorate in Mansoura was blown up, and the Egyptian military immediately blamed the Muslim Brotherhood, which was completely banned. Even speaking up in its defense would be punished by a five-year sentence and a big fine. The military's vendetta against the Muslim Brotherhood appears to have been spurred on in part by three Gulf oil monarchies: Kuwait, the United Arab Emirates, and Saudi Arabia. They viewed the Brotherhood as a subversive form of political Islam that potentially challenged their conservative, monarchical uses of Muslim conservatism, and ponied up some $24 billion in aid pledges to the military government.

A new constitution was drafted by supposed liberals, which did have some virtues (it strictly forbade torture and gave more rights to children, and it removed the more theocratic elements of the Morsi constitution). But three years after the overthrow of Mubarak, the ideals of the left-liberal youth movements were far from being attained, and in some areas of law and practice there was a reversion to Mubarak-era techniques. The crushing of the Muslim Brotherhood seemed likely to radicalize some of its members and to lead to terrorist attacks and perhaps long-term instability in a country that needs tourism and foreign investment. Many millennials, traumatized by the year of Brotherhood rule, acquiesced in this crackdown. But their generation is so mobilized that the aspiration of General al-Sisi, the Mubarak-era judges, and the Gulf oil monarchies to restore the pre-2011 status quo faced many obstacles.

April 6 and other New Left movements served the function of a check on perceived attempts at continued dictatorial power, whether by Tantawi's SCAF or Morsi's Muslim Brotherhood, during the two and a half years after the fall of Mubarak. As with Kefaya's experience in 2005, the youth activists proved not very good at winning seats in Parliament, though it may be that the peculiar electoral rules in place in the fall of 2011 disadvantaged them. Some activists, such as Ahmed Maher, were against allowing the movement to become a political party, seeing value in preserving the independent political network as a force outside parliamentary politics.

The New Left, however, racked up an impressive series of victories that powerfully shaped Egypt's new political era. Early on it achieved the dismissal of police implicated in violence against protesters and forced pro-Mubarak cabinet members out of the interim Sharaf government. It is not clear that Mubarak and his sons and associates would have been tried, or at least tried so soon, had it not been for the July 2011 Tahrir protests. The New Left and their big rallies gave cover to the independent labor movement in 2011–13, as millions of workers resigned from state unions and formed their own. In 2011–12 the military was forced to allow a much wider range of political speech than it would have liked, including grudgingly tolerating calls for its own return to the barracks. In late May 2012 SCAF was forced to announce the end of the state of emergency that had been declared in 1981 and that suspended many civil rights. By the winter of 2012 it was forced to stop using military tribunals to process arrested activists on a massive scale.

When President Morsi declared himself above the courts, forced a non-consensus constitution on the country, tried to legislate right-wing, religiously tinged laws with his rump upper house of Parliament, and pursued a vindictive and invidious policy of prosecuting critics and bringing an ever increasing number of blasphemy charges against Christian schoolteachers, the New Left turned on their erstwhile partner of convenience. In November and December 2012 they mounted huge nationwide demonstrations against the president's claim on extrajudicial power, moving from Tahrir Square to the Ittihadiyya presidential palace and forcing the president to flee. Their street actions gave support to the complaints of the parties grouped in the National Salvation Front, which otherwise might have seemed isolated and full of sour grapes. The youth played a crucial role in crystallizing the nation's social and economic discontent with Brotherhood rule.

The skills in crowd mobilization and street politics demonstrated by April 6 and kindred groups allowed them to continue to pressure the new Egyptian establishment to move in a revolutionary direction. Their ability to put thousands of youth in the streets allowed the New Left repeatedly to give the junta, and then the Brotherhood, the choice between risking public opprobrium by brutally repressing them or giving in to some of their demands for the sake of social peace. Where SCAF turned to violence, as in the December 2011 crackdown that produced the notorious video of the beating of the girl in the blue bra, it suffered a fall in public estimation and was forced to back down. The youth movements faced repression under Morsi, and mobilized to remove him. It was the last big hurrah of the revolutionary era, after which the military and elements of the old regime reasserted themselves, attempting to put an end to the era of demonstrations and political upheaval. Even if they succeed in the short term, it seems unlikely that we have heard the last of the Egyptian millennials.

8

Libya's Youth Rebels

Libya was even more tightly controlled by Muammar Gaddafi, his sons, his loyalists, and his ubiquitous "revolutionary committees" than was the case with Ben Ali's Tunisia or Mubarak's Egypt.[1] Unlike the UGET in Tunisia or April 6 in Egypt, there was no organized youth movement in Libya, where independent organizations were not tolerated. A Gallup poll done in major urban areas in 2010 showed that only about 66 percent of Libyans age fifteen to twenty-nine thought that young Libyans could help their country "make substantial progress," and only 55 percent thought that young women could. In contrast, in middle-income Arab countries, 94 percent thought young men could make a difference, and nearly 80 percent thought young women could.[2] Libyan millennials were far less self-assured, though it is important to note that a majority did believe in their generation's importance. In 1996 Gaddafi forbade the teaching of foreign languages, so Libyan youth were not as cosmopolitan as their counterparts in neighboring countries. The internet was relatively underdeveloped in the country. Since Libya was an oil state and the regime provided some welfare for the disadvantaged and unemployed, far fewer Libyans went abroad for work than was the case with Tunisia or Egypt.

Still, the grievances of Libyan youth were familiar: youth unemployment was high, the government neglected key infrastructure, and the state was extremely repressive. As with other countries tending toward republican monarchy, the sons of Gaddafi acted like spoiled princes. Some of them were themselves millennials, but their peers saw them as villains. In addition to their resentments against government regimentation, Libyan youth objected to Gaddafi's favoritism toward some regions and his neglect of others, especially the east of the country and the Berber region of Jabal Nafusa. After the Tunisian and Egyptian upheavals, Libyan youth quickly formed flash mobs and Facebook groups, spontaneously organizing to challenge the control of the revolutionary committees. How would the Gaddafi regime, which claimed to have no central leader, respond to this networked and largely leaderless rebellion?

The Massocracy of Fear

Like most of the Arab world, Libya had been a province of the Ottoman Empire in the nineteenth century. It had three major territorial and demographic components: Cyrenaica in the east, Tripolitania in the west, and Fezzan in the southwest. The Ottomans lightly garrisoned the territory and had little power beyond the towns along the Mediterranean coast. A well-organized Sufi brotherhood (devoted Muslim mystics who met to chant and worship) named the Sanusi provided the backbone of local political power in the east of the country. It sometimes turned militant.

In 1911, during the heyday of the European craze for acquiring colonial possessions, Italy took Libya. (Italy got into the game late and was therefore only a minor player.) Some Libyans chafed under Italian rule, especially during the harsh decades under fascist strongman Benito Mussolini. Umar Mukhtar launched a rebellion in 1912, centered in the east at Benghazi, and intensified his activities in the late 1920s with the help of the Sanusi Sufi brotherhood. He was wounded and captured by Mussolini's forces in 1931 and swiftly hanged. During World War II the British in Egypt at length expelled Italy and its German allies from Libya and administered it along with France as a caretaker until the United Nations took over and ushered the country into independence in 1951. The leader of the Sanusi order at that time, Idris, who had established an emirate in eastern Libya after the war, was made a reluctant king of the whole of Libya. He declined to move from his base in Benghazi to Tripoli. His appointed prime ministers, their cabinets, and the legislature (which was elected on a nonparty basis in what were widely believed to be fixed polls) were weak leaders. Libya in the late 1960s was still mostly rural. Oil exportation had begun in 1961 and mushroomed to 3 million barrels a day by the end of the decade, making the country one of the more important petroleum producers in the world. But the money had yet to make a big impact. Illiteracy was over 80 percent, and the poverty rate was high. The British and the Americans both had military bases in the country, licensed by King Idris, though in the late 1960s his government took steps to close them down.

Especially in the east of the country, Libyans looked to Egypt as an opinion leader, and those who went to college often did so in Cairo or Alexandria. In the 1950s and 1960s enthusiasm grew among the Libyans born after the war for the ideas of Gamal Abdel Nasser, who veered increasingly toward socialism and an alliance with the Soviet Union. In 1969 Colonel Muammar Gaddafi and other junior officers staged a coup, deposed Idris, and announced a revolutionary state. By the mid-1970s Gaddafi had committed himself to a political and economic system that mixed together some of the elements of Nasser's Arab nationalism, Mao Zedong's Cultural Revolution, and East Germany's domestic spying apparatus, the Stasi. He issued his revolutionary manifesto, the Green Book, which was inflicted on generations of Libyans as their guide to correct ideology. Gaddafi's was a kind of Arab Stalinism, shorn of antireligious materialist philosophical underpinnings, and by the late 1970s he had outlawed private property altogether. He co-opted Muslim rhetoric and forbade alcohol, in keeping with Islamic law (sharia). He hinted that he was a Mahdi, a Muslim messiah figure. But he did not allow competing Muslim currents and cracked down hard on the Libyan branch of the Muslim Brotherhood, radicalizing them. By 1973 he had formed two thousand local committees tightly controlled by him and his Revolutionary Command Council. He proclaimed a new form of government: rule by the masses, or massocracy. Later in the 1970s the revolutionary committees began purging the university faculties and bureaucracy of thousands considered insufficiently committed to the revolution. They arbitrarily announced the abrogation of legal statutes on the books and took control of radio and television stations. A paramilitary, the Popular Resistance Forces, was armed and trained. Auto-da-fés were held of Old Regime books; the list of banned authors included Jean-Paul Sartre, Baudelaire, Ezra Pound, Graham Greene, Henry James, and D. H. Lawrence. In the late 1970s Libyan authorities began simply lynching dissidents, even on university campuses.[3]

I wanted to get a personal sense of the tragedies inflicted on Libyans by the jailings and secret murders of dissidents. Before I left the United States for Egypt in 2012, I had investigated getting a visa to Libya and learned that Americans had to be invited into the country by a Libyan. My colleague Khaled Mattawa, a distinguished Libyan poet and translator in the English Department at the University of Michigan, was in the country, and I wrote him asking for an invitation. He did a great deal better than that, arranging a formal invitation from the Transitional National Council. It was not clear, however, whether the invitation would be enough or whether I needed an actual visa, so I went to the Libyan embassy in Zamalek, an upscale neighborhood on an island in the Nile, near downtown Cairo. About sixty people were milling around outside. I asked the guard which entrance to use and he sent me around to the side, but the door there was locked. I went back to him to complain. He said, "The embassy is closed today. Come back Sunday." I tried coming back several times over the succeeding days. Finally the guards told me that the embassy wouldn't open for at least a week. It became clear that I was not going to get a visa from Zamalek.

Then I ran into an Egyptian who worked with nongovernmental organizations in Libya, who told me that an invitation would be enough for Benghazi but might not work at the airport in the capital, Tripoli, where the bureaucracy was more strict. "The airport in Benghazi," he said, "is just one room." So I contacted Khaled and suggested that I fly to Benghazi. He agreed that it was a good plan, and as he had business there, he would meet me at the airport. I was still not sure that I would be allowed to board the Air Egypt flight in Cairo without a visa or that I would be allowed into Libya once I arrived. At Cairo Airport, when the security official asked to see the visa in my passport, I showed him the invitation letter, which was stamped "good for a two-week stay." He examined it suspiciously, then smiled. "Two weeks, huh?" he said, as he waved me through. I couldn't shake a little anxi-ety during the flight about what awaited me on arrival. It wouldn't be so bad to be deported back to Cairo, but I didn't want to be arrested and put in a Libyan holding cell. When we deplaned and got to the one room where the passport officials sat, I could see Khaled behind them greeting me with a broad smile. The man in the uniform looked at my papers, arranged for a visa, and waved me through, saying my friend had already talked to him. I was in Benghazi, a city about which I had been worried sick in February and March 2011, when troops of Gaddafi's armored division were advancing on it with mass murder on their minds.

A couple of days later, Khaled kindly took me to meet the historian and physician Muhammad al-Mufti. Born in Dirna in 1943, he had graduated with a medical degree from the University of Leeds in 1968.[4] The dapper, gentlemanly al-Mufti received us in his book-lined study. As I looked at the shelves and shelves of books, I thought of the story the new head of the Na-tional Library in Benghazi told me. He said that in the early 1980s Gaddafi appointed a general to run the library. The man was dismissive of books. "All we need," he declared, "is the Green Book." Libya under Gaddafi, I thought, was no place for a bibliophile.

Dr. al-Mufti confirmed my conclusion. He told me that, as a young man, he had been enthusiastic about the 1969 revolution that deposed the conservative King Idris. In those early days Colonel Gaddafi went around the country meeting people fairly freely, and in the early 1970s al-Mufti had an opportunity to meet him. Gaddafi asked his opinion about where to take the country, and Al-Mufti suggested that it would be good for Libya to move from a military regime toward parliamentary democracy. He said it in all innocence, convinced that Gaddafi wanted an honest answer and was casting about for a new direction. He admits now, "Perhaps I was naïve." Gaddafi was in fact looking for a new model in 1973, but it was the Maoist model of Cultural Revolution and anti-intellectualism that attracted him. Shortly after al-Mufti spoke out, secret police came to his home and ar-rested him. He spent eleven years in prison for his remark.

Al-Mufti's wife, Najat al-Kikhia, had just won a seat on the Benghazi city council when I visited him that morning in late May. A professor of statistics at the university, she got more votes than any other candidate. Unlike her liberal husband, she is a member of the Muslim religious right. (A liberal Libyan to whom I spoke after a talk I gave in Benghazi viewed her as "dangerously fundamentalist.") Professor al-Kikhia's family had had their own encounter with Gaddafi's murderous repression. Her brother, Mansour Rashid al-Kikhia, had studied law in Egypt and France. He entered the foreign ministry in 1958, during the reign of King Idris, and became foreign minister in 1972–73, early in the revolutionary experiment, but later broke with the regime and emerged as a major voice of opposition. He went to Cairo in late November 1993 for a conference of the Arab Human Rights League, and on December 10 he disappeared. Egyptian intelligence had the Libyan embassy under surveillance and carefully traced two cars that went overland from Cairo to Libya via Marsa Matrouh that weekend. (After the fall of Mubarak, *al-Ahram*, Egypt's newspaper of record, acquired and printed the intelligence report on their movements.) Al-Kikhia was hidden in one of the cars. Once back in his home country, he was transported to Tripoli and shot down by a firing squad, according to *al-Ahram*'s investigation.[5] The narrative of the Egyptian intelligence officials raised the question of why, if al-Kikhia and the Libyan agents under cover at the embassy were under surveillance, Egyptian authorities had allowed the kidnapping. There is also the question of why Hosni Mubarak did not appoint a governmental commission to look into the disappearance on Egyptian soil of a former Libyan foreign minister in town to attend a human rights conference! The squalid state of human rights in Mubarak's Egypt requires no more eloquent statement than the regime's silence in the wake of this incident.

A clue as to the motives for this insouciance was provided by Abdel Rahman Shalgam, another high-ranking Libyan diplomat who gave an interview in the Arabic press in July 2011.[6] As the dictators fell, their secrets began tumbling out. Shalgam, who had served as Libyan foreign minister from 2000 to 2009, alleged that Gaddafi and his oil money played a role in propping up the corrupt and dictatorial regimes of Mubarak in Egypt and Ben Ali in Tunisia. Shalgam said that the cooperation of the "security apparatus" (secret police) was so complete between Libya and Tunisia that Gaddafi had actually put Ben Ali on a monthly retainer. Likewise, he said, Gaddafi offered a wide range of personal "support" to Mubarak, buying him a private plane and providing other emoluments. He alleged that General

Omar Suleiman (d. 2012), the former head of Egyptian military intelligence, was "Libya's man in Egypt." Under Suleiman, military intelligence was accused of having used unsavory techniques of interrogation redolent of those deployed by Gaddafi himself. That Gaddafi had bribed Mubarak, along with someone in the Egyptian intelligence establishment, to allow him to deal with any Libyan dissidents who sought refuge in the neighboring country is perfectly plausible, and it would explain why Egyptian secret police allowed al-Kikhia to be abducted while they were actually following him and his kidnappers.

As I sat in that study in Benghazi, I marveled at the baneful effect that Gaddafi's police state had had on just this one household, with one of its members jailed for over a decade for speaking frankly and the brother of its other resident abducted and summarily executed. How many thousands of such households were there in Benghazi alone? The regime was particularly harsh toward anyone who had been an insider, such as al-Kikhia, and then left, since they were thought to know damning details and to continue to have influence on the inside. The Gaddafi government and its revolutionary committees were run like a cult.

Along with arbitrary imprisonment and torture of political dissidents at home, Gaddafi emerged onto the North Atlantic scene as an element of disorder. He helped fund and train the Irish Republican Army at a time when it was setting off bombs in London. (Ireland had legitimate grievances toward British policy, but bombings in public places that kill innocents are reprehensible.) He was alleged to have been involved in the bombing in 1986 of a Berlin dance club known to be frequented by U.S. troops. (Gaddafi had close relations with East Germany, which trained his own domestic spies.) After President Ronald Reagan bombed Tripoli and Benghazi that year, Gaddafi claimed that an adopted daughter was killed in the bombing, even though she later turned up as a dentist in Tripoli with a new identity. Gaddafi commissioned a small sculpture showing an arm and fist reaching up to grab an F-16 fighter-jet, which he placed outside his Bab al-Aziziya palace. He was allegedly behind the 1988 bombing of Pan Am 103 over Lockerbie, Scotland, probably in revenge for the U.S. bombing raids. With a population of only 3 million at that time, and an oil industry that required at least some cooperation from the world economy, Libya had reached its limits as a radical, independent actor, and the North Atlantic powers and their Arab allies moved to contain it.

Blocked in other arenas, Gaddafi used Libya's petroleum revenues to fund substantial involvement in sub-Saharan Africa. He styled himself "the king of kings of Africa," often sporting opulent robes to underline the point. Nearby to Libya he pursued racist Arabization projects, attempting to empower Arabic-speaking groups. He supported one faction in the long civil war in Chad, occupying the north of the country at times, but was expelled by a united Chadian effort in 1987. He was also an element of disorder in Sudan's Darfur region, backing expansion of the power of Arabic-speaking tribes and training fighters for the Janjaweed militia. He also pursued "dinar diplomacy" in western and southern Africa, far from traditional regions of Arab or Muslim influence. About a third of African leaders were said to be taking money from him. He also was alleged to have been deeply involved in wars in Sierra Leone and Liberia. On the positive side, he gave some funding and training to Umkhonto we Sizwe, the paramilitary wing of South Africa's anti-apartheid movement, the African National Congress.[7]

In part because Gaddafi and his advisers did not want to use up the country's oil reserves, and in part because of U.S. sanctions, which began hurting investment and infrastructure upgrades in Libya in the 1980s, Libya produced only about a million barrels a day through the 1980s. United Nations sanctions were imposed in 1992. Nevertheless, beginning in the early 1990s the country managed to increase production to about a million and a half barrels a day, which remained the plateau until the 2011 revolution.[8] By the mid-1980s, after a decade and a half of sometimes wild economic and political experiments, Gaddafi accepted the need for some economic reforms and a greater role for the market. These changes were relatively minor until the mid-1990s. Libya lost a regional ally when East Germany dissolved into a reunited Germany in 1989, and then lost a Great Power patron in 1991 with the collapse of the Soviet Union. In about 1995 the regime began allowing small private companies to operate again.

The stifling political atmosphere in Libya and the disruptions in rules governing property wrought enormous violence on the public sphere and denied space to civil society. Despite Gaddafi's protestations that he was an elder brother rather than leader, the revolutionary committees enforced a cult of personality and crushed dissent. At the same time, Gaddafi's regime vastly expanded educational opportunities for the entire population, and the oil industry led to substantial urbanization. Gaddafi's rule produced two generations of much more urban, much more literate and educated Libyans, who, however, had no outlet for their economic, professional, and political aspirations.

Princes of the House of Gaddafi

As in most of the other Arab republics, the next generation of the ruling family emerged as serious political and economic players in the twenty-first century.[9] European and UN sanctions were finally lifted in 2004, when Libya agreed to pay indemnities to the Lockerbie families. By then Gaddafi's second son, Saif al-Islam, had enough influence with his father to convince him to abandon work on chemical, biological, and nuclear weapons in order to end U.S. sanctions as well. The government became more pragmatic and was able to attract back to the country technocrats who had fled in the repressive 1970s and 1980s.[10]

Saif's emergence into prominence signaled Libya's turn toward republican monarchy. He was clearly the leading candidate among the two or three sons being primed to succeed. All of the Gaddafi children, however, had opportunities in the reformed, more technocratic Libyan state.[11] To begin with, as U.S. embassy officials in Tripoli observed, "All of the Qadhafi children and [regime] favorites are supposed to have income streams from the National Oil Company and oil services subsidiaries."[12] One-Nine Petroleum, under the control of Saif, sought sweetheart deals that would enrich the family and its hangers-on. The Gaddafi family also had a large stake in Libyan tourism through ownership of the Bab Africa Corinthia Hotel, one of the few nice complexes where conferences could be held. Daughter Aisha Gaddafi allegedly deployed her charitable foundation to acquire businesses in health care, including plastic surgery. She and her mother, Safia Farkhash (Gaddafi's second wife), also had financial interests in the private clothing stores established after 1995; it was alleged that they sometimes had customs hold up the shipments to their competitors before holidays and other major shopping periods.

These openings for wealth and power sometimes created fierce rivalries among the eleven Gaddafi offspring, as illustrated in the Great Coca-Cola Battle of 2005–6.[13] On December 28, 2005, troops showed up suddenly at the local Coca-Cola franchisee's bottling factory in Tripoli, only two weeks after it began production. An eyewitness told the U.S. embassy that "two military cars carrying armed personnel without clear identification illegally broke into the facility, asked the employees to leave the premises and shut down the plant." The troops may have been loyal to Mu'tasim Gaddafi (1974–2011), whereas the Coca-Cola franchise was held by his brother Muhammad (b. 1970, now in Algeria). The wrinkle is that Mu'tasim had originally made the deal in the 1990s, through a Tunisian partner, to set up a holding company that could get around U.S. sanctions. Then, in 2001, he is alleged to have attempted to stage a coup against his father and was exiled to Egypt. Muhammad, head of the Olympic Committee, put the Coca-Cola franchise in the hands of that state organ, which he controlled. Mu'tasim made up with his father in 2005 and knew that his brother had muscled in on his franchise, so he had his loyalists disrupt the plant in preparation for his return early in 2006.

Mu'tasim's troops beat up a worker at the plant in February and camped out for a while on its grounds. His goons then threatened Jordanian middle managers so they would stop working for Muhammad. The plant remained idle for months. U.S. embassy officials heard a rumor that Aisha Gaddafi stepped in to negotiate a settlement between her two brothers, which they agreed to in May 2006, allowing the plant to reopen and thirsty Libyans to have a Coke and a smile. That this story sounds like a competition over ownership of a Las Vegas casino by two brothers in the Chicago mob in the 1960s is no accident. The Gaddafis increasingly operated as a family cartel.

The incident also reveals the predilections of the two brothers involved. Muhammad is a businessman, and despite being the eldest, had no interest in succeeding his father as the republican monarch. He gained notoriety for insisting that Pope Benedict XVI convert to Islam and calling for a fight against infidels in 2006, when the pontiff criticized Islam.[14] He went on to chair the state General Posts and Telecommunications Company, which was in charge of cell phone and satellite services in Libya. (His contribution to the counterrevolutionary effort in 2011 was to cut off internet service for six months.) In contrast, Mu'tasim, famed for his love of the good life and of women, was an army officer and in 2008 became national security adviser. He negotiated with the U.S. government for better and more sophisticated weaponry, and during the revolution he commanded troops at Brega in 2011 in the attempt to advance on Benghazi. A younger brother, Khamis (1983–2011) was also interested in military affairs (his two higher degrees were both at military academies, in Libya and the Russian Federation), and he developed his own professional military unit, the "Khamis Brigade."

Some of the sons exhibited the problems of a troubled Hollywood starlet more than those of an ambitious member of a family firm. Saadi Gaddafi (b. 1973) is a case in point. Educated as an engineer, he became obsessed with soccer; he actually managed to make an appearance with the Serie A Perugia team in Italy in 2003, though he was lambasted for being painfully slow and was washed out when he failed the drug test. He nevertheless insisted on heading most important offices in Libyan soccer and was majority owner of the major Libyan al-Ahli team. Then he became enthusiastic about being an officer in a military Special Forces unit but allegedly grew bored by that life. Then he fancied himself a movie mogul, creating and owning World Navigator Entertainment. Behind the scenes he may have played his own part in the Great Coca-Cola Battle of 2006. By 2009 he had moved to the town of Zuwara in the far west of the country along the coast, near Tunisia, where he wanted to build up a duty-free zone and construct a new, artificial city, with its own port and airport. A shadow was cast over all these plans by this son's flakiness, however. The U.S. ambassador noted, "Saadi has a troubled past, including scuffles with police in Europe (especially Italy), abuse of drugs and alcohol, excessive partying, travel abroad in contravention of his father's wishes."[15]

Even more troubled was the youngest son, Hannibal. He had an interest in Libya's naval affairs and its merchant marine. In 2004 he was arrested in Paris for drunkenly racing his Ferrari at 90 miles an hour up the Champs-Élysées, running several red lights. When French police initially tried to arrest him, two cars full of his bodyguards pulled up and beat the officers. The French authorities let Hannibal go on grounds of diplomatic immunity, infuriating the French police.[16] In 2008, while he and his wife, Aline Skaf, were staying in a $7,000-a-night imperial suite at the President Wilson Hotel in Geneva, Switzerland, they allegedly beat their servants nearly to death. The Moroccan, Hasan, and his Tunisian wife filed charges. The Swiss police went to the chalet and arrested the Gaddafi couple; bail was set at over $450,000. Aline, very pregnant, was held under guard at a hospital; Hannibal was jailed for two days. The old dictator, infuriated that a son of his might be subject to the rule of law, declared an economic jihad (holy war) on Switzerland, demonstrating in his response a foreign policy thuggishness to match his son's domestic brutality. He demanded that the police who arrested Hannibal be disciplined. The U.S. ambassador in Tripoli lamented later that year that the Libyan government "recently notified Swiss companies active in Libya that they must cease their operations and liquidate their locally-held assets by January 31. Employees of Swiss companies have been threatened with incarceration unless they leave Libya immediately."[17] As for the servants, they initially pursued a civil suit against Hannibal, but after Hasan's mother, who was living in Libya, was detained for a month, allegedly badly beaten, and his brother disappeared, Hasan and his wife's Swiss attorney announced that, "in full liberty" and "after deep reflection," they had decided to drop their suit.[18]

The most prominent of the sons, Saif, was considered a leading candidate for heir apparent.[19] His main rival was his brother Mu'tasim, the national security adviser. Despite his lack of an official position, Saif functioned as an informal prime minister. U.S. embassy officials in Tripoli observed of his financial interests, "Saif stands behind the Economic and Social Development Fund (ESDF), which holds one of the most extensive investment portfolios in the country. His oil company NESSO is a member of one of the few successful oil production consortiums in the country, and he is the primary investor in Libya's Coca-Cola operation, among other ventures."[20] So it seems in the end that his brothers' rivalry over the Coca-Cola concession was for naught, and that Saif managed to acquire it. His One-Nine Group made a bid to distribute all imported foreign print publications in Libya. It was a sign of progress that more foreign publications would be available, but, as the U.S. embassy noted, "the Qadhafi family will clearly accrue significant financial gains from having exclusive rights to distribute foreign press in Libya, as well as effective censorship over any troubling articles that might appear."[21] When it came out that he had paid rhythm-and-blues star Mariah Carey a million dollars to perform at a New Year's Eve bash in St. Bart's, Saif's newspaper immediately denied the story and said that the financing had been handled by Mu'tasim. Saif's political rhetoric about openness to the West made him popular among many of the youth in Tripoli. His actual authoritarianism, however, was apparent when demonstrations broke out in Benghazi in February 2011 and he insisted that they be swiftly put down. "Let's go!" he said to the murderous armored corps heading for Libya's second city. "Let's go!"

Around the Gaddafis were prominent business families benefiting from their political ties to the ruling family. Only five families controlled food distribution; consumer goods distribution was in the hands of three families. The U.S. embassy reported, "The Akida Group, run by the Akak family, is rumored to have close ties to the ruling regime and it runs a virtual monopoly over air conditioning equipment, heating units, and small appliances as the local LG agent."[22] The economy was dominated by four banks, all owned by the Central Bank. Loans were hard to get and awarded on the basis of political connections.[23]

When I was walking around Tripoli in early June 2012, I stopped at an electronics store off Omar Mukhtar Avenue. This thoroughfare stretched toward what used to be called Green Square (now Martyrs' Square), where Gaddafi staged his interminable harangues. It has a colonnade on either side, with shops set back along it. The store, I was later told, was amazingly well-stocked compared to the past. I asked the owner, in Arabic, how things had changed since the fall of the regime the previous autumn. He broke out in a broad smile and said that for the first time, he knew whether he would make a profit. He explained that he used to send buyers to Dubai, and they would bring back electronics at the best price they could find. Whether the price was one on which he could make a profit depended on the tariff rate he would have to pay when the goods arrived at customs in Tripoli. His brow furrowed. The problem was that Gaddafi kept tinkering with the tariff rates, and you could never know in advance whether they would be favorable or not.

Dissidents

By the beginning of this century, it was clear that the regime was widely hated inside Libya. At the commemoration of Gaddafi's thirty-six years in power in 2005, the U.S. embassy reported, "The government did whatever was necessary to get tens of thousands of supporters into the center of Tripoli for Revolution Day celebrations on August 31. Reportedly, government officials in the outlying areas of Libya were told to be in Tripoli for the celebration or risk losing their jobs. We heard rumors that each 'shabbiat' (district) official was ordered to be at the ceremony along with a minimum of two other attendees. Universities and other institutions sent busloads of participants. USLO LES staff relayed rumors that the government would hand out 200 dinars to everyone in Green Square the afternoon of August 31. . . . In the end, the regime got what it needed—a large enough crowd to look impressive on television."[24] According to the embassy cable, in the aftermath of this farce the Egyptian ambassador suggested that the clear lack of enthusiasm among the crowd was a bad sign for the regime. Startled, a colleague asked him if he thought Gaddafi might be overthrown. The Egyptian ambassador shrugged. "Who knows? Something like this can glide for a long time before it crashes." The ambassador did not know it, but he was describing much of the Arab world, including his own country.

The discontent was both political and economic. Despite Libya's oil wealth, the country I visited in late spring 2012 was not anything like an oil state of the sort you see in the Persian Gulf. Indeed I was taken aback by how ramshackle Benghazi in particular is. Even the capital, Tripoli, is a hit-or-miss affair, with some gleaming new buildings and neighborhoods and others run down. South of the medieval citadel lies the medina (old city) of Tripoli, a vast slum primarily inhabited by Africans and Libyans of African heritage. Some 60 percent of Libyan jobs are with the government. A lot of the others are in what sociologists call the informal sector—selling things from a stall or a cart or occasional provision of services. From the cracked sidewalks, the graying buildings, and the hidden-away slums it seemed obvious that Gaddafi had looted the country of billions for himself and his cronies and had squandered trillions of the country's oil income on foreign policy boondoggles in Africa and elsewhere. Some estimates of what Gaddafi squirreled away in foreign banks reach $200 billion, twice the annual economic output of his country.[25] The educated youth who had no jobs because the country's wealth was frittered away or stolen became increasingly restive.

Some dissidents in Libya got their start working within the country's institutions. Daif al-Ghazal, for instance, was born in the mid-1970s in Benghazi.[26] As a teenager in the late 1980s, he joined the Revolutionary Committee Movement in his school through a summer camp, going to meetings and conferences in support of the ideals of Gaddafi's Green Book, an idiosyncratic mixture of nationalism, socialism, and Maoism. In the early 1990s he joined the *mathaba* (local headquarters) of his revolutionary committee. These organizations were full of Gaddafi's popular spies and enforcers, watching the local population for any sign of deviation from the official line or criticism of the Brother Leader. Their headquarters in urban neighborhoods had a distinctive design that looked to me like a concrete teepee but reminded locals of a volcano. Known for his precocious and eloquent defense of the Green Book, al-Ghazal became chairman of the Culture and Media Section, a remarkable achievement for one so young. He did a history undergraduate degree at Qar Yunis University and became a regime journalist. From about 1999 he wrote for the official *al-Zahf al-Akhdar* (Green March), the organ of the Revolutionary Committees Movement and in his early twenties quickly rose to become its editor in chief.

Around the time he was twenty-four or twenty-five, in the opening years of the new millennium, al-Ghazal appears to have seen something in his revolutionary committee that disturbed him. Likely committee members with grudges against one another, possibly because of the different clans to which they belonged, were waging internal vendettas and kidnapping and killing one another. He gradually began denouncing "extremists" in the committee. In 2003 he resigned from his newspaper and from the committee, titling his last column "An Urgent Call to Moderation and the Expulsion of Infiltrators." Had it not been for the rise of the internet, we may never have known much about his case. But dissident Libyan websites, mostly based in the West, publicized it. According to one, he wrote in that column, "Why do revolutionaries slaughter each other and why do they apply methods of the secret police in eliminating one another (their colleagues!). Is it because of power? How so when we believe that power belongs to the people and it cannot be abducted in favor of a tribe or two? Everyone is invited to rethink their position."[27]

As a young man formed within the regime and its institutions, al-Ghazal appears to have been unable to see how dangerous his behavior was. Once you were an insider in the revolutionary committees, and privy to their secrets, it was not so easy to leave. He gave a public talk in 2004 on the need to fight corruption. He ran for head of the local journalists' guild in early 2005 but was defeated, some say by ballot stuffing. By February 2005 he was giving interviews in the London expatriate digital press (*Libya Today* and *Libya Jeel*) in which he complained of being persecuted and interrogated. He also began publishing his critical articles abroad, since the regime newspapers would not touch them. On May 21, 2005, two armed men kidnapped him in Benghazi. A week and a half later his disfigured body was found in an alley, allegedly covered with the marks of torture. Al-Ghazal's death must have had a demoralizing effect on the Benghazi youth who still supported the regime. His story points to the activities of youth a decade younger than he who would emerge in 2011 to mount a decisive challenge to the revolutionary committees.

The publication in a Danish newspaper of caricatures of the Prophet Muhammad caused riots and demonstrations at Western embassies throughout the Muslim world, and Libya was no different. On February 17, 2006, an angry crowd of young men in Benghazi attacked the Italian consulate, provoked when the Italian reforms minister Roberto Calderoli appeared on state television sporting a T-shirt emblazoned with one of the caricatures. The Benghazi police intervened with live ammunition, leaving eleven dead and more wounded. In the two succeeding days the city mounted an insurrection of sorts. The angry young men began targeting Libyan government buildings, attacking four police stations, the tax collection office, and a bank, among others. Only gradually did the regime manage to reassert itself. Tripoli appears to have been embarrassed by the image of its police murdering Libyan protesters on behalf of Westerners ridiculing the national religion, and Gaddafi fired the head of public security, Nasser al-Mabrouk Abdullah, over the incident. On a follow-up visit to Benghazi some months later, Ethan Goldrich, the deputy chief of mission of the U.S. embassy, found the Italian consulate in ruins and the city around it run down and neglected by the central government: "The disparity of wealth compared with Tripoli is obvious, and most clearly marked by the cars on the road. New black and white cabs are nearly impossible to find, and other vehicles are severely dilapidated and sand-blasted. . . . Contacts reported that work on several large apartment block developments has been on hiatus for many months; their cinderblock and rebar husks loom forlorn and half-finished. A major bridge connecting the city has been closed for years, with rumors of imminent repairs stretching to fill the time." Benghazi under Gaddafi was not like Abu Dhabi or Kuwait City, metropolises of oil states, but like a poor provincial Egyptian or Jordanian city.[28]

Youth dissatisfactions seethed beneath the surface in the east of the country, the old Cyrenaica region. On September 1, 2006, the country's Independence Day, youth threw stones at a government convoy in the eastern city of Derna: "The U.S. diplomat attending the event counted about 50 indentations in each bus."[29] The Libyan authorities attempted to dismiss the incident as boys' high jinks, but the U.S. diplomat on the scene insisted that the buses were deliberately targeted.

Despite Saif Gaddafi's promises, the regime continued to deny citizens the most elementary liberties. In the first decade of the century, the Libyan fiction writer Abdelnasser Al-Rabbasi was serving a fifteen-year sentence imposed in 2003 for submitting a short story to the *Arab Times* that took on corruption and human rights violations. In December 2009 secret police hauled off the attorney and dissident Jamal el Haji, who was being too vocal in criticizing Libya's poor human rights record. The chief of internal security admitted that his agency was still holding hundreds of prisoners who had been acquitted or had served their full sentences at the Ain Zara and Abu Salim prisons; the General People's Committee for Public Security declined to obey calls from the secretary of justice to release these individuals. Dissident Fathi al-Jahmi was arrested in 2004 after giving international satellite television interviews demanding democratization and calling Gaddafi a dictator; he died in prison in 2009. In 2010 secret police contacted the al-Jahmi clan and, among other demands, told them that Fathi's cousin, the blogger Hasan al-Jahmi, should "shut his mouth." His clan urged him to comply. This anecdote shows the way the regime was able to blackmail entire extended families into political quiescence and even into policing the public speech of their members (and with Fathi's death, the al-Jahmis could be assured that Gaddafi meant business). Instead of falling silent, however, Hasan al-Jahmi agreed with his clan elder to disavow his family publicly so as to protect them from association with him, and then he fled to Switzerland.[30]

One of the most difficult things for the families and friends of those arbitrarily arrested and imprisoned by the regime and its revolutionary committees was simply not knowing what happened to their loved ones. When the Gaddafi regime took people, it usually would not admit to holding or killing them. They just evaporated. On my visit to Benghazi in May 2012, I visited the courthouse on the Mediterranean, in the square in front of which thousands of protesters had gathered in February 2011 to protest the regime. Above the door was graffiti that read "Anti-Christ of the Age," denouncing Gaddafi in the terms of Muslim expectations about the last days. Inside the courthouse I found the walls covered with posters commemorating the martyrs who died fighting for the revolution or who were summarily executed in prison. There were also pictures of those who had disappeared over the years, along with plaintive inquiries as to whether anyone knew their fate. Yellowing black-and-white photos curled with age and the heat of desolate summers under tyranny. One typical display was labeled "Missing." It gave the name of the young man, a police officer who had been charged by the regime in 1979 with helping a political prisoner escape. Some of the disappeared were from Abu Salim Prison, and theirs was a darker story. Members of the radical Libyan Islamic Fighting Group had been rounded up and imprisoned in the early 1990s for terrorist activity. In 1996 there was a prison riot, which was settled when Gaddafi ordered hundreds of the inmates simply mown down.[31] The regime, however, never admitted to the massacre and never confirmed the dead, leaving relatives in Benghazi forever wondering about their sons. The pleas for information about the missing tugged at your heart even more than the posters of the martyrs, since they attested to years or decades of wondering and anguish, without closure even today.

Youth Crowds and the First Libyan Revolution

Like all the authoritarian governments in the region, the Gaddafi regime was dismayed at the outbreak of youth activism in Tunisia and Egypt. Gaddafi deplored the overthrow of Ben Ali (whom he had on retainer), saying it was unreasonable of the Tunisian people to not simply wait until 2014, when the president had promised to step down. The regime's normal way of doing business, targeting human rights activists for arbitrary arrest and imprisonment by secret police trained by the East German Stasi, suddenly became insupportable among Gen Y Libyans in close contact with their Tunisian and Egyptian colleagues. In January, at the height of the Tahrir Square events, the Libyan internet specialist Hasan al-Jahmi, in exile in Switzerland, created a Facebook page calling for the launch of a revolution throughout Libya on February 17, the anniversary of the 2006 insurrection and crackdown in Benghazi around the Danish caricature controversy. It quickly gained thirty thousand "friends." He also organized demonstrations by a wide range of Libyan youth groups, including nationalists and the Muslim Brotherhood, in front of the UN building in Geneva.[32]

The abrupt and arbitrary arrest on February 15 of attorney Fethi Tarbel (who handled the suit brought by families of the Abu Salim Prison massacre victims) provoked demonstrations by attorneys and others in Benghazi, whose population was already raw from years of crackdowns. The attorneys refused, however, to demand the fall of the regime. The regime intervened brutally, injuring dozens. On the following evening, February 16, a crowd of several hundred youth gathered peacefully in downtown Bayda, an industrial city of 250,000 on the Mediterranean in the east of the country. They chanted, "Bayda has not lived in fear. May Gaddafi fall, fall!" The youth wanted to forestall Gaddafi's plans to turn the country over to his son Saif. Local troops opened fire on them with live ammunition, killing at least three young protesters. On the same day university students in the al-Fatayeh district of the eastern city of Derna demonstrated in sympathy with Benghazi.[33]

The Libyan revolution dates from the rally in the square in front of Benghazi's courthouse on February 17. When I visited the following year, I took a photo of a graffito addressed to the dictator that said, "The generation of wrath: Wrath has come to you." As with Tunisia and Egypt, young people were disproportionately in the front ranks of the protests. The first big demonstration in Tahrir Square had been labeled by activists the "Day of Wrath," and Libyan internet activists used that name to refer to February 17.

The Day of Wrath produced clashes in Bayda and Benghazi in the east and the small city of Zintan in the west. In Bayda the protests were driven in part by anger among shopkeepers at the red tape and corruption of the Gaddafi authorities, and a march of youth met repression from the militias of the revolutionary committees and troops of the Khamis Brigade, who deployed live fire, leaving four dead. In the aftermath rumors circulated on the internet that the people of Bayda had liberated themselves from Gaddafi's government. In Benghazi crowds came out throughout the city. Among the important organizations on the ground there was the February 17 Committee, coordinated by Abdel Salam al-Mismari, a prominent young attorney. The sound of gunfire rang out from several districts. Police killed seven demonstrators and wounded thirty-five. In Zintan young people occupied the city square with tents and stayed the night, until they were attacked by police at 3 the next morning and several were arrested. Official media accused the crowds of attacking and burning police stations, but even the newspaper close to Saif Gaddafi, *Quryna*, condemned security forces for attacking peaceful protesters.[34]

The next day, February 18, crowds in Bayda and Benghazi held funerals for the young people killed by the revolutionary committees on the Day of Wrath and again came into conflict with the security forces. Even the official press reported twenty-four protesters killed. Demonstrations were launched in sixteen cities that day, throughout the east of the country but also in the west. On February 19, 100,000 were reported to have gathered in front of Benghazi's courthouse, where they came under sniper fire. Others surged toward the al-Fadil b. Umar police station, which was known as the "Bab al-Aziziya" of Benghazi, the name of Gaddafi's palace. The police opened fire on them. Eyewitnesses got the word out on internet sites that dozens of protesters were killed. One said that at one point the crowds drove security forces to take refuge in a building, from which they then sniped at the protesters. Others reported the regime's use of machine guns and even artillery pieces. The protests spread throughout the country, not only to the east but to western cities such as Zawiya and into the Jabal Nafusa area of the southwest. Even some conservative religious districts of the capital staged demonstrations.[35]

The security forces' use of medium and heavy weapons and the high death toll they imposed on Benghazi backfired on them. On February 20 massive and determined crowds of tens of thousands of youth took over the city and chased the revolutionary committees and their militias and mercenaries out of police stations. Most of the protesters surged ahead on the basis of sheer people power, but some had already begun forming youth militias and looting government stockpiles for weapons, showing themselves brave if amateur fighters. Unlike in Yemen or Iraq, most urban Libyans did not own firearms and did not know stock from barrel. An exception was a small number of radicals who had belonged to the Libyan Islamic Fighting Group and had fought in Afghanistan or later in Iraq against American troops. They formed ad hoc platoons and emerged as the best fighters against the regime, despite their small number. The government exaggerated the importance of the guerrilla actions carried out against its police and troops, which were dwarfed in size by the tens of thousands of peaceful protesters in the streets.

On February 21, as fighter-jets and helicopter gunships circled above, troops turned anti-aircraft guns on the crowds in Benghazi in one last push. Some people were under the impression that they were subject to aerial bombardment, and this report was broadcast by Al Jazeera. It may not have been true, but, as the journalist Lindsey Hilsum argues, the report was probably the result of the fog of war.

Popular uprisings took place elsewhere in the east, including at Tobruk near the Egyptian border, where security forces are said to have killed one hundred but to have lost control of the city in the end. Gaddafi had kept his military small for fear that an ambitious officer might make it the basis for a coup, and most regular army soldiers had no notion of how to deal with crowd protests or even insurgency. Only the Khamis Brigade had had some training in counterinsurgency in the old Soviet Union. Most of the regular officers and their units based in the east began defecting to the rebel side.[36]

In late February the rebels announced the formation of a National Transitional Council. Cyrenaica had largely been reconstituted, recovering the status it lost in 1963, when King Idris united the country's three regions into one government unit. While some political forces in Benghazi wanted to secede or move to a Canada-style federal system with very substantial provincial autonomy, most important politicians and youth leaders in the city of nearly a million wanted to march west to liberate the capital of Tripoli from the dictator and reestablish a unitary Libyan state. For many youth in the east, the idea of recovering Umar Mukhtar, who had organized the failed uprising against Italy in the 1920s, as their national symbol and replacing the erratic and arbitrary Gaddafi, was exhilarating. When I visited Libya in 2012, I found graffiti of Umar Mukhtar everywhere. Gaddafi had not banned representations of him but was clearly jealous of him and had downplayed his importance in favor of his own role as Brother Leader. Ironically the anti-imperialist Gaddafi was depicted by revolutionaries as himself an imperial actor, analogous to Mussolini, from which the grandchildren of Umar Mukhtar had liberated themselves. By March 5 Benghazi and the east were entirely liberated.[37]

Hasan al-Jahmi and other internet activists broadcast the news of the youth demonstrations and the vicious repression they faced. He posted items to his website, which was followed by colleagues in Tunisia, Egypt, and the Gulf. When he posted a video, they shared it with their networks and it spread around the Middle East in less than ten minutes. "In that way," he remarked, "a spontaneous network was formed, without any planning, since each contact led to another, and so on." A revolutionary publicity committee formed in Misrata that sent him videos by satellite internet and asked him to put them in touch with Reuters and Al Jazeera. (The latter sent them video camera equipment.) Publicity committees were set up in Nalut, Ajdabiya, Tripoli, and Derna. Al-Jahmi's group in Europe attempted to vet videos for authenticity and warned news media if an old video was being recycled as new. In March Ayat Mneina in Canada and Omar Amer in England founded the Libyan Youth website, Facebook page, and Twitter feed, and over time attracted codirectors of the page from within Libya. It served as a major clearinghouse of news of the revolution. Mohammed Nabbous (1982–2011), a young Benghazi businessman and internet activist, founded Free Libya Television, initially on the Libyan internet but later via a two-way satellite link, and broadcast news of the revolution despite the danger, until he was killed by a sniper on March 19.[38]

Gaddafi had the choice of going gracefully into exile, as Ben Ali did. There was, however, no independent officer corps in Libya that could give him a push in that direction, what with two of his sons being major commanders. He had lost half his army when the field officers and troops in the east defected to the youth rebels, but the Tripoli-based forces were more formidable. The alternative was to plot a countrywide campaign of counterrevolution that would inevitably involve piling bodies up to the sky. Gaddafi appears never to have been much bothered by a conscience, and he chose the latter. In the first half of March the regime launched a full-blown military campaign against the cities that had rebelled against it. Those urban areas in the west in easy reach of government troops and mercenaries suffered horribly. Zawiya, a city of 200,000 just a half-hour drive west from the capital, was subjected to aerial bombardment and then to heavy tank and artillery barrages by Khamis Gaddafi's armored forces from March 6 through 10. Journalist Alex Crawford described the scene at the beginning of the battle: "There were great holes in the sides of buildings, and smashed-in walls down the roads leading in to the town. There were broken lamp-posts, and total devastation."[39] But this was only the beginning. Once the city was taken, the revolutionary committees were reestablished, and they began tracking down and detaining prominent young rebels.

The tanks then advanced on other cities. The Facebook page of Revolutionaries Libya 17 for Building a Free Libya reported ominously on March 11, "God is most Great. From Misrata: An attack has been launched on the outskirts of Misrata by Gaddafi's mercenaries, with 35 tanks and numerous armored vehicles."[40] Undeterred, young commenters on the page defiantly pointed out that throughout history, small bands of determined people had often prevailed over larger forces. The regime's military waged similar campaigns at Zuwara near Tunisia and in Ras Lanuf and Brega in the east, deploying tanks and Russian BM-21 trucks mounted with multiple rocket launchers, called Grad (hail) in Russian. Beyond Brega lay Benghazi itself, toward which Gaddafi's tanks were rolling. The U.S. director of national intelligence James Clapper testified to Congress that it was likely Gaddafi's armed forces would fairly easily take back the eastern cities. What had happened to Zawiya raised the specter that such a reconquest would involve massacres of thousands and that hundreds of thousands would flee to the Egyptian desert, creating a massive refugee crisis. (These are precisely what happened, on a large scale, in Syria when that regime decided to crush its revolution, putting the lie to those rather naïve commentators who questioned whether a Gaddafi reassertion would really be attended by significant loss of life.) As if to settle the issue, Gaddafi gave a fiery and menacing speech, calling on his supporters to chase down the rebels, which he called vermin and drug addicts, in every street and alleyway, and making it clear that he wanted them cleansed. He was aware that his opponents were the youth: "They are young—sixteen, seventeen, eighteen years old. They sometimes mimic what is happening in Tunisia and Egypt. . . . However, there is a small sick group, implanted in the cities, and is giving out pills, and sometimes money, to these young men, and thrusting them into these side battles." He warned that if the rebellion continued, "I and the millions will march in order to cleanse Libya, inch by inch, house by house, home by home, alley by alley, individual by individual, so that the country is purified from the unclean."[41]

The rebels were aware that they were no match for Gaddafi's helicopter gunships, so they asked their many supporters in the Arab League to lobby for a no-fly zone. They did not want foreign troops on Libyan soil, but they did want the world to level the playing field. The Arab League was full of states that had been stabbed in the back by Gaddafi, and most of them probably voted against him not only out of horror at the massacre he was conducting but also on less noble grounds. Saudi Arabia and Qatar were no democracies, but Gaddafi had repeatedly insulted the Gulf monarchies as American lackeys. He had supported a separatist movement in Morocco. He had provoked trouble in Sudan, backing the Arabic-speaking Janjaweed militias. In addition, Egypt and Tunisia were now revolutionary states that feared Gaddafi as a counterrevolutionary force, and they lobbied vigorously for the young rebels. In the end, Syria and Algeria were the only no votes, though earlier Yemen had also had reservations. (The Yemeni and Syrian regimes were then facing their own restive street crowds.)[42]

The Arab League went to the United Nations Security Council (UNSC) in early March to plead for the authorization of the international community to use force and to institute a no-fly zone. The UNSC was divided on the proposition. China and Russia abstained. The French and British governments, fearful that a successful Gaddafi repression of a national movement would push Libyans into terrorism and create a huge new refugee problem for Europe, were eager for a no-fly zone. President Obama was skittish about getting involved in another Middle Eastern war. The Arab League resolution, however, tipped the scales inside the White House on March 15 toward the humanitarian interventionists and against the cautious realists. When the UNSC voted two days later, it adopted Resolution 1973 with ten votes in favor and five abstentions (from Brazil, Russia, India, China, and Germany). Acting under Chapter VII of the UN Charter, the UNSC gave permission to the international community for the deployment of "all necessary measures" in Libya "to protect civilians and civilian populated areas under threat of attack" and to establish a no-fly zone. The UNSC also took Gaddafi's war crimes to the International Criminal Court. Late on the afternoon of March 19, as Mu'tasim Gaddafi's tank corps raced toward Benghazi, French Mirage jets intervened to stop them in their tracks. Later that day the United States launched a massive attack on Gaddafi's anti-aircraft batteries, making it safe for NATO to patrol the skies. The danger receded from Benghazi and points east even as the west of the country along the Mediterranean was largely resubdued by Gaddafi's forces. Still, Gaddafi was limited to controlling about 2 million of Libya's 6 million people, and demographically his regime was doomed.[43]

Youth Brigades and the Second Libyan Revolution

With the imposition of the no-fly zone, the Libyan revolution turned into a civil war, and the youth rebels militarized to confront Gaddafi's deadly armor. Fighting concentrated on three fronts. The first was Jabal Nafusa in the southwest, whose population is largely Berber and rural, and so comprises natural fighters good with a gun because of their hunting experience. The second was Misrata, to the east of the capital, the country's third-largest city and the site of a major steel factory, which was besieged by the Khamis Brigade and other armored units. The third was the area between Benghazi and the oil towns directly to its west, Ajdabiya and Brega, where a line formed that oscillated only slightly for months. The Benghazi forces proved unable to make headway against the tanks, artillery, and Grad arrays that Mu'tasim Gaddafi was able to deploy against them, so that the eastern front saw a great deal of fighting but no real movement. High school and university students flocked to lessons on how to use firearms, offered by defecting noncommissioned officers from the Libyan army. The training was often inadequate to the task. Benghazi hospitals reported the alarming statistic that most of the firearms injuries they treated among the young rebels were self-inflicted. With the exception of the former Libyan Islamic Fighting Group forces under Abdul Hakim Belhadj, the eastern rebel army was not ready for prime time.[44]

There was also an information war. Muhammad Gaddafi, in charge of electronic communications, simply turned off the internet. The country still had satellite television access, and dissident youth used cell phone and SMS to share information. Those who had the resources could use satellite equipment to upload video, which was then broadcast on Al Jazeera. In addition, the American activist John Scott-Railton developed a way for youth revolutionaries to get around internet blackouts by calling a phone number and having a voice message turned into a tweet on Twitter.[45]

The militias cobbled together by the youth in Misrata were able to construct gelatina bombs from TNT, which they used to stop Gaddafi's tanks from taking the city. The city's shopkeepers and small merchants bankrolled the revolution, as they did in Benghazi and Jaba Nafusa.[46] The rebels also, over time, received some shipments of rocket-propelled grenades, which they used to fend off repeated assaults by Khamis's armor. They were bedeviled in April by regime snipers, who positioned themselves atop key buildings. When I visited Misrata in June 2012, young people told me that they had used the industrial knowledge they had learned from working at the steel mill. A visiting journalist, Xan Rice, found that they welded steel plates to their trucks to armor them, and the longshoremen used shipping containers to block streets against the advance of the tanks. Because Gaddafi's tanks were able to penetrate the city from the west, NATO appears to have felt unable to provide intensive close air support, for fear of hitting an apartment building full of noncombatants and creating a public relations

disaster. The Gaddafi armored forces may have received fewer reinforcements than they otherwise would have because NATO bombed some tank
convoys moving out from the capital toward the east. But the Khamis Brigade and other units were able to get enough logistical support to keep the
city under siege for months, turning much of it into rubble. The 600,000
residents of Misrata soldiered on, virtually alone except for occasional,
chancy resupply at its port (which was often itself under artillery bombardment by the Gaddafi forces).

One young fighter confessed to a visiting journalist in April that it was
not Islam that really sustained him; like many Arab millennials, he was less
pious than his forebears. "I did shout Allahu akbar when we fought, but I
don't believe in God and that virgins for the martyrs stuff, and neither do
many of my friends. We like to listen to music, get drunk on the beach
on home-made alcohol. I just can't tell my family how I feel, because my
uncle is the head of a mosque."[47] During my visit a year later I was struck
by a conversation at a coffeehouse in which some Libyan intellectuals were
clearly critical of Islam. Libya's long years under a semisocialist government
had some impact on at least the private beliefs of many youth, as was also
true of the left in Tunisia and Egypt. About a fifth of Libyans support a
strong separation of religion and state, and my guess is that they are disproportionately younger than thirty-five.[48]

I gained some insight into the hell that was Misrata during the revolution when I visited the city about eight months after its agony ended. Tripoli Avenue, the miles-long stretch of buildings along the road to the capital,
used to be full of upscale shops, cafés, and apartment, office, and bank
buildings. It had been almost completely destroyed. The rows of bowed
and crippled buildings lined up to the horizon as though in a surrealist
painting, blackened and as full of holes as Swiss cheese where they had not
collapsed. Khamis's tank crews and artillerymen had fired indiscriminately
for months, inevitably killing large numbers of noncombatants who used to
live in those now misshapen edifices. I spent hours at a folk museum dedicated to their struggle that the Misratans had swiftly erected. It is a single
room, perhaps formerly a retail store. Outside stands the statue of the fist
grasping the F-16, weirdly displaced, become a mockery of itself by its re-
location to a city that Gaddafi tried to kill but was prevented from doing so

in part by U.S. airstrikes. There are also captured artillery pieces. A kitschy welcome mat with Gaddafi's image on it is available for wiping one's shoes before entering. Inside, one wall is completely covered with pictures of the city's martyrs, including the rows of bright-eyed smiling babies, distracted toddlers, and cocky adolescents, their quotidian existence frozen on glossy photograph paper shortly before the barrage of snipers' bullets or tank or Grad shells extinguished it. Some display cases show captured weapons and other memorabilia of the vanquished tyrant, including his slippers and colonel's hat. Others showcase the city's fighting spirit, with knickknacks and vases made of shrapnel gathered up by the survivors and welded together, then painted. A few secret police documents are posted.

Along with the largely Arab city of Zintan, which lies south of Zawiya at the edge of the Jabal Nafusa region, the Berber-majority towns, such as Nalut and Galaa, put up the bravest of fights against Gaddafi's armored units. The Berbers benefited from their rugged terrain, which they knew much better than the troops from Tripoli, and from their control of the border checkpoint with southern Tunisia, which allowed them to be resupplied by land. They also received NATO air drops. As with Misrata, they received shipments of rocket-propelled grenades from foreign patrons, allegedly Qatar, and were able to destroy many of the tanks sent against them. How young and inexperienced the fighters were should not be forgotten. An eyewitness in a nearby city mused, "The transitional national council in Surman made the abandoned police station its temporary headquarters, and teenagers were carrying light weapons in front of its main gate. I had to wonder about those youth, who had been listening to Western music with earbuds night and day and obsessed with wearing jeans and getting the latest fashionable haircut. . . . Who imagined that they would leave all that and take up light, medium and heavy weaponry and go off to the front?"[49] Their region never fell to the regime, though they briefly lost Yefren in the spring, regaining it in June. NATO bombing of government weapons depots and exposed tanks in the desert deprived the government of a key advantage.[50]

Although the NATO intervention was controversial in the West, it was universally welcomed by the Libyan youth revolutionaries. Most NATO air strikes, aside from the ones targeting Gaddafi's compound in Tripoli, were aimed at military targets outside the cities, especially arms depots and armored convoys. Despite exaggerated claims by critics, they do not appear to have killed very many noncombatants. (Fewer than one hundred such casualties were at issue, according to Human Rights Watch.)[51] Neither before nor after the war was there any evidence that NATO acted primarily out of concern for oil contracts, which had already been secured under Gaddafi and, if anything, were put in danger by the intervention.

Despite the centrality of the youth fighters, the technically savvy computer engineers and amateur hackers among the youth played a role, even in some rural areas. A physician, Moez Zaiton, who visited the Jabal Nafusa area during the revolution found that Libyan youth set up internet-connected media centers in virtually every one of its towns, which they used to share photographs, videos, and news reports. When international journalists visited, the media centers amplified their ability to tell local stories. The internet blackout was not effective against these local media centers. Zaiton observed, "Satellite equipment was used to upload footage and keep us and journalists abreast of the situation in other areas of the country. It also allowed Libyans to tell expats of major needs." Zintan's media center also had satellite internet access, though it was very slow. Nalut operated its own regional radio station.[52] When the Zintanis and Berbers of this region demonstrated that they could fight off the tanks deployed against them, they began working on an offensive strategy. Zintan had a geographical connection with Zawiya on the coast, and the fighters knew that if they took that city, they could cut off the capital from the west and advance on it. By mid-August the Zintan militia had liberated Zawiya and was rolling toward Tripoli itself.

The great surprise of the Libyan revolution was that the capital rose up against its tyrant and overthrew him even before the Zintani militia could get into the city center.[53] As dawn broke on August 21 revolutionaries were telling Al Jazeera Arabic that much of the capital was being taken over by supporters of the February 17 youth revolt. They called it "the Night of Venezuela," in reference to speculations in the press that Gaddafi might be given asylum in that country. Ringleaders had coordinated this uprising with Benghazi, but it may have gained so much support in part because residents of the capital were terrified that Gaddafi would launch a scorched-earth last stand in their city and turn it into rubble. The suburb of Tajoura to the east and districts in the eastern part of the city such as Suq al-Juma, Arada, the Mitiga Airport, Ben Ashour, Fashloum, and Dahra were in whole or in part under the control of the revolutionaries. Those who were expecting a long, hard slog of fighting from the Western Mountain region and from Misrata toward the capital overestimated Gaddafi's popularity in his own capital and did not reckon with the severe shortages of ammunition and fuel afflicting his demoralized security forces. Nor did they take into account the steady NATO attrition of his armor and other heavy weapons.

This development, with the capital creating its own nationalist myth of revolutionary participation, was the very best thing that could have happened. Instead of being liberated (and somewhat subjected) from the outside by Berber or Cyrenaican revolutionaries, Tripoli entered the Second Republic with its own uprising to its name, as an equal able to gain seats on the Transitional National Council once the Gaddafis and their henchmen were out of the way. Tunisia and Egypt both recognized the TNC as Libya's legitimate government as the Tripoli uprising unfolded through the night.

The underground network of revolutionaries in the capital, which had been violently repressed by Gaddafi's security forces the previous March, appears to have planned the uprising on hearing of the fall of Zawiya and Zlitan. It was the month of Ramadan, so people in Tripoli were fasting during the day and breaking their fast at sunset. Immediately after they ate their meal, the muezzins mounted the minarets of the mosques and began calling out, "Allahu Akbar" (God is most Great) as a signal to begin the uprising.[54]

Revolutionaries had been smuggling weapons into the capital, and the youth of working-class districts in eastern Tripoli were the first to rise up. Tajoura, a working-class suburb a few kilometers from Tripoli to the east, mounted a successful attack on the Gaddafi forces, driving them off. At one point the government troops fired rockets at the protesters, killing 122. But it was a futile act of barbarity, followed by complete defeat of the Gaddafi forces. One eyewitness, Asil al-Tajuri, told Al Jazeera Arabic by telephone that the revolutionaries in Tajoura captured six government troops and freed five hundred prisoners from the Hamidiya Penitentiary.

The Tajoura popular forces also captured the Mitiga military base in the suburb and stormed the residence of Mansour Daw, the head of security forces in Tripoli.

The revolt in the eastern district of Suq al-Juma appears to have begun before the others in the city of Tripoli proper, on August 20. Throughout that day Gaddafi security forces attempted to put it down, but in the end they had to flee. Gaddafi released an audio address in which he made his usual fantasyland observations, claiming that real Libyans liked to kiss pictures of him, and called the revolutionaries rats and agents of imperial France. It was an incoherent, rambling performance, and the last such. At one point an Al Jazeera Arabic correspondent was able to get the frequency of the security forces and broadcast their fretting that they were running low on ammunition and fuel for their riposte to the revolutionaries' advance. By 8 a.m. on August 21, fighters from Nalut and elsewhere in the Western Mountain region had begun marching into Tripoli to give aid to the people who made the uprising. The revolutionaries' advance into the capital was called "Operation Mermaid Dawn." Throughout the day the youth militias from Zintan and other neighboring cities flooded into the capital, receiving close air support from NATO and finding only weak resistance. They were able to go right into Green Square by the citadel, which they renamed Martyrs' Square in honor of the dictator's many victims. Two days later the militias chased Gaddafi and his presidential guard from the massive Bab al-Aziziya complex that had been his headquarters for decades. Only rubble was left after sixty-two NATO air strikes on its secret military command centers that had been directing the attempt to crush the revolution. The Misrata militias later came from the west to loot what was left of the mementos strewn about there.

Dissidents in Tripoli who had been nearly silenced by the ubiquitous revolutionary committees suddenly emerged from the shadows. The rap group G-A-B (Good against Bad) issued a music video, "Libya Bleed," calling for Gaddafi and his sons to be arrested and ridiculing the Brother Leader's Green Book:

> *Libya bleed, just like us*
> *Picture me being scared for my brothers who own the same blood as me*

Libya bleed, just like us
Picture me being shook by the bloodbaths and the smell of death in
my 'hood
Libya bleed, just like us
Picture my daughter's crying and her life's in Qaddafi's hands, while
he's just deciding.[55]

Over the following weeks Gaddafi's family members and close associates either escaped or were killed. In late October Muammar and his son Mu'tasim, the military commander, were tracked down by rebel youth from Misrata and summarily killed, in what was an unfortunate beginning for a revolutionary state that aspired to initiating the rule of law. Only if one remembers the pictures of those giggling babies on the wall of Misrata's resistance museum can one comprehend the cold fury of the militiamen who dispatched the dictator. Gaddafi's body was displayed for days in Misrata in an industrial freezer, as a vengeful populace directed their hatred at his cadaver for the long and brutal siege they had endured at the hands of his armored corps. Khamis, the commander of the armored division, was probably killed in a NATO airstrike, though some observers believe he went into hiding. The Zintan militiamen captured Saif. Saadi, the failed soccer player, fled to Niger. IT chief Muhammad and young hothead Hannibal escaped with their sister, Aisha, and her mother to neighboring Algeria. Misratans also wrought a terrible revenge on the nearby small town of Tawergha (population thirty thousand), which had largely remained loyal to the regime and had helped besiege their city. Misratans blamed Tawerghans, who were disproportionately from the small African-heritage minority, for brutality and for sexual aggression against their daughters, and the militias chased virtually everyone out of the town, creating thousands of refugees. The Misratans I talked to in 2012 were still angry and sensitive about this issue, complaining that international journalists seemed to have more sympathy for the perpetrators of the siege than for the victims. Getting the Tawerghan families back into their homes and finding a framework for reconciliation were two of the important tasks for Libya's transition but were not accomplished in the three years after the fall of Tripoli.[56]

The Long Transition

As in Tunisia, the youth were disadvantaged by the transitional government, which was staffed by older politicians. Hasan al-Jahmi, the internet activist, declined the offer of a job as an official publicist with the Benghazi government, believing his work as a blogger would be more useful to the revolutionary society in critiquing the errors of politicians from the outside. He was convinced that politics was not as important as reestablishing institutions: "We don't need political coalitions, we need a national army, so that the country does not devolve into armed groups."[57] During the revolution and civil war, Mahmoud Jibril, an economist trained at the University of Pittsburgh, had served as de facto prime minister on behalf of the Transitional National Council, an ad hoc body made up of technocrats who were either longtime regime opponents or had defected to the revolution relatively early on. After the TNC declared Libya officially liberated on October 23, 2011, the country's surviving notables moved to form a transitional government, headed by Abdel Rahim al-Keib, a former professor of electrical engineering at the University of Alabama. Al-Keib presided over the transitional period ending in summer 2012, during which Libya prepared for elections. In the al-Keib government, militia leaders from Zintan and Misrata were rewarded with key cabinet posts, but little headway was made in turning the militias into a new national army.

The country was inevitably in substantial disarray, given that Gaddafi's revolutionary committees and secret police had micromanaged it for decades. The youth militias fell into four categories. Some were organic to their districts and functioned as a sort of neighborhood watch. Some were revolutionary advance forces and were still away from home but had not gained the recognition of the state. Some in the east represented federalism, or demands that Cyrenaica be allowed to run itself with less interference from Tripoli. The transitional government relied on a few loyal major militias, which were paid regularly and served as a national guard alongside what was left of the regular army, which was dominated by eastern troops and officers who had defected in February 2011. Militias sometimes ran a parallel government, controlling jails and political prisoners. They also served as intermediaries between pro-Gaddafi and pro-revolution factions in the country's cities, many of which went on struggling over distribution of government patronage well after the shooting war was over.

The day after I flew out of Tripoli, a militia from the nearby town of Tarhouna appeared at the airport in a convoy of SUVs, drove onto the tarmac, and parked under the wings of the planes, trapping any passengers who had already boarded. The young men said that their leader had disappeared, and they suspected the transitional government of taking him. A negotiator from the government arrived and said that the TNC had no idea where their leader was but that rival militias in Tarhouna were likely suspects. Later that day the Zintan militiamen, who had only recently turned the airport over to the central government, came back in and engaged in a firefight with the Tarhounis, wounding four of them and capturing twelve of their vehicles. The Tarhouna militiamen then surrendered control of the airport, which reopened a couple of days later; they had not harmed any passengers or airport equipment. After some months a few of the Tarhounis involved were apprehended and tried for their deed. This story speaks to Libya's postrevolutionary chaos, but it also speaks to the way militias often balanced one another, some supporting the government and acting in the place of a weak army and police. Of course, there were instances of militia faction fighting that ended less happily, though they tended to be rare and sporadic in the first two years after the revolution.[58]

The government's inability to reestablish the police and military on a firm footing and to disband the militias, inducting their members as soldiers in a chain of command, bedeviled the country and led to a number of later political crises. When I was in Tripoli in early June 2012, I saw a convoy of police cars driving through Martyrs' Square, horns blaring, full of recent graduates from the academy, and the crowd was going wild in admiration for them. On another day I came upon a small demonstration at the square by young men demanding a national army. They told me that the country could not be unified without one. I suspect that they also saw the army as an employment opportunity. Despite outbreaks of militia violence from time to time, people told me that personal security was good: you were unlikely to be mugged. I noticed that gold and jewelry shops were open until after dark. Thereafter, however, security deteriorated substantially, not only because the militias were not disbanded, disarmed, or effectively integrated into a new army but also because extremist cells in Benghazi and elsewhere increasingly conducted bold campaigns of terrorist assassinations and bombings.[59]

In July 2012 Libya held elections for its Constituent Assembly, which went as smoothly as could be expected. One problem was that the youth for the most part felt marginalized in this process. The British Council reported, "[The] youth did not get a chance to run for the local council or the National Congress to exercise political action. . . . There are some youth coalitions, but they did not gain the opportunity to vote for them because people consider them young and without understanding."[60] Nevertheless, many youth found much in these events to celebrate, even from the sidelines. In Tripoli the election was described on Twitter as a big family wedding, with lots of loud celebrations and tears of joy. Turnout was about 60 percent, with 1.6 million casting their ballots. This high turnout was especially impressive given how confusing the election procedures were; there were three thousand candidates, and only eighty seats out of two hundred were set aside for some three hundred political parties (most newly formed and not well known). There was relatively little election violence. The *Libya Herald* quoted the High Electoral Commission as saying, "Of 1,554 polling centres across the country, 24 were unable to operate, including two in Kufra, six in Sidra and eight in Benghazi." Kufra is a small town in the south of the country riven by ethnic rivalries and not a national bellwether. The eight districts in Benghazi that could not open were more worrisome, though the city had many polling centers that functioned perfectly normally. The problematic ones were centers of eastern separatism where residents objected to being reintegrated into a unified, nonfederal Libya. Some of the trouble in Benghazi may also have come from radical Muslim groups opposed to democracy, a vocal fringe that is not popular but has the weaponry and fighting experience to cause trouble. Even cities in which there was postrevolution faction fighting by militias, such as Zintan, were able to vote securely and enthusiastically. Women registered to vote, ran for office, and went to the polling stations in surprisingly high numbers. In some small cities eyewitnesses thought the women's lines were much longer than those of the men. Women won about 17 percent of the seats in the national legislature, mainly on the party lists. There was no evidence of former pro-Gaddafi groups boycotting the vote, and voter registration was high even in former regime bastions such as Bani Walid and Sirte. The Muslim fundamentalist parties that were expected to dominate the new Parliament did not do so. Only 80 of the 200 seats were allocated to parties. The nationalist party, led by Mahmoud Jibril, the former head of Gaddafi's National Economic Development Board, did well, and the Muslim Brotherhood's party did poorly, though many independents were elected who thought well of political Islam.[61]

Postrevolutionary Libya's close relationship with the United States was deeply harmed on September 11, 2012, when radical Muslim militiamen attacked a poorly secured building serving as the U.S. consulate in Benghazi. They deployed not only light arms but rocket-propelled grenades, which set the building afire and caused the death, by smoke inhalation, of U.S. ambassador Christopher Stevens and three others. The rest of the embassy staff were rescued by Libyan special forces, who moved them first to a nearby CIA safe house and ultimately to the airport; from there they were flown to Tripoli. Benghazi youth were outraged by this incident, which harmed the city's reputation and prospects for international investment, and they attacked two radical militia centers in the city, driving the jihadis out.[62] While the incident became a political football in Washington, many Libyan youth saw it as one example in a long series of militia lawlessness and extremism in the transitional period and as an argument for a more effective government and national military.

In the fall of 2012, after initial attempts to form a government faltered, the General National Council's two hundred members voted in as prime minister Ali Zeidan, a longtime Geneva-based human rights lawyer who is considered a left-liberal. He defeated the Muslim Brotherhood candidate in the council election and took office in November 2012. The first speaker of the council, called the president of that body, was Mohamed al-Magariaf, who had been an ambassador to India in the 1970s but in 1980 defected to the leftist guerrilla National Front for the Salvation of Libya. Al-Magariaf called for Libya to be a secular state. He was elected in August and served until May 2013, when the council passed the Political Isolation Law under pressure from the militias, barring former regime figures from holding office. He was succeeded as council president by Nouri Abusahmain, a Berber from Zuwara in the far west of the country, who was supported by the Muslim Brotherhood and its allies. The revolutionary youth hailed his election as a sign of Libya's new multiculturalism, given that Gaddafi had long suppressed Berber culture. The elected transitional government had the duties of trying to run the country, establishing a subcommittee of sixty members of Parliament to craft a new constitution, and moving to a permanent elected Parliament.

As the years rolled by there was substantial dissatisfaction with the slowness of the constitution-drafting process. In the meantime, the militia problem continued to bedevil the security situation. The transitional leaders appear to have been too beholden to major militias to rebuild the central army with sufficient speed and efficiency, threatening the return of the country to stability and prosperity and even harming petroleum revenues, the source of 95 percent of Libya's income. Libya's ability to produce oil was increasingly impeded not only by workers' strikes but also by the assertion in Lanouf of federalist militias determined to keep petroleum revenue in Cyrenaica rather than seeing it go to the central government in Tripoli.[63] Militia violence and faction-fighting in cities such as Benghazi worsened in the fall of 2013. After U.S. operatives came into Tripoli and captured and abducted an al-Qaeda leader hiding there, a fundamentalist militia briefly kidnapped Prime Minister Ali Zeidan in protest, sure that he had been involved in this affront to Libyan sovereignty. Late in 2013 the interim General National Congress voted to extend its life until the end of 2014, as it continued to work on a constitution. The Muslim fundamentalist forces in parliament were strengthened because of the spring 2013 exclusion of former regime officials such as Mahmoud Jibril from politics, and Libya moved closer to enshrining Islamic law in the constitution, something that its elected leaders in 2012 had seemed to reject.

Among the youth rallies held in spring and summer 2013 were protests against the continued power and disruptive activities of the militias. In June a well-organized demonstration was held in Algeria Square in Tripoli demanding that the militias disband and go home, leaving policing to the professionals. People came in from outlying cities such as Zintan to participate.

The youth had planned some logistics, including providing cold drinks in Libya's torrid summer.[64] Youth also protested in several cities on July 26 and 27 against the assassination in Benghazi of Abdelsalam al-Mismari (forty-five years old), the first Libyan revolutionary to be shot down in broad daylight. (Numerous police and military officers had been killed in Benghazi and other eastern cities, but presumably they were mainly targeted because of grievances dating back to the Gaddafi period.) Al-Mismari had spoken out against the continued dominance of militias in postrevolutionary Libya and bluntly criticized the Muslim Brotherhood. He also opposed the political exclusion law forced on the General National Congress by the militias, which removed al-Magariaf from his position as speaker and dashed the political hopes of important transitional figures such as Mahmoud Jibril, the first revolutionary prime minister. Youth protesters demanded that the government and new security services step up and do their jobs. That weekend progressive youth also targeted for protest the headquarters of the Muslim Brotherhood in Benghazi. The struggle that had broken out between progressives and adherents of political Islam in Tunisia and Egypt that summer thus had its echoes in Libya. Youth also decried the actions in late July of one of the terrorist cells active in Benghazi, including blowing up the courthouse in front of which the February 17 revolution began. Benghazi's terrorist cells were a phenomenon distinct from the militia problem, and as time went on they appeared to aspire to an Iraq-type destabilization of the country.[65] In December 2013 unarmed protesters assembled outside several government buildings in Tripoli, demanding the resignation of Prime Minister Zeidan on the grounds that he had failed to rein in the militias.[66] Zeidan failed a vote of no confidence in March 2014.

Unlike in Egypt no active youth organizations such as April 6 or Rebellion shaped national politics in the transitional period, nor was there a strong student union as in Tunisia. Libya's youth were more networked than organized, and the lack of organization appears to have harmed their ability to continue to assert themselves. Youth continued to suffer from high unemployment in the transitional years, though some NGOs were established to train them for specialized jobs. Students did occasionally stage campus rallies, mainly to protest poor security or issues such as scholarships and exam schedules. In May 2013 students at Benghazi University held a demonstration against lawlessness in the city, after a car carrying tank ammunition, presumably for arms smugglers, accidentally exploded. (It was initially thought to be a car bomb.) They displayed banners against the transitional government's army chief of staff, Major General Yousef Mangoush. Students at Tripoli University, including the Engineering Students Union, rallied a month later, complaining that militiamen were coming freely onto campus, and demanding that nonstudents be banned.[67] Youth activists pointed to the very ability to hold demonstrations peacefully as one of the achievements of the revolution, along with the vast expansion of a freer press, the explosive growth of civil society organizations and political parties, and improved opportunities for women.[68] These achievements were threatened, as the youth recognized, by violence and insecurity. In the summer of 2013 a journalist was assassinated in Benghazi, and another was fired at and threatened by text message.[69]

Websites such as that of the Libyan Youth Movement appear to have functioned as little more than information clearinghouses, not as enablers of street action or organizational activities. Ayat Mneina complained that the new Libyan government was not used to thinking in terms of cooperation with such nongovernmental organizations. In an interview with Mneina, journalist Laura Hughes remarked, "Commentators say Libyan Youth movement is marginalised because of lack of experience, skills and direction." Mneina replied that this lack of direction was an advantage: "With Libya still in flux, I don't think it's wise for us to decide on a specific goal; our flexibility is a strength."[70] She stressed the need for better educational facilities, job training for young people, more loans for small businesses and internet technology ventures, and an opening of entrepreneurial opportunities by strengthening property rights.[71] Libyan youth see the NGO and civil society organization sectors as their primary arena, as indeed identical with the youth, given that under Gaddafi no true NGOs had been tolerated and most of the organizations that have grown up since 2011 have been efforts of the millennials. They feel that there are barriers of experience to their entrance into formal politics and that the barriers for young women in particular are even higher. In contrast, they have so many opportunities to gain government funding to form and run civil society organizations that the real brake on their proliferation is not money but having enough expertise to run these organizations effectively.[72]

Libyan youth conceived of themselves as a youth movement in making their revolution and were the primary actors in overthrowing Gaddafi. Their elders, full of despair, often admitted that they would have advised against trying. Because of the extreme form of Gaddafi's authoritarianism, the youth movement in Libya was more inchoate than in other revolutionary Arab countries. Independent youth, student, and political organizations such as Kefaya and April 6 in Egypt or the General Union of Tunisian Students had no counterparts in Libya. Public demonstrations, pamphleteering, and other organizational techniques common in Egypt were impossible in Libya before February 17.

Internet and media activists such as Hasan al-Jahmi, Ayat Mncina, Omar Amer, and Mohammed Nabbous played an important informational role. Their impact, and that of other technologically savvy youth on the ground in Jabal Nafusa, Misrata, and Benghazi, was probably greater than is usually recognized, given their use of satellite internet to upload video for rebroadcast on Arab satellite television, which was never blocked. Still, their impact was inevitably far less robust than that of their colleagues in neighboring countries, given the relatively low rates of internet penetration in Libya and the government's blackout of internet service for the duration of the revolution. The revolution was nevertheless primarily made by young people, who organized the crowds in the streets as of February 17, deploying their high school, university, and workplace networks as well as extended kinship.

In the aftermath of the revolution, youth organized to demand better security on campus and continued to pressure the transitional government for more job opportunities and better training. In the first two years of the transition, they were unable to erect or maintain specifically political organizations analogous to April 6 or Rebellion in Egypt, and even more than in Tunisia and Egypt were marginalized in the new political process.

If few young people found a place as politicians or leaders of powerful

organizations, newly liberated youth have gone into fields such as professional journalism. Some have continued their role as citizen journalists. In
the transitional period they no longer faced government censorship, though
militias sometimes menaced newspaper staff over their reporting, and one
journalist was assassinated. The millennials devoted themselves to founding
civil society or nongovernmental organizations dedicated to a wide range
of cultural and social issues. Some NGOs put on concerts, poetry readings,
and art exhibits; others fight hunger among the poor or work for women's
rights or human rights. Nongovernmental organizations are likely to be
the social space in which Generation Y will have the biggest impact in the
coming decade.

Conclusion

$\mathcal{M}$any observers have questioned whether the events in Tunisia, Egypt, and Libya in 2011 and afterward amounted to a revolution. They did. At a basic level, a revolution is a rapid and systemic political change brought about by a social movement. A social movement, as defined by sociologist Charles Tilly, involves an organized campaign for the achievement of specified goals by influencing a target audience; acting out in public with rallies, vigils, strikes, public statements, and pamphleteering; and displays of worthiness, unity, numbers, and commitment.[1] What historians typically call "revolutions" in reality comprise diverse social movements acting in concert. While some observers take the American and French revolutions of the eighteenth century as a template for the phenomenon, insisting on liberal or progressive outcomes and ideals to distinguish it from a coup, in modern history revolutions have been diverse in their composition and outcomes. They have been led by peasants and by business classes and have resulted in all sorts of new political and economic systems, from liberal parliamentary governments to socialist one-party states and even praetorian regimes. To be useful the category must comprise the Russian and Chinese revolutions, no less than the Polish. The important thing is that these upheavals involve a "rapid, mass, forceful, systemic transformation of a society's principal institutions and organisations."[2] They provoke swift changes in institutions (the way society organizes to accomplish key tasks) as well as in norms and outlooks. A revolution is different from a reform in being a sudden and profound set of changes.

Sociologist Theda Skocpol distinguishes between political revolutions and social revolutions. In a political revolution there is a change in rule but not necessarily in the social structure. In a social revolution, as she defines it, at least 5 percent of property has to change hands, and typically the laws governing property are changed.[3] When pundits ask if what happened in Tunisia, Egypt, Libya, and Yemen was really a revolution, they are asking if structural alterations were made, or was there simply a change in who staffed the heights of government. Were these just, in other words, "personnel wars"? Too little changed in Yemen to term it a revolution, but in the other three countries it seems to me that the previous ruling clique was so narrow and so grasping that breaking its hold on power was certainly revolutionary. I would argue that because the three revolutionary Arab states had been ruled by family cartels that concentrated tremendous wealth in their hands and in the hands of cronies, the removal of these ruling strata involved the vast redistribution of wealth. Tunisia's dictator, Zine El Abidine Ben Ali, and his in-laws in the Trabelsi clan, as well as the high officials of the ruling Democratic Constitutional Rally, held the lion's share of wealth and power in the country, and their departure from the scene wrought a significant economic as well as political change. The U.S. embassy estimated that half of Tunisia's economic elite was related to the president in the beginning of the century, and as of 2011 that assertion was no longer true. Likewise in Egypt the Mubarak family and hangers-on became billionaires through government contracts and largesse, and their fall freed up spaces in the economy for thousands of others. Postrevolution Libya not only saw the control of enormous oil wealth pass from the Gaddafis to elected leaders, but new propertied classes emerged and old ones attempted to recover lands taken by the government. Of the three, Libya may have witnessed the biggest transfers of property. On the other hand, the wealthy in all three countries, aside from the top tier of regime cronies pursued on charges of corruption, mostly remained wealthy. These were hardly socialist revolutions; they were much more like the French Revolution than the Soviet or Chinese. Nevertheless, on both criteria, of institutional change and of change in who controls the wealth, these were genuine revolutions, despite all the obvious continuities below the 1 percent in class structure, bureaucratic personnel, and law.

The millennials were raised to believe in the developmental state, in the government as a vehicle for national independence from imperial and neoimperial domination, as an economic engine for industrialization and job creation, and as a means to educate a new, urban generation. Implicitly the revolutionary Arab governments had urged the people in the decades after escape from European domination to postpone demands for democracy in favor of these developmental goals, which, they argued, needed a strong and unfettered state. But by the twenty-first century it was clear that the Nasserist state, which had doubled per capita income in Egypt between 1960 and 1970 and founded large numbers of factories, was long moribund. With the advent of moves toward privatization and the long period of autocracy, the state had become a Western-dominated enterprise run for the benefit of the ruling family and its hangers-on, and society was headed for greater and greater inequality. The cartel state was kept in place by a huge cadre of secret police, plainclothes thugs, and practices of surveillance and torture. The demand for bread, liberty, and social justice on the part of the revolutionary youth in 2011 was an attempt to craft a political coalition. The poor and workers wanted "bread," that is, an improved standard of living. The urban middle classes wanted freedom and dignity, that is, a democratic, liberal politics and freedom of expression on the Western European model. And the unions and student left wanted a more equitable society with a social safety net, minimum wage, and less impunity for the rapacious billionaire oligarchs. Something like Scandinavian social democracy seems to have been the common ideology of the youth revolutionaries, though each group put more emphasis on some of these demands than others.

The Arab baby boomers and Gen X had ways of escaping the increasingly stagnant and sclerotic police states. Millions worked for a while in the oil states of the Gulf; others went to Europe and North America as students, guest workers, or immigrants. The oil boom of the last quarter of the twentieth century created enormous labor demand in the Gulf. The demographic decline and the general economic advances in Europe created a similar labor demand in many of its countries. But the 2008 global crisis in finance capital sent economies in the Middle East and Europe into a tailspin, idling millions of guest workers, cutting remittances, and leaving youth coming onto the labor market with no prospects at home or abroad. Long-term droughts devastated the rural population. The revolutions were in part unemployment riots organized into political campaigns. Since they did not in fact produce governments with the will and ability to expand employment, the likelihood is that the now-mobilized youth will continue to agitate for change.

The revolutions were demands for personal dignity and public input into government decision making. Since the new governments have had difficulty shaking traditions of elite decision making, the progressive youth will likely continue to press for democratization, given that the turmoil of the summer of 2013 in Egypt and Tunisia did not serve as a warning to new contenders for political power that adopting the high-handed governing techniques of the old ruling parties was dangerous indeed. The transitional governments put in place after 2011 typically did almost nothing for the labor unions and their members or for the disgruntled peasants and workers of the provincial towns where much of the unrest unfolded, causing them to flex their muscles again during the crises of summer 2013.

A new generation has been awakened and has learned how to network and mobilize, and as I write they have already shaken the political establishment in Egypt and Tunisia twice. As the millennials enter their thirties and forties, they will have a better opportunity to shape politics directly, so that we could well see an echo effect of the 2011 upheavals in future decades.

F. Scott Fitzgerald wrote, "There are no second acts in American lives." But revolutionary generations in modern history have often had second acts. The political ideals and themes of the short-lived Second Republic of 1848–52 in France seemed to be eclipsed by the authoritarian Second Empire of Napoleon III in 1852–70. But republicanism had its resurgence after the Franco-Prussian War of 1870, with the establishment of the liberal Third Republic that reformed French education in a secular direction and engaged in lively parliamentary politics. The Prague Spring of the late 1960s in communist Czechoslovakia, which sought "socialism with a human face," looked as though it was crushed by Soviet tanks. Dissident and playwright Vaclav Havel (1936–2011) took to the radio waves in 1968 to denounce Moscow's invasion and afterward was banned from staging his plays. But two decades later Havel reemerged during and after the Velvet Revolution as the communist governments of Eastern Europe fell, and he became president of Czechoslovakia and then of the Czech Republic. The

Arab millennials' quest for bread, liberty, and social justice is very unlikely to be over.

The decline in religious observance among the new generation of Arabs may be accelerated by the bad experience they had with Muslim Brotherhood rule in Egypt in 2012–13 and by the excesses of the Renaissance Party and the Salafis in Tunisia. Indeed, the almost militant secularism expressed by Rebellion spokesmen such as Mahmoud Badr and their obvious hostility to religion in politics may signal a turning point in modern Egypt. Likewise, the crushing defeat of the Muslim candidates in the Tunisian student union signals a significant change in youth politics. It seems clear that the issue of nationalist or leftist politics versus the political right constitutes a divide that the millennials have to work through in coming years, and that unlike Gen X, many of them have a distinct antipathy to religion in politics, even if they are personally religious. The religious-nationalist divide is also clear in Libya, though there the greater salience of militia and other violence gave the religious hard right a coercive advantage on the ground.

The incredible proliferation of civil society organizations, newspapers, websites, and political parties in the postrevolutionary period creates new arenas in which new sorts of politics can be pursued. The decoupling of women's rights movements from the state feminist project of elite actors such as Leila Ben Ali and Suzanne Mubarak may increase the legitimacy of these movements and free young women from the shackles of the official parties and their agendas. Women of Gen Y have already challenged the postrevolutionary states on numerous occasions, getting thousands into the streets, as with the protests in Egypt against the brutal army attack on the "blue bra girl" or the marches in Tunisia against Salafi attempts to coerce women. Women activists in youth movements such as April 6 and Rebellion tended to foreground demands for regime change over specifically feminist concerns, though such concerns were part of their agenda. The Arab world suffers from remarkably low female workplace participation, in part because of religious strictures on gender mixing in public and because of low investment rates and high unemployment in general. If transitional governments can stabilize and bring in new investment, and if a new, more open media landscape can allow a challenge to shibboleths such as gender segregation, young women will be able to press for substantial, structural change. Now that the transitions are ongoing, greater women's activism in the freer political milieux of postrevolutionary North Africa and Egypt may be the shoe that has not yet dropped. Tellingly, new constitutions in both Egypt and Tunisia protect women's rights.

Transitions away from an authoritarian government can take place through a sort of gentleman's agreement between two opposing sections of a country's elite, as happened in Spain in the early 1980s and in Taiwan during the early twenty-first century. Transitions can also take place under the pressure of popular demonstrations and turbulence from below, as happened in Poland and in South Korea in the late twentieth century. Observers argue about which form of transition is healthier for subsequent democratic politics. In one study of regime transitions between 1970 and 2005, among the thirty-five countries that consolidated their democracy and remained free, "(69 percent) had strong nonviolent civic coalitions . . . (23 percent) had moderately strong civic coalitions, and only . . . (8 percent) had movements that were weak or absent in the two-year period leading up to the opening for the transition."[4] That is, the kind of revolution by popular movements achieved in Tunisia, Egypt, and Libya has more staying power as a force for democratic practices than a gentleman's agreement among divided elites. The youth upheavals in the three countries treated here were not "pacted" transitions but rather popular overthrows of entrenched elites. The turbulent character of the transition may have made for a less stable set of outcomes, but it also involved millions of people in the making of their destiny, which is surely a more *democratic* process in the original meaning of the term than a gentleman's agreement would have been.[5]

Of the twenty-two member countries of the Arab League, the outbreak of youth demonstrations in 2011 and after resulted in four overthrows of a president for life and one civil war. All five of the most seriously affected countries were republican monarchies, suffering from weak legitimacy. Remarkably, republics with relatively authoritarian states but no dynastic heir on the horizon (such as Algeria and Sudan) were able to weather the period of turmoil, at least through 2013. While the monarchies often faced long-lived protest movements, most were able to defuse discontent with relatively limited administrative or legal changes or through an increase in public aid or benefits, which was easy for the oil monarchies. Bahrain, riven by problems of religious ethnicity, is the exception. It faced ongoing social turmoil and protests by the disadvantaged majority Shiite population.

The mass youth movements were not the only actors who helped determine outcomes. How the elite behaved was important, and in particular the officer corps. In Egypt and Tunisia in 2011 the military declared neutrality and fostered a transition away from the dictator rather than risk damaging the prestige of their institution by opposing what was clearly a very popular revolutionary movement. The United States and France acquiesced in this outcome for similar reasons. Yemen's military was more willing to kill protesters for Ali Abdalluh Saleh but ultimately allowed a transition to his vice president, which also was acceptable to the United States. The militaries of Libya and Syria were very close to the ruling clique and willing to repress the population with heavy armaments. In Libya this attempt was forestalled by the Arab League, the United Nations, and NATO. The regional support of the Baath government in Syria by Iran and by Lebanon's Hizbullah, and the international support by Russia and China, forestalled an international intervention there, creating the prerequisites for a long, grinding civil war.

In Tunisia the Ben Ali clique was abandoned on January 14, 2011, by the military, by the UGTT leadership, and by the older, Bourguiba elite. Those elites then presided over the transition to elections, in alliance with institutions such as the major labor union and some of the left-of-center parties. The officer corps presided over a small military force and kept itself in the background. President Fouad Mebazaa and Prime Minister Beji Caid Essebsi, one in his late seventies and the other in his eighties, represented the first postindependence generation that had constructed the Bourguiba state, before the Ben Ali circle excluded them and monopolized power. This nationalist elite was in principle still willing to do deals with politicians who had served under Ben Ali, but the mobilized youth movements rejected such a pact, insisting on an exclusion of thousands of members of the Democratic Constitutional Rally. The youth thus prevented a conservative accord that might have preserved the power and prerogatives of high RCD officials and instead insisted on the marginalization of thousands of previously powerful Remnants. (Of course, below the cut-off of the fourteen thousand or so persons temporarily banned from public life, many mid- and lower-level former RCD members and bureaucrats retained much of their power and wealth.) While forestalling a political bargain between the Bourguibist camp and the remnants of the Ben Ali dictatorship made Tunisia more volatile than it might otherwise have been, it also punished corruption, impeded any immediate counterrevolution, and opened the political and economic systems to greater competition.

In Egypt, once the youth and workers created an opening, the officer corps stepped in in February 2011 to preside over the transition. Unlike in Tunisia, the military did not relinquish control of the executive, so that Field Marshal Hussein Tantawi effectively became the president and the Supreme Council of the Armed Forces served as his advisory council. Tantawi had far more power than his Tunisian counterpart, Fouad Mebazaa. Tantawi appointed two prime ministers in the transitional period. Both men had served in a Mubarak cabinet, a kind of elite continuity that the Tunisian youth were able to avert, in part because they faced a much less powerful officer corps. Only the very top circle of Mubarak-era officials was excluded from politics and put on trial, leaving the masses of well-connected and wealthy former National Democratic Party officials, known as the Remnants (*fulul*), to continue to play a social and economic role. Initially Interior Minister Habib Al-Adly and steel magnate Ahmed Ezz were proffered to the angry youth as examples of the new justice, both men sentenced to prison terms for their oppressive or corrupt roles in the Mubarak government (though Ezz was released on bail in the fall of 2013). The military and the Remnants were initially reluctant to prosecute the Mubaraks themselves, lower-level NDP officials, and police guilty of brutality and killings during the revolution, but the revolutionary youth successfully put pressure on them to do so. The military also attempted to retain as many Remnants as possible on the cabinet and in other institutions, but the youth pushed back against that move as well, though not always successfully.

In Libya, the massive youth demonstrations in Benghazi, Bayda, Derna, and other eastern cities led to the collapse of the revolutionary committees and the defection of the field officers and troops based in the east, many of them with local roots. Misrata, though separated from the east by a stretch of loyalist territory, also managed to rise up, its steel mill workers deploying their specialized skills in fortifying the city and turning their trucks into armored vehicles. In the southwest of the country, the Berbers and some Arab towns went into revolt as well. While some western cities rebelled, their proximity to Tripoli allowed Gaddafi to deploy armor and helicopter gunships against them and to crush the resistance in Mediterranean cities between the capital and the Tunisian border. Tripoli initially remained largely in the hands of the regime, both because elites there had benefited from government largesse and because the military, led in part by Gaddafi's sons, remained loyal and could menace dissidents. Libya was thus partitioned by the demonstrations into a Benghazi-led east and southwest, and a loyalist or cowed northwest.

The Benghazi revolutionaries threw up a Transitional National Council, consisting in part of technocrats who defected from the Gaddafi state, such as interim president Mustafa Abdul Jalil (former justice minister) and interim prime minister Mahmoud Jibril (formerly head of the Economic Development Board). Some of these figures had returned to Libya in the beginning of the century because of the promise of Saif al-Islam Gaddafi's reforms, but now they perceived that the state was inflexible and ultimately incapable of dealing with the country's challenges. The TNC included several former Gaddafi cabinet members, along with a number of longtime expatriates who came back for the revolution. The loyal Gaddafi armored units and helicopter gunships were deployed in an attempt to crush the uprising, provoking Arab League, United Nations Security Council, and ultimately NATO intervention. Although NATO fighter jets saved Benghazi from being invested in mid-March, and although their intervention helped the revolutionaries, the stiff resistance put up by newly armed Libyan youth in Misrata, Jabal Nafusa, and Ajdabiya was crucial to the success of the revolution. NATO avoided air strikes inside Misrata, and it was the young steel workers, ship container movers, and newly armed militiamen who pushed Gaddafi's snipers and tanks out of the center of the city and kept them at bay. When Tripoli itself rose up in late August, and Zintani and other revolutionaries flooded into the city, the Gaddafis were overthrown. The civilian transitional government was supported by most officers from the eastern military forces, who had also defected early on. The disbanded revolutionary committees, for all their insistence on control, had been repositories of managerial talent, which was lost to the transitional bodies. The posture of the military toward an attempted youth revolution in each country went a long way toward explaining its outcome.

Transitional Elected Government

Elections do not mark the end of democratic transitions. Democracy is not consolidated until two free and fair contested elections in a row are held and political actors come to agreement on the legitimate rules of the game. Tunisia and Libya held elections for a combined body that functioned both as a Constituent Assembly and a Parliament, though in both cases these bodies were reluctant to legislate too extensively, aware of their limited mandate. Egypt elected a regular Parliament, which was supposed to oversee the establishment of a separate Constituent Assembly that would draft a new constitution.

The Constituent Assembly in Tunisia came to be dominated by the religious right, in the form of the Renaissance Party. The progressive youth had disrupted any counterrevolutionary pact between Bourguibists and Ben Ali Remnants in 2011, but they were unable to prevent a left-liberal alliance with Renaissance in 2012–13. This development was on the whole a disappointment to the revolutionary youth in the major urban areas, who had been largely centrist to left of center in their politics and whose generation is less religious than their predecessors. A silver lining was that the presidency went to Moncef Marzouki, a secular human rights campaigner, and the speaker of the assembly, Mustapha Ben Jafar, belonged to a democratic socialist party. That the Renaissance Party had only a plurality in Parliament led it to abandon any attempt to insert sharia law into the new constitution, which probably forestalled substantial social unrest from the left and the secular political forces. Nevertheless, prosecutors had a sudden interest in pursuing morals and blasphemy cases, and Renaissance figures were put at the head of some media, casting a chill on Tunisia's lively information sector and angering influential bloggers, Facebook page administrators, and journalists. Still, government censorship of the internet was abolished in the law. The transitional government also played favorites with the hard-right Salafis, giving them more legal leeway than its secular critics. However,

2012 passed with relative social peace. The assassinations in 2013 of the leftists Chokri Belaid and Mohamed Brahmi by far-right Muslim extremists galvanized the youth and labor unions, who responded with large demonstrations and sit-ins. Dissidents accused the Renaissance government of being soft on terrorism. As a result of this leftist youth activism, the Renaissance Party finally showed some spine in taking on the would-be spoilers among the Muslim extremists and at least talked a better game of compromise and flexibility on some paragraphs of the draft constitution than it might otherwise have done. Continued youth and labor unrest pushed the government to other compromises in the fall of 2013, and to allow a transition to a government of technocrats to oversee the vote on the constitution and elections for a regular parliament.

In Egypt, the Muslim Brotherhood's Freedom and Justice Party and the Salafis dominated the first transitional Parliament. Their victory, however, was vitiated by the presidential system, whereby the president appointed the prime minister without reference to the majority party in Parliament. The military and the Remnants thus retained executive power until the presidential elections of June 2012, despite the Muslim Brotherhood Parliament, which was relatively toothless. When Parliament attempted to assert itself by packing the Constituent Assembly with members of the religious right to ensure a fundamentalist constitution, the courts struck down the attempt. The courts then dissolved the entire Parliament for substantial electoral fraud because the Muslim Brotherhood and Salafis had run party candidates in independent constituencies, giving themselves an unfair advantage. In the period between the inauguration of the new Parliament in December 2011 and the presidential elections the following summer, the youth activists concentrated on pushing back against military rule, insisting that the army retire to its barracks, that early presidential elections be held, and that the Emergency Law of 1981 be abrogated. Youth activism and the sometimes massive crowds they could inspire probably shortened the transition to the election of a civilian president and finally did ensure the demise, at least on paper, of the Emergency Law suspending constitutional rights.

Unlike in Tunisia, where a parliamentary system prevailed and the prime minister represented a parliamentary majority, President Mohamed Morsi was forced to rule without an elected Parliament. His legitimacy was thus somewhat weakened. His preference for Muslim Brotherhood appointees in key cabinet and other high posts isolated him and made him look sectarian. Unlike the Renaissance prime ministers, Hamadi Jebali and Ali Larayedh, Morsi did not have the support of secular or leftist figures like Marzouki and Ben Jafar. Rather their Egyptian equivalents, Mohamed ElBaradei and Hamdeen Sabahi, were increasingly alienated from him. Morsi's decree placing himself above the courts and his subsequent rashness in pushing through a Brotherhood constitution not voted for by 80 percent of the electorate provoked massive opposition, as did his creation of a Parliament out of thin air and his attempt to pack the courts. So too did the increasing atmosphere of intellectual repression created by Morsi's pursuit of sometimes frivolous political libel cases against critics such as Bassem Youssef and the bloggers. The revival of neoliberal policies by Brotherhood eminence grise Khairat al-Shater enraged the workers and the New Left. The progressive youth again went to the streets in November and December 2012 to protest his constitutional decree and his constitution. The violence Morsi used in dealing with some of the demonstrations against him in late fall of 2012 determined some of the revolutionary youth organizations to unseat him. These organizations allied with the parties of the National Salvation Front. Since some of these parties were led by former regime officials such as Amr Moussa, Morsi had inadvertently provoked a budding alliance between the left-of-center youth organizations and some of the less objectionable elements of the old regime. He also alienated the working class with his economic policies, provoking a record number of strikes and protests. Behind the scenes, the National Salvation Front established contacts with the increasingly disgruntled officer corps, asking that it put pressure on Morsi to rule more consensually. The danger Egypt faced was of a slide into a new authoritarianism with theocratic overtones, made possible by the corporate power of the Muslim Brotherhood cadres backing an elected president. Morsi made the mistake of excluding from his government the reformist parties that had been part of Kefaya and the Brotherhood's partners in opposing the Mubarak dictatorship, turning them into deadly enemies. Having barely won the presidency, he ruled from his narrow base.

The success of the youth networks around the Rebellion Movement in putting millions of protesters in the streets on June 30, 2013, made an opening for the military to stage a coup and appoint members of the National Salvation Front to a new transitional government. Egypt was back to the transitional period as of summer 2013, exactly where it had been in March 2011; the difference was that now it was even more divided. The difficulty it had in consolidating its move to democracy derived in part from the poor economic performance of the Morsi government; economic downturns are often fatal to democratic transitions. But it also stemmed from other important social and political realities. The old Mubarak-era elite was still powerful in the judiciary, the public sector, and private business, since the 2011 revolution had been two parts political revolution and only one part social revolution. The Remnants on the whole rejected Muslim Brotherhood rule. The officer corps, whether one considers it Remnants or an independent force, likewise found it difficult to accept the Brotherhood in power, perhaps with the exception of some officers in the Third Army at Suez, with whom Morsi had better relations, but who were not willing to break their line of command on his behalf.

Morsi's dictatorial ruling style deeply angered the mobilized youth movements, who, unlike those in Tunisia, had never stood down and could deploy an impressive repertoire of social action in city streets throughout the country. The sinking economy provoked a record number of labor actions. The lack of a pact between the Brotherhood and the left-liberals of the kind that was struck between Renaissance and its partners in Tunisia was fatal to the first attempt at transition. But the continued volatility of youth and worker politics was also key to the ability of the army, the reformists, and the Remnants jointly to move against an increasingly authoritarian Morsi. Without the agitations of April 6, the Revolutionary Socialists, the January 25 youth, the labor unions, and other such organizations in the fall of 2012, Morsi's constitution might have been perceived legitimate. Without the millions of demonstrators up and down the Nile on June 30, 2013, the July 3 military coup would have had far less public acceptance. The army's deposing of a freely and fairly elected president and attempted marginalization of the Muslim Brotherhood risked long-term social strife, as happened in Algeria from 1992 after the military abrogated the victory of the Islamic Salvation Front in the 1991 parliamentary elections there. Arrests of some two thousand Brotherhood leaders, the bloody dispersal of sit-ins in late summer 2013, and the banning of some Brotherhood media boded ill for another attempt at a transition to a liberal, inclusive order. After two and a half years Egypt still had found no formula for a successful new politics, though some sort of return to the legitimacy of elected government was promised. The dynamism of its youth movements, the power of its military, and the polarization over religion in politics told against a smooth approach to the country's new politics.

In Libya, the elected General National Council, established in July 2012, proved weak and open to pressure by the militias. Prime Minister Ali Zeidan failed to demobilize these armed youth gangs, which at key points were able to impose their will on the elected officials. Their most significant victory was banning Gaddafi-era officials such as Mahmoud Jibril from political office, forcing the resignation of council speaker Mohamed al-Magariaf, who had once pledged to disband the militias. Zeidan made little progress in rebuilding the national army and security forces, the sine qua non for restoring security, though the economy improved in 2013. Beyond the problem of militias that represented urban groups and neighborhoods, the transitional government was bedeviled by terrorist cells such as Ansar al-Sharia, some of which, especially in Benghazi, adopted from the Iraqi insurgents of the "Islamic State of Iraq" the strategy of destabilizing the government by a campaign of bombings and assassinations. While youth and student organizations protested the insecurity of their campuses and other spaces and went to city squares to protest the assassination of Abdel Salam al-Mismari in the summer of 2013, the civil youth movements were relatively powerless, and small NGOs did not have a major impact on politics. To the extent that the youth played a role in revolutionary Libya's troubled transition, it was mainly not youth movements in the sense of organizations organized for and by the youth as an interest group, but militias, which represented neighborhoods, cities, or narrow ideologies, that shaped it most strongly. Like the Tunisian youth movements, but deploying much more sinister methods, these youth militias succeeded in banning members of the old regime from holding political office during the attempted transition and perhaps even after.

The youth who made the revolutions were guilty of a certain amount of magical thinking. When I interviewed Nobel Peace Prize–winning Yemeni activist Tawakkul Karman late in 2011, she replied to all my questions about Yemen's social and economic problems by insisting they would be solved if only President Ali Abdullah Saleh could be removed, and she was typical in this regard.[6] Many activists appear to have believed that the corrupt dictators were the major obstacle to economic and social progress and that sweeping them away would abruptly improve the economy. Instead, the economies of Egypt and Tunisia contracted during the two years after the revolution, and workers and students felt betrayed. Moreover, the center-right governments of the Egyptian Brotherhood and the Tunisian Renaissance Party continued to pursue neoliberal, market-oriented economic policies, even though the youth and workers had rebelled against them. In Libya, petroleum exports accounted for much of the economy, and those were largely restored to prerevolution levels by late 2012, though in 2013 undisciplined militiamen, eastern autonomists, and numerous strikes by workers on the rigs sometimes drastically reduced exports. Despite their economic problems, Tunisia and Egypt had the advantage of having had nonviolent protest movements that united youth across the political spectrum, an approach associated with successful democratic transitions.

In Tunisia, the Remnants, with their state corruption, domestic surveillance, and police repression, were deeply weakened by the youth movements, though some of them regrouped in the center-right Call Party in 2013. The young people could not completely deter the Renaissance Party from taking up some of the old state methods of intimidation. In Egypt, the youth mounted powerful challenges, first to Field Marshal Tantawi's de facto military dictatorship, and then to President Morsi's creeping theocratic coup. They proved flexible and pragmatic inasmuch as they were at first willing to ally with the Muslim Brotherhood against the officer corps, but then, when the Brotherhood seemed a bigger danger to the ideals of their revolution, many of them welcomed Brigadier General Abdel Fattah al-Sisi's coup. To be fair, the long-standing youth organizations were more troubled by the coup than were the inchoate and networked youth of the spontaneous Rebellion Movement. Given the history of the youth movements, the officers should not be sanguine that the young people will stay with them if they overreach. Egypt's first attempt at transition failed and then entered a potentially polarized political environment not conducive to successful democracy. Unfortunately, those who hoped that the Brotherhood would take advantage of the democratic opening to rule in a parliamentary and consensual way were deeply disappointed by its rapid descent into renewed forms of authoritarianism that also would not have boded well for a democratic transition. Libyan elites also failed to make a new set of bargains that would smooth the way to a stable democratic government. In part, the youth militias prevented the challengers from striking a deal with the Gaddafi Remnants. In part, small but powerful armed extremists rejected the whole idea of a democratic transition and possessed the firepower to act as spoilers.

The conservative pacted transition or gentleman's agreement was effectively achieved only in Yemen. There youth movements camped out at Change Square in Sanaa throughout 2011 and allied with other social and political groups opposed to President Saleh. He, however, retained powerful support from influential tribes and his ruling political party, the General People's Congress. In early 2012 he finally agreed to step down as president, though he remained the head of the ruling party and so retained a great deal of power. Abed Rabbo Mansour Hadi, his vice president from the same party, was elected in a one-person referendum to be his successor in February 2012. Some 80 percent of Yemenis expressed satisfaction with this outcome. Cabinet posts were shared with some of the challengers. It is unclear, however, whether much changed in Yemen, with the same party in power and Saleh still the head of it. (Hadi was considered weak and still influenced by Saleh.) The country was riven by a southern secessionist movement and by both Sunni and Shiite forms of extremism. Desperately poor, it faced severe economic and environmental problems, including widespread hunger and the threat of running out of water. Saleh could no longer act quite as high-handedly as before, and Hadi tried to break the power of the Saleh family by removing them from high security positions. Elections were scheduled for early 2014. One would like to say that the transition by pact of Yemen saved the country some of the divisiveness and security problems produced by the more revolutionary outcomes across the Red Sea, but Yemen's security situation was already so bad and its polarization so great that the bargain struck on the cabinet in Sanaa seemed somewhat distant and irrelevant. Yemen, in any case, is hardly an argument for the virtues of a relatively conservative pacted transition among elites.[7]

In contrast, Syria stands at the other end of the spectrum, a country that went from youth in the streets in the spring of 2011 to fierce military repression and then to civil war and radicalization. It provides a horrific glimpse into what likely would have happened in Libya had the international community not intervened. The opposition of Russia and China to any intervention in Syria left the revolutionaries on their own. Under those circumstances, it was unwise of the youth to militarize their struggle, even if the decision was understandable given the brutal repression exercised by the regime. Syria's elites are deeply divided, with the army and the business classes in the larger cities standing with the regime, while the workers and the lower middle class in the small cities of the center rebelled. The civil war is not about religion, but the two sides are polarized in part on sectarian grounds. The regime counts on the support of the Alawite Shiite minority (10 to 14 percent of the population), the Christians (also 10 to 14 percent), small Shiite communities and the Druze, along with secular middle-class Sunnis of the large cities. The opposition is largely small-town and rural Sunnis, and over the course of the struggle the more radical, al-Qaeda–linked Sunnis came to the fore as the best fighters. The radicalization provoked by a vicious civil war that killed over 140,000 and displaced millions in a country of only 22 million made any bargain among the country's elites increasingly remote. It also marginalized the civil youth movements that sprang up in 2011, with lean and hungry militiamen for the most part taking their place.

The transitions in Tunisia, Egypt, and Libya have been troubled, even though they avoided the two extremes of long-term civil war and conservative gentleman's agreement. Just as the promotion of ethnic hatred by post-Soviet politicians such as Slobodan Milosevic of Serbia led to civil war after the breakdown of the old Yugoslavia, so the conflict between nationalists and the religious right posed an obstacle to consolidation of democratic practices in the Middle East. Just as a conflict among postrevolutionary elites over whether to retain authoritarian techniques of governance or to democratize roiled politics in post-Soviet Russia, Ukraine, and Kyrgyzstan, so the neo-authoritarian tendencies of the Muslim Brotherhood in Egypt angered the liberals and the left. Where a challenger group came to power and began violating the values of the youth revolutionaries by deploying authoritarian tactics redolent of the old regime, as Renaissance sometimes did in Tunisia, the youth had some success in pushing back. Where a challenger seemed to be replicating the old one-party state in a new guise, as Morsi appeared to be doing in Egypt, the progressive youth allied with other social forces to unseat him. Where the government became hostage to forces such as the militias or fundamentalist groups, as in Libya, the youth demonstrated against and shamed the politicians, asserting that the government must serve the whole people. The youth activists powerfully shaped the transitions.

The Worldwide Impact

The iconic images of Mohamed Bouazizi and the crowds in Tahrir Square had an impact not only in the Middle East but throughout the world. Combining pamphleteering, street politics, marches, strikes, and occupations of public space with Facebook and Twitter campaigns became common strategies throughout the world after January and February 2011. Most of these movements were evanescent and focused on economic or lifestyle discontent, and none of them succeeded in overturning a government. The magic formula, of cross-class alliances and a focus on the removal of a single top leader, eluded these other youth tsunamis.

The revolutions had an impact throughout the Middle East, even where protesters were unable to create a critical mass for structural change. The Sunni Arabs of central and western Iraq launched numerous protests in 2011–13 against the Shiite-dominated government installed during American rule of that country. The king of Morocco made only slight changes in response to the street demonstrations of 2011, but he did agree to appoint the prime minister thenceforth from the largest party in Parliament. He thereby took a small step toward popular sovereignty and, indeed, went beyond the system in Egypt in that regard, where there was still no such provision in the transitional period. Iranian high politics is opaque, but it is possible that the Supreme Leader allowed the moderate Hassan Rouhani to become president in the June 2013 presidential election because he feared another round of popular unrest if he resorted to ballot-stuffing, as he was accused of doing in 2009 in favor of Mahmoud Ahmadinejad. In contrast, some of the small oil monarchies of the Gulf took steps to back away from what little democracy and freedom of the press they had allowed before the 2011 upheavals. Kuwait, Bahrain, and Saudi Arabia became more repressive, fearing that their own youth might turn revolutionary. Bahrain's Sunni monarchy in particular saw the largely Shiite demonstrators as cat's paws of Iran. They feared both the left and the organized religious right. The United Arab Emirates prosecuted alleged members of the Muslim Brotherhood as subversives.

In Spain, Tahrir Square was evoked by the Indignados (Indignants), protesting against unemployment, government cuts in education, and high rents. Youth activists from Cairo visited their counterparts in Madrid and gave them pointers. Tahrir likewise inspired the student movement in Chile, which demanded free higher education and mobilized hundreds of thousands of students to go to the streets, in a struggle that lasted for years.

The Estonian Canadian activist Kalle Lasn and his anticonsumerist colleagues at the Vancouver-based Adbusters Media Foundation were inspired by the success of the revolutionaries in Tahrir Square in deposing the dictator Hosni Mubarak. Their organization specializes in combating advertising culture through spoofs and pranks. It was *Adbusters* magazine that sent out the call on Twitter in the summer of 2011 for a rally on Wall Street on September 17, with the now-famous hashtag #OccupyWallStreet, though it was not the only such organizer. A thousand protesters gathered on the designated date, commemorating the 2008 economic meltdown that had thrown millions of Americans out of their jobs and homes. Some camped out in nearby Zuccotti Park, in another unexpected global spark of protest. April 6 leaders and Egyptian bloggers went to New York to share ideas with the demonstrators. After Mayor Michael Bloomberg ordered the police to disperse the protesters that November, Lasn and a coauthor wrote:

> The Occupy Wall Street meme was launched by a poster in the 97th issue of our international ad-free magazine, Adbusters and by a "tactical briefing" that we sent to our 90,000-strong "culture jammer" global network

of activists, artists and rabble-rousers in mid-July. The movement's true origins, however, go back to the revolutions in Tunisia and Egypt. That was when the world witnessed how intransigent regimes can be toppled by leaderless democratic crowds, brought together by social media, that stand firm and courageously refuse to go home until their demands for change are met. Our shared epiphany was that America, too, needs its Tahrir Square moment and its own kind of regime change. Perhaps not the hard regime change of Tunisia and Egypt, but certainly a soft one.[8]

In 2013 the Gezi Park movement in Turkey protested police brutality, neoliberal economic policies, and the restrictions on lifestyle by the center-right government of the Justice and Development Party. The AKP, having analyzed the events in the Arab world, refused to allow a long-term occupation of the park near Taksim Square, deploying water cannon and heavy doses of tear gas to clear it. Also in 2013 Brazil was shaken by urban protests mirroring cyberspace campaigns, complaining about high transportation costs and government and police corruption.

The youth movements in Tunisia, Egypt, and Libya pioneered not so much new tactics as new combinations of tactics in social movements. They allied with both blue- and white-collar workers to protest high unemployment, low pay, police brutality, and a closed, corrupt elite. Above all, they were adamant that they were not going to be inherited like so many sticks of household furniture by the heir of their president for life. The Arab millennials challenged their police states with a whole repertoire of public dissent, including pamphleteering, marches, demonstrations, hunger strikes, labor strikes, appropriation of long-standing public rituals, and long-term massive sit-ins. They mirrored their activism in urban spaces with internet campaigns that were not merely informational but also interactive and formational. The youth in all three countries deployed the multiplier effect of the internet to organize nationwide protests on designated days and to delegitimize the regime with videos of police torture, with charges of high-level corruption, and with ridicule and caricature. In Egypt, after years of cooperation and cross-class networking by the New Left, they were able to enlist allies among workers and labor unions and even public sector office workers. Among their targets were neoliberal policies imposed by the

West via the International Monetary Fund and other bodies, which stressed privatization of the economy and the use of market mechanisms even with regard to public goods like education. Given Egypt's very large public sector, these policies affected millions of people, often negatively. Similar discontent with the tyranny of the market was felt by youth throughout the world in the twenty-first century.

The millennial leaders also created a sympathetic image for themselves as crusaders for an end to torture, corruption, and police repression, an image with which other, initially less engaged youth could identify. They saw the advantages of young people for social protest and mobilized them, making use of the spare time of many young men and women, some of them unemployed, who were still unmarried and so lacked the family responsibilities that might deter them from risking the violence inherent in street protest. The youth revolutionaries of the Middle East inspired their peers throughout the globe by their ideals of liberty and social justice and their collective action techniques. Fundamentalist movements seeking to take advantage of the political opening to impose new forms of theocratic authoritarianism suffered severe setbacks at the hands of the same youth activists.

There will be no more republican monarchies. This generation of New Arabs has shaken a complacent, stagnant, and corrupt status quo and forever changed the world.

Acknowledgments

The field research for this book was carried out in the summer of 2011, spring 2012, and March and June 2013 and was supported by research funds attached to my Collegiate Chair in the School of Science, Letters and the Arts at the University of Michigan, by a research stipend from my duties as center director at the International Institute at that university; by the Centre d'études maghrébines à Tunis (American Institute for Maghreb Studies), and by kind donations from readers of my site, *Informed Comment*. I am also grateful to the Center for the Study of Islam and Democracy in Tunis for having me speak in 2012 and 2013 and to the Law Faculty of Kairouan University for hosting me in May 2012. My fellowship at the Nouvelle Sorbonne in Paris in March 2013, while for another project, did also allow me to meet Arab revolutionaries based there, discuss the upheavals with French academic colleagues, and collect recent French-language writing on the subject.

For their insights on contemporary Tunisia I am indebted to Amira Yahyaoui, Hélé Béji, Youssef Cherif, Stuart Schaar, and Larissa Chomiak. In Egypt I am grateful to Ahmed Maher and other members of April 6, to Saad Eddin Ibrahim of the Ibn Khaldun Center for Human Rights, to the Egyptian Institute for Personal Freedom, to Barbara Ibrahim and Sherine El Traboulsi of the John D. Gerhart Center for Philanthropy and Civic Engagement at the American University in Cairo, to Samir Fadel, to Jihan Khodeir of al-Lutus li al-Tanmiya wa Huquq al-Insan, to Khaled Fahmy, Amr Ezzat, Ann Lesch, and Mariam Kirillos of Human Rights Watch, and many others too numerous to thank properly here. My Libya trip would not have been possible without the help of my dear friend Khaled Mattawa.

I am eternally grateful to him for arranging Arabic-language talks and discussion sessions for me in Benghazi and Tripoli, and to the audiences for their comments and suggestions. I am beholden as well to Dr. Muhammad Mufti of Benghazi and to Muhammad Fannous, who was then the manager of the Misrata Revolution Museum. Also thanks for comments to Eric Schewe and Atef Said.

My agents, Steve Wasserman and Brettne Bloom of Kneerim & Williams Literary Agency, were the first to believe in this project. I am deeply grateful to Simon & Schuster for their faith in and patience with me. I began discussing the shape of this book with Alessandra Bastagli when she was at that publisher and am indebted to her for her enthusiasm and encouragement as it was being conceived. My editor on this book, Priscilla Painton, was crucial in helping me formulate its precise focus. Her many suggestions for improving the book have made it better and clearer. I am grateful to her for challenging me to go the extra mile in striving for precision and cogency, as well as for her support and encouragement.

My wife, Shahin, courageously accompanied me to a society in revolutionary turmoil and shared in this voyage of discovery. It is impossible for me to thank her adequately.

Notes

PREFACE

1. Early overviews include Jean-Pierre Filiu, *The Arab Revolution: Ten Lessons from the Democratic Uprising* (Oxford: Oxford University Press, 2011); Manuel Castells, *Networks of Outrage and Hope* (Cambridge, UK: Polity Press, 2012); Philip N. Howard and Muzammil M. Hussain, *Democracy's Fourth Wave? Digital Media and the Arab Spring* (Oxford: Oxford University Press, 2013); Marc Lynch, *The Arab Uprising* (New York: Public Affairs, 2012); James Gelvin, *The Arab Uprisings: What Everyone Needs to Know* (New York: Oxford University Press, 2012); Adeed Dawisha, *The Second Arab Awakening* (New York: Norton, 2013); Hamid Dabashi, *The Arab Spring: The End of Postcolonialism* (London: Zed, 2012); Gilbert Achcar, *The People Want: A Radical Exploration of the Arab Uprising* (Berkeley: University of California Press, 2013).

2. Asef Bayat, "Reclaiming Youthfulness," in Samir Khalaf and Roseanne Saad Khalaf, eds., *Arab Youth: Social Mobilization in Times of Risk* (London: Saqi Books, 2011), 47, 49.

3. Dina Shehata, "Youth Movements and the 25 January Revolution," in Bahgat Korany and Rabab El-Mahdi, eds., *Arab Spring in Egypt: Revolution and Beyond* (Cairo: American University in Cairo Press, 2012), chapter 6.

4. "Arab World Growth as World Population Reaches 7 Bln," *Albawaba*, October 29, 2011, www.albawaba.com/editorchoice/arab-world-growth-world-population -reaches-7-bln-398993.

5. For an argument about how the classic methods of academic history can be deployed for very recent events, see Juan Cole, "Blogging Current Affairs History," *Journal of Contemporary History* 46 (July 2011): 658–70.

6. Castells, *Networks of Outrage*, 100.

7. My approach is influenced by Charles Tilly, *Social Movements, 1768–2004* (Boulder, CO: Paradigm, 2004); Charles Tilly, *Regimes and Repertoires* (Chicago: University of Chicago Press, 2006); Mayer Zald and John D. McCarthy, eds., *Social Movements in an Organizational Society* (New Brunswick, NJ: Transaction

Books, 1987); Joel Beinin and Frederic Vairel, *Social Movements, Mobilization and Contestation in the Middle East and North Africa* (Stanford: Stanford University Press, 2011); and Castells's notion of networked youth movements.

CHAPTER 1: THE ARAB MILLENNIALS

1. "Irtiyah," Buraydh, no. 1, July 2, 2012, www.buraydh.com/forum/showthread.php?t=332447.
2. "Youth Unemployment in the Arab World Is a Major Cause for Rebellion," International Labour Organization, April 5, 2011, www.ilo.org/global/about-the-ilo/newsroom/features/WCMS_154078/lang--en/index.htm; Achcar, *The People Want*.
3. "Libya: Economy and Trade," Qfinance, 2010, www.qfinance.com/contentFiles/QF02/gpflqc6p/10/0/libya.pdf; Abdul Rahman Al Ageli, "Youth Employment in Libya: A Structural Solution Is Needed (Parts 1, 2, 3)," *Libya Herald*, December 12, 16, 19, 2012, www.libyaherald.com/2012/12/12/youth-employment-in-libya-a-structural-solution-is-needed-part-13/.
4. Yousef Courbage, "The Demographic Youth Bulge and Social Rupture," in Khalaf and Khalaf, *Arab Youth*. For a critique see Achcar, *The People Want*, 41–43.
5. Courbage, "The Demographic Youth Bulge," 81.
6. Juan Cole, "Egypt's Modern Revolutions and the Fall of Mubarak," in Fawaz Gerges, ed., *The New Middle East: Protest and Revolution in the Arab World* (Cambridge, UK: Cambridge University Press, 2013); Juan Cole, *Colonialism and Revolution in the Middle East: Social and Cultural Origins of Egypt's 'Urabi Movement* (Princeton, NJ: Princeton University Press, 1993).
7. David Leonhardt, "Urbanization in Libya," *New York Times*, February 22, 2011, http://economix.blogs.nytimes.com/2011/02/22/urbanization-in-libya/.
8. Cities Alliance, "Tunisia Urbanization Review," World Bank. www.citiesalliance.org/ca_projects/detail/21923.
9. Tova Benski, Lauren Langman, Ignacia Perugorría, and Benjamín Tejerina, "From the Streets and Squares to Social Movement Studies: What Have We Learned?," *Current Sociology* 61, no. 4 (2013): 541–61.
10. Julia Zinkina and Andrey Korotayev, "Urbanization Dynamics in Egypt: Factors, Trends, Perspectives," *Arab Studies Quarterly* 35, no. 1 (2013): 20–38.
11. Farha Ghannam, "Mobility, Liminality, and Embodiment in Urban Egypt," *American Ethnologist* 38, no. 4 (2011): 790–800.
12. Merlyna Lim, "Clicks, Cabs, and Coffee Houses: Social Media and Oppositional Movements in Egypt, 2004–2011," *Journal of Communication* 62, no. 2 (2012): 231–48, this point on 235.
13. Anna di Bartolomeo, Tamirace Fakhoury, and Delphine Perrin, "Migration Profile Tunisia: The Demographic-Economic Framework of Migration, the Legal

Framework of Migration, [and] the Socio-Political Framework of Migration," Consortium for Applied Research on International Migration, Robert Schuman Centre for Advanced Studies, European University Institute, Florence, Italy, June 2010, www.carim.org/public/migrationprofiles/MP_Tunisia_EN.pdf.

14. Teresa Graziano, "The Tunisian Diaspora: Between 'Digital Riots' and Web Activism," *Social Science Information* 51, no. 4 (2012): 534–50.

15. Tarek Osman, *Egypt on the Brink: From Nasser to Mubarak* (New Haven, CT: Yale University Press, 2012), chapter 7.

16. Amira Saleh, "CAPMAS: Egyptians Working Abroad Up 10% in 2008," *Egyptian Independent*, October 22, 2009, www.egyptindependent.com/news /capmas-egyptians-working-abroad-10-2008.

17. Castells, *Networks of Outrage*; Howard and Hussain, *Democracy's Fourth Wave?*

18. Reporters sans Frontières, "Tunisie," in *Internet sous surveillance*.

19. Ragui Assaad and Ghada Barsoum, "Rising Expectations and Diminishing Opportunities for Egypt's Young," in Navtej Dhillon and Tarik Yousef, eds., *Generation in Waiting: The Unfulfilled Promise of Young People in the Middle East* (Washington, DC: Brookings Institution, 2009), chapter 3; Andrea Kavanaugh, Seungwon Yang, Steven Sheetz, Lin Tzy Li, and Ed Fox, "Between a Rock and a Cell Phone: Social Media Use During Mass Protests in Iran, Tunisia and Egypt," 2011, at http://eprints.cs.vt.edu/archive/00001149/01/journal_paper.Kavanaugh_et_al .social_media_middle_east.pdf.

20. "Egypt Reaches 72 per cent Mobile Penetration," Comm, April 9, 2010, http:// comm.ae/egypt-reaches-72-per-cent-mobile-penetration; Kavanaugh et al., "Between a Rock and a Cell Phone."

21. Sara Leckner and Ulrika Facht, compilers, "A Sampler of International Media and Communication Statistics," Nordic Media Trends 12 (Goteborg, Sweden: University of Gothenburg, 2010), www.nordicom.gu.se/common/publ_pdf /NMT12.pdf.

22. "Reaching Teens and Young Adults in the Middle East," *MEInfo* (Dubai), January 30, 2005.

23. Linda Herrera, "Youth and Citizenship in the Digital Age: A View from Egypt," *Harvard Educational Review* 82, no. 3 (2012): 333–52, this point on 342.

24. Sultan al-Qassemi, Barjeel Art Foundation, presentation on panel, "The Emergence of New Media," Middle East Studies Association, Denver, Colorado, November 17, 2012.

25. Herrera, "Youth and Citizenship in the Digital Age," 334, citing C. Shirky.

26. Sihem Najar, "Les femmes cyberactivistes et les revendications d'un changement démocratique en Tunisie," in Sihem Najjar, ed., *Le cyberactivisme au Maghreb et dans le monde arabe* (Paris: Karthala, 2013), 149–73, this point on 160.

27. "Facebook Usage: Factors and Analysis," Arab Social Media Report, Dubai School of Government, January 2011, http://unpan1.un.org/intradoc/groups

/public/documents/dsg/unpan044212.pdf; Herrera, "Youth and Citizenship in the Digital Age," 358.

28. Philip N. Howard, Aiden Duffy, Deen Freelon, Muzammil Hussain, Will Mari, and Marwa Mazaid, "Opening Closed Regimes: What Was the Role of Social Media During the Arab Spring?," Working paper 2011/1, Project on Information Technology & Political Islam, 13, www.scribd.com/doc/66956384/Opening-Closed-Regimes.

29. Castells, *Networks of Outrage*, 224–25, discusses "virality"; the invocation of the multiplier effect is my own.

30. Ghannam, "Mobility, Liminality, and Embodiment in Urban Egypt."

31. Courbage, "The Demographic Youth Bulge," 79.

32. Hassan R. Hammoud, "Illiteracy in the Arab World," DVV International, 2005, www.iiz-dvv.de/index.php?article_id=208&clang=1.

33. Hassan R. Hammoud, "Illiteracy in the Arab World," Literacy for Life, Background paper prepared for the Education for All Global Monitoring Report, UNESCO, 2006, http://unesdoc.unesco.org/images/0014/001462/146282e.pdf

34. Osman, *Egypt on the Brink*, chapter 7.

35. "Ta'thir al-wasa'il al-tiknulujiya al-haditha 'ala al-'ilaqah al-'a'iliyya," *al-Jazeera Arabic*, July 22, 2002, transcript at www.aljazeera.net/programs/pages/4636e685-e936-47b3-9bfe-5c3b126f78a5.

36. Sa'id Ben Yaminah, "Al-Taghayyur al-ijtima'i wa atharuhu 'ala suluk al-shabab fi al-mujtama' al-'arabi," *Socio-Algérie*, July 28, 2010, https://sites.google.com/site/socioalger1/lm-alajtma/mwady-amte/altghyr-alajtmay-wathrh-ly-slwk-alshbab-fy-almjtm-alrby.

37. Muhammad al-Shaghnubi, "Mawqif ghayyara Hayatahu: Fallah Misri yaqhar al-ummiyyah," MBC.net, December 22, 2008, http://almasse.ba7r.org/t452-topic.

38. "Fallah ummi yatarashshah li al-ri'asah," *al-Anba'*, March 20, 2012, www.alanba.com.kw/absolutenmnew/templates/oula2010.aspx?articleid=276801&zoneid=12&m=0.

39. Alaa al-Aswany, Arabic tweet, December 8, 2012, 4:32 p.m.

40. Robert L. Tignor, *Egypt: A Short History* (Princeton, NJ: Princeton University Press, 2011), 224.

41. Pew Forum on Religion and Public Life, *The World's Muslims: Unity and Diversity* (Washington, D.C.: Pew Research Center, 2012), www.pewforum.org/uploadedFiles/Topics/Religious_Affiliation/Muslim/the-worlds-muslims-full-report.pdf.

42. Umm al-Mudawwanah, http://semsam.blogspot.com/.

43. "Ana `almani," April 2012, http://semsam.blogspot.com/2012/04/blog-post_8766.html#.UG_FMq7hcfY.

44. Nadine Sika, "Dynamics of a Stagnant Religious Discourse and the Rise of New Secular Movements in Egypt," in Korany and El-Mahdi, *Arab Spring in Egypt*, chapter 4.

45. Karl Mannheim, "The Problem of Generations," in *Essays in the Sociology of Knowledge* (New York: Oxford University Press, 1952), 276–320.

46. Mansoor Moaddel, "What Do Arabs Want?," Project Syndicate, January 4, 2012, www.project-syndicate.org/commentary/what-do-arabs-want-.

47. Ibid.

48. Good places to start with regard to the Brotherhood are Richard P. Mitchell, *The Society of Muslim Brothers* (Oxford: Oxford University Press, 1969); Carrie Rosefsky Wickham, *The Muslim Brotherhood: Evolution of an Islamist Movement* (Princeton, NJ: Princeton University Press, 2013); Bruce K. Rutherford, *Egypt after Mubarak* (Princeton, NJ: Princeton University Press, 2008), chapter 3; Juan Cole, *Engaging the Muslim World*, revised ed. (New York: Palgrave Macmillan, 2010), chapter 2.

49. Mohamed-Ali Adraoui, *Du golfe aux banlieues: Le salafisme mondialisé* (Paris: Presses Universitaires de France, 2013).

50. Raghida Dirgham, "al-Maqariyaf li al-Hayat: al-mutatarrafun qillah," *al-Hayat* (London), October 1, 2013, at http://alhayat.com/Details/440055.

51. Lina Ben Mhenni, "Na`m ana mulhidah," @benmhennilina, Twitter, October 26, 2012.

52. Jano Charbel and Sherif Zaazaa, "The Unbelievers: Post–Alber Saber, More Atheists Struggle to Assert Their Identity," *Egypt Independent* (Cairo), October 28, 2012, www.egyptindependent.com/news/unbelievers-post-alber-saber-more -atheists-struggle-assert-their-identity.

53. Mahmoud Jibril, "Arab Awakening and Regional Order: Libya," Istanbul World Forum, Istanbul Congress Center, October 13, 2012 (my translation from Jibril's Arabic oral presentation).

54. "Managing Gen Y Recruitment Module," Culture Coach International, 2009, www.culturecoach.biz/CCI%20Store/Resources/Gen%20Y%20Module _Package3.pdf.

55. Robert J. Brym, *Intellectuals and Politics* (London: George Allen & Unwin, 1980); Cole, *Colonialism and Revolution in the Middle East*.

CHAPTER 2: THE REPUBLICAN MONARCHS

1. E. P. Thompson, "The Moral Economy of the English Crowd in the Eighteenth Century," *Past and Present* 50, no. 1 (1971): 76–136. Thompson's essay spawned a vast literature. Relevant to our discussion is Edmund Burke III, "Understanding Arab Protest Movements," *Arab Studies Quarterly* 8, no. 4 (1986): 333–45; Larbi Sadiki, "Popular Uprisings and Arab Democratization," *International Jour-*

nal of Middle East Studies 32, no. 1 (2000): 71–95; Andrea Khalil, "The Political Crowd: Theorizing Popular Revolt in North Africa," *Contemporary Islam* 6, no. 1 (2012): 45–65.

2. Husayn Husni, *Sanawat maʿa al-Malik Faruq: Shahadah lil-haqiqah wa-al-tarikh* (al-Qahirah, Egypt: Dar al-Shuruq, 2007). For land ownership, see Stella Margold, "Agrarian Land Reform in Egypt," *American Journal of Economics and Sociology* 17, no. 1 (1957): 9–19. For the anecdote of the stolen bride, see "Abd al-Ghani al-Sayyid: Tallaqa zawjatahu bi amr al-Malik Faruq," Akhbar al-Naharda (Cairo, Egypt), December 18, 2012, www.akhbar-today.com/59088.

3. David Harvey, *A Brief History of Neoliberalism* (Oxford: Oxford University Press, 2007). See also, e.g., Edmund Amann and Werner Baer, "Neoliberalism and Its Consequences in Brazil," *Journal of Latin American Studies* 34, no. 4 (2002): 945–59.

4. Saad Eddin Ibrahim, "'Ala masrah al-jumlukiyyah," *al-Masry al-Youm* (Cairo, Egypt), October 31, 2009, www.almasryalyoum.com/node/156361.

5. Ambassador Margaret Scobey, Cairo, to Secretary of State Condoleezza Rice, September 23, 2008, www.guardian.co.uk/world/us-embassy-cables-documents/171176.

6. Daniel Swift, "Saad Eddin Ibrahim: Through the Arab Looking Glass," Open Democracy, April 10, 2003, www.opendemocracy.net/people-middle_east_politics/article_1146.jsp; also Juan Cole, "Saad's Revolution," Truthdig, February 1, 2011, www.truthdig.com/report/item/saads_revolution_20110131/; Bari Weiss, "A Democrat's Triumphal Return to Cairo," *Wall Street Journal*, February 26, 2011, online.wsj.com/article/SB10001424052748703408604576164482658051692.html.

7. The literature on modern Egypt is vast. Among the more accessible studies of the late Mubarak era that I recommend are Galal Amin, *Egypt in the Era of Hosni Mubarak* (Cairo: American University in Cairo Press, 2010); Lisa Blaydes, *Elections and Distributive Politics in Mubarak's Egypt* (Cambridge, UK: Cambridge University Press, 2010); Rutherford, *Egypt after Mubarak*; John R. Bradley, *Inside Egypt* (New York: Palgrave Macmillan, 2008); Osman, *Egypt on the Brink*; Roger Owen, *The Rise and Fall of the Arab Presidents for Life* (Cambridge, MA: Harvard University Press, 2012); Samer Soliman, *The Autumn of Dictatorship: Fiscal Crisis and Political Change in Egypt under Mubarak* (Palo Alto, CA: Stanford University Press, 2011); Joshua Stacher, *Adaptable Autocrats: Regime Power in Egypt and Syria* (Stanford: Stanford University Press, 2012).

8. Owen, *Rise and Fall*, chapter 4.

9. Blaydes, *Elections*, chapter 3; Stacher, *Adaptable Autocrats*, chapters 2, 3.

10. Ambassador Francis J. Ricciardone, Cairo, to Secretary of State Condoleezza Rice, April 3, 2006, wikileaks.org/cable/2006/04/06CAIRO2010.html.

11. Khalid Elbalshy, "Khadijah Ah, Misr la!," *Mudawwanat Khalid al-Balshy*, April 27, 2007, http://elbalshy.blogspot.com/2007/04/blog-post_26.html.

12. Ambassador Margaret Scobey, Cairo, to Secretary of State Hillary Clinton, November 17, 2009, Wikileaks, at http://wikileaks.org/cable/2009/11/09CAIRO2155.html.

13. Khalid Elbalshy, "Jamal Mubarak wa 'shuraka'uhu kharrabu buyut sighar al-mudaribin," Mudawwanat Khalid al-Balshi, March 7, 2007, http://elbalshy .blogspot.com/2007/03/blog-post_7500.html; Mohamed Fadel Fahmy, "Sons of Ousted Egyptian President on Trial," CNN, July 9, 2012, www.cnn.com/2012 /07/09/world/africa/egypt-mubarak-sons-trial; "Mubarak Brothers Accused of Exploiting Influence for Gain," *Egypt Independent* (Cairo, Egypt), April 18, 2011, www.egyptindependent.com/news/mubarak-brothers-accused-exploiting -influence-gain.

14. For use of banks for political purposes see Owen, *Rise and Fall*, chapter 3.

15. Ambassador Francis J. Ricciardone, Cairo, to Secretary of State Condoleezza Rice, April 8, 2008, Wikileaks, http://wikileaks.org/cable/2008/04/08CAIRO714 .html.

16. "Fasad Jamal Mubarak," *Fasad al-Hukumah al-Misriyya*, February 11, 2008, http://fasad.yoo7.com/t5-topic; "Ahmed Ezz Sentenced to 34 Years for Squandering Public Funds," *Egypt Independent*, March 3, 2013, www .egyptindependent.com/news/ahmed-ezz-sentenced-34-years-squandering -public-funds; "Ahmed Ezz released pending retrial in steel licenses case," *Egypt Independent*, August 5, 2013, www.egyptindependent.com/news/ahmed-ezz -released-pending-retrial-steel-licenses-case.

17. Ambassador Margaret Scobey, Cairo, to Secretary of State Condoleezza Rice, September 15, 2008, Wikileaks, http://wikileaks.org/cable/2008/09 /08CAIRO2027.html.

18. Umar al-Hadi, "Al-Barada'i . . . `ala maqas al-amal," *Asad*, February 17, 2010, http://asadx.net/node/131 (seen November 10, 2011).

19. "Bad Blood: Is Government Corruption Beyond Cure?" *Egypt Independent* (Cairo), February 25, 2010, www.egyptindependent.com/news/bad-blood-govt -corruption-beyond-cure; "Egyptian delegation In London demands return of fugitive Mamdouh Ismail," Ahram Online, July 14, 2011 http://english.ahram .org.eg/NewsContent/1/64/16398/Egypt/Politics-/Egyptian-delegation-In -London-demands-return-of-fu.aspx.

20. 'Imad Fawaz, "Jam`iyyat jil al-mustaqbal," Ahamm Khabar, July 12, 2009, http://efawaz.elaphblog.com/posts.aspx?U=1449&A=21938.

21. Blaydes, *Elections*, chapter 6.

22. Ambassador Francis J. Ricciardone, Cairo, to Secretary of State Condoleezza Rice, Dec 12, 2007, Wikileaks, http://wikileaks.org/cable/2007/12/07CAIRO3465. html.

23. Ambassador Francis J. Ricciardone, Cairo, to Secretary of State Condoleezza Rice, April 3, 2008, Wikileaks, http://wikileaks.org/cable/2008/04/08CAIRO677.html.

24. Christopher Alexander, *Tunisia: Stability and Reform in the Modern Maghreb* (London: Routledge, 2010); Béatrice Hibou, *The Force of Obedience: The Political Economy of Repression in Tunisia*, trans. Andrew Brown (Cambridge, UK: Maiden Press, 2011); Mahmoud Ben Romdhane, *Tunisie: État, économie et société: Ressources politiques, légitimation et régulations sociales* (Tunis: Sud Editions, 2011); Hakim Ben Hammouda, *Économie politique d'une revolution* (Brussels: De Boeck, 2012); Owen, *Rise and Fall*, chapter 4.

25. "Tunisia: What Succession Scenario?," Ambassador Robert F. Godec, Tunis, to Secretary of State Condoleezza Rice, May 9, 2008, Wikileaks, http://wikileaks .org/cable/2008/05/08TUNIS493.html.

26. "Tunisia: What Succession Scenario?," Ambassador Robert F. Godec, Tunis, to Secretary of State Condoleezza Rice, May 9, 2008, Wikileaks, http://wikileaks .org/cable/2008/05/08TUNIS493.html.

27. "Tunisie: La fulgurante ascension de Mohamed Sakher El Materi," Nawaat.org (Tunis), November 23, 2010, http://nawaat.org/portail/2010/11/23/tunisie-la -fulgurante-ascension-de-mohamed-sakher-el-materi/.

28. Ambassador Robert F. Godec, Tunis, to Secretary of State Hillary Clinton, July 27, 2009, Wikileaks, http://wikileaks.org/cable/2009/10/09TUNIS790.html.

29. "Al-Matri yashtari Dar al-Sabah," Journaliste Tunisien-9, April 18, 2009, http:// journaliste-tunisien-9.blogspot.com/2009/04/blog-post_1927.html. See also "Businessman Buys Dar al-Sabah, Tunisians Fear Loss of Last Independent Media Outlet," *Menassat*, May 22, 2009, www.menassat.com/?q=en/news-articles/6567 -businessman-buys-publishing-company-tunisians-fear-loss-last-independent -media-ou.

30. Claude Moniquet, *Printemps Arabe, Printemps Pourri* (Paris: Editions Encre d'Orient, 2012), 145.

CHAPTER 3: "GIANTS OF MEAT AND STEEL"

1. Melissa Y. Lerner, "Connecting the Actual with the Virtual: The Internet and Social Movement Theory in the Muslim World—The Cases of Iran and Egypt," *Journal of Muslim Minority Affairs* 30, no. 4 (2010): 555–74.

2. John Pollock, "How Egyptian and Tunisian Youth Hacked the Arab Spring," Streetbook, MIT Technology Review, September/October 2011, http:// m.technologyreview.com/web/38379; Howard and Hussain, *Democracy's Fourth Wave?*, chapters 2–3.

3. Foetus in Mazin al-Sayyid, "Majmu`at muqawimah fi al-ahya', nishat iliktruni dakhm," *al-Safir* (Beirut), February 21, 2011.

4. Pascale Egré, "Internet, nouveau territoire de lutte pour les opposants politiques en exil," *Hommes et Migrations*, no. 1240 (September–October 2002), www

.hommes-et-migrations.fr/docannexe/file/1240/1240_08.pdf. See also Amnesty International, "Mme Imen Derouiche, ancienne prisonnière d'opinion tunisienne," December 2004, www.amnesty-volunteer.org/aiscf/coord-tunisie/I%20 Derouiche.htm.

5. Egré, "Internet, nouveau territoire de lutte pour les opposants politiques en exil."

6. Reporters sans Frontières, *Internet sous surveillance: Les entraves à circulation de l'information sur le réseau. Rapport 2003* (Paris: Editions La Découverte & Syros, 2003), www.rsf.org/IMG/pdf/doc-2233.pdf; Mike Jensen, "North African Internet Round-up," *Telecommunications* 33, no. 10 (1999): 188–89.

7. Jensen, "North African Internet Round-up."

8. Amira Yahyaoui, interview with the author, by email in French, July 29, 2012; all subsequent remarks attributed to Amira Yahyaoui are from this interview and quotes are my translation. For the beginnings of TUNeZINE and the crackdown, see also Reporters sans Frontières, *Internet sous surveillance*. For more on Amira Yahyaoui, see "Tunisie: Amira Yahyaoui, une vie d'activiste," Tekiano.com, May 18, 2012, www.tekiano.com/ness/portraits/5338-tunisie-amira-yahyaoui -une-vie-dactiviste-.html.

9. Najar, "Les femmes cyberactivistes."

10. "Risalah Maftuha ila Ra'is al-Dawlah," TUN-e-ZINE, July 6, 2001, www .tunezine.com/tunezine07.htm. See also "Le juge Mokhtar Yahyaoui," Facebook, posted July 26, 2010, https://www.facebook.com/note.php?note_id= 113794162006500&comments; Mohamed Hamdane, "Visages de la Révolution: Mokhtar Yahyaoui, le juge rebelle," Center Blog, July 5, 2011, http:// droit-tunisie-revolution.centerblog.net/413-mokhtar-yahiaoui.

11. Lilia Weslaty, "Entrétien avec Sophie Piekarec, la fiancée de Zouheir Yahyaoui," Nawaat, March 14, 2012, http://nawaat.org/portail/2012/03/14/entretien-avec -sophie-piekarec-la-fiancee-de-zouheir-yahyaoui/.

12. Al-Qassemi, "The Emergence of New Media."

13. Pollock, "How Egyptian and Tunisian Youth Hacked the Arab Spring."

14. World Summit on the Information Society,"Declaration of Principles: Building the Information Society: A Global Challenge in the New Millennium," Document WSIS-03/GENEVA/DOC/4-E, December 12, 2002, www.itu.int/wsis/ docs/geneva/official/dop.html.

15. Reporters without Borders, "World Summit on the Information Society: Bloggers and Cyber-dissidents Offer Advice," RSF Newsletter, February 17, 2005; "Victor's Pictures from WSIS," Committee to Protect Bloggers, February 19, 2005, http://committeetoprotectbloggers9.blogspot.com/2005/02/victors-pictures -from-wsis.html.

16. Pollock, "How Egyptian and Tunisian Youth Hacked the Arab Spring."

17. "Rights: Stick in Hand, Tunisia Talks Freedom," Inter Press Service, February 19, 2005, www.ipsnews.net/2005/02/rights-stick-in-hand-tunisia-talks-freedom/.

18. Julien Pain, "La censure se raidit au pays du SMSI," Bureau Internet et libertés, posted by Mokhtar Yahyaoui to JoeUser Forums, March 3, 2005, http://forums .joeuser.com/67198.
19. Quoted in Rebecca MacKinnon, "Tunisian Online Protest Blocked," *Global Voices*, October 4, 2005, http://globalvoicesonline.org/2005/10/04/tunisian -online-protest-blocked/.
20. Internet World Stats, "Tunisia Internet Usage and Marketing Report," December, 2009, www.internetworldstats.com/af/tn.htm.
21. "Tunisia," Open Net Initiative, August 7, 2009, http://opennet.net/research/ profiles/tunisia.
22. Ambassador Robert F. Godec, Tunis, to Secretary of State Hillary Clinton, February 20, 2009, Wikileaks, http://wikileaks.org/cable/2009/02/09TUNIS99 .html.
23. Ambassador Gordon Gray, Tunis, to Secretary of State Hillary Clinton, February 22, 2010, Wikileaks, http://wikileaks.org/cable/2010/02/10TUNIS135.html.
24. "Tunisia: Number of Local 'Facebook' Users Exceeds 1 Million," *AllAfrica*, February 17, 2010, http://allafrica.com/stories/201002180156.html.
25. "Surprises Force Delay in Lawsuit against Tunisian Internet," Magharebia, November 5, 2008, www.magharebia.com/cocoon/awi/xhtml1/en_GB/features/ awi/features/2008/11/05/feature-01.
26. Lina Ben Mhenni, *Tunisian Girl: Blogueuse pour un printemps arabe* (Montpelier, France: Indigene editions, 2011), 4–5.
27. "'A Tunisian Girl' Talks about Blogging under Repressive Regimes," *Deutsche Welle*, December 4, 2011, www.dw.de/dw/article/0,,14984166,00.html.
28. Blog entry, picture and Arabic poem, "A Tunisian Girl," January 12, 2010, http://atunisiangirl.blogspot.com/2010/01/blog-post_12.html.
29. Lina Ben Mhenni, "Tunisia: Ammar 404 Is Back and Censoring Blogs Again," Global Voices, May 15, 2009, http://globalvoicesonline.org/2009/05/15/tunisia -ammar-404-is-back-and-censoring-blogs-again/.
30. Cecily Hilleary, "Tunisian Blogger Undeterred by Censorship," Voice of America, January 4, 2011, www.voanews.com/content/tunisian-blogger-undeterred -by-censorship-112948869/157156.html.
31. Abdelaziz Belkhodja and Tabak Cheikhrouhou, *14 Janvier: L'Enquète* (Tunis: Apollonia, 2013), 16; Nasser Widdady, "Online Activism Meets Real World Activism: A Day against Censorship," Nawaat, May 31, 2010, http://nawaat.org /portail/2010/05/29/online-activism-meets-real-world-activism-a-day-against -censorship/.
32. Maryam Ben Salem, "Femmes tunisiennes et usages différenciés de la sphère du Web comme outil de participation politique," in Najar, *Le cyberactivisme*, 141–48.
33. "Il etait une fois deux revolutions: Facebook ma republique, Twitter ma

ligue arabe!," *AllAfrica*, February 13, 2011, http://fr.allafrica.com/stories /201102141393.html.

34. "Egypt and Libya: A Year of Serious Abuses," Human Rights Watch, January 24, 2010, www.hrw.org/news/2010/01/24/egypt-and-libya-year-serious-abuses.

35. Ahmad Gharbeia, "I'lan istiqlal li al-fada' al-sibirani," Ahmad Gharbiya, October 2005, ahmad.gharbeia.org/archive/200510 (seen February 12, 2013).

36. Mounir Bensalah, *Réseaux sociaux et révolutions arabes?* (Paris: Michalon, 2012), 41–43; Sherif Azer, *Cyberactivism in Egypt: A New Social Movement* (Saarbruecken, Germany: Lap Lambert Academic, 2012), 39–42; Cynthia Johnston, "YouTube Stops Account of Egypt Anti-torture Activist," Reuters, November 27, 2007, www.reuters.com/article/2007/11/27/egypt-youtube -idUSL2759043020071127. For the quote about Abu Ghraib, see Steven Stanek, "Egyptian Bloggers Expose Horror of Police Torture," *San Francisco Chronicle*, October 9, 2007, www.sfgate.com/politics/article/Egyptian-bloggers -expose-horror-of-police-torture-2536284.php.

37. Amr Ezzat, "Sanidu 'al-ta'dhib fi Misr,'" Ma Bada li, November 6, 2006, http:// mabadali.blogspot.com/2006/11/blog-post_06.html.

38. Ambassador Margaret Scobey, Cairo, to Secretary of State Hillary Clinton, March 30, 2009, Wikileaks, http://wikileaks.org/cable/2009/03/09CAIRO544 .html.

39. Shahinaz Abdel Salam, *L'Égypte, les débuts de la liberté* (Paris: Michel Lafon, 2011), 34.

40. Shahinaz Abdel Salam, Wa7damasrya, http://wa7damasrya.blogspot.ca/.

41. Azer, *Cyberactivism in Egypt*, 42–44.

42. Nathan J. Brown and Amr Hamzawy, *The Draft Party Platform of the Egyptian Muslim Brotherhood: Foray into Political Integration or Retreat into Old Positions?*, Middle East Series, no. 89 (Washington, DC: Carnegie Endowment for Peace, 2008). For the intellectual background to these controversies, see Mona El-Ghobashy, "The Metamorphosis of the Egyptian Muslim Brothers," *International Journal of Middle East Studies* 37, no. 3 (2005); Bruce K. Rutherford, "What Do Egypt's Islamists Want? Moderate Islam and the Rise of Islamic Constitutionalism," *Middle East Journal* 60, no. 4 (2006): 707–31.

43. Marc Lynch, "Young Brothers in Cyberspace," Middle East Research and Information Project, no. 245 (2007). See Muhammad Hamza, "Ma wara' maswaddat barnamaj al-hizb: 'Al-marja`iyyah'?," *Wahid min al-Ikhwan*, December 16, 2007, http://tinyurl.com/agdf2kj.

44. Ivesa Lübben, "Junge Islamisten im Cyberspace: Die Bloggerszene der Muslimbrüderjugend," INAMO, no. 55, Jahrgang 14, (Herbst 2008), reprinted at www.acfc.cc/de/magazin/magazin/article/junge-islamisten-im-cyberspace-die -bloggerszene-der-muslimbruederjugend/.

45. Muhammad Hamza, "Tasa'ulat hawla taghyir al-murshid al-`amm li al-ikhwan,"

Wahid min al-Ikhwan, March 28, 2009, http://mohamza80.blogspot.com/2009/03/1-2006-2006-2006-2001-2005-2006-2-3.html.

46. Joel Beinin, "A Workers' Social Movement on the Margin of the Global Neoliberal Order, Egypt 2004–2009," in Beinin and Vairel, *Social Movements*, chapter 9; Joel Beinin, Kamal Abbas, Sarah Whitson, and Michele Dunne, "Labor Protest Politics and Worker Rights in Egypt," Carnegie Endowment for International Peace, February 17, 2010, www.carnegieendowment.org/2010/02/17/labor-protest-politics-and-worker-rights-in-egypt/2ye.

47. "Idrabat Tawilah, ta'thir mumtadd, harakah 'ummaliyyah," al-Ishtirakiyyah al-Thawriyyah, 2007, www.e-socialists.net/node/1727.

48. Samer S. Shehata, *Shop Floor Culture and Politics in Egypt* (Albany: State University of New York Press, 2010).

49. Ambassador Francis J. Ricciardone, Cairo, to Secretary of State Condoleezza Rice, December 28, 2006, Wikileaks, http://wikileaks.org/cable/2006/12/06CAIRO7256.html.

50. 'Isam Hasan Shaaban, "Limadha adraba 'ummal al-Mahallah?," *al-Hiwar al-Mutamaddin*, February 28, 2007, www.ahewar.org/debat/show.art.asp?aid=89853.

51. Chargé d'Affaires Stuart Jones, Cairo, to Secretary of State Condoleezza Rice, September 25, 2007, Wikileaks, http://wikileaks.org/cable/2007/09/07CAIRO2887.html.

52. Atef Said, "Egyptian Labor Erupting," *Against the Current* 24, no. 4 (2009): 11–14, 18.

53. Jones to Rice, September 25, 2007.

54. Hossam al-Hamalawy, "Egyptian Strikes: More Than Bread and Butter," *Socialist Review*, May 2008, www.socialistreview.org.uk/article.php?articlenumber=10388.

55. Ambassador Francis J. Ricciardone, Cairo, to Secretary of State Condoleezza Rice, October 8, 2007, Wikileaks, http://wikileaks.org/cable/2007/10/07CAIRO2983.html.

56. Beinin quoted in Said, "Egyptian Labor Erupting."

57. Ambassador Francis J. Ricciardone, Cairo, to Secretary of State Condoleezza Rice, September 19, 2007, Wikileaks, http://wikileaks.org/cable/2007/09/07CAIRO2839.html.

58. Caitlin E. Werrell and Francesco Femia, eds., *The Arab Spring and Climate Change* (Washington, DC: Center for American Progress, 2013), available as a pdf file from www.americanprogress.org/issues/security/report/2013/02/28/54579/the-arab-spring-and-climate-change/.

59. Ricciardone to Rice, September 19, 2007.

60. Muhammad Abd al-'Aziz, "Bi'l-ams sami't," Muhawarat al-Misriyyin, July 4, 2007, www.egyptiantalks.org/invb/index.php?showtopic=32399 (seen April 10, 2013).

61. "Egyptian, Independent Press Review for 7 July 2007," BBC Worldwide Monitoring, Lexis Nexis, July 7, 2007, via Lexis Nexis; "To Drink, Perchance to Live," Baheyya: Egypt Analysis and Whimsy, July 28, 2007, http://baheyya.blogspot.com/2007_07_01_archive.html; "Ahali 'izbat Sharif bi madinat Samannud amwat 'ala qaid al-hayat," 'Ummal Misr, July 28, 2007, http://egyworkers.blogspot.com/2007_07_01_archive.html.

62. "Sayf al-Burulus al-Sakhin," *al-Thawriyyun al-Ishtirakiyyun*," June 29, 2008, http://revsoc.me/workers-farmers/syf-lbrls-lskhn-yhrq-sb-lhkwm; Korm Dakrouri and Nasser el-Sharkawi, "El-Barlas Residents Protest against Flour Non-Distribution on Food Supply Coupons," *al-Masry al-Youm*, June 8, 2008, http://today.almasryalyoum.com/article2.aspx?ArticleID=108453.

63. "Maryam," La shay yastahiqq, January 13, 2009, http://fnangeology.blogspot.com/2009/01/blog-post.html.

64. Diya' al-Din Gad, "Kalimah min nizam al-'amil Mubarak," al-Sawt al-Ghadib, February 2, 2009, http://soutgadeb.blogspot.com/2009/02/blog-post_01.html.

65. Ambassador Margaret Scobey, Cairo, to Secretary of State Hillary Clinton, April 6, 2009, Wikileaks, http://wikileaks.org/cable/2009/04/09CAIRO580.html.

66. Ambassador Margaret Scobey, Cairo, to Secretary of State Hillary Clinton, March 30, 2009, Wikileaks, http://wikileaks.org/cable/2009/03/09CAIRO544.html.

67. Amr Ezzat, interview, Egyptian Initiative for Personal Rights offices, Garden City, Cairo, May 5, 2013.

68. Lim, "Clicks, Cabs, and Coffee Houses," 231–48.

69. Ambassador Margaret Scobey, Cairo, to Secretary of State Hillary Clinton, July 28, 2009, Wikileaks, http://wikileaks.ch/cable/2009/07/09CAIRO1447.html.

70. "Egypt and Libya: A Year of Serious Abuses."

71. Herrera, "Youth and Citizenship in the Digital Age."

72. Lim, "Clicks, Cabs, and Coffee Houses," 234.

73. Howard and Hussain, *Democracy's Fourth Wave?*, chapter 2 and conclusion.

74. Sihem Najar, "Mouvements sociaux en ligne, cyberactivisme et nouvelle forms d'expression en Méditerannée," in Najar, *Le cyberactivisme*, 13–25.

CHAPTER 4: THE NEW LEFT

1. Alexander Solzhenitsyn, *The Gulag Archipelago*, vol. 1: *An Experiment in Literary Investigation*, trans. Thomas Whitney (1974; New York: HarperCollins, 2007), 213.

2. Habiba Muhsin, "Hawl al-musharaka al-siyasiyya ghair al-taqlidiyya li al-shabab min al-tayyar al-yasari al-misri," in Muntada al-bada'il al-'Arabi li al-Dirasat, *Al-Anmat ghair al-taqlidiyya li al-musharaka al-siyasiyya li al-shabab fi misr* (Cairo: Rawafid, 2012), 75; Marie Duboc, "Egyptian Leftist Intellectuals' Activism from the Margins," in Beinin and Vairel, *Social Movements*, chapter 3.

3. Manar Shorbagy, "Understanding Kefaya: The New Politics in Egypt," *Arab Studies Quarterly* 29, no. 1 (2007): 39–60. For discontents, see Ann Lesch, "Egypt's Spring: Causes of the Revolution," *Middle East Policy* 18, no. 3 (2011): 35–48.

4. Quoted in Rabab El-Mahdi, "Enough! Egypt's Quest for Democracy," *Comparative Political Studies* 42, no. 8 (2009): 1011–39, this point on 1018, citing an interview with George Ishaq.

5. Quoted in ibid., 1020.

6. Quoted in ibid., 1023.

7. Counselor for Economic and Political Affairs Michael Corbin, U.S. Embassy, Cairo, to Secretary of State Condoleezza Rice, July 11, 2005, Wikileaks, http://wikileaks.org/cable/2005/07/05CAIRO5272.html.

8. Ibid.

9. Shorbagy, "Understanding Kefaya," 51.

10. Gordon Gray III, Deputy Chief of Mission, Cairo, to Secretary of State Condoleezza Rice, May 5, 2005, Wikileaks, http://wikileaks.org/cable/2005/05/05CAIRO3424.html.

11. Gordon Gray III, Deputy Chief of Mission, Cairo, to Secretary of State Condoleezza Rice, June 1, 2005, Wikileaks, http://wikileaks.org/cable/2005/06/05CAIRO4121.html.

12. Alia Mosallim, "An-Nas al-sughayyirah," Qira'at fi al-Sahab, May 30, 2005. http://cloudformation.blogspot.com/2005/05/blog-post_1117456611196566121.html; Sunny Daly, "Young Women as Activists in Contemporary Egypt: Anxiety, Leadership, and the Next Generation," *Journal of Middle East Women's Studies* 6, no. 2 (2010): 59–85, 133.

13. Alaa Abdel Fattah, "The Bastards Stole My Laptop," Manal and Alaa's Bit Bucket, May 26, 2005, www.manalaa.net/the_bastards_stole_my_laptop.

14. Wael Abbas, "Nawal wa al-Ahram," al-Wa`i al-Misri, May 25, 2005, http://tinyurl.com/b5yytcg.

15. Conversation with Wael Abbas, Dearborn, Michigan, November 16, 2013.

16. Wael Salah Fahmi, "Bloggers' Street Movement and the Right to the City: (Re)claiming Cairo's Real and Virtual 'Spaces of Freedom,'" *Environment and Urbanization* 21, no. 1 (2009): 96, see for other points 96–98.

17. Ibid.

18. Corbin to Rice, July 11, 2005.

19. Amr Ezzat, interview with the author, Cairo, June 7, 2013.

20. Shorbagy, "Understanding Kefaya," 50.

21. Alaa Abdel Fattah, "Muzaharat al-Tarshih," Manal and Alaa's Bit Bucket, July 30, 2005,www.manalaa.net/node/361; Chargé d'Affaires Stuart Jones, Cairo, to Secretary of State Condoleezza Rice, August 2, 2005, Wikileaks, http://wikileaks.org/cable/2005/08/05CAIRO5946.html.

22. Chargé d'Affaires Stuart Jones, Cairo, to Secretary of State Condoleezza Rice, August 4, 2005, Wikileaks, https://dazzlepod.com/cable/05CAIRO6010/.

23. Ibid.

24. Ambassador Francis J. Ricciardone to Secretary of State Condoleezza Rice, October 11, 2005, Wikileaks, http://wikileaks.org/cable/2005/10/05CAIRO7793 .html; Michaelle Browers, "The Egyptian Movement for Change: Intellectual Antecedents and Generational Conflicts," *Contemporary Islam: Dynamics of Muslim Life* 1, no. 1 ((2007): 75, 82; Muhsin, "Hawl al-musharaka."

25. Abdel Salam, *Égypte*, 131–32.

26. Yoram Meital, "The Struggle over Political Order in Egypt: The 2005 Elections," *Middle East Journal* 60, no. 2 (2006): 257–79.

27. Chargé d'Affaires Stuart Jones, Cairo, to Secretary of State Condoleezza Rice, December 15, 2005, Wikileaks, http://wikileaks.org/cable/2005/12 /05CAIRO9314.html.

28. Simsima, "A'tasimu fi hubb misr," Tafasil, March 10, 2006, http://tafassel .blogspot.com/2006/03/blog-post_114200809417404228.html (identifies self as a socialist and feminist); Wael Abbas, "Laila fi Hubb Misr, 16 & 17 Mars," *al-Wa'i al-Misri*, March 17, 2006, http://misrdigital.blogspirit.com/files/coverage2 /judges_night_16mar06.htm; Fahmi, "Bloggers' Street Movement," 99–102.

29. Simsima, "Muzaharat 20 Mars bi al-Qahirah," Tafasil, March 21, 2006, http://tafassel.blogspot.com/2006/03/20_21.html; "Demonstration in Egypt Denounces U.S. Presence in Iraq," MENA, March 20, 2006.

30. Rutherford, *Egypt after Mubarak*, chapter 2.

31. Ambassador Francis J. Ricciardone, Cairo, to Secretary of State Condoleezza Rice, May 24, 2006, Wikileaks, http://wikileaks.org/cable/2006/05/06CAIRO3106 .html.

32. Ambassador Francis J. Ricciardone, Cairo, to Secretary of State Condoleezza Rice, May 30, 2006, http://wikileaks.org/cable/2006/05/06CAIRO3270 .html.

33. Browers, "The Egyptian Movement for Change," 69–88.

34. U.S. Embassy, Cairo, to Secretary of State Condoleezza Rice, July 27, 2006, Wikileaks, http://wikileaks.org/cable/2006/07/06CAIRO4611.html.

35. Ambassador Francis J. Ricciardone, Cairo, to Secretary of State Condoleezza Rice, March 26, 2008, Wikileaks, http://wikileaks.org/cable/2008/03 /08CAIRO587.html.

36. Ahmad Mansur, "Shuhada' tawabir al-khubz," *al-Muhit*, March 19, 2008, www .masress.com/moheet/209421.

37. Global Food Markets Group, U.K. Government, "The 2007/08 Agricultural Price Spikes: Causes and Policy Implications" (London, 2008), www.growthenergy .org/images/reports/UKgov_Ag_Price_Spikes.pdf. See also Tony Sternberg, "Chinese Drought, Wheat, and the Egyptian Uprising: How a Localized Hazard

Became Globalized," in Werrell and Femia, *The Arab Spring and Climate Change*, 7–14.

38. Soliman, *The Autumn of Dictatorship*.

39. Ambassador Francis J. Ricciardone, Cairo, to Secretary of State Condoleezza Rice, March 23, 2008, Wikileaks, http://wikileaks.org/cable/2008/03/08CAIRO563.html.

40. "U.S. Acknowledges Navy Warning Shot Killed Egyptian," Reuters, March 26, 2008, www.reuters.com/article/2008/03/26/us-egypt-usa-shooting-idUSL2667123320080326. Wael Abbas blogged the incident and published a photo of the offending vessel: Wael Abbas, "Nanfarid bi nashr surat al-safinah," al-Wa'i al-Misri, March 24, 2008, http://tinyurl.com/b7762td.

41. Ambassador Francis J. Ricciardone, Cairo, to Secretary of State Condoleezza Rice, March 31, 2008, Wikileaks, http://wikileaks.org/cable/2008/03/08CAIRO621.html.

42. Abd al-Rahman Rashwan, "Limadha la nusharik fi idrab 6 Abril?," Ikhwan Youth, April 4, 2008, http://ikhwanyouth.blogspot.com/2008/04/6.html.

43. Wael Abbas, "Tabi' akhbar al-idrab 'ala al-hawa mubashiratan," al-Wa'i al-Misri, April 6, 2008, http://tinyurl.com/bxpcqlc.

44. Ambassador Francis J. Ricciardone, Cairo, to Secretary of State Condoleezza Rice, April 7, 2008, Wikileaks, http://wikileaks.org/cable/2008/04/08CAIRO697.html.

45. Wael Abbas, "Fidiyu nadir li suqut sanam Mubarak fi al-Mahallah," al-Wa'i al-Misri, April 9, 2008, http://tinyurl.com/asfcj5z.

46. Ambassador Francis J. Ricciardone, Cairo, to Secretary of State Condoleezza Rice, April 16, 2008, Wikileaks, http://wikileaks.org/cable/2008/04/08CAIRO783.html. For al-Mahalla testimonials that push back against government charges of vandalism, see Amira al-Tahawy, "Journalists Testify about Events in Mahalla," Menassat, April 17, 2008, www.menassat.com/?q=en/news-articles/3516-journalists-testify-about-events-mahalla.

47. Tahawy, "Journalists Testify."

48. Ambassador Margaret Scobey, Cairo, to Secretary of State Condoleezza Rice, April 23, 2008, Wikileaks, http://wikileaks.org/cable/2008/04/08CAIRO843.html.

49. David Wolman, *The Instigators* (Seattle: Kindle Single, 2011).

50. Ambassador Margaret Scobey, Cairo, to Secretary of State Condoleezza Rice, July 18, 2008, Wikileaks, http://wikileaks.org/cable/2008/07/08CAIRO1581.html; Ambassador Margaret Scobey, Cairo, to Secretary of State Condoleezza Rice, August 4, 2008, Wikileaks, http://wikileaks.org/cable/2008/08/08CAIRO1679.html.

51. Ambassador Margaret Scobey, Cairo, to Secretary of State Condoleezza Rice, November 26, 2008, Wikileaks, http://wikileaks.org/cable/2008/11/08CAIRO2431.html.

52. Mona al-Wardani, "Another Egyptian Blogger Disappears into the System," Menassat, November 25, 2008, www.menassat.com/?q=ar/news-articles/5218 -another-egyptian-blogger-disappears-system.

53. Scobey to Rice, November 26, 2008.

54. Ambassador Margaret Scobey, Cairo, to Secretary of State Condoleezza Rice, December 30, 2008, Wikileaks, http://wikileaks.org/cable/2008/12 /08CAIRO2572.html.

55. "Ihtijaj 'amm li sha'b misr," March 2009, bulletin board notice at the Traidnt Forum at www.traidnt.net/vb/traidnt1154333/. For the figure of seventy thousand Facebook fans, see Lim, "Clicks, Cabs, and Coffee Houses," especially 240.

56. Ambassador Margaret Scobey, Cairo, to Secretary of State Hillary Clinton, March 18, 2009, Wikileaks, http://wikileaks.org/cable/2009/03/09CAIRO468 .html.

57. Ambassador Margaret Scobey, Cairo, to Secretary of State Hillary Clinton, March 24, 2009, Wikileaks, http://wikileaks.org/cable/2009/03/09CAIRO504 .html.

58. Salwa Ismail, *Political Life in Cairo's New Quarters: Encountering the Everyday State* (Minneapolis: University of Minnesota Press, 2006); Salwa Ismail, "The Egyptian Revolution against the Police," *Social Research* 79, no. 2 (2012): 435–62.

59. Scobey to Clinton, April 6, 2009; "Security Forces Arrest Bloggers, 39 April 6th Activists," IkhwanWeb, April 5, 2009, http://ikhwanweb.com/article .php?id=19800.

60. Ambassador Margaret Scobey, Cairo, to Secretary of State Hillary Clinton, April 7, 2009, Wikileaks, http://wikileaks.org/cable/2009/04/09CAIRO591.html.

61. Wael Abbas April entries, Misr Digit@l, April 2009, archives at http://misrdigital .blogspirit.com/archive/2009/04/index.html.

62. Asma' Mahfouz in "Sibu Asma' li haliha ya wilad al-qahbah!," Misr Digit@l, May 8, 2009, http://tinyurl.com/a65rxq9.

63. Ambassador Margaret Scobey, Cairo, to Secretary of State Hillary Clinton, April 23, 2009, Wikileaks, http://wikileaks.org/cable/2009/04/09CAIRO695.html.

64. Deputy Chief of Mission Matthew H. Tueller, Cairo, to Secretary of State Hillary Clinton, July 30, 2009, Wikileaks, http://wikileaks.org/cable/2009/07 /09CAIRO1464.html.

65. Shehata, "Youth Movements," 115.

66. Ambassador Margaret Scobey, Cairo, to Secretary of State Hillary Clinton, September 17, 2009, Wikileaks, at http://wikileaks.org/cable/2009/09 /09CAIRO1819.html.

67. Ambassador Margaret Scobey, Cairo, to Secretary of State Hillary Clinton, November 17, 2009, Wikileaks, http://wikileaks.org/cable/2009/11 /09CAIRO2155.html.

68. Ambassador Margaret Scobey, Cairo, to Secretary of State Hillary Clinton, October 22, 2009, Wikileaks, http://wikileaks.org/cable/2009/10/09CAIRO2022.html.

69. "Egypt Frees Opposition Protesters," Voice of America, April 7, 2010, via Proquest.

70. Gray to Clinton, February 22, 2010.

71. Ambassador Robert F. Godec, Tunis, to Secretary of State Condoleezza Rice, July 11, 2008, Wikileaks, http://wikileaks.org/cable/2008/07/08TUNIS769.html.

72. Ambassador Robert F. Godec, Tunis, to Secretary of State Condoleezza Rice, August 7, 2008, Wikileaks, http://wikileaks.org/cable/2008/08/08TUNIS894.html.

73. Gray to Clinton, February 22, 2010.

74. Ambassador Robert F. Godec, Tunis, to Secretary of State Condoleezza Rice, November 12, 2008, Wikileaks, http://wikileaks.org/cable/2008/11/08TUNIS1153.html.

75. Beat Stauffer, "Civil Society in the Maghreb: Delicate Plants in a Harsh Environment," Qantara.de, November 18, 2005, http://en.qantara.de/Delicate-Plants-in-a-Harsh-Environment/6192c159/index.html.

76. Fathi al-Hamami, "Safaqs: Tadamunan ma'a filistin fi masirat al-ghadab wa al-hurriyya," *al-Tariq al-Jadid*, January 11, 2009, http://attariq.org/spip.php?article369.

77. Ibid.

78. "Safaqs: Al-Talamidh wa al-asatidha wa al-mu`allimun yantasiruna li Ghazza," *al-Sha`b* (Tunis), January 17, 2009, www.turess.com/echaab/7191.

79. Ambassador Robert F. Godec, Tunis, to Secretary of State Condoleezza Rice, January 9, 2009, Wikileaks, http://wikileaks.org/cable/2009/01/09TUNIS14.html.

80. Ibid. For other provincial reports of demonstrations, see "Tadamunan ma'a Ghaza: Taharrukat sha'biyya ta'umm al-bilad," al-Tariq al-Jadid, January 11, 2009, http://attariq.org/spip.php?article369.

81. Ambassador Robert F. Godec, Tunis, to Secretary of State Hillary Clinton, April 6, 2009, Wikileaks, http://wikileaks.org/cable/2009/04/09TUNIS214.html.

82. Ambassador Robert F. Godec, Tunis, to Secretary of State Hillary Clinton, April 16, 2009, Wikileaks, http://wikileaks.org/cable/2009/04/09TUNIS236.html.

83. Godec to Clinton, April 6, 2009.

84. Reporters without Borders, "Online Reporter Transferred to Southern Prison to Serve Sentence," December 3, 2009, http://en.rsf.org/tunisia-online-reporter-transferred-to-03-12-2009,35202.html; "Threatened Voices: Zouhaier Makhlouf," *GlobalVoices*, February 12, 2010, http://threatened.globalvoicesonline.org/blogger/zouhaier-makhlouf.

85. Gray to Clinton, February 22, 2010.

86. "Al-Talabah al-Tunisiyyun li wizarat al-ta'lim al-'ali: Ghabat al-hurriyyat wa al-huquq wa al-imkaniyyat, ma fa'ida man' al-tadkhin?," *Mudawwanah Muwatiniyya Jami`iyya*, May 21, 2010, http://tinyurl.com/bo6hsje (seen via Google cache April 6, 2013).

87. Al-Amin al-Bu'azizi in Ghassan Ben Khalifa, "Al-Shabab al-Tunisi yatahaddith 'an thawratihi," *Majallat Al-Adab*, March 1, 2011, http://adabmag.com/node /368.

88. "Tunisian Farmers Say Bank Stole Their Land," Nawaat, July 16, 2010, http:// nawaat.org/portail/2010/07/16/tunisian-farmers-say-bank-stole-their-land/.

CHAPTER 5: FROM BOUAZİZİ TO TAHRİR

1. Stuart Schaar, "Revolutionary Challenges in Tunisia and Egypt: Generations in Conflict," *New Politics* 13, no. 3 (2011): 19–26; Peter J. Schraeder and Hamadi Redissi, "Ben Ali's Fall," *Journal of Democracy* 22, no. 3 (2011): 5–19.

2. "Sidi Bouzid Brule!," A Tunisian Girl, December 19, 2010, http://atunisiangirl .blogspot.com/2010/12/sidi-bouzid-brule.html.

3. Habib Toumi, "Man at the Centre of Tunisia Unrest Recuperating, Doctors Say," GulfNews.com, December 31, 2010, http://gulfnews.com/news/region/tunisia/ man-at-the-centre-of-tunisia-unrest-recuperating-doctors-say-1.738967.

4. Shihab Abbas, "Taghtiya kamila li al-thawra al-tunisiyya," Jammoul.net, December 24, 2010, www.jammoul.net/forum/archive/index.php/t-18200.html; Kibusmed, "Al-Mutalaba bi haqq al-shabb Muhammad Bu 'Azizi," December 20, 2010, www.youtube.com/watch?v=AjVPgmobLyw; Kibusmed, "Sidi bouzid w 3anf il 7akem tunis," December 20, 2010, www.youtube.com/ watch?v=VXE7dZ8MPYc; "Fidiyu: Suwar hayyah 'an muwajahat al-mutazahirin fi Sidi Buzid ma'a al-bulis," *Vimeo*, fall 2010, http://vimeo.com/17977490#; "'Buziyan' al-Tunisiyya tushi' dahiyat idtirabat al-batala," *al-Arabiyya*, December 26, 2010, www.alarabiya.net/articles/2010/12/25/130842.html; Pierre Puchot, *Tunisie: Une Revolution Arabe* (Paris: Galaade Editions, 2011), 168.

5. Amin al-Bu'Azizi, "Lihadhihi asbab intafadat wilayat Sidi Buzid," Nawaat, December 24, 2010, http://tinyurl.com/bklaqsb.

6. Alcinda Honwana, "Youth and the Tunisian Revolution," *Conflict Prevention and Peace Forum*, Social Science Research Council, 2011, 10, http://webarchive .ssrc.org/pdfs/Alcinda_Honwana,_Youth_and_the_Tunisian_Revolution, _September_2011-CPPF_policy%20paper.pdf.

7. El Général, "Tounes Beledna," posted to Youtube by Sam1306, January 3, 2011, http://youtu.be/PP_7zmLGB2I (this is the earliest example I could still find at Youtube, but there may still be some from that fall); English lyrics from "El Général, Hip Hop, and the Tunisian Revolution," *Revolutionary Arab Rap*, October 22, 2011, http://revolutionaryarabrap.blogspot.com/2011/10/el-general-hip-hop-and -tunisian.html.

8. This quote in David Peisner, "Inside Tunisia's Hip-Hop Revolution," *Spin*, August 24, 2011, www.spin.com/articles/inside-tunisias-hip-hop-revolution/; other sources: El Général, "Général—Rayes le bled: ughniya rab tunisiyya," posted by al-Hiwar Net to Youtube, November 10, 2010, http://youtu.be /-ZE0oRgzVIs; Ulysses Rap, "El Général—Rais Lebled," Allthelyrics.com, May 14, 2011, www.allthelyrics.com/forum/arabic-lyrics-translation/114682-el-g-n -ral-rais-lebled.html; Vivienne Walt, "El Général and the Rap Anthem of the Mideast Revolution," *Time*, February 15, 2011, www.time.com/time/world/ article/0,8599,2049456,00.html; Robin Wright, *Rock the Casbah* (New York: Simon and Schuster, 2012), chapter 5.

9. El Général, "Rayat al-Islam fi Tunis," uploaded to Youtube by Ali Benmoham-med, January 16, 2011, http://youtu.be/f8noZbTP7ME.

10. Ferida Labidi, interview with the author, Parliament, Tunis, April 1, 2013. See also Eileen Byrne, "The Women MPs Tipped to Play Leading Roles in Tunisia's New Assembly," *Guardian*, October 28, 2011, www.guardian.co.uk/world/2011 /oct/29/women-mps-tunisia-government.

11. "I'tisamat fi Qafsa wa Qasrayn wa Safaqs wa masira fi Tunis," *al-Khabar*, December 28, 2010, www.elkhabar.com/ar/monde/240015.html.

12. Honwana, "Youth and the Tunisian Revolution," 10–11.

13. "Ma wara' al-khabar," Al Jazeera, December 28, 2010, http://youtu.be /Ek1ld2mhizU. For the role of Al Jazeera, see Howard and Hussain, *Democracy's Fourth Wave?*, chapter 5.

14. Revolution-era caricatures could still be seen in May 2013 at https://www .facebook.com/media/set/?set=a.154393737977090.38262.154185547997909; Belkhodja and Cheikhrouhou, *14 Janvier*, 35–36.

15. "Tajaddud al-muwajahat," *al-Khabar* (Tunis), December 29, 2010, www .elkhabar.com/ar/monde/240056.html.

16. Lina Ben Mhenni, "Lawyers' Demonstration Tuesday 28th, 2010," A Tunisian Girl, December 29, 2010, http://atunisiangirl.blogspot.com/2010/12/lawyers -demonstration-tuesday-28th-2010.html; Lina Ben Mhenni, "Bloody Day for Lawyers #sidibouzid," A Tunisian Girl, December 31, 2010, http://atunisiangirl .blogspot.com/2010/12/bloody-day-for-lawyers-sidibouzid.html.

17. "Muzahirat fi Safaqs wa al-Qasrayn wa Sidi Bouzid bi Tunis," *al-Khabar*, January 5, 2011, www.elkhabar.com/ar/monde/240512.html.

18. "Balagh al-Hay'a al-Wataniyya li'l-Muhamin, Qasr al-'Adala Tunis," Tunis, January 6, 2011, reprinted at *Chawki Tabib*, January 7, 2011, www.chawkitabib.info /spip.php?article645; Lina Ben Mhenni, "Lawyer's Strike," A Tunisian Girl, January 6, 2011, http://atunisiangirl.blogspot.com/2011/01/lawyers-strike.html.

19. "Akhbar al-Hurriyyat fi Tunis," al-Hiwar.net, January 6, 2011, www.alhiwar.net /ShowNews.php?Tnd=13042.

20. Peisner, "Inside Tunisia's Hip-Hop."

21. Lina Ben Mhenni, "Hier le jeudi 06 01 2011 fut une journée horrible," A Tunisian Girl, January 7, 2011, http://atunisiangirl.blogspot.com/2011/01/hier-le-jeudi-06012011-fut-une-journee.html.

22. Lina Ben Mhenni, "You Can't Stop Us from Writing!!," A Tunisian Girl, January 3, 2011, http://atunisiangirl.blogspot.com/2011/01/you-cant-stop-us-from-writing.html; "Ughniyat 'li al-Bu'Azizi' li Amal al-Mathluthi," France 24, January 18, 2011, www.france24.com/ar/20110118-amel-mathlouthi-song-bouazizi-memory; "Slim Amamou and Azyz Ammami," *Posting on the Net*, January 2011, http://tinyurl.com/af5c8mn.

23. Lina Ben Mhenni, "Wissem tu me Manques Déjà!," A Tunisian Girl, January 8, 2011, http://atunisiangirl.blogspot.com/2011/01/wissem-tu-me-manques-deja.html.

24. Niqabi al-Safaqs, "Safaqs: Iqafat fi sufuf al-talaba wa al-talamidh," Jammoul.net, January 8, 2011, www.jammoul.net/forum/archive/index.php/t-18200.html; Juan Cole and Shahin Cole, "An Arab Spring for Women," *Nation*, April 26, 2011.

25. Marie Kostrz, "Émeutes en Tunisie: 'La police a pris d'assaut la faculté,'" Rue89, January 8, 2011, www.rue89.com/2011/01/08/emeutes-en-tunisie-la-police-a-pris-dassaut-la-faculte-184517.

26. "Tunis tushi' qatla al-jaysh," *al-Duwaliyya* (Paris), January 10, 2011, www.doualia.com/2011/01/10/tunisie-mort-militaire-commune-sous-une-grele-de-balles; Yasmine Ryan, "The Massacre behind the Revolution," Al Jazeera, February 16, 2011, www.aljazeera.com/indepth/features/2011/02/2011215123229922898.html.

27. Lina Ben Mhenni, "Erregueb January 9, 2011," A Tunisian Girl, January 10, 2011, http://atunisiangirl.blogspot.com/2011/01/erregueb-january-9th-2011.html.

28. Belkhodja and Cheikhrouhou, *14 Janvier*, 42.

29. Ben Hammouda, *Economie politique d'une revolution*, 146.

30. "Al-Qasrayn: Mustajiddat muhimma wa mutalahiqa," *al-Hiwar*, January 10, 2011, www.alhiwar.net/ShowNews.php?Tnd=13171; 'Umayrah 'Aliyah Saghir, *Al-Thawra fi 'aynay mu'arrikh* (Tunis: al-Magharibiyya, 2012), 77.

31. See entries (press releases, Facebook items, eyewitness reports, and wire services) for January 10, 2011, listed at Jammoul.net, www.jammoul.net/forum/archive/index.php/t-18200.html; Puchot, *Tunisie*, 157–58.

32. Muhammad bin Rajab, "Abu al-Qasim al-Shabi: Intafad min qabrihi li yaqud al-thawrat al-'Arabiyya," *Ilaf*, February 14, 2011, www.elaph.com/Web/Culture/2011/11/695490.html.

33. Honwana, "Youth and the Tunisian Revolution," 13; see Saghir, *Al-Thawra*, 67.

34. Jammoul.net., entries for January 11, www.jammoul.net/forum/archive/index.php/t-18200.html.

35. "Sarkozy Admits to Errors in France's Tunisia Policy," France24, January 24, 2011, www.france24.com/en/20110124-sarkozy-admits-errors-tunisia-response-policy-alliot-marie-ben-ali-anti-government-protests.

36. "'Rashid `Ammar: al-rajul alladhi rafada itlaq al-nar `ala sha`bihi wa faddala al-istiqala," *al-Masri al-Yawm*, Jan. 15, 2011 www.almasryalyoum.com/news/details/108506; Belkhodja and Cheikhrouhou, *14 Janvier*, 50; Puchot, *Tunisie*, 164.

37. "Violent Unrest over Unemployment Spreads to Capital Tunis," France24, January 12, 2011, www.france24.com/en/20110112-violent-unrest-breaks-out-tunisian-capital-tunis-ben-ali.

38. See entries (press releases, Facebook items, eyewitness reports, and wire services) for January 13, 2011, listed at Jammoul.net, at www.jammoul.net/forum/archive/index.php/t-18200.html; Belkhodja and Cheikhrouhou, *14 Janvier*, 53.

39. Belkhodja and Cheikhrouhou, *14 Janvier*, 55–138.

40. Wael Abbas on Riz Khan, "Is Social Media Driving Reform in the Arab World?," Al Jazeera English, January 21, 2011, http://youtu.be/4C56fzPc4i8; Amal Kandeel, "Egypt at a Crossroads," *Middle East Policy* 18, no. 2 (2011): 37–45.

41. "Facebook Videos Posted by Asmaa Mahfouz," January 22, 2010, http://youtu.be/8CJdoEEdpkQ; Mahmud al-Rashidi, *Al-Intirnit & Facebook: Thawrat 25 Yanayir namudhajan* (Cairo: al-Dar al-Misriyya al-Lubnaniyya, 2012), 38.

42. Yasir Thabi, *Dawlat al-ultras: Asfar al-thawra wa al-madhbaha* (Cairo: Dar Uktub, 2013), 60–61.

43. Amro Ali, "Saeeds of Revolution: De-Mythologizing Khaled Saeed," *al-Jadaliyya*, June 5, 2012, www.jadaliyya.com/pages/index/5845/saeeds-of-revolution_de-mythologizing-khaled-saeed; Wolman, *The Instigators*; Ismail, *Political Life*, chapter 5.

44. Muhammad 'Alam al-Huda, "'Kulluna Khalid Sa'id' akthar min mujarrad safha," *al-Sabah* (Tunis), October 31, 2012, www.elsaba7.com/NewsDtl.aspx?Id=34303; Herrera, "Youth and Citizenship in the Digital Age."

45. Wael Ghonim, *Revolution 2.0* (New York: Mariner Books, 2012), chapters 3–4; Sahar Khamis and Katherine Vaughn, "Cyberactivism in the Egyptian Revolution: How Civic Engagement and Citizen Journalism Tilted the Balance," *Arab Media and Society*, no. 14 (Summer 2011), www.arabmediasociety.com/?article=769; Lim, "Clicks, Cabs, and Coffee Houses," 241; al-Rashidi, *Al-Intirnit & Facebook*, 31–35.

46. John D. Sutter, "The Faces of Egypt's 'Revolution 2.0,'" CNN, February 21, 2011, www.cnn.com/2011/TECH/innovation/02/21/egypt.internet.revolution/index.html; Ghonim, *Revolution 2.0*, 75–81.

47. 'Abd al-Rahman Yusuf, *Yawmiyyat thawrat al-sabbar* (Cairo: Dar al-'Ulum li al-Nashr wa al-Tawzi', 2011), 19.

48. Sabri Hasanayn, "'Arba'at alaf misri tazaharu didd al-irhab fi 'Shubra,'" *Ilaf* (London), January 2, 2011, www.elaph.com/Web/news/2011/1/622220.html.

49. "Videos Posted by Asmaa Mahfouz," YouTube, January 19, 2011, http://youtu
.be/gPKcK5lY8Js; Castells, *Networks of Outrage*, 69–70; Amira Taha and Christopher Combs, "Of Drama and Performance," in Samia Mehrez, ed., *Translating
Egypt's Revolution: The Language of Tahrir* (Cairo: American University of Cairo
Press, 2012), chapter 2.

50. Howard and Hussain, *Democracy's Fourth Wave?*, chapter 3.

51. Dina Shihata, "Al-Harakat al-Shababiyya wa thawrat 25 yanayir," *al-Ahram
al-Raqami*, January 1, 201[2], http://digital.ahram.org.eg/articles.aspx?Serial
=657099&eid=6729; "Bayan min 'ulama' wa mashayikh al-da'wa al-salafiyya
bi Iskandariya," January 23, 2011, http://forum.mustafahosny.com/showthread
.php?t=136308.

52. Khamis and Vaughn, "Cyberactivism"; "Ahmad Maher: Khattatna li iqalat al-
'Adli fa ajbarna al-ra'is 'ala al-tanahhi," *al-Shuruq* (Cairo), February 18, 2011,
www.masress.com/shorouk/391758, and "Ziyad al-'Alimi: Khada'na al-amn,"
al-Shuruq, reprinted at "Asrar wa khafaya thawrat shabab misr," February 19,
2011, www.sh4online.com/vb/showthread.php?t=75859; Lim, "Clicks, Cabs,
and Coffee Houses," 243.

53. The literature on Tahrir is already enormous. My account focuses on the prominent youth networks and their intersection with labor and guilds. In addition
to works cited below for specific points, see for overviews and studies, Mona
el-Ghobashy, "The Praxis of the Egyptian Revolution," Middle East Research
and Information Project, no. 258 (2011), www.merip.org/mer/mer258/praxis
-egyptian-revolution; Claude Guibal and Tangi Salaun, *L'Egypte de Tahrir: Anat-
omie d'une revolution* (Paris: Editions du Seuil, 2011); Castells, *Networks of Outrage*, 53–92; Samia Mehrez, ed., *Translating Egypt's Revolution: The Language of
Tahrir* (Cairo: American University of Cairo Press, 2012); Hatem Rushdy, ed.,
18 Days in Tahrir (Hong Kong: Haven Books, 2011); Korany and El-Mahdi,
Arab Spring in Egypt; Denis Campbell, *Egypt Unshackled: Using Social Media to
@#:) the System* (Carmarthenshire, Wales: Cambria Books, 2011).

54. Al-Ma'adh 'Abd al-Karim, "Al-Shuyu'i zayy al-ikhwani fi i'tilaf shabab al-
thawra," *al-Shuruq*, February 18, 2011, reprinted at http://news.egypt.com/
arabic/permalink/880261.html.

55. "Misr: Isabat wa i'tiqalat," *al-Arab*, January 26, 2011, www.alarab.com.qa/details
.php?docId=171497&issueNo=1136&secId=15; Ghonim, *Revolution 2.0*, 148–
50; Wolman, *The Instigators*.

56. Yusuf, *Yawmiyyat*, 26–34; Ibrahim Abd al-Majid, "Misr ta'ud tahta al-shams," in
"Kitab al-Thawra," *al-Kitaba al-Ukhra*, no. 2 (March 2011): 120; Ihab 'Umar,
Al-Thawra al-misriyya al-kubra (Cairo: Dar al-Hayah, 2011), 97.

57. Mustafa Rizq in Hiba 'Abd al-'Alim, *Yawmiyyat al-Ghadab* (Giza: Dar al-Hayah,
2012), 21.

58. "Muzaharat al-ghadab tajtah al-Qahira wa al-muhafazat li al-mutalaba bi al-

islah," *al-Misriyyun* (Cairo), January 26, 2011, http://masress.com/almesryoon /48662.

59. "Indhar...al-alaf yatazahirun didd al-faqr wa al-batala wa al-ghala' wa al-fasad...wa yutalibun bi rahil al-hukuma," *al-Misri al-Yawm*, January 26, 2011, http://today .almasryalyoum.com/article2.aspx?ArticleID=286068; "Suqut awwal shahid fi Suways 'Misr' fi yawm al-ghadab," *Tunisia Café*, January 25, 2011, www.tunisia -cafe.com/vb/showthread.php?t=14706; Wael Abbas, "Fidiyu Shahid Su-ways," al-Wa`i al-Misri, January 26, 2011, http://misrdigital.blogspirit.com /archive/2011/01/26/the-martyr-of-suez.html; Muhammad Sha'ban and Khu-lud Sha'ban, "Lahzat," in 'Abd al-'Alim, *Yawmiyyat al-Ghadab*, 189–94.

60. Zeynep Tufekci and Christopher Wilson, "Social Media and the Decision to Participate in Political Protest: Observations from Tahrir Square," *Journal of Communication* 62 (2012): 363–79.

61. Moaddel, "What Do Arabs Want?"; Walid El Hamamsy, "BB = BlackBerry or Big Brother: Digital Media and the Egyptian Revolution," *Journal of Postcolonial Writing* 47, no. 4 (2011): 454–66.

62. "Al-Amn ya'zil al-Suways," *al-Shuruq*, January 27, 2011, www.masress.com /shorouk/384114.

63. "Ahmad Maher," *al-Shuruq*.

64. Amal Salih, "Shabab al-Tahrir li 'al-'Ashara Masa': 'al-maydan asbah ramzan li al-thawra," *al-Yawm al-Sabi'* (Cairo), February 10, 2011, www1.youm7.com /NewsPrint.asp?NewsID=349312.

65. Yusuf, *Yawmiyyat*, 67–68; Ahmed Maher, reply to my question about nonvio-lence at the Istanbul World Forum, October 14, 2012, Panel on Youth and Just Politics; Samuel P. Jacobs, "Gene Sharp, the 83 Year Old Who Toppled Egypt," *Daily Beast*, February 14, 2011, www.thedailybeast.com/articles/2011/02/14 /gene-sharp-the-egyptian-revolts-prophet-of-nonviolence.html; Andy Khouri, "Egyptian Activists Inspired by Forgotten Martin Luther King Comic," *Com-ics Alliance*, February 11, 2011, www.comicsalliance.com/2011/02/11/martin -luther-king-comic-egypt; Ghonim, *Revolution 2.0*.

66. "Alaf al-mutazahirin bi 'wasat al-qahira,'" *al-Misri al-Yawm*, January 29, 2011, http://today.almasryalyoum.com/article2.aspx?ArticleID=286802; Sahar Kerai-tim and Samia Mehrez, "Mulid al-Tahrir: Semiotics of a Revolution," in Mehrez, *Translating Egypt's Revolution*, chapter 1.

67. Yusuf, *Yawmiyyat*, 70; "Masira hashida min al-jami' al-azhar," *al-Misri al-Yawm*, January 29, 2011, http://today.almasryalyoum.com/article2.aspx?ArticleID= 286808.

68. "Ihraq al-maqarr al-ra'isi li al-hizb al-watani bi al-qahira wa tahtim 'iddat maqarr fi al-muhafazat," *al-Misri al-Yawm*, January 29, 2011, http://today.almasryal youm.com/article2.aspx?ArticleID=286779; Ahmad 'Ali, "Wa idha kana la budd al-mawt," in 'Abd al-'Alim, *Yawmiyyat al-Ghadab*, 93–111; "Al-Amn ya`zil 'al-

suways' ba'd saytarat al-muzahirin," *al-Misri al-Yawm*, January 29, 2011, http://today.almasryalyoum.com/article2.aspx?ArticleID=286823; "'Asharat al-alaf yusharikun fi 'jum`at al-ghadab' bi al-muhafazat," *al-Misri al-Yawm*, January 29, 2011, http://today.almasryalyoum.com/article2.aspx?ArticleID=286815; Sha'ban and Sha'ban, "Lahzat," 192–93; "Muzaharat al-Iskandariya," *al-Misri al-Yawm*, January 29, 2011, http://today.almasryalyoum.com/article2.aspx?ArticleID=286819; 'Umar, *Al-Thawra*, 130; Marco Allegra et al., "Rethinking Cities in Contentious Times: The Mobilisation of Urban Dissent in the 'Arab Spring,'" *Urban Studies* 50, no. 9 (2013): 1675–88.

69. "'Al-Shuruq' tanshur nass shahadat dubat amn al-dawla fi 'Iqtiham sijn Wadi al-Natroun," *al-Shuruq*, July 8, 2013, http://shorouknews.com/news/view.aspx?cdate=08072013&id=701d5f8b-00aa-4e41-aa5a-6000d507146f.

70. Yusuf, *Yawmiyyat*, 91–92.

71. Muhammad al-Shamma', *Ayyam al-hurriyya fi maydan al-tahrir* (Cairo: Shams, 2011), 41–46; Yusuf, *Yawmiyyat*, 81–91; Thabit, *Dawlat al-ultras*, 64–76.

72. Taha and Combs, "Of Drama and Performance," 79–84.

73. "Hasilat al-laila al-tasi'a min thawrat al-ghadab," *al-Yawm al-Sabi'*, February 3, 2011, http://masress.com/youm7/345783; al-Shamma', *Ayyam*, 41–54; Amira Salah Ahmad et al., *Mudhakkarat al-Tahrir* (Cairo: Dar al-Shuruq, 2012), 127–34.

74. "Al-Iskandariya: 150 li Mubarak . . . 30 alfan diddahu," *al-Wafd* (Cairo), February 3, 2011, http://masress.com/alwafd/14286.

75. "Alaf yatazahirun bi al-Zaqaziq didd Mubarak," *al-Wafd*, February 3, 2011, http://masress.com/alwafd/14291; Yusuf, *Yawmiyyat*, 94–97.

76. "Abril 6 yu'akkid i'tiqal sitta min a'da'ihi," *al-Shuruq*, February 4, 2011, www.masress.com/shorouk/384890; "Ahmad Maher," *al-Shuruq*; Yusuf, *Yawmiyyat*, 126–30; Joel Beinin, "Egyptian Workers and January 25: A Social Movement in Historical Context," *Social Research* 72, no. 2 (2012): 323–48, this point on 339.

77. "Al-Muwajahat fi al-masirat bayn 'al-Watani' wa 'al-Ikhwan' fi al-Iskandariya," *al-Misri al-Yawm*, February 4, 2011, www.masress.com/almasryalyoum/308723; "Musadamat mutawaqqa'a fi Kafr Shaykh," *al-Yawm al-Sabi'*, February 4, 2011, www.youm7.com/News.asp?NewsID=346159; "Alaf al-mu'aridin li 'Mubarak' yujaddidun muzahiratihim," *al-Misri al-Yawm*, February 4, 2011, http://today.almasryalyoum.com/article2.aspx?ArticleID=286521, cited in *al-Misri al-Yawm*, February 4, 2011, cited in Juan Cole, "Repression Fails as Thousands Demand Mubarak Departure," Informed Comment, February 4, 2011, www.juancole.com/2011/02/repression-fails-as-thousands-demand-mubarak-departure.html.

78. "Egypt Unrest: Obama Increases Pressure on Mubarak," BBC, February 5, 2011, www.bbc.co.uk/news/world-us-canada-12371479.

79. "Al-Mutazahirun yuqimun 'Qaddas al-Ahad' bi al-Tahrir takriman li al-shuhada'," *al-Yawm al-Sabi'*, February 6, 2011, http://masress.com/youm7/347068;

"Muhawala litashkil i'tilaf thawrat 25 yanayir wa al-mutazahirun yutalibun bi muhakamat al-fasad," *al-Ahram* (Cairo), February 7, 2011, www.ahram.org.eg /archive/The-First/News/61846.aspx.

80. Ahmad Zaghlul al-Shayti, *Mi'at Khutwa min al-thawra: Yawmiyyat min maydan al-Tahrir* (Cairo: Dar Mirit, 2011), 77.

81. "Wael Ghonim's Interview with Mona Shazly on February 7th," *Unsettling the Dust*, March 21, 2011, http://translatingrev.wordpress.com/2011/03/21/wael -ghonims-interview-with-mona-shazly-on-february-7th/; Taha and Combs, "Of Drama and Performance," 84–90.

82. Ghonim, *Revolution 2.0*, 258–65; Wolman, *The Instigators*.

83. Al-Shamma', *Ayyam*, 68–69.

84. "Thawrat al-'ummal," *al-Badil*, February 9, 2011, http://masress.com/elbadil /19466; Dina Bishara, "The Power of Workers in Egypt's 2011 Uprising," in Korany and El-Mahdi, *Arab Spring in Egypt*, chapter 5; Beinin, "Egyptian Workers and January 25," 339–40; Megan Cornish, "Women Workers in Egypt: Hidden Key to the Revolution," Al-Jazeerah, April 11, 2011, www.aljazeerah .info/Opinion%20Editorials/2011/April/11%20o/Women%20Workers%20 in%20Egypt,%20Hidden%20Key%20to%20the%20Revolution%20By%20 Megan%20Cornish.htm.

85. "Masira milyuniya thalitha fi 'al-Tahrir," *al-Misri al-Yawm*, February 9, 2011, http://today.almasryalyoum.com/article2.aspx?ArticleID=287306; "Tawasul al-muzaharat," *al-Misri al-Yawm*, February 10, 2011, http://today.almasryalyoum .com/article2.aspx?ArticleID=287505; 'Abd al-Rahman al-Shalabi, "Al-shabab yutliqun mubadara li inqadh al-bursa," *al-Masry al-Youm*, February 9, 2011, http://today.almasryalyoum.com/article2.aspx?ArticleID=287285.

86. "Hushud talabat al-tibb tanzil al-maydan," *al-Wafd*, February 10, 2011, http:// masress.com/alwafd/15406.

87. "5 alaf sinima'I yanzilun al-tahrir," *al-Wafd*, February 10, 2013, http://masress .com/alwafd/15403.

88. Wala' Wahid, "Ta'sis I'tilaf li shabab 25 yanayir bi al-Isma'iliya," *al-Wafd*, February 10, 2011, http://masress.com/alwafd/15436.

89. "Waqfa ihtijajiyya li 'ummal al-bitrul imam al-wizara," *al-Wafd*, February 10, 2011, http://masress.com/alwafd/15417.

90. "al-Yawm al-sadis 'ashar, 9 Fibrayir 2011," Mobile-sn, http://mobile-sn.net/vb /showthread.php?t=6575.

91. "Tazayud muzaharat wa waqfat ihtijajiyya fi Asyut," *Shabab Misr* (Cairo), February 10, 2011, www.masress.com/shbabmisr/5583; Muhammad Abu Ghait, "Madina 'ala hamish al-thawra," in 'Abd al-'Alim, *Yawmiyyat al-Ghadab*, 221–46.

92. "24 alf 'amil 'bi Ghazl al-Mahalla' yu'linun idraban jama'iyyan 'an al-'amal," *al-Yawm al-Sabi'*, February 10, 2011, http://masress.com/youm7/349257.

93. Hiba Ahmad, "Idrab 45 alf 'amil bi hay'at al-naqal al-'amm," *al-Wafd*, February 10, 2011, http://masress.com/alwafd/15450.
94. "Ahmad Maher," *al-Shuruq*; 'Umar, *Al-Thawra*, 247–48.
95. "3 alaf muwatin bur sa'id yahriqun sayarat al-muhafiz," *al-Misri al-Yawm*, February 9, 2011, www.almasryalyoum.com/node/314616; "Al-Thawra tata-wassi' wa tazhaf li qasr Mubarak," Aljazeera.net, February 11, 2011, www.aljazeera.net/mob/f6451603-4dff-4ca1-9c10-122741d17432/9a35cbf0-3c66-4184-a311-d89e3cce22fc.

CHAPTER 6: TUNISIA

1. Juan Linz and Alfred Stepan, *Problems of Democratic Transition and Consolidation: Southern Europe, South America, and Post-Communist Europe* (Baltimore: Johns Hopkins University Press, 1996); Larry Diamond, "The Impact of the Economic Crisis: Why Democracies Survive," *Midan Masr*, July 20, 2013, www.midanmasr.com/en/article.aspx?ArticleID=85; David Epstein, Robert Bates, Jack Goldstone, Ida Kristensen, and Sharyn O'Halloran, "Democratic Transitions," *American Journal of Political Science* 50, no. 3 (2006): 551–69.
2. Pierre Puchot, *La révolution confisquée: Enquete sur la transition democratique en Tunisie* (Paris: Sindbad, 2012), chapter 1.
3. "Muzahara didd al-hukuma al-jadida fi wasat al-'asima al-tunisiyya," *al-Fajr Niyuz* (Tunis), January 18, 2011, www.turess.com/alfajrnews/44852; François Hauter, "Tunisie: La nouvelle équipe ne calme pas la rue," *Le Figaro*, January 18, 2011.
4. Honwana, "Youth and the Tunisian Revolution," 14.
5. "Istiqalat 3 wuzara'," *Al-Bilad*, January 19, 2011, www.albiladpress.com/news_print.php?nid=86528; "Istiqalat 'arba'a a'da' fi hukumat al-wahda min manasibihim," *al-Fajr Niyuz*, January 18, 2011, www.turess.com/alfajrnews/44854; Angelique Chrisafis, "Tunisia's Caretaker Government in Peril as Four Ministers Quit," *Guardian*, January 18, 2011.
6. Alyssa, "Jeter le bébé avec l'eau du bain?," Nawaat, January 19, 2011, http://nawaat.org/portail/2011/01/19/jeter-le-bebe-avec-leau-du-bain/.
7. "Tawasul ihtijaj al-mu'tasimin bi sahat al-hukuma bi al-'asimah," Wikalat Tunis Ifriqiya li al-Anba', January 27, 2011, www.turess.com/tap/34184; "Tashkila jadida," *al-Sabah*, January 29, 2011, www.turess.com/assabah/48891; "We Are Not Free Yet!," A Tunisian Girl, January 29, 2011, http://atunisiangirl.blogspot.com/2011/01/we-are-not-free-yet.html; "La ahlam bi mansab fi ayy mustawa," *al-Sabah*, January 30, 2011, www.turess.com/assabah/48934.
8. "Al-Mu'arid al-Islami Rashid al-Ghannushi ya'ud al-yawm ila Tunis," *al-Wasat* (Tunis), January 30, 2011 at www.turess.com/alwasat/16788.
9. Azzam S. Tamimi, *Rachid Ghannouchi: A Democrat within Islamism* (New York: Oxford University Press, 2001).

10. "Tawasul al-i'tisam fi sahat al-hukuma bi al-qasba," Wikalat Tunis Ifriqiya li al-Anba', February 21, 2011, www.turess.com/tap/36077; "Al-Ghannushi yastaqil," *al-Shuruq*, February 28, 2011, www.turess.com/alchourouk/182815; Karim M., "Tunisie: Le rôle de la Casbah et l'avenir de la Révolution," Nawaat, March 4, 2011, http://nawaat.org/portail/2011/03/04/tunisie-le-role-de-la-casbah-et-lavenir-de-la-revolution; Lina Ben Mhenni, "Quand le Mot Liberté Rime avec Foutre le Bordel," A Tunisian Girl, March 1, 2011, http://atunisiangirl.blogspot.com/2011/03/quand-liberte-rime-avec-foutre-le.html; Emna El Hammi, "Les manifestants de la Kasbah garants de la Révolution," Ma Tunisie sans Ben Ali, March 4, 2011, http://tunisie.blogs.liberation.fr/blog/2011/03/les-manifestants-de-la-kasbah-garants-de-la-revolution-tunisienne.html.

11. "Rasmi: 'Al-Nahda' tahsil 'ala al-ta'shira," *al-Shuruq* (Tunis), March 2, 2011, www.turess.com/alchourouk/183036; "Fu'ad al-Mubza' yu'lin: majlis ta'sisi," *al-Shuruq*, March 4, 2011, www.turess.com/alchourouk/183260; "Al-Yawm yughadir al-mu'tasimun al-qasba," *al-Shuruq*, March 4, 2011, www.turess.com/alchourouk/183265.

12. "Mu'tasimu qasbatay Tunis wa Safaqs qabl rahilihim: 'In 'adu . . . 'adna'," *al-Shuruq*, March 5, 2011, www.turess.com/alchourouk/183397; Ian Black, "Tunisia Dissolves Secret Police to Meet Key Demand of Protesters," *Guardian*, March 7, 2011, www.guardian.co.uk/world/2011/mar/07/tunisia-abolishes-secret-police-force; Querine Hanlon, "Security Sector Reform in Tunisia: A Year after the Jasmine Revolution," United States Institute of Peace, March 2012, www.usip.org/sites/default/files/resources/SR304.pdf; Nouveau Système, "Baba Sebsi win méchin," Youtube, posted August 12, 2012, www.youtube.com/watch?v=Vveq7Gv-KtI.

13. Honwana, "Youth and the Tunisian Revolution," 15.

14. "Man' tarashshuh itarat al-tajammu' al-dusturi al-dimuqrati," *Wikalat Tunis Ifriqiya li al-Anba'* (Tunis), April 11, 2011, www.turess.com/tap/39776; Emna el Hammi, "Le bourguibisme de Béji Caid Essebsi contre la menace islamiste," Ma Tunisie sans Ben Ali, April 18, 2011, http://tunisie.blogs.liberation.fr/blog/2011/04/le-bourguibisme-de-b%C3%A9ji-caid-essebsi-contre-la-menace-islamiste.html; "15 juillet : Appel aux modérés !!!!!!," Nawat, July 14, 2011, http://nawaat.org/portail/2011/07/14/15-juillet-appel-aux-moderes/; Khaoula Zoghlami, "Témoignages sur l'attaque de Kasbah 15/07," Nawat, July 17, 2011, http://nawaat.org/portail/2011/07/17/temoignages-sur-lattaque-de-kasbah-1507; Puchot, *La révolution confisquée*, 70.

15. Emna El Hammi, "L'État d'urgence en Tunisie: Une arme de dictature à surveiller," Ma Tunisie sans Ben Ali, May 5, 2011, http://tunisie.blogs.liberation.fr/blog/2011/05/letat-durgence-en-tunisie-une-arme-de-dictature-%C3%A0-surveiller.html; "Hudu' hadhr wasat al-'asima wa intishar amni mukaththaf ba'd tafriq tajammu' li 'adad min al-muwatinin," Wikalat Tunis Ifriqiya li al-Anba',

May 6, 2011, www.turess.com/tap/41580; Winston Smith, "Wa yatawasal al-qam' al-bulisi," Nawat, May 6, 2011, http://nawaat.org/portail/2011/05/06; "My Participation in the Oslo Freedom Forum," A Tunisian Girl, May 10, 2011, http://atunisiangirl.blogspot.com/2011/05/my-word-for-oslo-freedom-forum.html.

16. Honwana, "Youth and the Tunisian Revolution," 15.

17. "Tunisie: 'Touche pas à mes créateurs' déplait aux obscurantists," *Investir en Tunisie*, June 27, 2011, www.investir-en-tunisie.net/index.php?option=com_content&view=article&id=10556; "Mubadarat Lamm al-Shaml fi Tunis," *al-Masdar* (Tunis), May 6, 2011, www.almasdar.tn/management/article-4409.

18. Sarah Orchani, "Marche pour la liberté et contre la violence en Tunisie ce 7 juil-let," *Mediapart*, July 6, 2011, http://blogs.mediapart.fr/edition/le-monde-arabe-en-mouvement/article/060711/marche-pour-la-liberte-et-contre-la-violence.

19. Najar, "Les femmes cyberactivistes," 163.

20. Dawish, *The Second Arab Awakening*, chapter 4.

21. "Tanzim taqaddumi sha'bi muwahhad: Hal huwa wahm am hulm am mashru' qabil li al-injaz?," Nawat, December 21, 2011, http://nawaat.org/portail/2011/12/21/; Naomi Scherbel-Ball, "Tunisia's Young 'General' Sees Future in Sharia," *Deutsche Welle*, February 13, 2013, http://dw.de/p/17cpM; "Tunisia's Communist Workers' Party Undergoes Facelift to Rally Adherents," *Xinhua*, July 11, 2012, http://news.xinhuanet.com/english/world/2012-07/11/c_131707215.htm.

22. "Tunisian Pair Sentenced to Seven Years for Prophet Caricatures," AFP, April 6, 2012, http://english.ahram.org.eg/NewsContent/2/8/38605/World/Region/Tunisian-pair-sentenced-to-seven-years-for-Prophet.aspx; "Tunisian Court Fines Newspaper Publisher over Photo," Reuters, March 8, 2012, http://mobile.reuters.com/article/cyclicalConsumerGoodsSector/idUSL5E8E8AL220120308; "Tunisian TV Chief Fined for Airing 'Persepolis,'" France24, March 5, 2012, www.france24.com/en/20120503-tunisian-tv-chief-fined-screening-persepolis-karoui-franco-iranian-film-revolution-nessma; Puchot, *La revolution confisquée*, chapter 5; Yosr Dridi, "Weld El 15: Two Years for 'Rapped Retaliation'?," Nawaat, June 15, 2013, http://nawaat.org/portail/2013/06/15/weld-el-15-two-years-for-rapped-retaliation/; "Tunisia: A New Prison Sentence for the Rappers 'Weld 15' and 'Klay'," *AllAfrica*, September 2, 2013, http://allafrica.com/stories/201309031346.html; "Libertés en Tunisie: Entretien avec la blogueuse Lina Ben Mhenni," *JOL Press*, June 20, 2013, www.jolpress.com/libertes-tunisie-entretien--blogueuse-lina-ben-mhenni-article-820244.html; Maher Chaabane, "La journaliste Hind Meddeb conteste la justice tunisienne," *Courrier International* (Paris), June 18, 2013, www.courrierinternational.com/article/2013/06/18/la-journaliste-hind-meddeb-conteste-la-justice-tunisienne.

23. "Tunis: 'Al-Nahda' yatakhalli 'an i'timad al-Islam masdaran li al-tashri'," *al-Siyasa* (Kuwait), March 27, 2012, www.al-seyassah.com/AtricleView/tabid/59/smid

/438/ArticleID/183781/Default.aspx; Emine M'tiraoui, "Al-Nahda tatma'in al-muhtajjin 'ala makanat al-shari'a," Nawat, March 28, 2012, http://tinyurl.com/m4adsqp.

24. Lina Ben Mhenni, "April 9th, 2012 Events Told by My Father," A Tunisian Girl, April 12, 2012, http://atunisiangirl.blogspot.com/2012/04/april-9th-2012-events-as-seen-by-my.html.

25. Rashid al-Ghannushi, interview with author, Tunis, May 10, 2012. My translation from the Arabic.

26. Houda Trabelsi, "Leaked Ghannouchi Tape Raises Salafism Concerns," *Maghare-bia*, October 15, 2012, http://magharebia.com/en_GB/articles/awi/features/2012/10/15/feature-01; "Mohamed Talbi: 'Il faut qu'on annule la charia musulmane,'" *Savoir ou se faire avoir*, July 4, 2011, http://tinyurl.com/k9fldvj.

27. "Al-Tunisiyun yudinun al-hujum 'ala al-sifara al-amrikiyya," *Magharebia*, September 16, 2012, http://magharebia.com/ar/articles/awi/features/2012/09/16/feature-01.

28. Lina Ben Mhenni, "Some Thoughts about the U.S. Embassy Incidents," A Tunisian Girl, September 15, 2012, http://atunisiangirl.blogspot.com/2012/09/some-thoughts-about-us-embassys.html.

29. "Vidéo: Des manifestants brûlent l'ambassade U.S. à Tunis," Nawaat, September 14, 2012, http://nawaat.org/portail/2012/09/14/video-des-manifestants-brulent-lambassade-us-a-tunis-deux-morts-et-des-dizaines-de-blesses/.

30. "'Al-Jabha al-sha'biyya' tu'lin 'an tashakkuliha," *al-Tunisiyya* (Tunis), October 7, 2012, www.attounissia.com.tn/details_article.php?t=64&a=71505; "Ijtima' al-jabha al-sha'biyya bi qasr al-mu'tamarat bi Tunis," Youtube, October 7, 2012, http://youtu.be/HMevhGP73wI.

31. "Tasfiyat Shukri Bu al-'Ayd," *al-Shuruq*, February 7, 2013, www.turess.com/alchourouk/615796; "Qays Sa'id wa Sadiq Bu al-'Ayd: 'Ala al-Jibali an yastaqil," *al-Sabah*, February 7, 2013, www.turess.com/assabahnews/18137.

32. Sana Sbouaï, "Tunisie: Situation toujours tendue au lendemain de l'assassinat de Chokri Belaid," Nawaat, February 7, 2013, http://nawaat.org/portail/2013/02/07/tunisie-situation-toujours-tendue-au-lendemain-de-lassassinat-de-chokri-belaid/; Lina Ben Mhenni, "Na`m, Ana Kafira," A Tunisian Girl, February 9, 2013, http://atunisiangirl.blogspot.com/2013/02/blog-post.html; Juan Cole, "Why Tunisia's Arab Spring Is in Turmoil," Informed Comment, February 9, 2013, www.juancole.com/2013/02/tunisias-spring-turmoil.html; "Tunisie: Quand l'Université salue l'âme du martyre Chokri Belaid," *El Fassikile* (Tunis), February 11, 2013, www.elfassikile.tn/actualites/tunisie-universite-martyre-chokri-belaid/2013/02/13/.

33. 'Abd al-Ra'uf al-Muqaddami, "Bi al-munasaba: 'Ali al-'Urayyid—Qudrat fikriyya . . . wa mahdudiyyat 'amaliyya," *al-Shuruq*, February 23, 2013, www.turess.com/alchourouk/619838.

34. "Tunisie Écrasante victoire des candidats de l'UGET contre les étudiants

d'Ennahdha," *Business News*, March 16, 2013, www.businessnews.com.tn/details _article.php?temp=1&t=520&a=29945.

35. Juan Cole, "Harlem Shake as Protest in Tunis," Informed Comment, February 28, 2013, www.juancole.com/2013/02/harlem-shake-protest.html.

36. "Al-Qayrawan: Istinfar amni . . . wa ghiyab al-ansar al-shari'a," *al-Tunisiyya*, May 19, 2013, www.turess.com/aljarida/16395; "Hayy al-Tadamun: Muwajahat," *al-Tunisiyya*, May 19, 2013, www.turess.com/attounissia/90885; John Thorne, "Tunisia Shuts Down Medieval City to Prevent Salafi Demonstrations," *Christian Science Monitor*, May 20, 2013, www.csmonitor.com/World/Middle-East/2013 /0520/Tunisia-shuts-down-medieval-city-to-prevent-Salafi-demonstrations.

37. Seif Soudani, "La Polit-Revue: Playoffs islamistes et simulacres de dialogues nationaux," Nawaat, May 19, 2013, http://nawaat.org/portail/2013/05/19/ la-polit-revue-playoffs-islamistes-et-simulacres-de-dialogues-nationaux.

38. Seif Soudani, "La Polit-Revue: Nidaa Tounes en a rêvé, l'Égypte l'a fait," Nawaat, July 7, 2013, http://nawaat.org/portail/2013/07/07/la-polit-revue-nidaa-tounes -en-revait-legypte-la-fait/.

39. Perrine Massy, "Qui est Boubaker Al-Hakim, tueur présumé de Mohamed Brahmi?," Nawaat, July 26, 2013, http://nawaat.org/portail/2013/07/26/qui -est-boubaker-al-hakim-tueur-presume-de-mohamed-brahmi/.

40. "Muzaharat fi mukhtalif al-mudun al-tunisiyya tutalib bi isqat al-hukuma," *al-Arabiyya*, July 26, 2013, http://tinyurl.com/owr4wj6; "Assassinat de Brahmi: Appel à la grève générale en Tunisie," *Le Parisien* (Paris), July 25, 2013, www .leparisien.fr/international/assassinat-de-mohamed-brahmi-manifestations -anti-ennahda-en-tunisie-25-07-2013-3007853.php; "Sidi Bouzid al-an," *Tunis al-Raqamiyya* (Tunis), July 26, 2013, http://tinyurl.com/mgkowg6; "Rashid al-Ghannushi: Jaysh, amn, sha'b, kulluna yad wahida," *Babnet*, July 26, 2013, www.babnet.net/rttdetail-68871.asp.

CHAPTER 7: EGYPT

1. Some of the following chapter first appeared in a different form in Juan Cole, "Egypt's New Left versus the Military Junta," *Social Research* 79, no. 2 (2012): 487–510.

2. "Mutazahiru al-tahrir yutalibun bi muhakamat 'Shafiq,'" *al-Yawm al-Sabi'*, March 4, 2011, www.youm7.com/News.asp?NewsID=362763&SecID=65; "Sharaf yaltaqi bi shabab al-thawra fi manzilihi," *al-Wafd*, March 4, 2011, www. alwafd.org/%D8%A7%D9%82%D8%AA%D8%B5%D8%A7%D8%AF /20694; "Isam Sharaf bi maydan al-tahrir," *al-Wafd*, March 4, 2011, www.masress .com/alwafd/20719.

3. "Young Leaders of Egypt's Revolt Snub Clinton in Cairo," ABC News, March 15, 2011, http://abcnews.go.com/blogs/politics/2011/03/young-leaders-of-egypts -revolt-snub-clinton-in-cairo/.

4. "Matalib fi Misr bi rafd al-ta'dilat al-dusturiya," *al-Arabiya* (Dubai), March 13, 2011, www.alarabiya.net/articles/2011/03/13/141325.html; "Wazir al-'adl: Tajrim al-ihtijajat hadafuhu himayat misr min al-thawrah al-mudada," *al-Yawm al-Sabi'*, March 26, 2011, www.masress.com/youm7/377022; Edward Cody, "Egypt's Ruling Generals Hand Down Interim Constitutional Rules," *Washington Post*, March 24, 2011.

5. Patrick Cockburn, "Egyptians on March to Keep Revolutionary Spirit Alive," *Independent*, April 2, 2011.

6. "Al-Mi'at ya'tasimuna fi maydan al-tahrir," *al-Wafd*, May 28, 2011, www.masress.com/alwafd/50132; "Al-Tahrir li Mubarak: Rabbuka huwa al-Hakim," *al-Wafd*, June 24, 2011, www.masress.com/alwafd/62055; "Egypt: Protesters and Police Clash in Tahrir Square," *AllAfrica*, June 29, 2011, via Lexis Nexis.

7. "Sharaf yu'lin tashkil al-hukumah al-yawm," *al-Ahram*, July 17, 2011, www.masress.com/ahram/89738.

8. "Jum'at 'Lamm al-Shaml' . . . al-Islamiyun yu'linun najahahum," *al-Yawm al-Sabi'*, July 30, 2011, http://masress.com/youm7/464409.

9. "Suhuf 'Alamiyyah: Al-Majlis al-'Askari ya'ish mu'dilat muhakamat Mubarak," *al-Misri al-Yawm*, July 31, 2011, www.almasryalyoum.com/node/481980.

10. Sharif Abdel Kouddous, "Facing Widespread Persecution, Egyptians Rally behind Woman Facing Charges for Internet Speech," Alternet, August 25, 2011, www.alternet.org/media/152100/facing_widespread_persecution,_egyptians_rally_behind_woman_facing_charges_for_internet_speech.

11. Zenobia, "Regarding Asmaa Mahfouz: The Second Expensive Tweet in Egypt," Egyptian Chronicles, August 14, 2011, http://egyptianchronicles.blogspot.com/2011/08/regarding-asmaa-mahfouz-second.html.

12. "Egypt Blogger Mahfuz Quizzed for 'Defaming' Military," BBC, August 14, 2011, www.bbc.co.uk/news/world-middle-east-14524094.

13. "Tahqiq 'askari ma'a nashitah misriyyah," *al-Jazirah*, August 14, 2011, www.aljazeera.net/humanrights/pages/8c3c4ba8-1a6b-439f-8d3a-8f51c066020b.

14. "Asma' Mahfouz ba'd ikhla' sabiliha: Yasqut al-'askari," CNN Arabic, August 16, 2011, http://arabic.cnn.com/2011/egypt.2011/8/16/Asmaa.Mahfouz/.

15. "Cairo Clashes Leave 24 Dead after Coptic Church Protest," BBC, October 9, 2011, www.bbc.co.uk/news/world-middle-east-15235212.

16. Sharif Abdel Kouddous, "Egypt: The Afterglow Has Faded," Pulitzer Center on Crisis Reporting, December 1, 2011, http://pulitzercenter.org/reporting/egypt-cairo-protest-military-government-violence-coptic; "RN Publishes English Version of Egypt's SCC Decision on Unconstitutionality of Parliament," Right to Nonviolence, June 15, 2012, www.righttononviolence.org/rn-publishes-the-english-version-of-egypts-scc-decision-on-unconstitutionality-of-parliament; Dawisha, *The Second Arab Awakening*, chapter 4.

17. Ibrahim Awad, "Breaking out of Authoritarianism: 18 Months of Politi-

cal Transition in Egypt," *Constellations* 20, no. 2 (2013): 275–92; Michele Dunne, "Egypt: Why Liberalism Still Matters," *Journal of Democracy* 24, no. 1 (2013): 86–100; Khalil al-Anani and Maszlee Malik, "Pious Way to Politics: The Rise of Political Salafism in Post–Mubarak Egypt," *Digest of Middle East Studies* 22, no. 1 (2013): 57–73; Beinin, "Egyptian Workers and January 25," 341–42.

18. "Mutalabat niswiyya bi dustur jadid yadmun al-'adala wa al-hurriyya," *Aswat Misriyya*, July 28, 2013, www.aswatmasriya.com/news/view.aspx?id=ab652e5a -06e7-4fde-874e-f96fecd7b545; Castells, *Networks of Outrage*, 72–73.

19. Amro Hassan, "Egypt's Rulers Try to Curb Anger over Guidelines for Constitution," *Los Angeles Times*, November 15, 2011, http://latimesblogs.latimes.com/ world_now/2011/11/egypt-military-constitution-drafting-principles.html.

20. "Egypt: Police, Protesters in Bloody Clash ahead of Vote," MSNBC, November 19, 2011, www.msnbc.msn.com/id/45369813/ns/world_news-mideast_n _africa/#.T6TB0FJELVZ.

21. "Istimrar al-ishtibakat fi Qasr al-'Ayni," *al-Yawm al-Sabi'*, December 18, 2011, www.masress.com/youm7/557282.

22. "Egypt Unrest: Women Protest against Army Violence," BBC, December 20, 2011, www.bbc.co.uk/news/world-middle-east-16267436.

23. "Sayyidat Misr yarfadna i'tidhar al-'askari," *al-Wafd*, December 20, 2011, http:// tinyurl.com/83vm4p9.

24. "Egyptian Protesters Head for Tahrir on New Protest," *MENA*, December 23, 2011.

25. Kristen Chick, "Egypt's Military Lifts Emergency Law—with One Big Loophole," *Christian Science Monitor*, January 25, 2012, www.csmonitor.com/World/Middle -East/2012/0125/Egypt-s-military-lifts-emergency-law-with-one-big-loophole.

26. "Al-Tayyarat al-Islamiyyah tasta'idd li mughadirat Maydan al-Tahrir . . . wa 'asharat al-alaf yatazahirun imam qiyadat al-mantiqa al-shamaliyya bi al-Iskandariyya," *al-Ahram*, January 25, 2012, www.ahram.org.eg/Al-Mashhad-Al -Syiassy/News/127147.aspx.

27. "La'ibu al-ahli ya'ishuna halat al-ru'b," *al-Ahram*, February 1, 2012, http:// tinyurl.com/mzg3ccy.

28. "Majzarat Bur Sa'id khuttita laha min sijn Tura," *al-Shuruq* (Cairo), February 2, 2012, www.echoroukonline.com/ara/articles/121511.html.

29. "Street Battles Rage near Egypt's Interior Ministry," Reuters, February 3, 2012.

30. "6 April raddan 'ala 'al-'Askari': al-'Isyan al-madani haqq dusturi liman hatafu bi suqut al-majlis," *al-Misri al-Yawm*, February 6, 2012, www.almasryalyoum.com /node/641761.

31. "Riyutirs: Hajm al-musharakah fi idrab Febrayir 11 yakshif 'umq al-inqisamat fi Misr," *al-Misri al-Yawm*, February 11, 2012, www.almasryalyoum.com/node /651791.

32. "Mahkamat 'al-Qada' al-Idari' tuqif tashkil ta'sisiyyat al-dustur," *al-Misri al-Yawm*, April 11, 2012, http://today.almasryalyoum.com/article2.aspx?ArticleID=334644&IssueID=2468.

33. "'Shabab al-Thawrah' yuhaddiduna al-'awdah ila 'al-Tahrir' ihtijajan 'ala tarshih Sulayman," *al-Shuruq*, April 10, 2012, http://shorouknews.com/news/view.aspx?cdate=10042012&id=8e7aba12-9522-486d-8ee2-0f20f8513b61.

34. "Misr: Murashshahu al-ri'asah yarfaduna irja' al-intikhabat, wa al-'askar yulawihhun bi 'Majlis Ri'asi,'" *al-Hayat*, April 17, 2012, http://international.daralhayat.com/internationalarticle/386170.

35. "Al-Quwa al-thawriyyah wa al-ahzab, ghaddan fi al-Tahrir: Al-Maydan huwa al-Hall," *al-Misri al-Yawm*, April 19, 2012, http://today.almasryalyoum.com/article2.aspx?ArticleID=335504.

36. "Misr: 'Al-Milyuniyyah al-Misriyyah' tuwahhid al-furaqa' khalf inha' hukm al-'askar," *al-Hayat*, April 21, 2012, http://international.daralhayat.com/internationalarticle/387458.

37. Mohamed Mahmoud, "Appearance of al-Zawahiri's Brother at Demonstration Stirs Debate in Cairo," *al-Shurfa*, May 10, 2012, http://al-shorfa.com/en_GB/articles/meii/features/main/2012/05/10/feature-01; "Egypt State of Emergency Ends for First Time in 30 Years," *Ahram Online*, May 31, 2012, http://english.ahram.org.eg/NewsContent/1/64/43368/Egypt/Politics-/Egypt-state-of-emergency-ends-for-first-time-in--y.aspx.

38. "Manassat al-Tahrir tu'lin istimrar al-i'tisam bi al-maydan ba'd al-ihtifal bi Mursi," *al-Yawm al-Sabi'*, June 25, 2012, www.youm7.com/NewsPrint.asp?NewsID=715098.

39. "Al-Jama'a al-Islamiyya turahhib bi ta'ahhud al-ra'is mursi bi al-ifraj 'an al-shaykh 'umar 'Abd al-Rahman," *al-Shuruq*, July 2, 2012, http://shorouknews.com/news/view.aspx?cdate=02072012&id=cb8aecca-842e-4cf1-88b3-df4250c37679.

40. Hamza Hendawi, "AP Exclusive: Egypt Military Builds Case on Morsi," Associated Press, July 26, 2013, http://news.yahoo.com/ap-exclusive-egypt-military-builds-case-morsi-213007144.html;_ylt=A2KJ2UYIo_VRhgYA0THQtDMD%20%20target=.

41. "Mumaththilu al-kana'is al-misriyya yattafiqun 'ala al-insihab min al-jam'iyya al-ta'sisiyya," *al-Watan* (Cairo), November 15, 2012, www.elwatannews.com/news/details/77667.

42. "Al-Ra'is yasdur qanun himayat al-thawra," *al-Yawm al-Sabi'*, November 23, 2012, www.youm7.com/News.asp?NewsID=854906.

43. "Rudud fi'il wasi'a 'ala qararat al-ra'is," *al-Yawm al-Sabi'*, November 23, 2012, www.youm7.com/News.asp?NewsID=855239; Juan Cole, "Egyptian Left/Liberals Confront Pres. Morsi with Rallies, Demos in 8 Provinces," Informed Comment, November 24, 2012, www.juancole.com/2012/11/egyptian-leftliberals-confront-pres-morsi-with-rallies-demos-in-8-provinces.html.

44. "Rudud fi'il wasi'a 'ala qararat al-ra'is," *al-Yawm al-Sabi'*, November 23, 2012, www.youm7.com/News.asp?NewsID=855239.
45. "Hizb April 6 yad'u al-sha'b li al-nuzul li al-ittihadiyya . . . wa yu'akkid: shar`iyyat al-ra'is saqatat," *al-Yawm al-Sabi'*, December 6, 2012 at www.youm7.com/News.asp?NewsID=867922; Mostafa Ali, "6 Dead, 450 Injured in Clashes at Egypt's Presidential Palace," *Ahram Online*, December 6, 2013, http://english.ahram.org.eg/NewsContent/1/64/59892/Egypt/Politics-/-dead,--injured-in-clashes-at-Egypts-presidential-.aspx.
46. Juan Cole, "New Fundamentalist Constitution Approved, Heralds Turn to Egyptian Theocracy," Informed Comment, December 26, 2012, www.juancole.com/2012/12/fundamentalist-constitution-theocracy.html; Nathan J. Brown and Clark Lombardi, "Islam in Egypt's New Constitution," Carnegie Endowment for International Peace, December 13, 2012, http://carnegieendowment.org/2012/12/13/islam-in-egypt-s-new-constitution/etph.
47. "Morsi Reaches Agreement with Senior Judges," *Middle East Monitor*, April 29, 2013, www.middleeastmonitor.com/news/africa/5871-morsi-reaches-agreement-with-senior-judges.
48. Zenobia Azeem, "Egypt's Supreme Court Rules against Shura Council," *Al Monitor* (Washington, D.C.), June 3, 2013, www.al-monitor.com/pulse/originals/2013/06/egyptian-shura-council-illegal.html.
49. Andre Azeem, "Morsi Appoints Nine Islamists to Key Ministries," *AsiaNews* (Vatican), May 8, 2013, www.asianews.it/news-en/Morsi-appoints-nine-Islamists-to-key-ministries-27868.html; "Tarhib wa ishada fi al-uqsur bi istiqala al-muhafiz 'Adil al-Khayyat," *Akhbar Misr* (Cairo), June 23, 2013, www.egynews.net/wps/portal/news?params=238802; "AESA Calls on President Morsi to Protect Egyptians' Right to Freedom of Speech, the Sanctity of the Rule of Law and Women Rights," Yahoo News, April 1, 2013, http://news.yahoo.com/aesa-calls-president-morsi-protect-egyptians-freedom-speech-130000846.html; "Jon Stewart Encourages Egyptian Counterpart," *Raw Story*, June 21, 2013, www.rawstory.com/rs/2013/06/21/jon-stewart-encourages-egyptian-counterpart-if-your-regime-is-not-strong-enough-to-handle-a-joke-then-you-dont-have-a-regime; Muhammad Fathi, *Mursi: Wa dumu'i wa ibtisamati* (Cairo: Dar Uktub, 2012), 102–4.
50. Ahmed Aboul Enein, "Labour Strikes and Protests Double under Morsi," *Daily News Egypt* (Cairo), April 28, 2013, www.dailynewsegypt.com/2013/04/28/labour-strikes-and-protests-double-under-morsi/.
51. David Kilpatrick, "Keeper of Islamic Flame Rises as Egypt's New Decisive Voice," *New York Times*, March 12, 2012; Conn M. Hallinan, "Egypt Faces a Potentially Chaotic Summer," *International Policy Digest*, March 18, 2013, www.internationalpolicydigest.org/2013/03/18/egypt-faces-a-potentially-chaotic-summer; "5 Million Tourists Bring in $4 Bn During 2013," *Ahram Online*,

June 14, 2013, http://english.ahram.org.eg/NewsContent/3/12/73998/Business
/Economy/-million-tourists-bring-in--bn-during--Egypt-touri.aspx; "Why the
Pound Devaluation Now?," Egyptian Initiative for Personal Rights Blog, January 20, 2013, http://eipr.org/en/blog/post/2013/01/20/1597; "Steel in Egypt
to Hike after Pound Devaluation," *Albawaba* (Amman, Jordan), May 28, 2013,
www.albawaba.com/business/egypt-steel-devaluation-495145; "Minister: Halting Egypt's Wheat Imports Was Morsi's Biggest Mistake," Reuters, July 21,
2013, at Lexis Nexis.

52. John Pollock, "Rebelbook: A Mix of Technologies Let Dedicated Citizens
Change Egypt," *MIT Technology Review*, July 5, 2013, www.technologyreview
.com/view/516836/rebelbook-a-mix-of-technologies-let-dedicated-citizens
-change-egypt/.

53. "Ihtijaj 'ummal al-Ghazl wa al-Tansij bi al-Mahalla li al-mutalaba bi huquqihim,"
al-Misriyyun (Cairo), June 21, 2013, http://tinyurl.com/l7fma2r; "'Ummal al-
Mahalla yu'linun 'al-Tamarrud' wa yusharikun fi hamlat sahb al-thiqa min al-
ra'is," *al-Watan*, May 12, 2013, www.elwatannews.com/news/details/180073.

54. Esam al-Amin, "An Impending Bloodbath in Egypt: Will It Break the Coup?
Banana Republic without Bananas," *Counterpunch*, August 2–4, 2013, www
.counterpunch.org/2013/08/02/an-impending-bloodbath-in-egypt-will-it
-break-the-coup/.

55. Mohamed Younis, "Egyptians' Views of Government Crashed before Overthrow;
Confidence in Electoral Process Also Shaken," *Gallup World*, August 2, 2013, www
.gallup.com/poll/163796/egyptian-views-government-crashed-overthrow.aspx.

56. "Al-Jaysh: Al-mutazahirun didd Morsi bi 'al-milayin' . . . innaha akbar muzaharat fi ta'rikh misr," *'Ammun* (Amman, Jordan), June 30, 2013, www.ammonnews
.net/article.aspx?articleno=158104; "Mayadin Misr tahtif: Yasqut hukm al-Murshid," *al-Safir*, June 29, 2013.

57. "Al-Tahrir wa al-ittihadiyya yastaqbilan al-misriyyin li al-musharaka bi fa'iliyyat 'mi-
lyuniyyat tafwid al-jaysh,'" *al-Yawm al-Sabi'*, July 27, 2013, www.youm7.com/News
.asp?NewsID=1179594; "Ittihad al-'ummal yu`lin musharakat 5 milayin 'amil fi
muzaharat 'tafwid al-jaysh,'" *al-Misri al-Yawm*, June 24, 2013, www.almasryalyoum
.com/node/1976506; "Layla ihtifaliyya fi al-muhafazat tarfa' suwar al-Sisi wa
sha'ar 'la li al-irhab,'" *al-Shuruq*, July 27, 2013, www.shorouknews.com/news
/view.aspx?cdate=27072013&id=7597151d-2bd1-4d93-bba9-d26864bd034c.

58. "Mubadarat 'al-maydan al-thalith' tarfud '30 Yuniu wa muzaharat al-Ikhwan' . . .
wa 'tamarrud,'" *al-Watan*, July 27, 2013, www.elwatannews.com/news/details
/232781.

CHAPTER 8: LIBYA'S YOUTH REBELS

1. Lisa Anderson, *The State and Social Transformation in Tunisia and Libya, 1830–
1980* (Princeton, NJ: Princeton University Press, 1987); Dirk Vandewalle, *A*

History of Modern Libya, revised ed. (Cambridge, UK: Cambridge University Press, 2012); Lindsey Hilsum, *Sandstorm: Libya in the Time of Revolution* (New York: Penguin, 2012); Ethan Chorin, *Exit the Colonel* (New York: Public Affairs, 2012); Vijay Prashad, *Arab Spring, Libyan Winter* (Edinburgh: AK Press, 2012); Jacques Roumani, "From Republic to Jamahiriya: Libya's Search for Political Community," *Middle East Journal* 37, no. 2 (1983): 151–68.

2. Julie Ray, "Before Conflict, Many Young Libyans Doubted Role in Progress," Gallup Poll News Service, March 21, 2011, via Lexis Nexis.

3. Anthony McDermott, "Gaddafi and Libya," *World Today* 29, no. 9 (1973): 398–408, this point on 405; Muhammad Yusuf al-Maqaryaf, *Jara'im al-lijan al-thawriyya fi Libiya: Man al-mas'ul 'anha?* (Beirut: al-Furat, 2009); Mahmud Muhammad al-Naku', *Al-Harakat al-Islamiyya al-haditha fi Libiya* (London: Dar al-Hikmah, 2010); Rana Jawad, *Tripoli Witness* (London: Gilgamesh, 2011), chapter 1.

4. Muhammad al-Mufti, interview with author, Benghazi, May 28, 2012.

5. 'Ala' al-'Attar, "Al-Ahram takshif laghz ikhtifa' Mansur al-Kikhya," al-Ahram, June 17, 2011, www.masress.com/ahram/84241.

6. "Shalqam: 'Umar Suleiman Rajul Libya fi Misr," *al-Arabiyya*, July 15, 2011, www.alarabiya.net/articles/2011/07/15/157779.html.

7. Steve Stottlemyre, "Flexibility: Libyan Foreign Policy under Qadhafi, 1969–2004," *Digest of Middle East Studies* 21, no. 1 (2012): 178–201; Asteris Huliaras, "Qadhafi's Comeback: Libya and Sub-Saharan Africa in the 1990s," *African Affairs* 100, no. 398 (2001): 5–25.

8. Luis de Sousa, "Where Are Libya's Oil Exports Headed?," *Oil Drum*, September 8, 2008, http://europe.theoildrum.com/node/4513.

9. Hilsum, *Sandstorm*, chapter 7.

10. Lisa Anderson, "Rogue Libya's Long Road," *Middle East Report*, no. 241 (Winter 2006): 42–47; Ronald John, "Libya and the United States: A Faustian Pact?," *Middle East Policy* 15, no. 1 (2008): 133–48.

11. Ihab Kamal, *Abna' al-Taghi* (Tripoli: Al-Karnak li al-Nashr wa al-Tawzi', 2012).

12. Gregory L. Berry, U.S. Liaison Officer, Tripoli, to Secretary of State Condoleezza Rice, May 10, 2006, Wikileaks, http://wikileaks.org/cable/2006/05/06TRIPOLI198.html.

13. Gregory L. Berry, U.S. Liaison Officer, Tripoli, to Secretary of State Condoleezza Rice, May 10, 2006, Wikileaks, www.wikileaks.org/cable/2006/05/06TRIPOLI197.html; Berry to Rice, May 10, 2006.

14. "Baba al-Fatikan yujaddid asafahu li isa'at al-fahm," *Al Jazeera*, September 9, 2006, www.aljazeera.net/news/pages/240af3fa-70b4-49cc-bbe5-62bc93c0d809.

15. Ambassador Gene A. Cretz, Tripoli, to Secretary of State Hillary Clinton, March 3, 2009, *Guardian*, www.guardian.co.uk/world/us-embassy-cables-documents/194957.

16. "Hannibal the Hoon," *Age*, September 29, 2004, http://theage.drive.com.au/motor-news/hannibal-the-hoon-20100824-13lb7.html.

17. Ambassador Gene A. Cretz, Tripoli, to Secretary of State Hillary Clinton, *Telegraph*, December 31, 2008, www.telegraph.co.uk/news/wikileaks-files/libya-wikileaks/8294901/THINGS-FALL-APART-LIBYA-TELLS-SWISS-COMPANIES-TO-CEASE-OPERATIONS.html.

18. "Al-Mudda`i al-`amm li Kantun Jiniv yughliq niha'iyyan al-da'wa al-marfu`a didd najl al-Qadhafi," SwissInfo (Bern), September 3, 2008 www.swissinfo.ch/ara/detail/content.html?cid=322786; "Gaddafi Son Arrested for Assault," BBC, July 8, 2008, http://news.bbc.co.uk/2/hi/africa/7512925.stm.

19. Yehudit Ronen, "Libya's Rising Star: Saif al-Islam and Succession," *Middle East Policy* 12, no. 3 (2005): 136–44.

20. Joan Polaschik, chargé d'affaires, U.S. Embassy, Tripoli, to Secretary of State Hillary Clinton, July 21, 2009, Wikileaks, http://wikileaks.org/cable/2009/07/09TRIPOLI590.html.

21. Berry to Rice, May 10, 2006.

22. Ibid. For a personal account of the Libyan elite, see Abd al-Rahman Shalqam, *Ashkhas hawl al-Qadhafi* (Beirut: Dar al-Farjani, 2012).

23. "Libya: Investment Climate Statement," in Ambassador Gene A. Cretz, Tripoli, to Secretary of State Hillary Clinton, February 10, 2009, Wikileaks, http://wikileaks.org/cable/2009/02/09TRIPOLI131.html.

24. Gregory L. Berry, U.S. Liaison Officer, Tripoli, to Secretary of State Condoleezza Rice, September 3, 2005, Wikileaks, www.wikileaks.org/cable/2005/09/05TRIPOLI224.html.

25. Paul Richter, "As Libya Takes Stock, Moammar Kadafi's Hidden Riches Astound," *Los Angeles Times*, October 21, 2011.

26. Mu'assasat al-Raqib li Huquq al-Insan, "Dayf al-Ghazal: Sirat Sahafi waqafa fi wajh al-Fasad," *al-Shabakah al-'Arabiyyah li ma'lumat Huquq al-Insan*, August 8, 2006, http://anhri.net/libya/lw/2006/pr0608.shtml. See also the English translation of this text at www.libya-watanona.com/hrights/lhrs/lh10066c.htm.

27. Ibid.

28. "Libiya tuqif wazir al-amn al-'amm wa tuhiluhu li al-tahqiq ba`d maqtal 10 fi muzaharat," *Al-Arabiyya*, February 18, 2006, www.alarabiya.net/articles/2006/02/18/21223.html; "In Libya, 11 Reportedly Die in Cartoon Protests," CNN, February 18, 2006, www.cnn.com/2006/WORLD/africa/02/17/libya.cartoons/; "Ahdath Binghazi . . . In'itaf fi sira' al-ajniha?," Swissinfo, February 27, 2006, www.swissinfo.ch/ara/detail/content.html?cid=5039628; Deputy Chief of Mission Ethan Goldrich, Tripoli, to Secretary of State Condoleezza Rice, October 5, 2006, Wikileaks, http://wikileaks.org/cable/2006/10/06TRIPOLI573.html.

29. Deputy Chief of Mission Ethan Goldrich, Tripoli, to Secretary of State Con-

doleezza Rice, September 14, 2006, Wikileaks, wikileaks.org/cable/2006/09/06TRIPOLI497.html.

30. "Libya: Events of 2009," Human Rights Watch, World Report 2010, www.hrw.org/world-report-2010/lybia; "Libya: Libyan Dissident, Long Imprisoned, Is Dead," Human Rights Watch, May 21, 2009, www.hrw.org/news/2009/05/21/libya-libyan-dissident-long-imprisoned-dead; "Jahmi yarwi tajribat al-shabab al-libi wa ma'rikat al-mawaqi' al-ijtima'iyya ma`a al-Qadhdhafi," Swissinfo, February 17, 2012, www.swissinfo.ch/ara/detail/content.html?cid=32142132.

31. Hilsum, *Sandstorm*, 7–11, 101–16.

32. "Jahmi yarwi"; "Libia, 'cinquanta morti': I manifestanti si ribellano e impiccano tre poliziotti," Blitz Quotidiano, February 18, 2011, www.blitzquotidiano.it/politica-mondiale/libia-morti-manifestazioni-poliziotti-impiccati-755435.

33. "Anba' 'an thalathat qatla fi Libiya," Al Jazeera, February 17, 2011, www.aljazeera.net/news/pages/d42b0705-5712-48b7-be3f-410afc90ac71; "Jahmi yarwi."

34. "Muwajahat 'anifa fi Benghazi al-Libiya," *Elaph* (London), February 17, 2011, www.elaph.com/Web/news/2011/2/632293.html?entry=articlemostcommented; "Bayan 'an ahdath madinat al-Bayda," *al-Manara* (Dubai), February 17, 2011, http://almanaramedia.blogspot.com/2011/02/blog-post_3739.html; "Risalamin al-Zintan," *al-Manara*, February 18, 2011, http://almanaramedia.blogspot.com/2011/02/blog-post_1739.html.

35. "Thawrat al-sha'b al-libi tuharrir 'adadan min al-mudun," *Misriyun*, February 20, 2011, www.alhiwar.net/ShowNews.php?Tnd=14961&q=%C8%E4%DB%C7%D2%ED; "Libiya: Akthar min 100 qatil," al-Hiwar, February 20, 2011, www.alhiwar.net/ShowNews.php?Tnd=14943&q=%C8%E4%DB%C7%D2%ED; "Al-Jaysh al-libi qasafa Benghazi," *al-Quds al-'Arabi* (London), February 19, 2011, www.alhiwar.net/ShowNews.php?Tnd=14938&q=%C8%E4%DB%C7%D2%ED.

36. "Libiya: Al-mutazahirun yusaytarun 'ala al-mantiqa al-sharqiyya," *Misriyun*, February 20, 2011, www.alhiwar.net/ShowNews.php?Tnd=14964&q=%C8%E4%DB%C7%D2%ED; Hilsum, *Sandstorm*, 199.

37. Husam Hanafi, "Qadat al-thuwwar: Sanataharrik li muhasarat Tarabulus," *al-`Arab* (Doha), February 24, 2011, www.alarab.com.qa/printarticle.php?docId=176005; Elycheikh Ahmed Telba, "Al-Thawra al-sha'biyya fi Libiya: Al-jaysh wa sinariyuhat suqut al-Qadhafi," *Magharebia*, March 2011, http://zawaya.magharebia.com/old_zawaya/ar/zawaya/opinion/398.html.

38. "Jahmi yarwi"; Priyanka Mogul, "Liberated Libya Exclusive: Interview with Co-founder of the Libyan Youth Movement, Ayat Mneina," Priyanka Mogul, February 21, 2012, http://priyankamogul.com/2012/02/21/youth-libyan-movement/; "Mohammad Nabbous, Face of Citizen Journalism in Libya, is Killed," *Guardian*, March 19, 2011, www.guardian.co.uk/world/blog/2011/mar/19/mohammad-nabbous-killed-libya.

39. Alex Crawford, "Libya: On the Frontline During the Bloody Battle for Zawiya," *Telegraph*, March 7, 2011.

40. Thuwwar 17 Fibrayir li bana' Libiya al-hurra, March 11, https://www.facebook.com/17Libyarebels.

41. "What Qaddafi Said: Excerpts from Libyan Leader Muammar al-Qaddafi's Last Televised Address," *Foreign Affairs*, June 4, 2011, www.foreignaffairs.com/articles/67878/the-editors/what-qaddafi-said.

42. "Wuzara' al-kharijiyya yad'un majlis al-amn li fard hazr jawwi 'ala Libiya," France24 Arabic (Paris), March 13, 2011, www.france24.com/ar/20110312-arab-libya-meeting-support-no-fly-zone-kadhafi-crisis-opposition; Radwan Mortada, "Qatar Leaks: The Business of Foreign Affairs," *al-Akhbar* (Beirut), January 23, 2013, https://english.al-akhbar.com/node/14752.

43. Paul R. Williams and Colleen Popkin, "Security Council Resolution 1973 on Libya: A Moment of Legal and Moral Clarity," *Case Western Reserve Journal of International Law* 44, nos. 1–2 (2011): 225–50; Paul D. Williams and Alex J. Bellamy, "Principles, Politics, and Prudence: Libya, the Responsibility to Protect, and the Use of Military Force," *Global Governance* 18, no. 3 (2012): 273–97; Jonathan S. Landay, "Despite Reluctance, U.S. Could Be Forced to Act in Libya," McClatchy Newspapers, March 2, 2011, www.mcclatchydc.com/2011/03/02/v-print/109737/despite-reluctance-us-could-be.html.

44. Bobb Scott, "Libyan Opposition Gives War Lessons to Youth," *Voice of America News*, April 14, 2011, via Lexis Nexis.

45. John Scott-Railton, "The Voices Feeds," July 27, 2012, http://johnscottrailton.com/the-voices-feeds.

46. Xan Rice, "Springtime of the Siege," *New Statesman*, no. 1996 (May 9, 2011): 28–33; Ibrahim Quwaydar, *Libiya: Idarat al-Taghyir* (Cairo: Dar al-'Ulum li al-Nashr wa al-Tawzi', 2011), 128.

47. Quoted in Rice, "Springtime of the Siege."

48. Chorin, *Exit the Colonel*, 284–86.

49. 'Abd al-Razzaq al-Dahish, *Min al-Bu'azizi ila Bab al-'Aziziya* (Tripoli: al-Qabas, 2012), 288.

50. Hilsum, *Sandstorm*, 217–21.

51. Human Rights Watch, "NATO: Investigate Civilian Deaths in Libya. At Least 72 Dead in Air Attacks on Unclear Targets," May 14, 2012, www.hrw.org/news/2012/05/14/nato-investigate-civilian-deaths-libya.

52. Moez Zeiton, "Connected Conflict: The Internet Amplified but Did Not Create the Bravery That Freed Libya," *Technology Review* 115, no. 3 (2012): 10.

53. Some of the following analysis was first published at Juan Cole, "The Great Tripoli Uprising," Informed Comment, August 21, 2011, www.juancole.com/2011/08/the-great-tripoli-uprising.html.

54. "Al-Thuwwar yusaytirun 'ala ahya' bi Tarabulus," *Al Jazeera*, August 21, 2011, www.aljazeera.net/news/pages/fc4c742c-aebb-46e0-a94d-359b43c837fa #.TlCRoZzwXEs.twitter; "Al-Thuwwar fi libiya: Bid' Tahrir Tarabulus," al-Hiwar, August 20, 2011, www.alhiwar.net/ShowNews.php?Tnd=20901&q= %D3%E6%DE+%C7%E1%CC%E3%DA%C9; al-Dahish, *Min al-Bu`azizi*, 291–300.

55. Valerie Stocker, "Libyan Rap Showcase Delights Tripoli Audience," *Libya Herald* (Tripoli), December 22, 2012, www.libyaherald.com/2012/12/22/libyan-rap -showcase-delights-tripoli-audience. The music video for "Libya Bleed" is at YouTube, www.youtube.com/watch?v=7hyULOKDL_o; lyrics at www.youtube .com/watch?v=mTpKEhR6LMw.

56. Hasan Muhammad Salih, "Al-Halqa al-sabi'a: al-Thawra fi Libiya ila ayn?," *Sudanese Online* (Khartoum), May 30, 2012, http://tinyurl.com/lt6j9uu; "The Gaddafi Clan: Where Are They Now?," BBC, October 20, 2012, www.bbc .co.uk/news/world-africa-19966059; "Libya: Stop Revenge Crimes against Displaced Persons," Human Rights Watch, March 20, 2013, www.hrw.org/news /2013/03/20/libya-stop-revenge-crimes-against-displaced-persons.

57. "Jahmi yarwi."

58. "Tripoli Airport Returned to Government," UPI, June 5, 2012, www.upi.com /Top_News/World-News/2012/06/05/Tripoli-airport-returned-to-government/ UPI-62731338899255; International Crisis Group, "Divided We Stand: Libya's Enduring Conflicts," Middle East/North Africa Report no. 130, September 14, 2012, www.crisisgroup.org/~/media/Files/Middle%20East%20North%20Africa /North%20Africa/libya/130-divided-we-stand-libyas-enduring-conflicts.pdf.

59. Hasan Muhammad Salih, "Al-Thawra al-Libiya ila ayn? (1)," *al-Dafatan* (Athens), May 10, 2012, http://su-press.net/new1/modules/publisher/item .php?itemid=157; Juan Cole, "A Tale of Two Bombings: Libya Too Weak, Egypt Too Strong," Informed Comment, July 24, 2013, www.juancole.com/2013/07/ bombings-egypt-strong.html.

60. "The Revolutionary Promise: Youth Perceptions in Egypt, Libya and Tunisia," John D. Gerhart Center for Philanthropy and Civic Engagement, American University of Cairo, and British Council, June 2013, p. 28, www.britishcouncil .org/d084_therevolutionarypromise_report_v4-5.pdf.

61. George Grant and Michael Cousins, "Jibril's National Forces Alliance Looks Set for Victory," *Libya Herald*, July 7, 2012, www.libyaherald.com/2012/07 /07/exclusive-jibrils-national-forces-alliance-looks-set-for-victory; Dominique Soguel, "Libyan Elections Give Women a 17% Starting Point," Women's E-News, July 18, 2012, http://womensenews.org/story/the-world/120719/libyan -elections-give-women-17-starting-point.

62. "Libyan Protesters Lash Out at Extremists," Associated Press, September 21,

2012; David D. Kirkpatrick, "A Deadly Mix in Benghazi," *New York Times*, December 28, 2013.

63. Ghaith Shennib, "Libyan Official Warns Disruptions Damaging Oil Sector," Reuters, July 2, 2013; "Libya's Largest Political Party Says Will Boycott Congress," *al-Arabiyya*, July 4, 2013, http://english.alarabiya.net/en/News/middle-east/2013/07/04/Libya-s-largest-political-party-says-will-boycott-congress.html; Mohamed Eljarh, "Why Libya's Oil Crisis Is Spilling Over into Politics," *Foreign Policy*, September 3, 2013, http://transitions.foreignpolicy.com/posts/2013/09/03/why_libya_s_oil_crisis_is_spilling_over_into_politics.

64. Tom Westcott and Seraj Essul, "Hundreds Gather in Algeria Square: Plan to Take On the Militias," *Libya Herald*, July 7, 2013, www.libyaherald.com/2013/07/07/hundreds-gather-in-algeria-square-plan-to-take-on-the-militias/.

65. "Shabab al-'asima Tarabulus yuwasilun al-layla muzaharatihim tandidan bi ightiyalat Binghazi," *Shabaka al-Akhbar al-Libiyya* (Tripoli), July 28, 2013, http://libyann.net/index.php?option=com_content&view=article&id=13613:2013-07-28-00-35-06&catid=62:2011-08-29-05-21-29&Itemid=130; "Muhtajjun yuhajimun makatib al-Ikhwan al-Muslimin fi Tarabulus wa Binghazi," *Shabaka al-Akhbar al-Libiyya*, July 27, 2013, http://libyann.net/index.php?option=com_content&view=article&id=13595:2013-07-27-13-38-52&catid=62:2011-08-29-05-21-29&Itemid=130.

66. "Protesters gather at Libyan ministries demanding PM quit," Reuters, December 29, 2013.

67. "Students Protest against 'State of Chaos' in Benghazi," *Libya Herald*, May 15, 2013, www.libyaherald.com/2013/05/15/students-protest-against-state-of-chaos-in-benghazi; Aimen Eljali, "Tripoli Students Protest at Campus Assaults," *Libya Herald*, June 10, 2013, www.libyaherald.com/2013/06/10/tripoli-students-protest-at-campus-assaults; https://www.facebook.com/UTSU.eng for June 2, 2013.

68. Noor Hewaidi, "Libyan Youth Voices: Ten Successes since the Revolution," April 24, 2013, http://internationalpoliticalforum.com/libyan-youth-voices-10-successes-since-the-revolution/.

69. Ashraf Abdul-Wahab, "Gunmen Target Another Benghazi Journalist, Threaten to Kill Her Next Time," *Libya Herald*, August 12, 2013, www.libyaherald.com/2013/08/12/gunmen-target-another-benghazi-journalist-threaten-to-kill-her-next-time/.

70. Laura Hughes, "A Post-Revolution Reality," *Nouse*, May 7, 2013, www.nouse.co.uk/2013/05/07/a-post-revolution-reality.

71. Francis Ventura, "Interview with Ayat Mneina: Founder of the Libyan Youth Movement," *Amani Duniani*, November 12, 2012, www.amaniduniani.com/2012/11/interview-with-ayat-mneina-founder-of.html.

72. "The Revolutionary Promise," 42.

CONCLUSION

1. Tilly, *Social Movements*, 53–54; Tilly, *Regimes and Repertoires*. See also Jeffrey C. Alexander, *Performative Revolution in Egypt: An Essay in Cultural Power* (London: Bloomsbury Academic, 2011).
2. George Lawson, "Negotiated Revolutions: The Prospects for Radical Change in Contemporary World Politics," *Review of International Studies* 31, no. 3 (2005): 473–93, this quote on 479.
3. Theda Skocpol, *States and Social Revolutions: A Comparative Analysis of France, Russia and China* (Cambridge, UK: Cambridge University Press, 1979).
4. Adrian Karatnycky and Peter Ackerman, "How Freedom Is Won: From Civic Resistance to Durable Democracy," Freedom House Special Reports, 2005, http://agnt.org/snv/resources/HowFreedomisWon.
5. Karatnycky and Ackerman, "How Freedom Is Won," 4; Jai Kwan Jung, "Popular Mobilization and Democratization: A Comparative Study of South Korea and Taiwan," *Korea Observer* 42, no. 3 (2011): 377–411. On the critique of a top-down approach to transitions, Jung cites Nancy Bermeo, "Myths of Moderation: Confrontation and Conflict during Democratic Transitions," *Comparative Politics* 29, no. 3 (1997): 305–22.
6. Juan Cole, "Cole Interview with Nobelist Tawakkul Karman," Informed Comment, December 16, 2011, www.juancole.com/2011/12/cole-interview-with-nobelist-tawakkul-karman.html.
7. Tobias Thiel, "After the Arab Spring: Power Shift in the Middle East? Yemen's Arab Spring: From Youth Revolution to Fragile Political Transition," in Nicholas Kitchen, ed., *LSE Ideas Special Reports* (London: London School of Economics and Political Science, 2012), http://eprints.lse.ac.uk/43465; Jennifer Steil, "Yemen: Descending into Despair," *World Policy Journal* 28, no. 3 (2011): 62–73.
8. Kalle Lasn and Micah White, "Just Wait, the American Spring Will Come," *Valley News* (White River Junction, VT), November 23, 2011, via Proquest.

Index

Karoui, Nabil, 178
Kasserine, Tunisia, 128, 135, 136, 140, 164, 172
Katatni, Saad al-, 153, 206, 220
Kefaya movement, 19, 68, 72, 75, 87–93, 105, 107, 112, 146, 162, 193, 203, 265, 278
decline of, 95–97
founding of, 145
Muslim Brotherhood and, 91–92, 93–94, 96
protests by, 89–90, 100, 101, 104
Keib, Abdel Rahim al-, 258
Kélibia, Tunisia, 172–75, 176
Khalifa, Khalifa bin Salman Al, 35
Khalil, Kamal, 88
Khalil, Muhammad, 14
Khamis Brigade, 236, 245, 252, 257
Kikhia, Mansour Rashid al-, 231
Kikhia, Najat al-, 230–31, 232
King, Martin Luther, 151
Kostrz, Marie, 134–35
Kuwait, 223, 285
Kyrgyzstan, 283

Labidi, Ferida, 129–30
labor unions, xiii, 5, 130, 163
see also specific unions
Lakah, Rami "Raymond," 109
Lamm al-Shaml (Reunion Coalition), 174, 175
Larayedh, Ali, 184, 185, 188, 278
Lasn, Kalle, 285–86
Lawrence, D. H., 229
Lawyers Syndicate, 96, 101
Lawyers' Union, 132, 133
Lebanon, 79, 273
Israeli war with, 19, 96, 97
Leninism, 84–85
Li, Merlyna, 80
liberals, 85–86
Liberia, 233
Libya, x, xi, 226–66, 283
Constituent Assembly of, 260
dynasty in, 32, 33
economy of, 238
foreign languages banned in, 226
growing discontent in, 239–43
internet in, 10, 226, 236, 251, 265
Italy's rule of, 30, 227
lack of elections in, xii
literacy in, 14, 228, 234
no-fly zone in, 250

oil revenues in, 3, 46, 226, 228, 232, 239, 262
Parliament of, 22, 24, 262
poverty in, 228
prominent business families in, 238
revolution in, x, 23, 45, 244–57, 267, 268, 274–75
sanctions on, 233, 234
secret police in, xii
transitional democracy in, 258–66, 280, 282, 283, 284
university crackdowns in, 228–29
urbanization in, 5
U.S. and British military bases in, 30
U.S. consulate attacked in, 261
women in, 260–61, 264
youth unemployment in, 3, 226–27
"Libya Bleed," 256–57
Libya Herald, 260
Libya Jeel, 241
Libyan Islamic Fighting Group, 246, 251
Libyan Revolutionary Youth, 193
Libyan Youth website, 247, 264
Libya Today, 241
literacy, 13–16, 26
Lockerbie, Scotland, 232, 234
London, 232
Los Angeles Times, 71
Lynch, Marc, 69

Mabrouk, Tamer, 80
Maddow, Rachel, 162
Madi, Abul Ela, 87–88
Magariaf, Mohamed al-, 22, 261–62, 263, 280
Mahdi, Rabab al-, 88
Maher, Ahmed, 99, 104, 105, 108, 110–11, 113, 146, 147, 148, 150, 156, 158, 161, 192, 197, 207–8, 212, 213, 216
Mahfouz, Asmaa, 110, 141, 145–46, 199–200, 213
Mahfouz, Naguib, 196, 199
Mahmoud, Mustafa Ragab, 149
Makhlouf, Zouhaïer, 119
Maktoob, 10
malls, 22
Mandate Palestine, 21, 30
Mangoush, Yousef, 264
Mannheim, Karl, 18
Mansour, Abdel Rahman, 143
Mansour, Adly, 221, 223
Mansoura, Egypt, 157, 159, 223
Mao Zedong, 228
Martyrs' Square, 238, 256, 259

About the Author

Juan Cole has been studying the Middle East for forty years, which includes living in the region a decade altogether, off and on, and being a frequent visitor. He is Richard P. Mitchell Collegiate Professor of History at the University of Michigan and director of its Center for Middle Eastern and North African Studies. He grew up in France, Eritrea, and the United States. Cole is an accomplished Arabist and has translated three books by the Lebanese author Kahlil Gibran. His recent works include *Napoleon's Egypt* (2007) and *Engaging the Muslim World* (2009). He writes a widely read blog on contemporary Middle East affairs, called Informed Comment.